DOWNLOADS FOR STUDENTS AND FACULTY

*D*etailed PowerPoint presentations and end-of-chapter/end-of-module review questions are available for students to download. New to the third edition website is a secure faculty section where instructors can download the Instructor's Manual, Model Syllabi, Teaching Suggestions, and more.

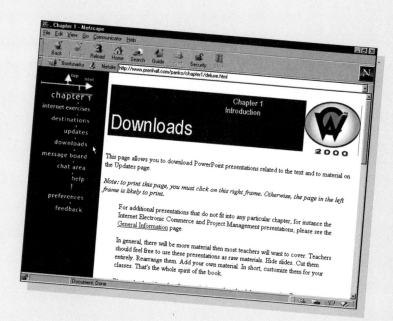

CHAPTER UPDATES

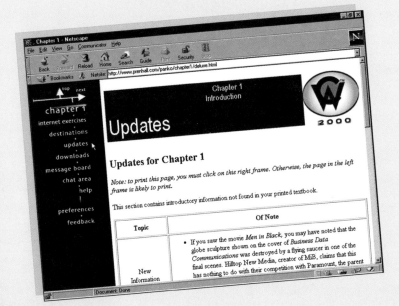

*C*hapter and module updates, including new information and supplemental readings, are provided by the author on the website. Updates are posted every month to help students and instructors stay abreast of the latest developments in data communications and networking.

Business Data Communications and Networking

THIRD EDITION

Raymond R. Panko
University of Hawaii

Prentice
Hall

Upper Saddle River, New Jersey 07458

Acquisitions Editor: David Alexander
Editor-in-Chief: Mickey Cox
Director of Strategic Marketing: Nancy Evans
Senior Marketing Manager: Kris King
Editorial Assistant: Erika Rusnak
Associate Managing Editor: Sondra Greenfield
Senior Manufacturing Supervisor: Paul Smolenski
Manufacturing Manager: Vincent Scelta
Print and Media Production Manager: Karen Goldsmith
Print Production Manager: Christy Mahon
Designer: Steven Frim
Design Director: Patricia Smythe
Cover Design: Steven Frim
Cover Illustration/Photo: Michael Hite Designs Inc
Production Services: Graphic World Publishing Services

Library of Congress Cataloging-in-Publication Data

Panko, R. R.
    Business data communications and networking / Raymond R. Panko.—3rd ed.
      p. cm.
    Includes bibliographical references and index.
    ISBN 0-13-088262-3
     1. Business enterprises—Computer networks—Study guides. 2. Computer net-
works—Management—Study guides. 3. Data transmission systems—Study guides.
I. Title.

HD30.37 .P36 2000
005.7'1—dc21

                                  00-027103

Prentice-Hall International (UK) Limited, *London*
Prentice-Hall of Australia Pty. Limited, *Sydney*
Prentice-Hall Canada, Inc., *Toronto*
Prentice-Hall Hispanoamericana, S.A., *Mexico*
Prentice-Hall of India Private Limited, *New Delhi*
Prentice-Hall of Japan, Inc., *Tokyo*
Prentice-Hall Pte. Ltd, *Singapore*
Editora Prentice-Hall do Brasil, Ltda., *Rio de Janeiro*

10 9 8 7 6 5 4
ISBN 0-13-088262-3

This book is dedicated to David Kalani Panko
for the inspiration of your curiosity and your
ability to solve almost any problem.

Brief Contents

Contents

CHAPTER 3   *A Closer Look at HTTP, TCP, IP, and PPP*   53

CHAPTER 4 *Physical Layer Concepts* 75

CHAPTER 5 *Modems and Beyond* 97

CHAPTER 6 *A Small PC Network* 119

CHAPTER 7 *Small Ethernet LANs* 143

CHAPTER 12   *Looking Forward*   271

MODULE C   *More on Local Area Networks*   335

MODULE D   *Telephone Service*   355

MODULE E   *More on Large-Scale Networks*   373

MODULE F   *More on Security*   381

Preface

The third edition of *Business Data Communications and Networking,* like its two predecessors, is based on extensive discussions with network administrators, reflects published data about what technologies are really used in organizations, and incorporates the comments of many teachers. The goal is to focus on what students really need to know for today's and tomorrow's networking jobs, including such things as LAN switching, security, and quality of service (QoS). The current edition is an 85 percent rewrite, although it generally follows the same flow as the second edition.

A UNIQUELY FLEXIBLE TEXTBOOK

Every teacher has different ideas about what to cover in a networking course. This book is designed to let teachers teach the course their way.

Covering the Basics in the 12 Core Chapters   Most teachers will wish to cover much or all of the 12 core chapters, which cover key networking concepts. Even within these chapters, more advanced material is placed in boxes for easy exclusion.

Free Time to Cover Your Special Topics   Teaching only the core chapters will leave one to three weeks free in a one-semester course. This leaves time for hands-on exercises or for the covering of additional topics.

Tools to Help You Cover Your Special Topics   To minimize the work that teachers have to do to prepare for this "extra time," there are eight advanced modules that cover more specialized topics. There is additional supplementary material at the book's website. For hands-on exercises, the book's website has Internet exercises that provide some options. The idea is to help teachers cover selected material without the need for them to create packets of special material.

End-of-Chapter Questions to Tie Things Together   End-of-chapter questions help students focus on what material to study. For instance, when I cover Chapter 7, which covers hub-based and switch-based Ethernet networking, I also include some material on older 10Base2 and 10Base5 technologies, which are covered in Module C. For homework, in addition to assigning questions from Chapter 7, I also assign relevant questions from Module C.

Also, end-of-chapter (and end-of-module) questions are divided into core review questions, detailed review questions, and thought questions. For faster coverage, teachers can assign core review questions and only selected detailed review questions or thought questions.

INSTRUCTOR RESOURCES

This book supports instructors intensively, again with a goal of minimizing the work that instructors have to do.

PowerPoint Presentations

Full Lecture Presentations For each chapter and module, there is a detailed PowerPoint presentation. This is a full lecture, not just "a few selected figures." Each presentation is created by the author and is closely tied to the material in the chapter itself.

Change Them to Fit Your Needs Instructors are invited to change the presentations to fit their needs. For instance, they can drop slides, add their own, or copy slides from advanced modules into core modules. (Advanced modules use the same presentation formats as the core chapters they support.) The only restrictions are that only adopters may use the presentations, that teachers must not remove the copyright notice, and that teachers may not reuse the clip art.

Gold Stars for Emphasis Gold stars in the PowerPoint presentations indicate material that is especially important or especially difficult. In either case, gold stars tell students that the material merits special care in study.

Transparencies, Too If instructors prefer transparencies or like to use transparencies selectively, there are transparency masters in Microsoft® Word for Windows format for every figure and table in the book, plus a few extra transparencies for material not presented in figures and tables.

The Companion Website: Updates

The book comes with a companion website, **http://www.prenhall.com/panko.** The third edition website will be directly controlled by the author and will be updated monthly.

Rather than putting material that ages quickly in the printed textbook, the companion website allows the author to disseminate rapidly changing and new information.

Case Studies Most importantly, the companion website has several case studies for all chapters (and for some modules). These are short cases with discussion questions to help students focus on the cases. Many cases are links to online trade journal articles on specific innovations in specific companies.

New Information   Networking is changing at the speed of light, and new information is appearing constantly. The website will present new information selectively. This new information will range from new developments in the field to new data and forecasts about the use of key technologies and standards.

Supplementary Information   In some cases, material will be offered that, while not entirely new, is a useful supplement that some teachers will wish to use in their classes. For instance, Chapter 1's supplementary reading page has a short tutorial on Base 2 arithmetic.

The Companion Website: Student Support

The website will also be a place for students to go to for interactive support.

Internet Exercises   All chapters and some modules will have Internet exercises to provide hands-on learning. For instance, do students know how to learn their PC's IP address? Do they know how many routers there are between themselves and their favorite websites? Do they know how fast their Internet connection really is? In the Internet exercises, they'll be able to find out.

End-of-Chapter/Module Question Downloads   Each chapter and module ends with a series of review questions that test students in their understanding of the material. Students can download the end-of-chapter and end-of-module questions. They can type in their answers and then give their work to the teacher on paper or electronically.

PowerPoint Presentation Downloads   For teachers who use PowerPoint presentations, students can download them from the website. In addition, adopters of the book are free to copy the presentations to their local sites for easier access. Even if the teacher does not use the presentations in class, many students will wish to download them as study guides.

Other Support for Instructors

Instructor's CD-ROM Disk with Test Bank and Answer Keys   An instructor's CD-ROM disk contains support materials you may use without the work of downloading material:

- PowerPoint presentations
- Transparency masters
- Computerized test bank and answer key
- Answers to end-of-chapter/module questions.

Contact the Author   Do you have a question or comment? Please contact the author at Ray@Panko.com.

Instructor's Mailing List for News   Also, if you adopt the book, send Ray an e-mail, and he will put you on a mailing list for adopters. You will get notices of updates to material.

COVERAGE AND PEDAGOGY

Topical Coverage

As noted earlier, the goal in writing this book was to cover the technology and standards that corporations actually use and will use, so that students will have the knowledge they really need.

TCP/IP and OSI   TCP/IP and OSI often are taught as competitors. In reality, however, they have become partners. On the Internet and within corporations today, the dominant "architecture" is really a hybrid of TCP/IP and OSI. Computers increasingly use TCP/IP at higher layers (internet, transport, and application) while using OSI at the data link and physical layers. This book takes this hybrid TCP/IP–OSI architecture as its basic architectural model. It does introduce full OSI layering, and it introduces IPX/SPX–OSI communication in Chapter 7 and SNA–OSI communication in Chapter 11. No matter what standards are used at upper layers, OSI standards are always used at the physical and data link layers.

In the first three chapters, students become very familiar with TCP/IP standards. In Chapter 3, for instance, they learn to think like a router by comparing the destination address of incoming packets with entries in a router forwarding table. They learn OSI physical and data link layer standards throughout the book, in appropriate places.

LAN Switching   LANs, including large site networks, are now "switch rich." We now introduce Ethernet switches and hubs equally in Chapters 6 and 7, and Chapter 8 discusses large switch-based site networks. The focus is Ethernet switching, but ATM switching is also covered. Chapter 8 covers switch selection, switch learning, VLANs, Layer 3 switches, Layer 4 switches, and other crucial LAN switching topics.

Quality of Service (QoS)   As networks get larger and more complex, quality of service (QoS) is an increasing concern. Chapter 1 introduces QoS in terns of latency and reliability. Chapter 8 looks at QoS for latency in depth, covering overprovisioning, priority, full QoS guarantees, and traffic shaping.

Wide Area Networking   In wide area networking, leased lines and public switched data networks are used about equally, so both are covered. However, in public switched data networking, Frame Relay is used much more than ATM. Consequently, Chapter 9 concentrates more heavily on Frame Relay, including its flexible virtual circuit numbering scheme and how to purchase Frame Relay service.

Security Security has grown in importance and also, unfortunately, complexity. Chapter 10 treats security in depth, including authentication, public key infrastructures, and automatic integrated security systems (using SSL as an example). Module F, among other things, discusses IPsec, Kerberos, and PPTP.

Wireless Networking and Non-PC User Devices Wireless networking has long been a promising way to support mobile devices. However, wireless networking at the LAN and metropolitan area levels is just now reaching the maturity it will need for explosive growth. In addition, desktop and notebook PCs will be joined by a large number of other different-size devices for user access. Chapters 5, 7, and 12 discuss wireless networking and Internet access. Chapter 4 spends considerable time on radio propagation, and Module B goes into even more detail.

Microsoft Windows Networking Setup Given the dominance of Microsoft Windows, Chapter 2 presents netwqork steup for Internet access, and Chapter 6 discusses network setup for client PCs.

Telephony Telephony is introduced throughout the book, including telephony's hierarchy of switches and circuit switching in Chapter 1, carriers in Chapter 9, IP telephony in Chapter 11, and cellular principles in Chapter 12. Many adopters choose to cover the telephony module, Module D.

Web-Enabled Database Access and Mainframes Contrary to popular belief, mainframes are not dying. Chapter 11 discusses web–host integration and offers a box covering mainframe communication and SNA.

Pedagogy As much as possible has been done to make the student's learning easier and more effective. The previous sections already discussed the use of end-of-chapter questions to guide student learning and the use of gold stars to mark important or difficult material in the PowerPoint presentations. The book has several other innovations.

Vignettes All chapters open with vignettes to pique student interest. Most vignettes raise issues that the student must address in an end-of-chapter thought question, using material learned in the chapter.

Begin with the Familiar and Concrete Many textbooks begin with wide area networks, which few students have experienced personally. *Business Data Communications and Networking,* in contrast, begins with two very familiar situations: Internet access (Chapters 2–5) and small PC networks (Chapters 6 and 7). Within these familiar and comfortable environments, students learn concepts in ways to which they can relate. Later, when more unfamiliar types of networking are encountered, students have the knowledge they need to approach them.

Layering Is Treated Early and Often Layering is the most difficult material in the course. Many textbooks introduce one layer at a time, only giving the whole picture very late in the book. *Business Data Communications and Networking* introduces networking at the beginning of the book and repeats it in several contexts, such as Internet access and PC networking. This repetition is needed to learn this difficult material.

Illustrations The book's extensive illustrations are tightly integrated into the text. Many have numbered items corresponding to items discussed in the text.

Case Studies and Internet Exercises As noted earlier, there case studies with discussion questions at the book's companion website. There are also Internet exercises for hands-on work.

CHANGES FROM THE SECOND EDITION

More but Smaller Chapters and the Same General Flow

The third edition looks somewhat different from the second edition. This edition has 12 core chapters, while the second edition only had eight. This has resulted largely from breaking Chapters 2 through 6 into smaller units for easier digestibility.

The mapping between the second and third editions is very direct at the first six chapters of the second edition, which map rather directly into chapters of the third.

Chapter 1 of the second edition generally matches Chapter 1 of the third edition.

Chapter 2, on layering and TCP/IP, is now Chapters 3 and 4.

Chapter 3, on physical layer technology and devices, is now Chapters 4 and 5.

Chapter 4, on PC networks, is now Chapters 6 and 7.

Chapter 5, on large network transmission, is now Chapters 8 and 9.

Chapter 6, on managing large networks, corresponds to Chapter 10 and parts of Chapter 12.

In the second edition, Chapters 7 and 8 covered applications, and there was no definitive "closing chapter." Chapters 11 and 12 now cover applications but do so more selectively. Chapter 11 focuses on crucial current applications, including web-based database applications, electronic mail, and IP telephony. Chapter 12 focuses on future applications, including wireless applications and networked object oriented programming.

Chapter 12 also covers product selection and purchasing considerations, which some teachers will wish to cover early in the course. The last chapter also provides closure to the book.

Topic Differences

TCP/IP In some sense, the TCP/IP material in early chapters in simplified for easier digestibility. For instance, fragmentation, flow control, and some other TCP details are now moved to Appendix A. However, UDP is now introduced with TCP, and there is now a section on how routers actually decide what to do with incoming IP packets by comparing destination addresses with entries in the router's forwarding table.

Increased Emphasis   Throughout the book, greater emphasis is given to several emerging topics, including the following:

Quality of Service (QoS). See Chapters 1 and 8.
LAN Switching. See Chapters 6–8, especially 8.
Security. See the all-new treatment in Chapter 10 and Module F.
Wide Area Networking. See Chapter 9.
Wireless Networking. See Chapters 7 and 12 especially.
Microsoft Windows Setup for Networking. See Chapters 2 and 7.

Integrating Telephony   The telephone module was very popular in the second edition. As noted earlier, some basic telephone material is now integrated into the core chapters, including some information about carriers, the telephone switching hierarchy, circuit switching, cellular basics, and IP telephony.

Design and Pedagogy Differences

More Open Book Design   Prentice Hall has nicely given the book a more "open" design so that the text will not feel cramped to students.

Vignettes   As noted earlier, each chapter begins with an opening vignette that engages student interest and usually raises issues students will have to resolve by understanding the material in the chapter.

Test Your Understanding   At the end of each section, there is a "Test Your Understanding" opportunity that points students to end-of-chapter questions they can answer to test their understanding of the section.

Bye, Bye, "PDU"   Chapter 2 used the term *protocol data unit (PDU)* for any message between peer processes at the same layer but on different computers. This OSI-specific term proved to cause a surprising number of problems for students. In response to the comments of several adopters, the term "PDU" is not used in the third edition. Messages between peer processes are simply called *messages, frames* (data link layer), or *packets* (internet layer), or are called by their standard-specific names, such as "TCP segment."

Renumbering Cellular Generations   The second edition numbered current personal communication system (PCS) systems as the third generation in cellular telephony. However, marketers have labeled PCS systems as "second generation" cellular and the merging multimedia cellular technology as the third generation. The third edition renumbers cellular generations to reflect this changing terminology.

A General One-Semester Course for IS Students

Most instructors will cover the 12 core chapters in a general one-semester course for information systems (IS) students. In a one-semester course with two examinations, covering the 12 core chapters will leave about two weeks for hands-on exercises or to cover two additional modules fully or in part. Furthermore, some material from the modules can be covered along with the core chapters.

One-Quarter Course for IS Students

Covering networking in a quarter instead of a semester is daunting. It can be done by focusing on the core chapters, eliminating boxed material, and, if this is still too much material, by focusing mainly on the core review questions at the end of each chapter.

A One-Semester Course for Community Colleges

Covering networking in a community college may necessitate lightening the material, depending on student preparation. Again, the instructor may wish to focus on the core chapters, eliminate boxed material, and possibly focus on the core review questions at the end of each chapter.

An MBA Course

In an MBA course, it is common to reduce the technical content by focusing on the core chapters and core review questions. In addition, in the more technical chapters (Chapters 2, 3, 4, and 7), a great deal can be skipped for MBA students. For instance, in Chapter 7, I usually cover only CSMA/CD, wireless LANs, and a brief overview of Token-Ring Networks. Most instructors use the freed time for case studies at the book's website and for individual projects and term papers.

A Two-Semester Course for IS Students

A small but growing number of schools have the luxury of a two-semester course. This leaves much more time for hands-on work. It also allows more advanced modules to be covered. My experience is that it is best to cover advanced modules at the same time as the basic material. In other words, after TCP/IP in Chapter 3, follow with Module A (More on TCP/IP). Another option is to cover core chapters first, and then advanced modules. This has the advantage of reinforcement and is theoretically better, although it may require the extensive review of earlier material.

About the Author

Dr. Raymond R. Panko (Ray) is a professor of information technology and management at the University of Hawaii. Before coming to the University, he was a project manager at Stanford Research Institute. He received his doctorate, in communication, from Stanford. At Stanford, he had the good fortune to do early work on VSATs with Prof. Bruce Lusignan and broadband LAN planning with Prof. Ed Parker and Paul Baran. His doctoral dissertation was done under contract to the Office of the President of the United States. At SRI, he had the good fortune to do early work on videoconferencing, electronic mail, and the ARPANET. He had the especially good fortune to work for Dr. Doug Engelbart, who invented the mouse and built the first hypertext system. His current research focuses on risks in information technology. His greatest pleasure is seeing the excitement in his students' eyes when they master difficult material and then realize that this is how the Internet, a PC network, or some other network they have long been using really works. His home page is www.panko.com. His e-mail is Ray@Panko.com.

Chapter 1

Basic Concepts and Principles

Glenn Davis sells papayas to wholesalers throughout the United States. His company is Paradise Groceries. A "road warrior," Glenn rarely is far from his notebook computer. Each morning, Glenn dials into the Internet from his hotel room to check his e-mail. He then uses the Internet to connect to his company's webserver to check for current prices and for internal company news. Now he is ready to call on customers.

At the customer site, Glenn can take orders online. While recording orders, he can check on product availability and delivery schedules. By adding the customer's order to the official list of orders, he can even guarantee a delivery date. He also shows the customer a website where he or she can check on the progress of the order.

Although Glenn is happy with the benefits his notebook has brought him, there are still some problems. Most importantly, there often is no telephone around when he wants to check his e-mail and get other information. At the customer's office, he has to ask for permission to use a phone, and this is awkward. Another big problem is that his telephone connections are very slow.

Glenn's company is evaluating a high-speed wireless Internet access service. However, the service is only available in some cities, does not work inside many buildings, and is very expensive. Glenn's private guess is that the company will wait until the technology is beyond the "bleeding edge" and alternatives have become clearer.

In general, Glenn is patient. In the last 10 years he has seen enormous improvements in his network services. He is fairly confident that his company will stay close to the leading edge of network technology without constantly jumping into immature market offerings that turn out to bring more problems than they solve. ■

Learning Objectives

After studying this chapter, you should be able to describe:

- Basic networking concepts in wide use today: voice and video communication versus data communications, circuit switching versus packet switching, multiplexing, congestion and latency, analog versus digital versus binary, modems, LANs versus WANs, terminal–host processing versus file server program access versus client/server processing, platform independence

- The elements of the Internet and the Internet standards used when you dial into the Internet from home or on the road in order to access a World Wide Web server (webserver)

- The need for quality of service guarantees and improved security

INTRODUCTION

The title of this book is "Business Data Communications and Networking." As Figure 1.1 illustrates, a **network** is an any-to-any communication system. This means that any station can communicate with any other station on the network.

For this to be possible, every station on the network must have a unique **network address**. For example, the telephone network can connect your phone to any other telephone in the world. You only need to know the other party's telephone number.

Data communications, in turn, is communication in which at least one party is a computer. When you use the Internet, therefore, it is data communications. We will discuss many other examples of data communications in this book.

Figure 1.1
Elements of a
Network

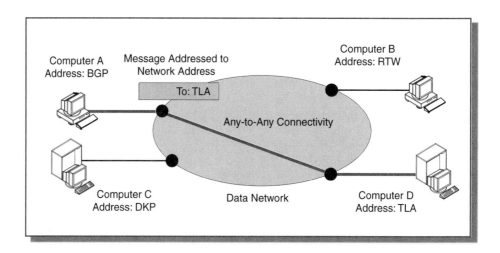

Basic Concepts   In this first chapter, we begin by looking at some core networking concepts we will use throughout this book. Many of these concepts will be familiar to you, but quite a few will be new.

The Internet   The Internet is arguably the most important network today. It is certainly changing the fastest. We will look at the technology of the Internet and the standards you use when you dial into the Internet from home or on the road to access a webserver.

Layered Standards   This chapter will introduce the *hybrid TCP/IP–OSI standards architecture*, which will be the focus of much of this book. This standards architecture governs the Internet and many other networks.

Looking to the Future   We will end this chapter with a discussion of two topics we expect to become increasingly important in the next few years: (1) security and (2) quality of service guarantees for latency (delays) and reliability.

Business Data Communications and Networking   As an **information systems (IS)** professional, you will not build switches or other networking devices. That is what computer scientists and electrical engineers do. Rather, as an IS professional you will be employed by a firm that uses networks to work more effectively and efficiently (or by a company that consults for such firms). Your duties will include everything from needs analysis through implementation and ongoing management. As a business student, it will not be enough to know the technology. You will have to work with users to help them articulate their needs and to help them see how networks can help them better do their work. At the same time, you will have to know the technology very well to do your job.

CORE CONCEPTS

We will begin by looking at some basic concepts in data communications and networking.

Voice and Video Communication

Traditionally, the world of communications has been divided into data communications, in which one or both parties is a computer, on the one hand and voice and video communications on the other hand.

Circuit-Switched Networks   As Figure 1.2 illustrates, the telephone network has traditionally handled both voice and video transmission.

Switches, Trunk Lines, and the Local Loop   Figure 1.2 shows that the telephone network consists of a hierarchy of **switches** connected by high-speed

Figure 1.2
Circuit Switching
for Voice and
Video
Communications

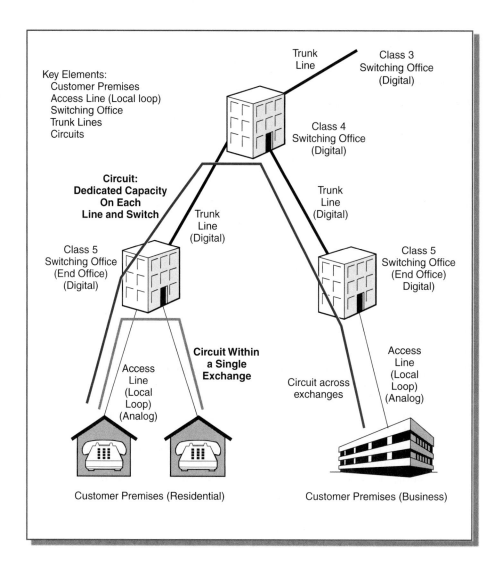

Key Elements:
    Customer Premises
    Access Line (Local loop)
    Switching Office
    Trunk Lines
    Circuits

Trunk Line

Class 3 Switching Office (Digital)

Class 4 Switching Office (Digital)

Circuit: Dedicated Capacity On Each Line and Switch

Trunk Line (Digital)

Trunk Line (Digital)

Class 5 Switching Office (End Office) (Digital)

Class 5 Switching Office (End Office) Digital

Circuit Within a Single Exchange

Access Line (Local Loop) (Analog)

Circuit across exchanges

Access Line (Local Loop) (Analog)

Customer Premises (Residential)

Customer Premises (Business)

transmission lines called **trunk lines.** Subscribers are connected to the nearest switching office with a transmission line called an **access line,** or, more colorfully, the **local loop.**

Circuits   When you dial another party, the telephone system creates a connection called a **circuit** between the two telephones. A circuit may pass through multiple switches and transmission lines, but to the two parties, it seems like a simple point-to-point link.

Guaranteed (Reserved) Capacity   The telephone uses **circuit switching,** which **reserves capacity** for your call along each trunk line and within each

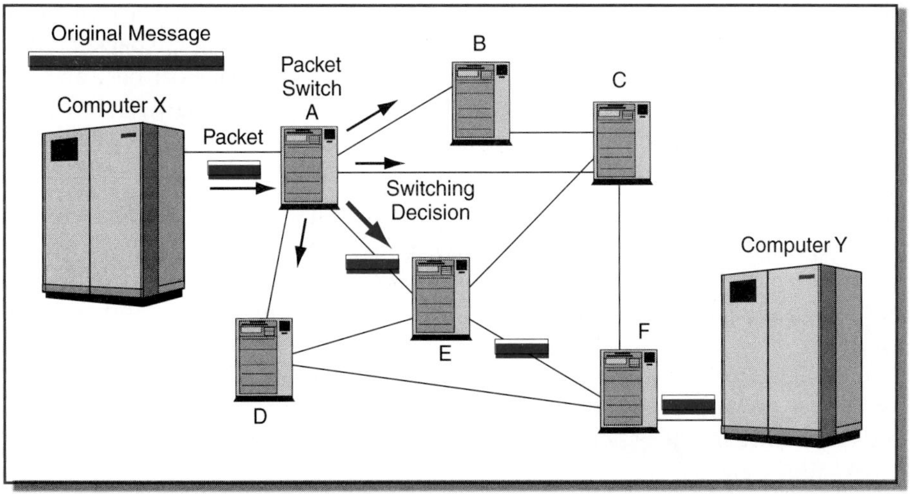

Figure 1.3
Packet-Switched
Network for Data

switch along the circuit's path. No matter how busy the telephone network gets, there will be no delay when you talk.

Wastefulness of Circuit Switching for Bursty Data Traffic On the downside, you must pay for this **dedicated capacity** whether you use it or not. Of course, in a voice call, one of the two parties is talking nearly all the time. In video, in turn, you receive a constant stream of images. Little capacity is wasted.

Data transmission, in contrast, is **bursty,** with short and intense transmissions separated by relatively long silences. Consider what happens when you use the World Wide Web. You download a page in a burst of a few seconds, then stare at the screen for up to several minutes before you start the next download burst. In data communications, you often transmit and receive less than 5% of the time. Yet with circuit switching, you pay for the capacity 100% of the time.

Packet-Switched Data Networks

Because circuit switching is not good for bursty data traffic, **data networks** (i.e., networks designed specifically to carry data) normally use a different type of switching called **packet switching.**

Packets As Figure 1.3 illustrates, large messages are broken into small pieces and sent in shorter messages called **packets.**[1] (We will see later in this chapter that these messages sometimes are called *frames*.) Small packets flow more easily through a switched network than long messages, much like sand flows more smoothly than rocks.

---

[1] A typical packet length is 100 to 1,000 bytes.

Switching Decisions   Figure 1.3 shows that when a packet arrives at a packet switch, there may be several ports available for sending the packet on to another router. The packet switch should select the output port best able to move the packet on to its ultimate destination. This **switching decision** may involve consideration of congestion, cost, and other factors.

Multiplexing to Reduce Transmission Costs   Figure 1.3 also shows that capacity is not reserved along the trunk lines that connect switches. Packets are **multiplexed** (mixed) on the trunk lines, sharing both the capacity and the cost of these trunk lines.[2] Packets also share the capacity and costs of switches.

On the positive side, packet switching avoids the wasted capacity of circuit switching, reducing costs dramatically. For data transmission, packet switching tends to be much less expensive than circuit switching. Almost all data networks today are packet-switched networks.

Congestion and Latency   On the negative side, because there is no capacity reservation, if traffic gets too heavy, there will be **congestion.** When there is congestion, packets may take much longer to get through the network. The length of delay is called the **latency** in the transmission. Users greatly dislike latency. As discussed later in this chapter, and more fully in Chapter 8, efforts are now under way to manage latency in packet-switched networks.

Analog and Digital Communication

Analog Communication   Some electrical signals, called **analog** signals, *rise and fall smoothly in intensity among an infinite number of states* (conditions). For instance, when you speak, your voice rises and falls smoothly in volume. The local loop from your home or office to the telephone company is designed to carry analog communication because the electrical signals created when we speak rise and fall smoothly in intensity and therefore are analog. Figure 1.4 illustrates analog communication. Note that we have used voice telephony as an example of an analog signal, but it is only an example. Any signal that rises and falls smoothly in intensity among an infinite number of states is an analog signal.

Digital Communication   Computers communicate differently. They use **digital communication.** As Figure 1.4 also shows, a digital signal has three characteristics:

- First, the signal remains at a constant **state** (say a voltage level) during each period of time called a **clock cycle.**
- Second, at the end of each clock cycle, the line can remain in the same state or jump to another state.

---

[2] The telephone network also uses multiplexing on trunk lines between switches. Several voice circuits can share a single high-speed trunk line. However, each circuit is still given dedicated capacity within each trunk line. This limits the economic benefits of circuit-switched multiplexing.

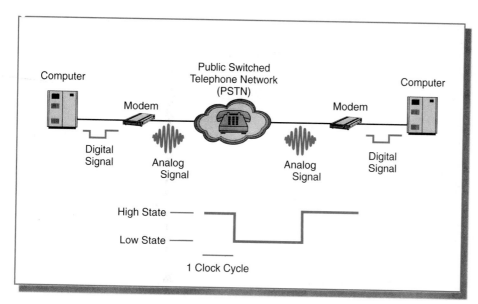

Figure 1.4
Analog
Communication,
Digital
Communication,
and Modems

- Third, there are only a few possible states to jump to at the end of a clock cycle. Sometimes there are as few as two possible states. There are rarely more than 32 possible states.

For example, there are 7 days in a week. On Monday, it is Monday all day, until midnight. Then the day changes immediately to Tuesday. In terms of electrical signaling, there might be two voltages, with one state (voltage) representing a one and the other state (voltage) representing a zero.

Binary Communication   When there are only two possible states, this is a special case of digital communication called **binary** communication. In each time period, we can send a single **bit,** that is, a single zero or one.[3] All binary signals are digital, but not all digital signals are binary. In particular, "digital" does not imply using two states (ones and zeros).

Representing Information Transmission Speeds   Of course, we send many **bits per second (bps)** when we transmit. In increasing multiples of 1,000 (not 1,024 as in computer memory), we have **kilobits per second (kbps),**[4] **megabits per second (Mbps), gigabits per second (Gbps),** and **terabits per second (Tbps).** So 55,300 bps is the same as 55.3 kbps. Twelve million bits per second is 12 Mbps.

---

[3]As Chapter 3 discusses, if there are more than two states, we can send more than one bit per clock cycle.

[4]Note that "kilobits" is abbreviated with a lowercase "k." This is proper metric notation. (Uppercase "K" is reserved for Kelvins, a measure of temperature.)

Modems   To send data over a traditional telephone line, you need a device called a **modem.** As Figure 1.4 illustrates, a modem translates outgoing digital computer signals into analog signals that can travel over the access line to the telephone network. When analog signals arrive from the other party, in turn, the modem translates these signals back into digital format and passes the digital signal on to the receiving computer. Chapter 3 looks at modems in considerable detail.

LANs and WANs

In terms of geographical scope, there is a core distinction between local area networks (LANs) and wide area networks (WANs).

LANs   As the name suggests, **local area networks (LANs)** cover a small region. Some LANs only serve one or two PCs in a home office. Others serve a dozen PCs in a small office. Still others serve dozens of computers in a single building. The largest LANs serve an entire site, such as a university campus, an industrial park, or a military base.

Figure 1.5 shows a small LAN that connects a few PCs. This LAN consists of a box called a *hub* or a *switch* plus *wiring.* The hub or switch transfers messages from one PC to another. Each computer must have a *network interface card (NIC)* that manages communication with the network.

As shown in Figure 1.5, a LAN often forms the transmission component for a PC network (although a LAN can connect any types of computers). In PC networks, **client PCs** are personal computers that sit on the desks of managers, professionals, and other information workers. The machines that provide services to these client PCs are called **servers.**

Figure 1.5
Small PC Network
Built on a LAN

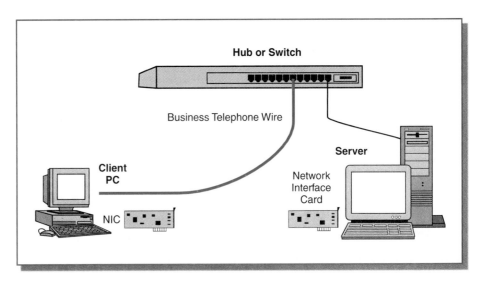

Chapter 1   Basic Concepts and Principles

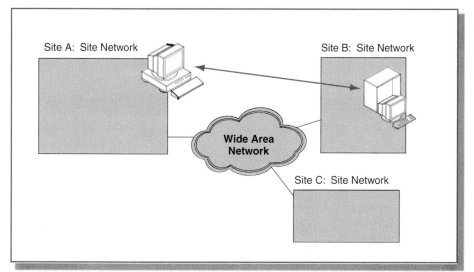

Figure 1.6
Wide Area
Network (WAN)

Wide Area Networks: Carriers   As Figure 1.6 illustrates, many organizations have multiple sites. They need **wide area networks (WANs)** to link the LANs in their various sites together.

Distributed Processing

When you use a stand-alone PC, all of the processing is done in one place. When you have a network, however, new possibilities for *where* to do processing appear. The ability to do processing in different places is called **distributed processing.**

Terminal–Host Systems   The first step in distributed processing came in the 1960s, when **terminal–host systems** appeared. As Figure 1.7 illustrates, users work at devices called **terminals.** Terminal–host systems were designed

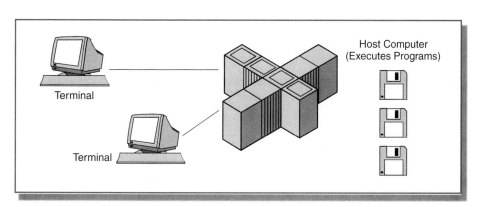

Figure 1.7
Terminal–Host
System

long before microprocessors were invented, so there was no way to put intelligence in these desktop machines. Instead, all intelligence is located in the central **host computer.** When the user types, the keystrokes go to the host for processing. The host then sends characters back to be painted on the terminal screen.

Importance of Mainframe Systems   Although some people think of terminal–host systems as ancient history, terminal–host systems are alive and well. This is especially true for systems that use the largest business host computers, called **mainframes.**[5] Most corporations still have a large amount of their central data stored on terminal–host systems.

Legacy Systems and Downsizing   In information technology, a **legacy system** is one that uses old technology but that would be very expensive to replace. Mainframe systems qualify for this label. While there is a long-term trend to **downsize** mainframe applications to run on smaller and newer processing platforms, mainframe terminal–host systems will be with us for many years to come.

File Server Program Access   Earlier, in Figure 1.5, we saw a small PC network. The most common type of server on PC networks is the **file server.** As its name suggests, it stores program files and data files for client PCs.

Processing on Client PCs   As Figure 1.8 illustrates, when you run a program on a client PC, that program is likely to be stored on a file server.[6] The file server will download a copy of the program to your client PC, which will actually run the program. Associated data files are also downloaded to the client PC.

Figure 1.8
File Server
Program Access

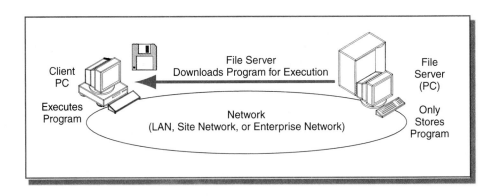

---

[5] Other large hosts include supercomputers, which are optimized for numerical scientific processing. Mainframes and other business hosts are optimized instead for file storage and retrieval, which are characteristic of most business applications.

[6] Of course, you can also store the program on your client PC's hard drive. A client PC can still work entirely locally.

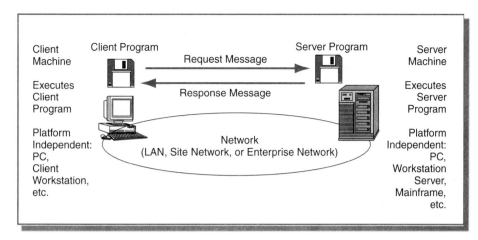

Figure 1.9
Client/Server
Processing

No Processing on the File Server   Many people are surprised that all processing is done on client PCs, which are often underpowered, instead of on file servers, which usually are much faster machines. However, file servers were only designed to store files, not execute them.

Client/Server Processing   Both terminal–host systems and file server program access do processing on a single machine. However, client/server processing does processing on *two* machines, as Figure 1.9 illustrates.

First, there is the **client program** running on the **client computer.** In web-server access, the client program is a browser. The client program sends **request messages** to the **server program** running on the **server computer.** For instance, a World Wide Web request message might ask for a webpage to be downloaded from the webserver to the browser. The webserver application program on the webserver is the server program. It sends a **response message** giving the requested information or explaining why the information cannot be supplied. Many applications other than webservice use client/server processing.

Comparing Forms of Distributed Processing   Different distributed processing approaches have different strengths and weaknesses. Figure 1.10 compares the major distributed processing alternatives.

Scalability   A crucial factor in any information technology is the degree to which it is **scalable,** that is, can be expanded to meet increasing demand. If demand outgrows a technology, the company will have to install a different technology. This always requires extensive staff retraining. Sometimes, it means the removal of all existing hardware with a forklift and the purchasing of all new equipment. In the worst case, the company cannot serve the demand.

Terminal–host systems are extremely scalable, because the largest mainframes have enormous processing power.

Figure 1.10
Comparing
Distributed
Processing
Alternatives

	File Server Program Access	Client/Server Processing	Terminal–Host Systems
Location of processing	Client PC (not on the file server)	Client computer and server (2 programs)	Host computer (terminals are dumb)
Graphics	Very good because of local processing in client PC	Very good because of local processing in client PC	Poor because rich graphics would require expensive high-speed network traffic.
Response Times	Very good because of local processing in client PC	Very good because of local processing in client PC, although some server delay	Poor because hosts often are overloaded.
Scalability	Low: Client PCs do not get very large.	High: Upgrade the server.	Very high: Mainframes get very large.
Platform independent?	No. For PCs only	Yes. Client and server machines may be of any platform type. The two machines may be of different platform types.	No. For terminals and hosts only

Note: A box shaded blue indicates a platform that is different than the other two along this dimension.

Client/server systems are also extremely scalable. Usually, the heavy processing is done on the server, so growth only requires getting a larger server.

Client/server processing is **platform independent,** meaning that it is not limited to PC servers. If the fastest PC is not fast enough, faster computers can be used. A popular choice is the **workstation server.** As Figure 1.11 illustrates, workstation servers generally use very fast (and very expensive) microprocessors that are faster than those in even the fastest PCs. They also usually run the UNIX operating system, which is more reliable but also more complex than Microsoft Windows.

File server program access has poor scalability, however. All processing must be done on the client PC, and client PCs simply do not get very large. File server program access can only run small programs.

Figure 1.11
Personal
Computers versus
Workstation
Servers

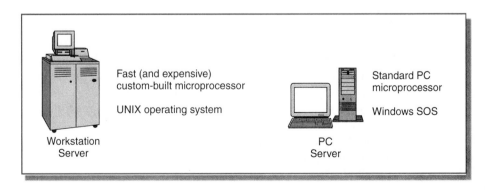

Fast (and expensive) custom-built microprocessor

UNIX operating system

Workstation Server

Standard PC microprocessor

Windows SOS

PC Server

Chapter 1   Basic Concepts and Principles

Response Time Another important performance consideration is **response time,** that is, how long the computer takes to respond when the user hits a key. For file server program access and client/server processing, response time usually is instantaneous because much or all of the processing is done on the user's PC. In contrast, terminal–host systems may take several seconds to respond when a user hits a key. This is very frustrating to users.

Graphics Terminal–host systems were designed in the 1960s, when long-distance transmission costs were very high. Graphics screens take many more bits to transmit than text screens. Consequently, many terminal–host systems used no graphics at all—only text, and text in a single color at that. Although some terminal–host systems used color and graphics, they tended to be limited in their use. In contrast, PC-based file server program access and client/server processing offer full graphical user interfaces.

Test Your Understanding

Answer Core Review Questions 1–6, Detailed Review Questions 1–2, and Thought Question 3.

THE INTERNET

Most people would argue that the Internet is the most important network today. Although LANs within corporations handle most of our basic day-to-day processing, the Internet's global reach and vast number of users make it enormously important.

Multiple Networks

Many data networks existed before the Internet. In fact, the existence of many networks was the problem that led to the creation of the Internet. Computers on different networks could not communicate with one another. As Figure 1.12 illustrates, the U.S. **Defense Advanced Research Projects Agency (DARPA)** solved this problem by creating a way for computers on different networks to work together. The collection of networks linked together so that their computers can communicate is called the **Internet.** The Internet, then, really is a network of networks, not a single network.

Routers and Routes

As shown in Figure 1.12, the various networks on the Internet are connected by devices called **routers,** which are capable of forwarding packets from one computer on one network to any other computer on any other network. (The path that a packet takes across the routers is called its **route.**) To users, routers make the Internet look like a single network. Initially, routers were called **gateways,** and they are sometimes still called gateways today, especially by the Microsoft Corporation.

Figure 1.12
The Internet

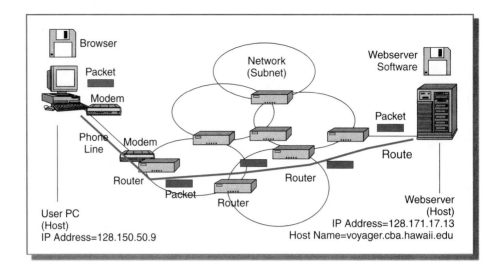

Host Computers

All computers attached to the Internet are called **hosts.** This includes large servers and *also your home PC.*

Note that in *terminal–host computing,* a host is a large machine that serves multiple terminal users. Conversely, in *Internet terminology,* any computer attached to the Internet is a host. In the early days of the Internet, only traditional hosts with terminals were powerful enough to attach to the Internet. Later, when PCs became powerful enough to connect directly, they were lumped into the "host" category on the Internet. You should keep this unfortunate dual use of the term *host* in mind.

IP Addresses

To transmit a message, a **source host** only has to know the Internet address of the **destination host**—just as you only need to know someone's telephone number to call them on the worldwide telephone network.

The Internet actually provides *two* addressing systems. One is the **IP address,** which consists of four numbers separated by dots, for instance, 128.171.17.13. The box, "Dotted Decimal Notation," shows that an IP address really is a string of 32 ones and zeros and that dotted decimal notation is merely a way of representing this string of bits.

The IP address is the host's official address, and every host on the Internet must have an IP address to use the Internet. This includes your home PC when you are on the Internet.[7]

---

[7] In Windows 95 and Windows 98, run the program winipcfg.exe in your Windows directory to see your PC's IP address and other configuration information explained in Chapter 2. Sometimes, winipcfg.exe is not installed by default in Windows 98, and you must load it from the installation disk.

Dotted Decimal Notation

As noted in the body, an IP address really is a string of 32 bits (ones or zeros). However, it is nearly impossible to memorize a long string of ones and zeros. Usually, IP addresses are written in an equivalent but slightly easier-to-remember way. This is dotted decimal notation.

In dotted decimal notation, we begin with a string of 32 bits, as shown in this example:

10101010000000001111111111001100

Next, we divide the string into four **octets,** which are collections of eight bits. In computer memory, collections of eight bits are called *bytes.* In networking, however, "octet" is more common than "byte."

10101010 00000000 11111111 11001100

The next step is to convert each octet into a decimal number. The least significant bit—the one farthest right—has the place value 1. Values double with each bit to the left: 2, 4, 8, 16, 32, 64, and 128 for the bit farthest left. This is shown in Figure 1.13.

Figure 1.13   Dotted Decimal Notation Conversion

Octet Bit	7 Farthest Left	6	5	4	3	2	1	0 Farthest Right
IP address Octet	1	0	1	0	1	0	1	0
Place Value*	128	64	32	16	8	4	2	1
Product	128	0	32	0	8	0	2	0
Total of Products	170							

*Place Value = $2^{\text{Octet Bit}}$. For instance, $2^7 = 128$.

Now, for each bit, the place value is multiplied by the value of the IP address bit in that position (either a zero or a one). Consider the example in Figure 1.13. The first octet is 170 in decimal. If you continue the calculations, the second octet is zero. The third is 255. The fourth is 204. So in dotted decimal notation, this IP address is 170.0.255.204.

Figure 1.14
Internet Service
Providers (ISPs)

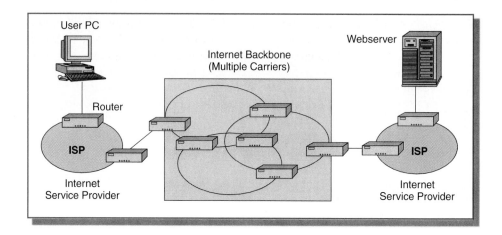

Host Names

While IP addresses are computer-friendly, they are not human-friendly. The other type of address on the Internet is the **host name,** which consists of several text labels separated by dots. For example, the computer with IP address 128.171.17.13 has the host name *voyager.cba.hawaii.edu.*[8] The host name is much easier for people to remember than the official IP address. Although all hosts on the Internet must have IP addresses, host names are optional. Usually, only server hosts have host names.

Internet Service Providers (ISPs)

Initially, commercial activity on the Internet was explicitly forbidden. In time, however, commercial activity began to grow anyway. Rather than fight this trend, the U.S. government privatized its portion of the Internet and turned commercial activity loose in the mid-1990s. As shown in Figure 1.14, all Internet transmission lines and routers in the United States today are owned by commercial organizations.

Technical Role of the ISP   To use the Internet from home or from a business, you must connect to an organization called an **internet service provider (ISP).** More specifically, when you connect to the Internet by telephone, you dial into the ISP's router, which connects you to the other routers on the Internet.

Economic Role of the ISP   The ISP charges you a fee. Some of this fee pays for its internal operations. To pay for the operations of Internet backbone companies, the ISP passes some of your fee on to them. So ISPs have two roles: (1) providing access and (2) handling the collection of fees.

---

[8] Although there are four labels in this host name, there is no correspondence between them and the four numerical segments in the IP address. Furthermore, many host names do not contain four labels.

Not Universal Although the idea of ISPs and a commercial backbone began in the United States, most countries—although not all—have adopted this approach today. ISP rates vary greatly from country to country.

Test Your Understanding

Answer Core Review Questions 7–9, Detailed Review Questions 3–4, and Thought Question 5.

STANDARDS

Although the Internet has many attractions, one of the most important is a strong body of standards. **Standards** *are rules of operation that most or all vendors follow.* Internet standards are **open standards** (i.e., not under the control of any vendor), so vendors can compete for the Internet hardware and software market. Competition has driven down prices and has led to an explosion of new products.

Layered Standards

As Figure 1.15 illustrates, the Internet uses a **layered standards architecture,** with standards in each of five layers doing specific tasks that together allow applications on different hosts to communicate, even if they are on different individual networks. The specific standards shown in Figure 1.15 are those you would encounter when dialing into the Internet from home or a hotel room to use a webserver.

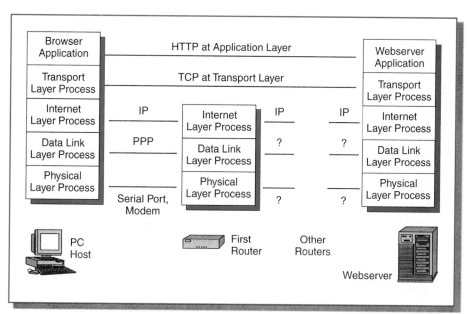

Figure 1.15
Hybrid TCP/IP–OSI Standards Architecture

Application Layer   Standards at the **application layer** *specify how two application programs communicate.* In webservice, these programs are the browser on your client PC and the webserver application program on the webserver.

For webservice, the application layer standard is the **HyperText Transfer Protocol (HTTP).** This is why you type "http://" at the beginnings of uniform resource locators (URLs) for Web information.

Different applications use different application layer standards. For instance, in Chapter 11, we will see that e-mail uses the SMTP and POP application layer standards to send and receive e-mail, respectively.

Transport Layer   Standards at the **transport layer** *specify how two host computers will work together, even if they are of different platform types (e.g., PCs, workstations, mainframes).*

It is the transport layer that gives platform independence. When you use a webserver, it does not matter whether the webserver is a PC, a workstation server, or even a mainframe. Your PC will be able to talk to it using a standardized protocol.

HTTP requires the use of the **Transmission Control Protocol (TCP)** standard at the transport layer. Chapter 3 discusses other transport layer standards.

Internet Layer   Standards at the **internet layer** *specify how hosts and routers will act to route packets end to end, from the source host to the destination host, across many single networks (subnets) connected by routers.* Note that messages at the Internet layer are called **packets.**

The main standard for packet routing on the Internet is the **Internet Protocol (IP).** This is why Internet addresses are called IP addresses.

An internet layer protocol does not say anything about the standards used by subnets. It is only concerned with transmission across single networks. This is the reason for the prefix "inter," which means between, in "Internet."

Data Link Layer   Along the route, each pair of routers is connected by a single network. A single network is called a **subnet.** There is also a subnet between the source host and the first router and another single network between the final router and the destination host.

The bottom two layers govern transmission across a single network. Standards at the **data link layer** *specify how to transmit* **messages** *within a single network.* This includes defining the structure of messages and controlling when stations may transmit their messages.

Messages at the data link layer are called **frames.** So in single networks, when we do packet switching (i.e., sending short messages), we are really "frame switching." However, this is still called packet switching.

When you dial in with a telephone line and a modem, the main standard at the data link layer is the **Point-to-Point Protocol (PPP).**

Physical Layer   The physical layer also governs transmission within a single network (subnet). While the data link layer is concerned with the organization and transmission of organized *messages,* standards at the **physical layer** *specify how to transmit* **single bits** *one at a time.* It leaves the interpretation of these bits as messages to the data link layer.

Physical layer standards govern things you can feel and touch, such as wires, connector plugs, and electrical voltages.

In dial-in access by telephone and modem, physical layer standards govern telephony and modem operation. Most modems today, for instance, follow the **V.90** standard, which governs transmission at 33.6 kbps but reception at 56 kbps.

Hybrid TCP/IP–OSI Standards Architecture

The five layers of standards shown in Figure 1.15 actually are taken from two very different standards architectures, as shown in Figure 1.16.

TCP/IP and the IETF   Internet standards at the application, transport, and internet layers are created by the **Internet Engineering Task Force (IETF).** These standards usually are called **TCP/IP** standards after the most important transport and internet layer standards, TCP and IP, respectively. This is confusing, because TCP/IP is a standards architecture, while TCP and IP are individual standards within the TCP/IP architecture.

IETF's TCP/IP standards tend to be very simple, resulting in rapid standards development. In addition, because standards are simple, products are inexpensive and are developed rapidly. "Inexpensive and fast to market" is a good recipe for success in any industry, and TCP/IP standards are becoming dominant above the subnet layers.

Figure 1.16
TCP/IP and OSI Standards in the Hybrid TCP/IP–OSI Standards Architecture

TCP/IP Layer	OSI Layer	Hybrid TCP/IP–OSI Layer	Purpose
Application	Application (7)	Application (5)	Allows two application programs to communicate effectively.
	Presentation (6)		
	Session (5)		
Transport	Transport (4)	Transport (4)	Allows two computers to communicate even if they are of different platform types.
Internet	Network (3)	Internet (3)	Governs the transmission of packets across multiple networks, via a mesh of routers. Each pair of routers is connected by a single network (subnet).
Subnet	Data Link (2)	Data Link (2)	Governs the transmission of *frames* within a single network (subnet).
	Physical (1)	Physical (1)	Governs the transmission of *individual bits* wthin a single network (subnet).

Notes: TCP/IP is the standards architecture created and maintained by the IETF.
OSI is the standards architecture created and maintained by ISO and ITU-T.

OSI, ISO, and ITU-T   Despite the dominance of TCP/IP at upper layers, the IETF rarely creates standards for subnets.[9] Instead, standards for single networks at the data link and physical layers usually are set by two other organizations. These are the **International Organization for Standardization (ISO)** and the **International Telecommunications Union–Telecommunications Standards Sector (ITU-T)**.[10] Their joint standards architecture is called **OSI**.[11] Even when ISO and ITU-T do not create standards, they must ratify standards created by others before these standards become official OSI standards.

---

[9] In a rare exception to the general pattern, the IETF did create PPP.

[10] No, the abbreviations do not match the names very well, but these are the official abbreviations.

[11] Reference Model of Open Systems Interconnection. Now you see why everybody uses the abbreviation.

OSI versus TCP/IP Layering

Figure 1.17 compares TCP/IP and OSI layers. Different authors will show different match ups because the two architectures define their layers differently, making comparisons difficult. However, in terms of *actual standards* produced in the two architectures, we argue that they match up very well at the lower four layers.

Figure 1.17   Layering in TCP/IP versus OSI

TCP/IP	OSI	OSI Layer Meaning
Application	Application (7)	Application–application interactions, free of presentation and session concerns.
	Presentation (6)	Allows two sides to negotiate and then use common transfer standards for representing data.
	Session (5)	Used to coordinate application–application interactions, such as setting up rollback points in a series of transactions.
Transport	Transport (4)	Allows two computers to communicate even if they are from different vendors and are of different platform types.
Internet	Network (3)	Now used for internetting.
Subnet: Use OSI Layers	Data Link (2)	Governs the transmission of frames within a single network (subnet).
	Physical (1)	Governs the transmission of individual bits within a single network (subnet).

Physical and Data Link Layers (OSI Layers 1 and 2)
TCP/IP calls for the use of OSI physical and data link layer standards, so by definition, the match-up in these two layers is perfect.

Continued.

Chapter 1   Basic Concepts and Principles

Network Layer (OSI Layer 3)

The OSI network layer (layer 3) was created for rather complex single networks of a type that never became popular.[12] However, OSI did create internet standards at the network layer.

Transport Layer (OSI Layer 4)

The OSI transport layer (layer 4) has standards that are functionally similar to those of the TCP/IP transport layer.

Application Layers

The three highest layers of OSI deal with the coordination of applications running on different computers. Together, they serve the function of the single TCP/IP application layer.

Session Layer (OSI Layer 5)

The OSI session layer (layer 5) was created for applications in which several single transactions may be necessary to complete an overall task. The session layer keeps track of the status of the transaction exchanges.

Presentation Layer (OSI Layer 6)

The OSI presentation layer (layer 6) allows the two communicating application processes to negotiate a common syntax for representing various types of information (e.g., text, graphics).

Application Layer (OSI Layer 7)

The OSI application layer (layer 7) deals with the specifics of particular applications, freed from data representation and transaction bookkeeping.

Test Your Understanding

Answer Core Review Questions 10–11 and Detailed Review Question 5.

---

[12]Specifically, networks that have switches connected in a mesh, much like the routers are connected in Figure 1.12. This creates the possibility of many alternative routes between any two end stations. The single network (subnet) standards we will see throughout this book only allow a single possible path between stations. This greatly reduces their complexity and therefore their cost.

Hybrid TCP/IP–OSI Standards Architecture   The five-layer architecture shown in Figure 1.15 that dominates Internet usage today combines standards from these two "pure" architectures, so we call it the **hybrid TCP/IP–OSI standards architecture.**

Standards Architectures   Another name for "standards architecture" is **standards framework.** Just as the architecture of a house is a framework for creating individual rooms within an overall plan, a **standards architecture** is a framework for creating individual standards within an overall layered plan.

OSI versus TCP/IP Layering   The box, "OSI versus TCP/IP Layering," compares OSI and TCP/IP layering in more detail.

Although networking is exciting today, what we now see is only the beginning of the networking era. In 10 years, we will think of today's networks and applications the way we now think of biplanes and Model-T Fords. Although predicting network trends has not had a good track record, there are two sets of issues that most analysts feel will be important in the next few years.

Quality of Service (QoS)

Anyone who has used the Internet extensively knows that it is far from perfect. Often, it is unbearably slow. There are also service quality problems on internal LANs and on commercial WANs. Network standards agencies are beginning to respond with standards for **quality of service (QoS)** in which network service providers can guarantee certain performance limits.

Congestion and Speed   One of the biggest problems facing network users is **congestion,** in which capacity is insufficient for the traffic being sent.

Latency   Congestion creates transmission delays. In networking, delay is called **latency.** We would like to have QoS guarantees for maximum latency. We might like, for example, to be guaranteed a maximum latency of 50 milliseconds (ms).

Throughput   These latency guarantees must be tied to **throughput** guarantees, which would guarantee us a certain transmission rate. For instance, we might require a guaranteed throughput of 1 million bits per second. QoS for latency and throughput are discussed in more detail in Chapter 8.

Reliability   If we pick up a telephone and do not hear a dial tone, we are extremely surprised. The telephone system is enormously reliable. Data networks, in contrast, often have serious reliability problems. We would like QoS guarantees for reliability. In general, we are most concerned with two reliability measures.

Availability   The first is **availability,** which is the percentage of time the network is available for use. We would like our networks to be available over 99.999% of the time.

Error Rate   The second is the **error rate,** which is the percentage of bits or messages that contain errors. Data from 1999 indicate an average loss rate for ISPs of 3% to 6% of all packets.[13] We would like this to be far lower.

---

[13] Greenfield, D., & Williams, M., Top 25 ISPs, *Data Communications,* June 1999, source was online at http://www.data.com/issue/990607/topisps.html.

Security

When network technology was new, security was not a significant concern. Today, however, security is a crucial issue in networks. A great deal of highly sensitive information today is stored in network-accessible databases and flows over the network to get from one location to another. In addition, there is growing evidence that computer crime within corporations and on the Internet has already grown to disturbing levels.

Encryption   One tool for security is **encryption,** in which we encrypt (i.e., scramble) messages before we transmit them. No one intercepting the encrypted messages will be able to read them. However, the receiver will be able to decrypt them back to their original form.

Access Control   Not everyone in an organization should be given access to all resources in the firm. **Access control** tools allow us to specify who should access specific resources and to restrict access to those people (or software processes) who should not have access. Today, access control typically uses **passwords,** most of which are far too easy to guess, thus being ineffective.

Authentication   In **authentication,** the sender proves his or her identity to the receiver. In the non-computer world, for instance, when you wish to cash a check, you often have to show your driver's license to authenticate yourself. Of course, authentication is important in access control. However, it is important in its own right, especially in electronic commerce. You want to be certain that you are dealing with a specific person or company, not with an impostor.

KEY POINTS

Distributed Processing   This chapter looked at three main computer platforms: (1) terminal–host systems, (2) file server program access, and (3) client/server processing. Client/server processing is platform independent, so the server often is a machine faster than a personal computer, for instance, a workstation server. Each platform type has advantages and disadvantages. It is important for you to be able to compare them as alternatives when you create or purchase applications.

Voice and Data Networks   For voice and video communication, the public telephone network uses circuit switching, which guarantees capacity but is wasteful for bursty data communications. In turn, data communications, in which at least one of the communication partners is a computer, normally uses packet-switched networks that send messages in small packets (or frames) and multiplex these packets efficiently along trunk lines between switches. Packet switching reduces costs through multiplexing, but there is a danger that congestion will occur.

The Internet The Internet is not a single network, but rather thousands of networks connected by devices called routers, which are sometimes called gateways. The Internet routes messages, called packets, from a source host to a destination host across a mesh of routers. Every computer on the Internet is a host computer regardless of size. Every host must have a unique IP address. Some hosts also have host names.

Layered Standards Multiple standards must be at work for two application programs on different computers on different networks to be able to work together. This chapter introduced the hybrid TCP/IP–OSI standards architecture, which dominates Internet use today and indeed dominates most non-Internet networking. This framework, or architecture, has five layers: (1) application, (2) transport, (3) internet, (4) data link, and (5) physical. When you access a webserver by telephone, the standards at these layers are HTTP, TCP, IP, PPP, and modem standards, respectively.

The Ubiquity of Change Although the Internet and corporate networks are already exciting, we are only in the early childhood of networking today. The mantra of "anything, anytime, anywhere" will soon become a reality. The last part of the chapter examined two of the many changes we can expect to see in networking in the near future: (1) a growing concern for security and (2) quality of service (QoS) guarantees for speed and reliability. Of course, the most exciting changes will be those we cannot foresee today. The important thing is to avoid thinking of today's networks as the networks we will see in 5 or 10 years.

Fundamental Concepts Finally, this chapter introduced a number of fundamental concepts that we will see throughout this book, including the following, which you should know thoroughly:

- analog, digital, and binary transmission
- multiplexing
- scalability
- circuit switching versus packet switching
- LANs versus WANs
- congestion and latency
- quality of service guarantees for speed (latency and throughput)
- quality of service guarantees for reliability (availability and error rates)
- encryption, access control, and authentication
- legacy systems
- platform independence
- terminal–host system, file server program access, and client/server processing

THE REMAINDER OF THE BOOK

The Remainder of the Core Chapters

This book has twelve core chapters that deal with the following topics:

- Chapter 2: Cooperation among standards at different layers
- Chapter 3: Details of the HTTP, TCP, IP, and PPP standards
- Chapter 4: Physical layer concepts
- Chapter 5: Reaching the Internet from home or the road
- Chapter 6: Small PC networks
- Chapter 7: Small Ethernet LANs
- Chapter 8: Site networks using Ethernet, ATM switches, routers, and layer 3 switches
- Chapter 9: Wide area networks
- Chapter 10: Security
- Chapter 11: Standards for networked applications
- Chapter 12: Looking ahead

The Advanced Modules   The advanced modules provide more in-depth information on key topics.

Test Your Understanding

Answer Core Review Questions 12–14.

REVIEW QUESTIONS

For questions with multiple parts, write the answer to each part in a separate line or paragraph.

Core Review Questions

1. **a)** What is a network? **b)** For delivery over a network, what does the sender have to know? **c)** Distinguish between voice and data communications.

2. **a)** Distinguish between circuit switching and packet switching. **b)** What is the switching decision? **c)** Which traditionally has been used for voice? Why? **d)** Which traditionally has been used for data? Why? **e)** What is multiplexing? **f)** Why is it desirable?

3. **a)** Define the following: 1) analog communication, 2) digital communication, and 3) binary communication. **b)** What does a modem do?

4. Distinguish between LANs and WANs.

5. **a)** Distinguish among terminal–host systems, file server program access, and client/server processing in terms of where processing is done. **b)** What is scalability? **c)** Explain the implications of the first part of your

answer (location of processing) for scalability. **d)** What is platform independence, and how does it enhance scalability in client/server processing? **e)** What are the implications of your answer to Part a) for graphics? **f)** What are the implications of your answer to Part a) for response time?

6. **a)** If you wish to increase the size of a client/server processing system, what do you do? **b)** How do PCs and workstations differ?

7. What are the main technical elements of the Internet? Describe each in a separate paragraph.

8. **a)** Distinguish between IP addresses and host names. **b)** Which is the official address of a host? **c)** Does a server host need an IP address? **d)** Does your home PC need an IP address when you are on the Internet? **e)** Does a server host need a host name? **f)** Does your home PC need a host name when you are on the Internet?

9. **a)** Is the Internet free in the United States and most other countries? **b)** What are the two roles of Internet service providers (ISPs)?

10. **a)** Name the five layers in the TCP/IP–OSI hybrid architecture. **b)** What do standards at each layer specify? (Write a separate paragraph for each layer.) **c)** What standard are you likely to use in each layer when you reach the Internet from home to work with a webserver? **d)** What are messages called at the internet layer? **e)** What are messages called at the data link layer?

11. **a)** What standards agency manages TCP/IP standards? **b)** What agencies manage OSI standards? **c)** Which layers in the hybrid TCP/IP–OSI standards architecture use TCP/IP standards? **d)** Which use OSI standards?

12. **a)** What is latency? **b)** What causes latency?

13. **a)** What is Quality of Service (QoS)? **b)** What performance measures does it cover?

14. What are the main elements in security? Briefly describe each.

Detailed Review Questions

1. List and explain the elements of a PC network on a small LAN, one element per paragraph.

2. **a)** Why are terminal–host systems referred to as legacy systems? **b)** Why don't we simply replace them all? **c)** What is replacing them called?

3. What are the two meanings we saw in this chapter for the word "host?"

4. Referring to the box, "Dotted Decimal Notation," convert the following IP address to dotted decimal notation. Show your work. 10101010 11110000 11001100 01010101. (Spaces are included to facilitate reading.)

5. Referring to the box, "OSI versus TCP/IP Layering," **a)** Name the OSI layers and their layer numbers. **b)** Briefly characterize each OSI layer. Write each in a separate paragraph. **c)** Describe how OSI and TCP/IP layers match up.

Thought Questions

1. What was the most surprising thing you learned in this chapter?

2. What was the most difficult part of this chapter for you?

3. **a)** Is the term "legacy system" limited to mainframe terminal–host system? **b)** What would a legacy network be?

4. In the opening vignette, Glenn Davis is a road warrior. **a)** What benefits is he experiencing? **b)** What problems is he experiencing? **c)** Decide whether his company should get the high-speed wireless Internet access service. Justify your decision. **d)** List technical concepts in the chapter that are explicitly illustrated in this vignette.

5. **a)** Why do you think the Internet is so attractive to businesses? **b)** To employees?

Case Studies

For case studies, go to the book's website, **http://www.prenhall.com/panko,** and look at the "Case Studies" page for this chapter.

Projects

1. **Getting Current.** Go to the book's website's "New Information" and "Errors" pages for this chapter to get new information since this book went to press and to correct any errors in the text.

2. **Internet Exercises.** Go to the book's website's "Exercises" page for this chapter and do the Internet Exercises.

3. **Client/Server Computing.** Create two applications in Visual Basic: a client program and a server program. In this programming project, which will continue through later chapters, you will simply create the forms for the two programs in this Chapter 1 portion of the project. Details on the "Internet Exercises" page for this chapter can be found at the book's website, **http://www.prenhall.com/panko.**

Chapter 2

Layered (Encapsulated) Communication for Internet Access

Glenn Davis of Paradise Groceries has been using the Internet for five years. Although he is fairly comfortable with the Internet, there are still many things that confuse him.

One is the "alphabet soup" of abbreviations he comes across. He constantly hears things like HTTP, TCP, IP, PPP, DNS, and DHCP. Apparently, all are standards, but why does the Internet need so many of them? Why isn't the Internet Protocol (IP) enough to do the job? And he wonders what the differences are among the terms TCP/IP, TCP, and IP—if there are differences at all.

Another thing that puzzles him is that sometimes when he types a uniform resource locator (URL), he is told that the host named in the URL does not exist. Yet often this is a host name he has been using successfully for months or even years. What is going on?

Also, when he looks at his computer's network setup, there are several meaningless (to him, at least) parameters he needs to type in: DNS host addresses, gateways, subnet masks, and other obtuse pieces of information. He hopes to learn at least enough to set up his new Windows PC to access the Internet.

Finally, in the office, he uses a file server on his PC network. He has been told that when he communicates with this file server, he does not use IP at all. ∎

Learning Objectives

After studying this chapter, you should be able to understand:

- Layered communication, using encapsulation in the context of Internet access.

- The Domain Name System (DNS) and autoconfiguration.

- The main network setup concepts and parameters in Microsoft Windows.

INTRODUCTION

In Chapter 1, we looked at the historical evolution of networking and examined key issues for the future. In this chapter, we begin to look at the complex world of network standards.

Standards Basics   We will begin by looking at standards in general, including what they are, why we need them, why message exchange is central, how to understand the structure of messages, and how to understand temporal interactions between processes.

Layering and Encapsulation   Next, we will see how standards at different layers work together to deliver messages between application programs, even if the applications are on different machines attached to different networks. Specifically, we will look at a process called *encapsulation*.

Helper Standards: DNS and Autoconfiguration   We will also look at two critical helper standards that you use almost every time you use the Internet. These are the Domain Name System (DNS) and autoconfiguration protocols.

Setting Up Internet Access in Windows 98   After looking at the main standards you use when you access the Internet, we will see how to set up a Windows 98 computer to work with the Internet via a telephone line and a modem.

Living in a Multiprotocol World   The chapter closes with a reminder that TCP/IP has many standards beyond the ones we will discuss in this chapter and that TCP/IP is not the only standards architecture. Today, we live in a multiprotocol world.

Standards *are rules of operation that are followed by most or all vendors.* Standards allow hardware and software from different vendors to work together. For example, consider what happens when you use your browser to download pages from a webserver. It does not matter (apart from advanced features) which browser you use; nor does it matter (again, apart from advanced features) whether the webserver application program came from Microsoft, Netscape, or a nonprofit organization. In such an open environment, competition among vendors brings lower prices and feature-rich products.

Standards Work Through Message Exchange

As Figure 2.1 shows, standards generally work by governing the exchange of messages between two hardware or software processes. However, computers do not have the flexibility of human intelligence, so network standards have to be limited and precisely defined.

Message Structure

First, messages must be structured in a highly predictable way. Figure 2.2 shows how messages are structured in the two central standards for the Internet: the Transmission Control Protocol (TCP) and the Internet Protocol (IP). We will discuss these standards later in this chapter and in more depth in Chapter 3.

Message Structure Diagrams A message is nothing more than a long string of bits (ones and zeros). However, unless your paper is several meters

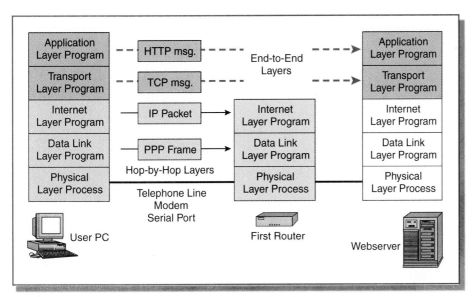

Figure 2.1
Standards Govern Interactions through the Exchange of Messages

Figure 2.2
Message Structure
Diagrams

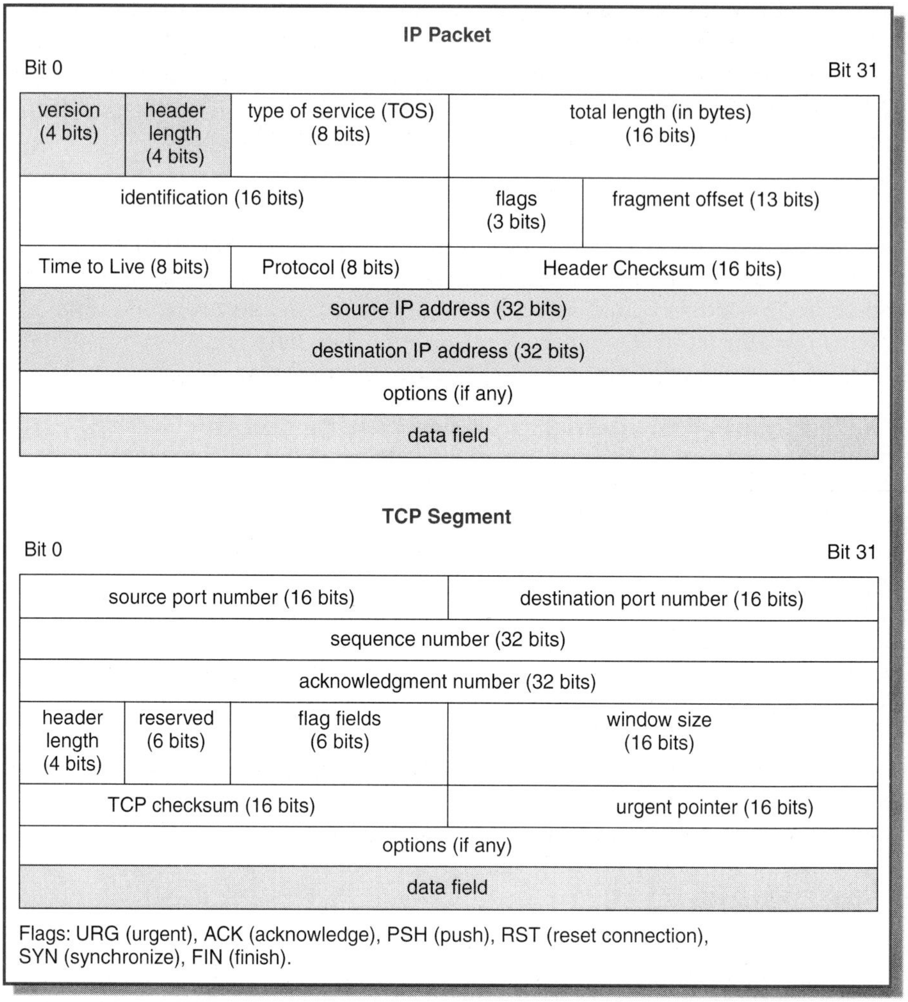

IP Packet

Bit 0   Bit 31

version (4 bits)	header length (4 bits)	type of service (TOS) (8 bits)	total length (in bytes) (16 bits)	
identification (16 bits)			flags (3 bits)	fragment offset (13 bits)
Time to Live (8 bits)		Protocol (8 bits)	Header Checksum (16 bits)	
source IP address (32 bits)				
destination IP address (32 bits)				
options (if any)				
data field				

TCP Segment

Bit 0   Bit 31

source port number (16 bits)		destination port number (16 bits)	
sequence number (32 bits)			
acknowledgment number (32 bits)			
header length (4 bits)	reserved (6 bits)	flag fields (6 bits)	window size (16 bits)
TCP checksum (16 bits)		urgent pointer (16 bits)	
options (if any)			
data field			

Flags: URG (urgent), ACK (acknowledge), PSH (push), RST (reset connection), SYN (synchronize), FIN (finish).

wide, it is difficult to display a long string of bits. To show message structures, we arbitrarily divide these long bit strings into units of fixed length and display each unit on a separate line. In Figure 2.2, each line (unit) represents 32 bits, with bits 0 through 31 on the first line, 32 through 63 on the second line, and so forth. (In binary, you begin counting at 0.)

Fields Moving away from display issues, messages really are logically divided into groups of bits called **fields,** which are identified by their position in the overall bit string. For example, in IP, the first field is the IP Version field (see Figure 2.2). This field is four bits long. Most hosts and routers today use Version 4 of the Internet Protocol. In such cases, the first four bits have the value 0100 (four in Base 2). The receiver knows that the fifth bit will be the first bit in the next field, the Header Length field.

Octets   In computer memory, information is stored in groups of eight bits called *bytes*. For historical reasons, networking specialists call groups of eight bits **octets.** This may seem a little strange at first, but the name certainly is more logical than "byte," because "octo" means eight (e.g., octopus, octagon). In any case, the term *octet* is used so widely in networking that you must be familiar with it.

Data Field   The data field is sometimes called the information field or the payload. It holds the information the message is trying to deliver to the other side. Think of the data field as the letter inside an envelope and other fields as the instructions on the envelope. Although the data field is only a single field, it is usually the longest and most important field in the message.

Header Fields   The initial fields in the message are collectively known as the **header.** The header consists of all fields before the data field. Although many header fields are shown for TCP and IP in Figure 2.2, most are only a few octets long. Collectively, these header fields usually are much smaller than the data field.

Postal envelopes have the recipient's address, a return address, and special handling instructions. These are included to guide the receiver. Analogously, header fields (and, as noted later, the trailer fields) provide information to allow the receiving hardware or software process to handle the data field appropriately.

Sometimes, however, there is no data field at all, and the message consists entirely of the header. For example, some TCP **supervisory messages,** which carry instructions instead of data, only need information in the header fields. These messages have no data fields.

Trailer Fields   Some messages also have fields following the data field. These fields are called, collectively, the **trailer.** Neither TCP nor IP in Figure 2.2 have trailers. Typically, trailer fields are only found in data link layer messages.

Message Time Diagrams

In addition to controlling message structures, networking standards govern the timing of messages. To give a trivial example, in client/server processing, the server program cannot send a response message until it has first received a request message. In general, two **processes** (either hardware or software) talk back and forth in a highly controlled way, such as actors in a play or birds in a mating dance.

To illustrate controlled dialogs, we often use **message time diagrams.** Figure 2.3 shows a message time diagram for two request–response cycles for the HyperText Transfer Protocol (HTTP). Time begins at the top and moves downward. In other words, lower message exchanges come later than higher message exchanges. In later chapters, we will see much more complex message time diagrams.

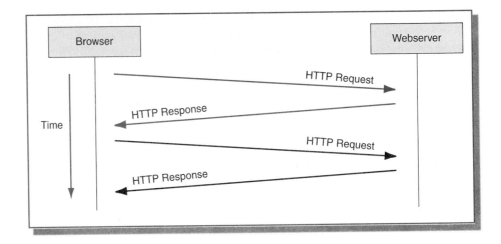

Figure 2.3
Message Time
Diagram for Two
HTTP Request–
Response Cycles

Standards When You Connect to a Webserver from Home

As discussed in Chapter 1, when you connect to the Internet from home using a telephone line and modem, you are dealing with standards at all five layers of the hybrid TCP/IP–OSI standards architecture. Figure 2.1 illustrates these layers.

Application Layer: HTTP   At the application layer, standards govern communication between the client program on your PC and the server application program (e.g., webserver application, mail application). For the World Wide Web, the application layer standard is HTTP. Other applications use different application layer standards.

Transport Layer: TCP   At the transport layer, standards ensure that the two host computers can work with each other even if they come from different vendors and are different computer types (PC, workstation, etc.). HTTP mandates the use of the Transmission Control Protocol (TCP) at the transport layer. Other applications use other transport layer protocols.

Internet Layer: IP   At the internet layer, standards govern the routing of packets end to end, from the source host to the destination host across a mesh network of routers connected by single networks (subnets). The main TCP/IP standard at the internet layer is the Internet Protocol (IP), although there are other internet layer standards. IP messages are called IP **packets** because "packet" is the general name for internet layer messages.

Data Link Layer: PPP   At the data link layer, standards govern the transmission of messages within a single network (subnet). Messages at the data link layer are called **frames.** For the subnet between your PC and the first router, i.e., for the telephone line linking you to your Internet service provider (ISP), the standard usually is the **Point-to-Point Protocol (PPP).** Other subnets linking routers along the route your packet takes to the destination host are likely to use different subnet (data link and physical layer) standards. PPP is used primarily on low-speed modem connections.

Physical Layer: Modems and Telephone Lines At the physical layer, standards govern the transmission of individual bits within a single network (subnet). In telephone transmission, telephone network standards as well as modem standards are physical layer standards. Modems are only used to link a user host to the first router. Other router–router links will almost certainly use faster transmission technologies, and even home users often use faster transmission technologies, which are discussed in Chapter 5.

Protocols

The term "protocol" appears in the names of many of the standards we have seen. A protocol is a specific type of standard. A **protocol** is a standard for communication between **peer processes,** that is, processes at the *same layer* but on *different machines*. For example, the HyperText Transfer *Protocol* is a standard for communication between application layer programs on the source host and the destination host. The Point-to-Point *Protocol*, in turn, is a standard for communication between data link layer processes on the source host and the first router. All of the standards shown in Figure 2.1 are protocols, and their names generally reflect this fact.

Test Your Understanding

Answer Core Review Questions 1–3 and Detailed Review Questions 1–2.

LAYER COOPERATION THROUGH ENCAPSULATION

The five layers of the hybrid TCP/IP–OSI standards architecture do not work independently. The most critical goal in the development of any standards architecture is to define a set of layers that, working together, will allow application programs on different computers on different networks to communicate effectively.

Layer Cooperation: Indirect Communication and Encapsulation

Figure 2.4 shows how processes at adjacent layers on the same machine cooperate to deliver messages. An application program on a source host creates a message for an application program on a destination host. Let us assume that the source application is a browser and that the message is an HTTP request message in which the browser asks the webserver application program for a particular webpage.

Figure 2.4
Indirect
Communication
Between
Application
Programs

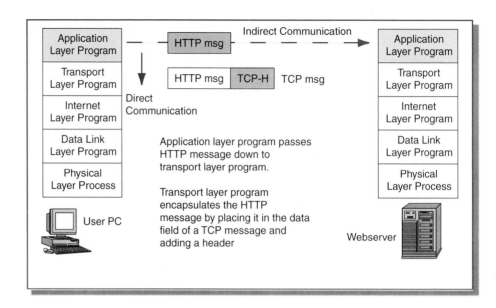

Indirect Communication The two application programs are on different machines, so the source application cannot transmit its message *directly* to the destination application program—just as you cannot directly deliver a letter directly to a friend in another city.

Instead, the application programs communicate indirectly. The source application passes the application layer message down to the next-lower layer, the transport layer, and asks the transport process to deliver the message.

Figure 2.4 illustrates this **indirect communication** by showing the indirect communication between the two application programs with a dashed line and the direct communication between the source application program and the source transport layer program with a solid line.

Encapsulation As Figure 2.4 illustrates, the transport layer creates a transport layer message according to the TCP standard. This requires creating a TCP header, using the format shown in Figure 2.2.

In the data field of this TCP message, the transport program places the application message—the HTTP request. *This process of placing the message of the next-higher layer process in the data field of a message and then adding a layer header (and perhaps trailer) is called* **encapsulation.**

Layered Communication on the Source Host

Figure 2.5 continues the processes needed on the source host for the delivery of the application program message.

Continued Encapsulation Figure 2.5 shows that encapsulation continues down to the data link layer. Each layer takes the message of the next-higher layer, adds its own header and perhaps trailer, and then passes the message down to the next-lower layer.

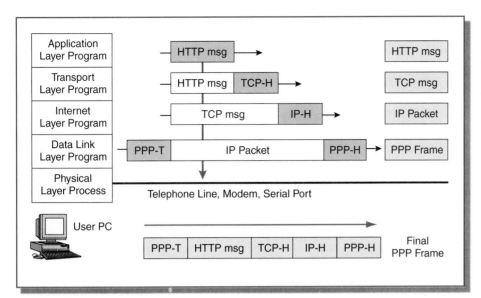

Figure 2.5
Indirect Communication through Encapsulation on the Source Host

The Final Frame Figure 2.5 also shows the final data link layer frame. The first five octets will be the PPP header (discussed in Chapter 3). Next will come the IP header (usually 20 octets), followed by the TCP header (also usually 20 octets), followed by the HTTP request message, and followed by the PPP trailer (3 octets).

The Physical Layer The physical layer works one bit at a time, so there is no physical layer message. When the data link layer process finishes building the PPP frame, it passes the frame down to the physical layer process. The physical layer process then transmits the frame, one bit at a time, to the physical layer process on the first router—the router to which the source host connects.

There is no need for the physical layer process to pass anything down to a lower layer. At the physical layer only, there is a *direct* connection to another machine. There is no need for indirect communication.

Refinements In the next chapter, we will see that the actual processes involved in encapsulation are somewhat more complex than we have seen. What will remain exactly true, however, is that *whenever a process creates a message, it passes the message down to the next-lower-layer process for handling.*

Layered Communication on the Destination Host

Figure 2.6 shows that the situation on the destination host is the reverse of the situation on the source host.

At the Physical Layer As Figure 2.6 illustrates, information arrives at the destination host from the final router as a stream of voltage levels

Figure 2.6
Indirect
Communication
through
Deencapsulation
on the Destination
Host

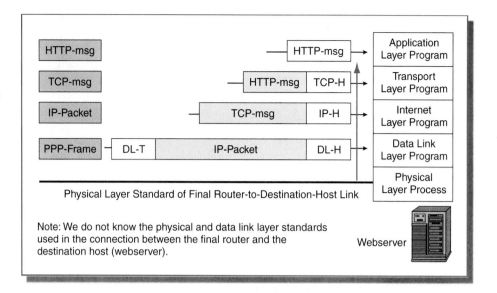

representing bits. The destination host's physical layer process converts these voltages into bits and passes the resulting data link layer frame up to the data link layer.

At the Data Link, Internet, and Transport Layers   The data link layer process on the destination host checks the data link layer header and trailer. If everything is correct, the data link layer removes the encapsulated IP packet from the frame's data field and passes the packet up to the next-higher layer—the internet layer.

This process of checking, deencapsulation, and passing the contents of the data field to the next-higher layer process repeats itself at the internet and transport layers.

At the Application Layer   When the transport layer passes the deencapsulated HTTP request to the application layer, the indirect communication is finished. The application layer message that began the process has reached its destination.

Of course, indirect communication will begin again when the webserver application finds the requested webpage, creates an HTTP response message containing the webpage, and passes the message down to its own transport layer process to begin the encapsulation process again, in the reverse direction.

Layered Communication on Routers

End-to-End and Hop-by-Hop Layers   At the application and transport layers, indirect communication governs communication between layer processes on the source host and the destination host, as Figure 2.1 illustrates. These are called **end-to-end layers.**

However, the internet, data link, and physical layer processes on the source host do not communicate with their peers on the destination host. Instead, they communicate with their peers on the *first router*, as Figure 2.1 shows. We call these **hop-by-hop layers.** Host–router, router–router, and router–host communication take place only at the hop-by-hop layers.

Multiple Ports (Interfaces): Router Forwarding Decisions Your PC has multiple ports, including one or two serial ports, a parallel port, a display port, and other ports. A **port** is the combination of a connector plug and internal electronics at the physical layer (and sometimes also at data link layer).

In the same way, as Figure 2.7 illustrates, a router has several ports leading to different networks (or subnets). In the router world, these ports often are called **interfaces.** The router receives a message through one port, selects another port to send the message out again, and transmits the message out that port. Selecting an output port or interface is called the **router forwarding decision.** It is the router's core task.

Figure 2.8 shows layered processes on the first router. For simplicity, only two ports are shown: the input port on which the IP packet arrives and the output port that the router selects to send the IP packet back out.

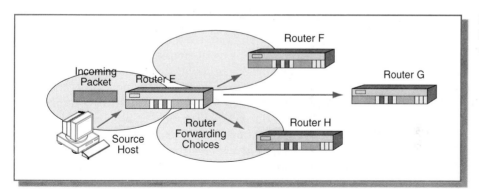

Figure 2.7
Routing Decision on the First Router

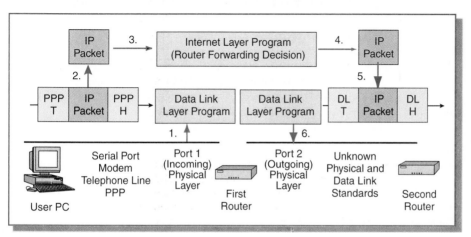

Figure 2.8
Layered Communication on the First Router

On the Input Port   The message arrives at the input port. As Figure 2.8 illustrates, this port has a physical layer and a data link layer. The physical layer passes the bits of the data link layer frame up to the data link layer process on that port. The data link layer processes the frame's header and trailer. If everything is correct, the data link layer on the input port passes the IP packet up to the internet layer process on the router.

At the Internet Layer   The internet layer process must select an output port to send the IP packet back on its way. In this example, there are only two interfaces (ports), and routers do not send IP packets back out their input ports because these packets have already come from that subnet. So the internet layer process passes the IP packet down to the other port's data link layer process. In the next chapter, we will see more sophisticated router forwarding decisions.

On the Output Interface   The output port connects the router to the next router (or to the destination host). The data link layer program on the output port receives the IP packet from the internet layer process, as Figure 2.8 shows. It adds its own data link layer header and probably trailer to encapsulate the IP packet. It then passes the data link layer frame down to the output port's physical layer process for delivery to the next router or to the destination host.

Layered Communication in Perspective

What we have just seen may seem complicated, but it is a complexity created by having many steps that are individually very simple. When a host or router transmits (sends), it keeps passing messages down one layer at a time, each time adding a header and perhaps a trailer to encapsulate the message of the next-higher layer. In turn, when a host or router receives, each layer reads a message, removes the data field, and passes the data field to the next-higher layer process.

There are only two subtleties, and both are fairly blatant to be called subtleties. First, at the physical, data link, and internet layers, processes on the source host communicate with peer processes on the first router, not with peer processes on the destination host. Second, on routers, processing takes place only at the physical, data link, and internet layers when an IP packet is being forwarded.[1]

Test Your Understanding

Answer Core Review Question 4 and Detailed Review Questions 3–4.

OTHER KEY TCP/IP PROTOCOLS

We have covered the main protocols you use at the five layers of the hybrid TCP/IP–OSI standards framework when you log into the Internet from home to use a webserver. However, we need to look at two more topics to enhance

---

[1] For some other types of work, a router does do processing at the transport and application layers.

the picture of TCP/IP standards when you dial into the Internet. These are the Domain Name System and autoconfiguration protocols.

Domain Name System (DNS)

We saw in Chapter 1 that *IP addresses,* such as 128.171.17.13, are the official addresses of hosts (and routers) on the Internet. However, there is a second type of address on the Internet, the *host name* (e.g., voyager.cba.hawaii.edu). Typically, users only know host names, not IP addresses. Host names are easy to remember, but they are not official addresses.

Domain Name System (DNS) Hosts   Figure 2.9 shows that when you type a webserver's host name in a browser window, a program on your PC called a **resolver** sends a **Domain Name System (DNS)** request message to your organization's or ISP's **local DNS host.** This message says, in effect, "Here is the host name of my target host; please send me its IP address."[2]

The local DNS host has a simple table listing host names and corresponding IP addresses.[3] It finds the IP address corresponding to the host name you sent

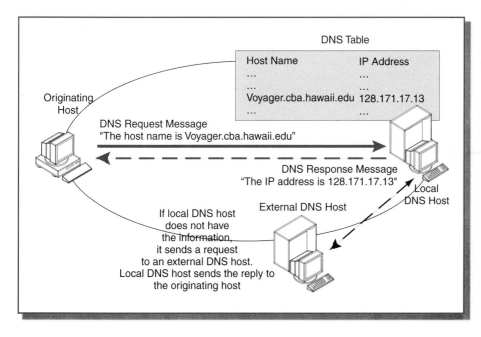

Figure 2.9
Domain Name System (DNS) Host Interactions

---

[2] In general on the Internet, a "name" identifies an object, while an "address" tells where that object is. The DNS allows you to learn where a host or other resource is if you only know its name.

[3] Only a single IP address is associated with a single host name in this example. However, a single computer with a single IP address may be given multiple host names, just as people can be known by more than one name. Whatever host name the user enters, he or she will be pointed to the same target host by the DNS host. It is even possible for a single host name to be associated with multiple IP addresses. Each time the DNS host is queried, it will give a different IP address on the list. This allows you, for instance, to have several webservers associated with a single host name and to allow the DNS to do crude "load balancing" among them. Finally, a single physical host computer can have multiple IP addresses.

in the DNS request message. It sends this information back in a DNS response message. Your PC can now send IP packets to the target host.

Multiple Host Interactions Actually, your local DNS host is only required to know host names and IP addresses for hosts and routers within your organization or that are served by your ISP. If you specify a host name for a host in another organization or ISP, your local DNS host will contact other DNS hosts to find the information, as Figure 2.9 illustrates.[4]

However, this indirect look-up is transparent to you, the user, because only your local DNS host will send you a response, as shown in Figure 2.9. Other DNS hosts send their information back to your local DNS host, which passes it on to you. The only way the user even suspects that multiple DNS hosts have been involved is that the process takes longer than usual.

Domains Host names are a specific example of a broader concept called **domain names.** A **domain** is a set of resources under the control of some organization.

As Figure 2.10 illustrates, the Internet Domain Name System is a hierarchy. Under the overall level, called the **root,** there are **first-level domains** that specify either a type of organization, such as *com* (commercial) or *net* (network), or a country, such as *UK* (United Kingdom) or *CA* (Canada).

Under these top-level domains, there are **second-level domains,** such as *cnn.com, panko.com, hawaii.edu,* and *Quercus.nl.* Every organization would like a simple second-level domain name to represent it. There is an international reg-

Figure 2.10
Domain Name
System Hierarchy

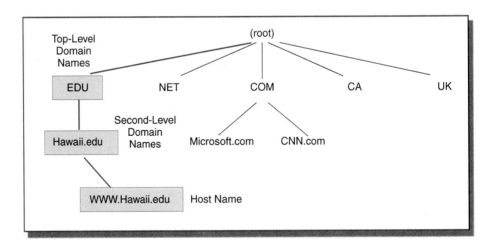

[4] Actually, there are root DNS hosts associated with particular top-level domains, such as EDU. If you ask your local DNS host to look up voyager.cba.hawaii.edu, your local DNS host will contact the EDU root DNS host, which will point your local DNS host to the hawaii.edu local DNS host. That local hawaii.edu DNS host will return the IP address for voyager.cba.hawaii.edu. There may even be other layers of lookup in a complicated DNS lookup.

istration system for applying for second-level domain names. In this system, a firm can register a second-level domain name for a small initial fee and a small annual fee.

Additional labels (text strings separated by dots) can be added to specify suborganizations. For instance, *cba.hawaii.edu* is the third-level domain name that the University of Hawaii gave to the College of Business Administration.

At the lowest level, a domain name can be an individual host name, such as "voyager.cba.hawaii.edu". So a host name is merely a type of domain name.

Autoconfiguration

When you first prepare your user PC to work with the Internet, you must configure it by giving it certain information about itself and the Internet.

Configuration Information   Among the things you must tell it are:

- Its *own IP address* to put in the source address field of each outgoing IP packet
- The IP addresses of your primary DNS host and perhaps your secondary DNS host (which is a backup to the primary DNS host)
- The IP address of your **gateway**[5] (the router to which you will send packets unless you get additional information)
- Your subnet mask (discussed in the next chapter)

Permanent IP Addresses   To work on the Internet, a host needs an IP address. Otherwise, other hosts will not be able to send it IP packets. One possibility is to assign each host in the organization a **permanent IP address**. However, this can be wasteful because many organizations do not have enough IP addresses to give out to all of their hosts, and many hosts would not be using their IP addresses all of the time anyway.

In addition, it is an administrative nightmare to assign each host an IP address, enter that permanent IP address in the host setup information, and maintain a list of which permanent IP addresses are in use and belong to which machine.

Temporary IP Addresses   Another approach is to use an **autoconfiguration host,** as shown in Figure 2.11. When a host first boots up, it sends an *autoconfiguration request* message to the autoconfiguration host. This message gives the requesting host's subnet address and asks for a temporary 32-bit IP address. The autoconfiguration host responds with an *autoconfiguration response* message giving the requested temporary IP address.

Clients and Servers   Server hosts must have permanent IP addresses so that they can always be reached at the same IP address. The IP addresses

---

[5] "Gateway" is an old name for "router." Microsoft still uses this terminology in its networking.

Figure 2.11
Autoconfiguration
Host

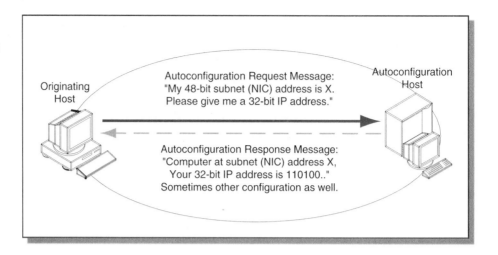

stored in DNS tables are permanent IP addresses. Therefore, temporary IP addresses obtained from autoconfiguration hosts are primarily for client hosts.

Other Configuration Information Early autoconfiguration protocols, such as RARP and bootp, only returned a temporary IP address in their response messages. However, the most popular autoconfiguration protocol today, the **Dynamic Host Configuration Protocol (DHCP),** returns additional configuration information. It can return the IP addresses of the local primary and secondary DNS hosts, the IP address of the gateway (default router), and other configuration information. DHCP offers a number of options for what information a DHCP autoconfiguration host will provide, but there is a growing tendency to supply all TCP/IP setup parameters to the user.

Test Your Understanding

Answer Core Review Questions 5–6 and Detailed Review Questions 5–6.

INTERNET SETUP IN MICROSOFT WINDOWS

Basic Layering Concepts

As Figure 2.12 illustrates, Microsoft Windows uses a simplified layering approach with only three layers.

- **Adapter.** This is the Microsoft designation for the physical and data link layers combined. The **Dial-Up Adapter** is the combination of a modem and PPP. The *Network Adapter,* in turn, is the network interface card (NIC) described in Chapter 6 for use in PC networks.
- **Protocol.** This is the Microsoft designation for the internet and transport layers combined. Popular "protocols" are TCP/IP, IPX/SPX, and NetBEUI.

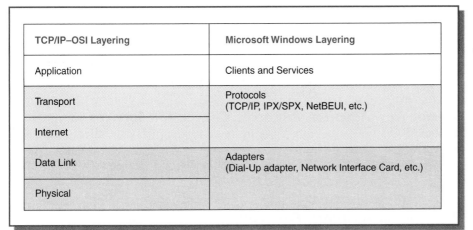

Figure 2.12
Basic Layering in
Microsoft
Windows

TCP/IP–OSI Layering	Microsoft Windows Layering
Application	Clients and Services
Transport	Protocols (TCP/IP, IPX/SPX, NetBEUI, etc.)
Internet	
Data Link	Adapters (Dial-Up adapter, Network Interface Card, etc.)
Physical	

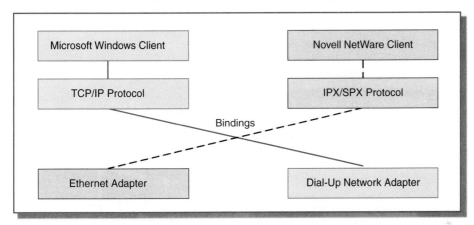

Figure 2.13
Bindings in
Microsoft
Windows
Networking Setup

- **Clients** and **Services.** These designations are used for file service in PC networks (see Chapter 6). If you wish your PC to be a client PC, you must choose the correct client for your server (Microsoft Windows, Novell NetWare, etc.). Your desktop PC can even act as a server using the services capability, although this is only useful in the small peer–peer PC networks discussed in Chapter 6.

Bindings

As Figure 2.13 illustrates, you may have multiple protocols and adapters. You must tell Windows which protocols should work with which adapters. This is called **binding** a protocol to an adapter. In some cases, Windows creates bindings automatically. In other cases, you must create them manually.

Adding Adapters, Protocols, Clients, and Services

To set up Windows for networking, in Windows 95 and Windows 98, go to the Start Button, choose *Settings,* choose *Control Panel,* and double click the *Network* icon.

Network Dialog Box Configuration Tab This set of steps opens the **Network Dialog Box** shown as Figure 2.14. Although the figure shows the Network Dialog Box in Windows 98, it is very similar in Windows 95.

Be sure the Configuration tab is selected. You can now see a list of adapters, protocols, clients, and services that have already been added.

Adding New Adapters, Protocols, Clients, and Services The "Add" button allows you to begin adding more adapters, protocols, clients, and services. Clicking on "Add" will take you to a list of possible add-ins from different vendors. You can also delete existing adapters, protocols, clients, and services from the Network dialog box.

Configuring Adapters, Protocols, Clients, and Services Below the list of items in the Configuration tab is a button marked "Properties." Click on an item, then on the "Properties" button. You will be taken to a **properties dialog box** showing properties that can be set for that entity.

Figure 2.14
Network Dialog
Box in
Windows 98

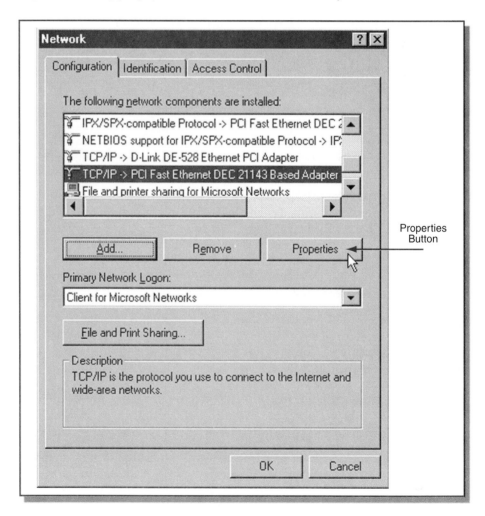

Chapter 2   Layered (Encapsulated) Communication for Internet Access

Bindings Typically, each properties dialog box has a tab where you can specify bindings between the adapter, protocol, client, and service you are configuring and entities at adjacent layers.

Configuring TCP/IP

TCP/IP configuration is particularly important. If you click on the TCP/IP protocol in the Network Dialog Box and then on the "Properties" button, you will be taken to the **TCP/IP Properties Dialog Box** shown as Figure 2.15.

Permanent IP Address By default, the IP Address tab is shown when you open the TCP/IP Properties Dialog Box. As Figure 2.15 shows, there are two radio buttons allowing you to "Specify an IP address" or allowing your computer to "Obtain an IP address automatically."

If you choose to specify a permanent IP address, you will bypass autoconfiguration to get a temporary IP address. For DHCP, this means also bypassing the ability to get other setup information, such as the IP addresses of DNS hosts and the default gateway.

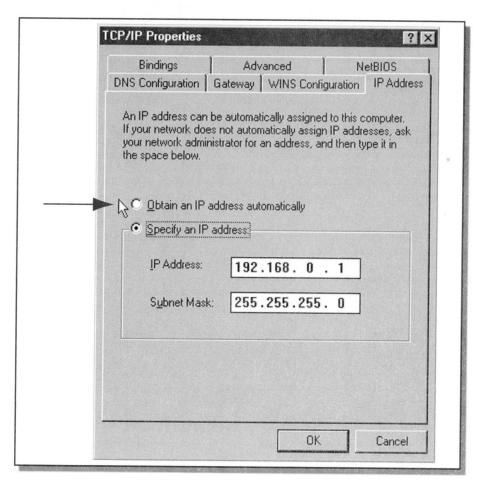

Figure 2.15
TCP/IP Properties Dialog Box in Windows 98

Autoconfiguration   However, if you select the radio button, "Obtain an IP address automatically," Windows implements DHCP, which is an autoconfiguration protocol noted earlier in this chapter. Windows then asks your DHCP host for a temporary IP address whenever it boots up.

As noted earlier, it is becoming common for organizations and ISPs to configure their DHCP hosts to provide all TCP/IP setup parameters instead of just giving a temporary IP address. So when you check the radio button, "Obtain an IP address automatically," you usually are doing far more than obtaining an IP address.

Test Your Understanding

Answer Core Review Question 7 and Detailed Review Question 7.

A Broader Perspective

In this chapter, we have looked primarily at dialing into the Internet from home to use a webserver, primarily using the HTTP, TCP, IP, PPP, and modem standards, together with DNS and autoconfiguration protocols.

Multiple Hybrid TCP/IP–OSI Standards

However, you should not make the mistake of thinking that you will always see HTTP, TCP, IP, PPP, and modems at the five layers of the hybrid TCP/IP–OSI standards architecture.

- Most importantly, different subnets will use different OSI standards at the data link and physical layers. We will see many physical and data link layer subnet protocols in this book. Modems, in fact, are so slow that they are only used in home and road access to the Internet. They are rarely used to connect routers to one another or to connect a high-speed server host to the Internet.
- At the internet and transport layers, in turn, IP and TCP are not the only important TCP/IP standards. Other internet and transport layer TCP/IP standards are discussed in the next chapter and in Module A.
- At the application layer, of course, different applications will use different application layer standards. For instance, mail transmission uses SMTP, not HTTP.
- There are many helper standards, of which DNS and autoconfiguration standards are only two examples.

Overall, then, HTTP, TCP, IP, PPP, DNS, and DHCP are only *examples* of the standards you will see in real-world networks that follow the hybrid TCP/IP–OSI standards architecture.

Other Standards Architectures

In addition, do not make the mistake of thinking that you will always see standards from the hybrid TCP/IP–OSI standards architecture.

- Many older Novell NetWare servers use the IPX/SPX architecture, which has its own layering and standards. There are many of these servers still in use in PC networks. Newer NetWare servers usually communicate via TCP/IP but can be configured to continue using IPX/SPX so that client PCs do not have to be changed to TCP/IP.
- Mainframe networks, in turn, use the SNA standards architecture, which not only has its own standards, but also has a radically different philosophical approach.
- Other popular architectures are AppleTalk for Apple Computers and NetBEUI, which are efficient and lightweight protocols that are sometimes used in very small networks.

When we compare TCP/IP to other architectures, we must keep in mind that even layering changes. We saw in Chapter 1 that OSI has different layering than TCP/IP. In Chapter 7, we will see that NetBEUI, IPX/SPX, and other protocol architectures also used different layering concepts. SNA's layering concepts are so different from TCP/IP–OSI layering concepts that even rough comparisons are hazardous, as discussed in Module H.

The one constant is that *all architectures use OSI standards at the physical and data link layers.*

Living in a Multiprotocol World

In time, TCP/IP is likely to become dominant above the subnet layers. OSI data link and physical layer standards are plentiful and well developed. TCP/IP standards, in turn, are simple, leading to inexpensive products that are developed quickly. Every year, TCP/IP–OSI's penetration increases.

However, we still live today in a **multiprotocol** world. Our routers must be able to forward not only IP packets, but also IPX packets, AppleTalk packets, SNA messages, and messages from some smaller standards architectures. Although we cannot cover all protocols in an introductory textbook and must focus on dominant TCP/IP–OSI standards, working network professionals need a broader view.

Test Your Understanding

Answer Core Review Question 8.

REVIEW QUESTIONS

Core Review Questions

1. a) What are standards? b) What two things do they govern?
2. a) What are the three main parts of a standardized message? b) What part is used the least often, and c) when is it usually used? d) What usually is the largest field in a message? e) Can we have messages that do not contain data fields? f) In general, what kind of messages are these? g) The header is divided into smaller units called what? h) What is an octet?

3. **a)** From the highest to the lowest, name the TCP/IP–OSI layers. **b)** What is the main standard you use at each layer when you dial into a webserver on the Internet from home using a telephone line and modem?

4. **a)** What is indirect communication? **b)** Why is it necessary? **c)** What is encapsulation? **d)** What is deencapsulation? **e)** What happens as soon as a layer process on the source host creates a message?

5. **a)** Why do we need DNS? **b)** What information do you send in a DNS request message? **c)** What information do you receive in a DNS response message?

6. **a)** Why is autoconfiguration good? **b)** What information do we get back, at a minimum, in an autoconfiguration response message? **c)** What other information may we get back?

7. **a)** Compare Windows layering and layering in the TCP/IP–OSI hybrid architecture. **b)** What is a binding? **c)** How do you get to the Network Dialog Box? **d)** How do you add a protocol? **e)** How do you begin to configure TCP/IP? **f)** How do you set up bindings? **g)** In the TCP/IP Properties Dialog Box, what does it mean if you choose, "Specify an IP address"? **h)** What does it mean if you choose, "Obtain an IP address automatically"?

8. Explain why it is dangerous to focus too heavily on HTTP, TCP, IP, and PPP.

Detailed Review Questions

1. What is a protocol?

2. **a)** Which are the end-to-end layers in TCP/IP–OSI? **b)** Which are the hop-by-hop layers?

3. On a router, what is an interface?

4. Explain encapsulation and deencapsulation on routers.

5. If your DNS request is passed from one DNS host to another, which DNS host will respond to you?

6. **a)** What is the most popular autoconfiguration protocol? **b)** What information can it provide?

7. **a)** What must you do in Windows to give your PC a permanent IP address? **b)** A temporary IP address? **c)** Why are temporary IP addresses preferable? **d)** In general, what types of hosts get permanent IP addresses?

Thought Questions

1. What was the most surprising thing you learned in this chapter?

2. What was the most difficult part of this chapter for you?

3. **a)** Based on what you learned in this chapter, explain why Glenn Davis sometimes is told that a URL does not exist, as noted in the vignette. **b)** How would you answer Glenn if he asked why we need so many standards to run the Internet?

Case Studies

For case studies, go to the book's website, **http://www.prenhall.com/panko,** and look at the "Supplementary Readings" page for this chapter.

Projects

1. **Getting Current.** Go to the book's website's "New Information" and "Errors" pages for this chapter to get new information since this book went to press and to correct any errors in the text.

2. **Internet Exercises.** Go to the book's website's "Exercises" page for this chapter and do the Internet exercises.

3. Set up a Windows PC to use the Internet.

Chapter 3

A Closer Look at HTTP, TCP, IP, and PPP

*C*hen May-Ling is the network administrator for Paradise Groceries. It is her job to set up the company's LANs and WANs. The company will soon be installing several routers to connect Paradise Groceries to the Internet and to bring better internal communication as well.

While Glenn Davis does not have to understand the detailed workings of routers, May-Ling does not have that luxury. She needs an intimate knowledge of how routers operate so that she can configure these routers to talk to one another and to the company's host computers. She also needs a plan for assigning IP addresses to the firm's growing number of computers linked to the Internet.

The president of Paradise Groceries has expressed concerns about the reliability of the company's website. Someone has told him that the Internet Protocol is unreliable and that so is HTTP, which the company's webserver uses to communicate with employees and outsiders. He wants assurances from May-Ling that TCP/IP is a safe standards framework before investments in TCP/IP technology increase. ■

Learning Objectives

After studying this chapter, you should be able to describe:

- How HTTP, TCP, IP, and PPP work.
- IP addresses, network and subnet masks, router forwarding tables, dynamic routing protocols, and router forwarding decisions.
- The concepts of connection-oriented versus connectionless service and reliable versus unreliable service.

INTRODUCTION

Chapter 2 looked broadly at standards. It focused most heavily on encapsulation—a process in which different layers work together to allow two application programs on different computers on different networks to work together.

However, the discussion in Chapter 2 simplified what really happens at each layer. In this chapter, we will look more closely at what happens at individual layers. Specifically, we will look at what really happens in interactions at the application, transport, and internet layers, using HTTP, TCP, and IP, respectively.

Pay special attention to the Internet Protocol (IP) discussion. This discussion will help you understand in more detail how the routers, which are the center of the Internet and of corporate intranets, do their job.

One problem you will have is that you need to be able to move back and forth fluidly between two mindsets. The first focuses on layering and concentrates on interactions between layer processes on the same machine. Chapter 2 had that mindset for most of its discussion. The second focuses on what happens at each layer. The two are obviously related, but they do focus on very different things. In addition, you will constantly need to remind yourself which layer you are currently working on, or you will get confused about which aspects of the discussion relate to which layer.

A CLOSER LOOK AT THE APPLICATION LAYER WHEN HTTP IS USED

Having now seen encapsulated communication broadly, we will look in more depth at what happens at each layer during layered communication, beginning with the application layer. In webservice, the **HyperText Transfer Protocol (HTTP)** governs application layer message exchanges.[1]

Client/Server Processing in HTTP

HTTP is a client/server protocol. This means that it is based on request–response cycles, in which the browser sends a request message and the webserver program on the webserver sends back a response message. Figure 3.1 illustrates a simple HTTP request–response cycle.

Note that the HTTP request message is entirely text. The response message also begins with several lines of text, although the file that follows these header lines can be anything.

---

[1] Some readers are undoubtedly saying, "Hey, I thought the HyperText Markup Language (HTML) was the standard for the World Wide Web." The answer is that HTML describes how to represent documents so that they can be processed and rendered onscreen, while HTTP describes how to transfer documents between the webserver and the PC browser and how to transfer other supervisory messages as well. Many applications require separate transfer and message structure standards. In Chapter 11, for example, we learn that the TCP/IP transfer standard for e-mail is SMTP, while the standard for the structure of text message headers and bodies is RFC 822.

Figure 3.1
Simple HTTP
Request–Response
Cycle

```
HTTP Request Message

    GET/panko/home.htm HTTP/1.1[CRLF]

HTTP Response Message

    HTTP/1.1 200 OK[CRLF]
    Date: Tuesday, 20-JAN-1999 18:32:15 GMT[CRLF]
    Server: name of server software[CRLF]
    MIME-version: 1.0[CRLF]
    Content-type: text/plain[CRLF]
    [CRLF]
    File to be downloaded.
```

HTTP Request Message   The request message in Figure 3.1 begins with the keyword GET, which indicates that the browser wishes to get a file from the webserver. Next comes the path to the file. This is the URL without the http:// and the host name. Finally, there is a designation of the version of HTTP the client program supports. In this case, it is HTTP 1.1.

This is a very simple request. More complex HTTP request messages contain additional command lines. Lines are separated by [CRLF] (carriage return and line feed).

HTTP Response Message   Response messages are somewhat more complex. Figure 3.1 shows a possible response message to the preceding GET request. Again, each line ends with [CRLF].

The first line is a *response status line*, which tells the browser what follows. Next come additional header lines resembling the header fields of an electronic mail message. (In fact, HTTP was modeled after electronic mail standards.) Then there is a blank line, followed by the all-text HTML document being retrieved.

- The status line confirms that the target file was found. The "200" is the code for a successful retrieval. If there had been a problem, a different code would have been used, such as the famous "404" code when the webserver program cannot locate the requested file.
- The header tells the date and time of the retrieval.
- The header names the webserver application software that the webserver is using. This allows the browser to adjust to the characteristics of that particular webserver program.
- HTTP is not limited to retrieving text files. Other types of content can be specified through the MIME content encoding standard. The response message tells the version of MIME used and the MIME content type of the file (in this case, plain text because we are retrieving an HTML file).
- The header ends with a blank line—[CRLF] with no content before it.
- This file can be either an all-text file or a general binary file consisting of any string of ones and zeros. In this example, the request message specifies an HTML file (home.htm). HTML files consist entirely of text.

Figure 3.2
Multiple HTTP
Request–Response
Cycles in Webpage
Downloading

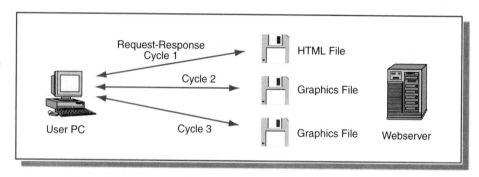

Multiple Request–Response Cycles in Webpage Downloads

Figure 3.2 shows a single HTTP request–response cycle, which downloads a single file from the webserver to the client PC. However, as Figure 3.2 shows, a "webpage" usually consists of several files that the browser combines into a single on-screen image.

Downloading the HTML File   The first HTTP request–response cycle downloads the HTML file, which contains the webpage's text and also contains references to other files needed to render (draw) the webpage. The HTML document in Figure 3.2, for instance, has two "tags" that specify graphics files to be downloaded and rendered in particular places on the webpage.[2]

Downloading Other Files   After the HTML file is downloaded, the browser reads the two tags and initiates the two additional HTTP request–response cycles needed to download the two graphics files.

Perspective   Overall, then, three HTTP request–response cycles are needed to download the three files. Complex webpages with many graphics, audio clips, Java applets, and other elements may need several dozen HTTP request–response cycles.

Unreliable Service

HTTP does not check for errors in HTTP request and response messages. This allows HTTP to be very simple. However, it does require lower-layer processes to correct any transmission errors that may have occurred. In standards terminology, HTTP is an **unreliable** protocol. An unreliable protocol does not ask for the retransmission of lost or damaged messages. HTTP can be unreliable without harming the user because TCP at the transport layer is highly reliable, as we will see below, ensuring the application layer of clean data.

---

[2] For readers familiar with HTML, these are <IMG> tags.

Connectionless Service

When you talk on the telephone, the first step is for the two parties to agree to talk, often by exchanging questions like, "'Is this a good time to talk?" At the end of a conversation, in turn, both sides mutually agree to end the conversation. It would be rude for one side simply to hang up abruptly. This is called **connection-oriented** service.

In contrast, when you send an e-mail message, you merely send it to the receiver. There is no need to establish a connection or break it afterward. This is **connectionless service.** It used to be called **datagram** service, because you sent data in an isolated message, like a telegram. Connectionless service is very simple, and HTTP uses it.

Test Your Understanding

Answer Core Review Questions 1–3 and Thought Questions 3, 4 and 6.

A CLOSER LOOK AT THE TRANSPORT LAYER WHEN TCP IS USED

The transport layer is for standards that enable two host computers to communicate with one another, even if they are different types of computers. In webservice, HTTP mandates the use of TCP at the transport layer.

Application–Transport Interactions

What happens when a browser creates an HTTP request or when the webserver creates an HTTP response? As Figure 2.4 illustrated, the application layer passes the HTTP message down to its transport layer process.

Figure 2.4 showed the transport layer merely adding a TCP header to the data field. As we will now see, the process at the transport layer actually is more complex. When the transport layer receives an application message, this arrival actually generates a flurry of transport layer messages. Many of these messages are transport layer supervisory messages.

Connection-Oriented Service

As Figure 3.3 illustrates, TCP is connection oriented. When the transport layer processes on the two computers begin to communicate, they first agree to open a connection by exchanging synchronization **(SYN)** messages.[3] These synchronization messages ask the other side to open a connection.[4]

Once the connection is open, the two transport processes can send TCP messages (called **TCP segments**) containing data back and forth freely. The source host can send TCP segments containing HTTP requests in their data fields, and

---

[3] In a SYN message, the SYN flag bit in the TCP header (see Figure 2.2) is set to one.

[4] These are header-only messages. They do not contain data fields.

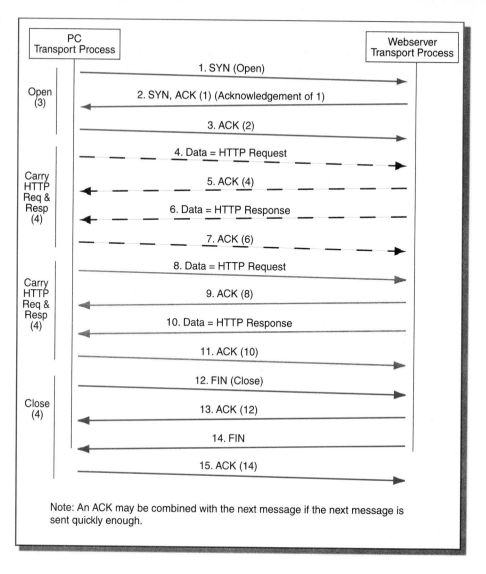

Figure 3.3 TCP Time Diagram

PC Transport Process — Webserver Transport Process

Open (3)
- 1. SYN (Open)
- 2. SYN, ACK (1) (Acknowledgement of 1)
- 3. ACK (2)

Carry HTTP Req & Resp (4)
- 4. Data = HTTP Request
- 5. ACK (4)
- 6. Data = HTTP Response
- 7. ACK (6)

Carry HTTP Req & Resp (4)
- 8. Data = HTTP Request
- 9. ACK (8)
- 10. Data = HTTP Response
- 11. ACK (10)

Close (4)
- 12. FIN (Close)
- 13. ACK (12)
- 14. FIN
- 15. ACK (14)

Note: An ACK may be combined with the next message if the next message is sent quickly enough.

the destination host can send TCP segments containing HTTP response messages in their data fields.[5] Figure 3.3 shows TCP segments carrying HTTP messages from three simple HTTP request–response cycles.

At the end, the two transport processes exchange finish **(FIN)** segments[6] to mutually agree to close the connection.

---

[5] As discussed in Module A, large HTTP response messages may have to be fragmented (broken into smaller pieces) and sent in several data-bearing TCP segments instead of just one. However, this does not change the basic process.

[6] In a FIN message, the FIN flag bit in the TCP header (see Figure 2.2) is set to one.

Reliable Service

Connection-oriented service is expensive because it must support opening and closing sequences. This requires the two hosts to do significant processing work. Of lesser importance, it also adds extra traffic to the network.

In addition, as Figure 3.3 shows, each TCP segment is **acknowledged** by a TCP segment containing an acknowledgement (**ACK**).[7] This adds considerably to the work that the host transport processes must do and adds somewhat to network overhead.

Speaking more precisely, the receiving transport process acknowledges every TCP segment it receives.[8] Of course, if it does not receive a particular TCP segment, it will not acknowledge that segment. In addition, the receiving transport process checks each TCP segment for errors. If it finds an error, it discards the TCP segment and does not acknowledge it. Overall, only correctly received TCP segments are acknowledged by the receiving transport process.

The sending TCP process keeps track of all acknowledgements. If a TCP segment is not acknowledged within a reasonable time period, the sending process assumes that the segment was damaged or lost. It retransmits the unacknowledged segment.

Note that TCP is a **reliable** protocol. It corrects all errors through retransmissions. In addition, it does not matter whether the errors occur at the transport layer or at lower layers. Whether an error occurs at the physical, data link, internet, or transport layer, TCP provides an accurate HTTP message to the application layer process.

User Datagram Protocol (UDP)

TCP is a heavyweight protocol.

- It places a heavy processing burden on the source and destination hosts, which have to create connections, break connections, send acknowledgements, and do the complex work of error detection and error correction (including the retransmission of lost or damaged TCP segments).
- In addition, it adds to network traffic with TCP segments to open and close connections and to acknowledge correctly received segments. This usually is of only secondary importance.
- Also, error correction host processing time and the time needed to retransmit damaged or lost TCP segments creates latency (delay).

For many applications, these costs and delays are reasonable prices to pay for TCP's reliable data delivery. However, not all applications need clean data delivery. For some applications, losing an occasional message is merely a nuisance. The high overhead of TCP is not worth the cost.

For other applications, such as voice communication, latency is intolerable, so TCP's high reliability actually is a problem rather than a solution. There

---

[7] In an ACK message, the ACK flag bit in the TCP header (see Figure 2.2) is set to one. Note, in Figure 3.3, that some messages both acknowledge TCP segments and also carry new information.

[8] Pure acknowledgements are not acknowledged or we would have infinite loops of acknowledgements.

simply is no time to retransmit lost or damaged messages in real-time voice conversations.

For applications that can tolerate occasional data losses or that cannot tolerate delay, TCP/IP offers an alternative to TCP at the transport layer. This is the **User Datagram Protocol (UDP).** UDP messages, called **UDP datagrams,** are sent individually, like letters or telegrams (hence the name *datagrams*). There are no opens and closes, so UDP is connectionless. There are no acknowledgements, so there is no error correction, and therefore UDP is unreliable. If a UDP datagram is lost through an error or the transport layer or some lower layer, the application program must deal with the loss.

Test Your Understanding

Answer Core Review Questions 4–5 and Detailed Review Questions 1–2.

A Closer Look at the Internet Layer When IP Is Used

As shown in Figure 2.5, whenever the transport layer creates a TCP segment, it passes the segment down to the internet layer process for delivery—just as a browser or webserver application program passes each HTTP request and response message down to the transport layer for delivery. The internet layer uses the Internet Protocol (IP) to govern communication.

IP Basics

Connectionless and Unreliable Service We have just seen that connection-oriented and reliable TCP does not merely accept an application request, add a TCP header, and pass it down to the internet layer for delivery. Rather, TCP also implements opens, closes, acknowledgements, and the retransmission of lost or damaged TCP segments.

In this respect, IP is much simpler. On the sending machine, the internet layer literally does take a TCP segment, add an IP header, and pass the new IP packet down to the data link layer. There are no open or close sequences of supervisory messages. There are no acknowledgements or retransmissions of lost or damaged IP packets. IP is a connectionless and unreliable protocol.

In fact, there is not even a guarantee that IP packets will arrive in the order they were transmitted. Successive IP packets may take different routes across the Internet, passing through different routers and arriving out of order.

IP Datagrams (IP Packets) IP messages go by two names. The Internet Protocol standard calls them **IP datagrams,** a term indicating connectionless delivery (as in UDP datagrams). However, it is more common to call them **IP packets.** As noted earlier in this chapter, "packet" is the generic name for any message at the internet layer.

Hop-by-Hop Operation   As we saw in Chapter 2, IP is a **hop-by-hop** layer. IP packets are exchanged between adjacent machines along the route. There may be many hops along the route—often 50 or more. So, it is important to minimize the processing that must be done at each hop. Otherwise, the routers along the way would be even more overloaded than they are today on the Internet.

This is why IP is connectionless and unreliable. Doing 50 or more opens, closes, and error correction sequences would be extremely expensive in terms of router processing costs. It is much better to do error correction only once, at the transport layer processes on the two host computers. *Connectionless and unreliable operations reduce the costs of routers, which are the most expensive elements in routed networks, exceeding the cost of transmission lines.*

IP Addresses

As shown in Figure 2.2 the IP packet header has two 32-bit address fields. These hold the IP addresses of the source and destination hosts. Although we usually write IP addresses (introduced in Chapter 1) in dotted decimal notation, for example 128.171.17.13, we should keep in mind that, as we saw in Chapter 1, dotted decimal notation is simply a compact way of expressing 32-bit IP addresses.

Hierarchical Addressing   Many addresses you encounter are hierarchical. For instance, your home address has at least a street address, a city, and a country. If you dial a telephone number in the United States from another country, you have a country code, an area code, and a local telephone number.

Hierarchical addressing makes delivery easier. When a post office receives a letter, it looks first at the country code. It then places the letter into a domestic or an international sorting bag. Letters in the domestic bag are then resorted by zip code in the United States and later by street address. At each stage in hierarchical sorts, there are only a limited number of alternatives, making the sorting decision easy.

Imagine what would happen if addresses were given out to houses randomly. If there were 50 million houses, there would have to be 50 million sorting bins! For large populations, hierarchical addressing is crucial.

Hierarchical Address Parts in IP   To simplify router forwarding decisions, IP also uses hierarchical addressing. As Figure 3.4 illustrates, there usually are three parts in an IP address: the network part, the subnet part, and the host part.

The Network Part   As Chapter 1 noted, the Internet is not a single network. Rather, it is a collection of networks owned and operated by different organizations: Internet service providers (ISPs), backbone service providers, and individual organizations.

Figure 3.4
Hierarchical IP
Addresses

Three-Part IP Address
(Total is 32 bits, for Example, 10101010111100000101010111100000)

Network Part:	Subnet Part:	Host Part:
Identifies network of destination host	Identifies subnet within network	Identifies host within subnet

Assigned by IP Address Registrar to Organization Number of Bits Varies From 8 to 24	Assigned by Organization to Suborganization Number of Bits Varies From 0 to 16	Assigned by Suborganization to Host Number of Bits Varies

Notes: Network Part (gray) is used by border routers to decide whether the destination address is outside the network or inside the network. See Figure 3.6.
Network Part (gray) plus Subnet Part (blue) are used together by internal routers to determine whether a router can deliver the IP packet directly to the destination host on one of the router's subnets. See Figure 3.5.
Host part tells router which host to deliver the packet to on a subnet.
If there are N bits in a network, subnet, or host part, there can be 2^N alternatives. However, two alternatives are excluded. Parts cannot consist of all zeros or all ones. So if there are N bits in a part, there really can be only 2^N minus 2 alternatives. For instance, if the host part is 8 bits, there can only be 2^8 minus 2 possible hosts on the subnet, that is, 254.

Note that we use the term "network" two ways on the Internet. First, there are physical networks, such as individual LANs. In IP addressing, however, a **network** is an *organizational concept*. Here, a network is a collection of routers and connecting subnets under the control of an organization. When we speak of the "University of Hawaii Network," for instance, we are talking about all routers and subnets on all University of Hawaii campuses.

An **IP address registrar** assigns a **network part** to each organizational network on the Internet. Each of that network's host IP addresses must begin with that network part. For example, the University of Hawaii was assigned network part 128.171. These are the first 16 bits in every host IP address in the university.

If a router on the Internet backbone sees the address 128.171.17.13, it notes that this is an address on network 128.171. It looks up forwarding instructions for 128.171 and sends the packet out again according to those instructions.

If we did not use network parts, then routers would have to treat each 32-bit IP address separately. A router would need router forwarding instructions for each IP address on the Internet. There are well over 100 million IP addresses in use on the Internet, so routers would need massive forwarding information files, and looking up forwarding information for a particular host might take seconds or even minutes at each router along the way.

However, thanks to hierarchical IP addressing, backbone routers only need to know forwarding instructions for network parts. Backbone router forwarding tables still contain tens of thousands of entries for network parts, but even this is far more manageable than having to maintain entries for every host on the Internet.

The Network Mask   How does the router know that the first 16 bits in 128.171.17.13 constitute the network part of the address?[9] The answer is that IP addresses are always paired with another 32-bit number called a mask. In a **network mask,** the bits corresponding to the network part are ones, and all later bits are zeros.

For the University of Hawaii, the network mask consists of 16 ones followed by 16 zeros. In dotted decimal notation, this is 255.255.0.0. Often, network masks are denoted in an even more compact form. For instance, the IP address 128.171.17.13 and its mask often are written together as 128.171.17.13/16. Here, the final 16 is called the **prefix.** It tells the number of ones that begin the network mask.

By the way, there is nothing magic about a network size of 16 bits. Network parts can range from 8 to 24 bits in length.

Subnet Part   Once a packet arrives at a network, it must be routed to the correct host computer. Most organizations today divide their network into groups of hosts under the control of specific suborganizations. These groups are called **subnets.** Like networks, subnets are organizational concepts rather than technical concepts, although it is common to find a subnet encompassing a single physical LAN.

The first job in delivery is to forward packets arriving from outside a network to the correct subnet. Packets originating inside a network must first be routed to the correct subnet.

For example, at the University of Hawaii, the College of Business Administration has a single local area network. The college and its LAN constitute a subnet. The university assigned the 8-bit **subnet part** number 17 to the college. All IP addresses in the college begin with 128.171, which is the university's network part, followed by the college subnet part, 17. So host 128.171.17.13 is in the college subnet.

Again, there is nothing magic about a subnet part size of 8 bits. Organizations can make the subnet part size anything they wish, subject to the constraint that they can only allocate the bits that follow the network part, which is set by the IP address registrar.

The Subnet Mask   Routing *within* an organization uses a different mask, a **subnet mask.** A subnet mask has initial ones in *both* the network and subnet parts, followed by zeros in the remaining part, the host part. This combination designates a specific subnet on the network.

The College of Business Administration has a 16-bit network part and an 8-bit subnet part, so its subnet mask consists of 24 ones followed by 8 zeros. In dotted decimal notation, this is 255.255.255.0. In prefix notation, it is /24.

---

[9] As Module A notes, it used to be possible to look at an IP address to tell the size of its network part. For instance, if the first bit was a zero, the network part was 8 bits long. If the first two bits were 10, the network part was 16 bits long. However, the Internet no longer uses this system because it was wasteful in assigning IP addresses. Today, the backbone Internet routers use Classless Interdomain Routing (CIDR), in which a network mask is necessary.

The Host Part The bits remaining after the subnet part constitute the **host part** of the IP address. The subnet organization assigns the host part bits to individual host computers. In the College of Business Administration, the host part is 8 bits. A specific host in the college was assigned the host part number 13 and therefore received the IP address 128.171.17.13.

Reserved Part Values In assigning part values, IP address registrars, organizations, and subnets have to follow two rules.[10]

First, a host cannot be assigned a network, subnet, or host part consisting of all ones. A part with all ones is a **broadcast address.** For instance, a host part of all ones indicates that all hosts on the subnet should read the IP packet. If you assigned an all-ones host part to an individual host, all IP packets individually addressed to it would be read by all other hosts.

The second limitation is that a network, subnet, or host part cannot consist of all zeros. A host can only use all zeros in a part when it first begins to operate and does not know its IP address yet. The source IP address field in IP (see Figure 2.2) must have a value. In this case, the host puts zeros into all unknown parts of the source address.

At the University of Hawaii, subnet parts are set to 8 bits. This means that there can be 2^8 minus 2 or 254 possible subnets, where the "minus 2" removes the all-ones and all-zeros possibilities.

Router Forwarding Decision Examples: A Simplified View

To see how router forwarding decisions actually are made, we will look at four examples illustrated in Figure 3.5 plus one more example illustrated in Figure 3.6. Our goal is to show the results rather than the mechanics of how decisions are made. We will return to those mechanics shortly.

Example 1: Source and Destination Hosts on the Same Subnet In the first example, the source and destination hosts (Hosts A and B) are on the same subnet. In this case, there is no need to involve a router. The source host, "A", merely forwards the IP packet directly to the destination host, "B", as Figure 3.5 illustrates with the arrow marked with a "1". To give an analogy, if you wish to give a written message to a neighbor, you deliver it yourself instead of passing it to a post office.

Example 2: Source and Destination Hosts on the Different Subnets In the second example, the source and destination hosts (Hosts A and C) are not on the same subnet. The source host, "A", therefore sends the IP packet to

---

[10] Actually, there is a third rule: IP address 127.0.0.0 may not be assigned to individual hosts. This special address is used in loopback testing, in which a host sends a message to itself. If 127.0.0.0 were assigned to a particular host, all IP packets sent to that host would be looped back to the sender instead of going to the receiver. However, address registrars never assign the network part 127, so in practice this rule does not affect corporate networking decision makers.

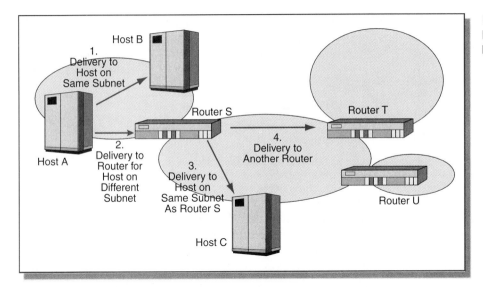

Figure 3.5
Routing Decision
Examples

Router S and asks Router S to take responsibility for the IP packet. This is shown by the line marked with a "2" in Figure 3.5.

Example 3: Router Delivery to a Destination Host on One of the Router's Subnets The third example continues the second. As Figure 3.5 shows, the source host, "A", has forwarded an IP packet to Router S for handling. The destination host, "C", is on one of the router's subnets, So Router S forwards the packet directly to the destination host, "C", on that subnet. This example is shown by the arrow marked with a "3" in Figure 3.5.

Example 4: Router Forwarding to Another Router The fourth example illustrates what a router, Router S, does when it receives a packet not addressed to a host on any of the router's subnets. In this case, the router passes the packet on to another router for delivery. This is shown in Figure 3.5 by the arrow marked with a "4".

Note that there are two possible **next-hop routers,** "T" and "U", to which the router could have forwarded the packet. Obviously, the router forwarding decision should choose the best possible next-hop router on the basis of some criterion. We will look at such criteria later.

Example 5: Border Router Forwarding Decisions The four examples shown in Figure 3.5 illustrate how routers make router forwarding decisions *within* a network. In such cases, routers connect subnets, and the network parts are always the same.

However, **border routers** connect a network with the outside Internet, as Figure 3.6 illustrates. Here, an IP packet for a destination host outside the

Figure 3.6
Border Router
Decision Making

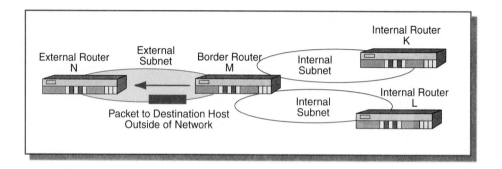

network arrives at a border router, "M". The border router forwards the packet on to a router, "N", outside the network.

Router Forwarding Tables

Now that we have seen the basic router forwarding decisions that can be made, we will see how routers make these router forwarding decisions when they receive an incoming IP packet with a particular destination address. As Figure 2.7 illustrated, we will look at the situation from the point of view of Router E, which receives the packet from Router D. Router E cannot deliver the packet directly to a station on one of its subnets. Router E must forward the packet to Router F, Router G, or Router H.

Router Forwarding Table Fields   As Figure 3.7 shows, Router E has a **router forwarding table.** This lists various combinations of IP addresses (or parts of IP addresses), mask prefixes, the **next-hop** routers that can deliver an IP packet closer to the address or address part, the metrics for using this next-hop router, and the interface to use to send the packet back out.[11]

A Simple Match   Note that entire IP addresses are not shown in the first column. Rather *parts* of IP addresses are shown, for instance, 172.1 (in the fourth row of entries). This stands for "all IP addresses beginning with 172.1 (1010110000010011)." If an IP address is 172.1.23.46, it will be handled according to the instructions in this row. This embodies hierarchical addressing. This single entry governs the forwarding of many possible IP addresses.

Masks   The mask tells how long the match should be to use the partial address in the first column. For the row with IP address part 171.1, the prefix /16 tells the router to use this row's instructions only if the first 16 bits of the destination IP address are 172.1. In other words, 172.2 will not match, because the second octet is different.

---

[11] For the address part, although IP addresses are 32 bits long, only the bits corresponding to the ones in the prefix are shown. Other bits are zero.

Figure 3.7
Router Forwarding
Table

Destination Address Part*	Prefix*	Metric (cost)	Interface**	Next-Hop Router
172.19	16	47	2	G
172.15.33	24	0	1	Local
172.1	16	12	2	G
172.40.	16	33	2	G
172.229.	16	34	1	F
172.40.6.	24	47	3	H
172.19.17.	24	55	3	H
172.229.	16	20	3	H
172.40.6.	24	23	1	F
172.15.12.	24	9	2	Local
172.15.122.	24	3	3	Local
0.0.0.0	0	5	3	H

Notes: *Destination address part 172.19 with a prefix of 16 means that:
The mask (network or subnet mask) begins with 16 ones and then has 16 zeros.
The first 16 bits in the destination address (where mask bits are one) must form the binary for
172.19 (1010110000010011) for there to be a match. The remaining bits can be anything.
**Routers F, G, and H are on Interfaces 1, 2, and 3, respectively.

By the way, is the mask a network mask or a subnet mask? The router neither knows nor cares. Addresses outside the network will be paired with network masks, while addresses inside the network will be paired with subnet
masks. However, the router forwarding table treats all masks the same.

Longest Match Selection Suppose Router E receives a packet with destination address 172.19.17.13. In Figure 3.7, there are entries for 172.19 for
Router G and 172.19.17 for Router H. Here, Router E uses the **longest match**
principle based on the mask prefix (the longer the prefix, the better). Router H
has a longer match (24 bits) than Router G (16 bits), so Router E forwards the
packet to Router H for the next hop.

Metric-Based Selection In some cases, two or more rows have the same
length of match. As Figure 3.7 shows, however, they may have different metrics. Metrics may measure costs. In such cases, Router E would decide the tie
based on lowest cost. Other metrics, such as reliability, should be maximized
instead of minimized. We must be vague at this point, because different routing standards use different metrics.

Suppose Router E receives a packet to 172.22.9.31. For address part 172.229,
which has the prefix 16, Router F will have a cost of 34, while Router H, which

also has the prefix 16, will have a cost of 20. The basic rule here is to use the next hop router offering the lowest cost. So Router E will send the packet to Router H.

Some routers only keep information about the lowest-cost route to a particular destination address part. This speeds individual routing decisions. However, this loss of information results in slower readjustment if there is a failure in the network.

What if two alternatives have identical metrics? In such cases, the router might select one arbitrarily or might "load balance," sending packets to both next-hop routers equally.

Default Router   In Figure 3.7 the address 0.0.0.0 is shown as using Router H. In router forwarding tables, the address 0.0.0.0, paired with the mask 0.0.0.0 (prefix=0), means that *if there is no match,* then use the router indicated "H" as the next-hop router. Router H is the **default router** in the router forwarding table.[12]

Local Delivery   Note that only after a router has determined that the destination host is not on one of its subnets does it consider a next-hop router. If the destination host is on one of the router's own subnets, of course, the router will forward the IP packet directly to the destination host, so there is no need for a next-hop router. The router forwarding table will indicate the local interface in such conditions, as Figure 3.7 indicates. In terms of masking, the longest match has the router's bits in the network and subnet parts.

Other Internet Layer Issues

Dynamic Routing Protocols   How do routers build their router forwarding tables? The answer, illustrated in Figure 3.8, is that routers constantly exchange information about routes and metrics. These exchanges are governed by **dynamic routing protocols**[13] that specify what routing information is exchanged, how often it is exchanged, and how it is exchanged.

There are several different dynamic routing protocols. Some are very simple and are good choices for small networks with only a few routers. Others can handle very large networks efficiently but are complex to administer. In general, the more sophisticated the routing protocol, the more sophisticated router forwarding table metrics will be, the more effective routers will be in making forwarding decisions, and the more routers will cost to buy and administer.

---

[12] The use of the address 0.0.0.0 is potentially confusing. Earlier in this chapter, we noted that zeros for network, subnet, or host parts can only be used in source addresses and can only be used in source addresses until the host has learned its IP address. Here, we apparently see 0.0.0.0 as a destination IP address. However, in the case of router-forwarding tables, 0.0.0.0 is a placeholder, not an IP address for a destination host.

[13] Another possibility is for a network administrator to type routing information into router forwarding tables. This is called static routing. However, static routing cannot keep up with large and rapidly changing networks.

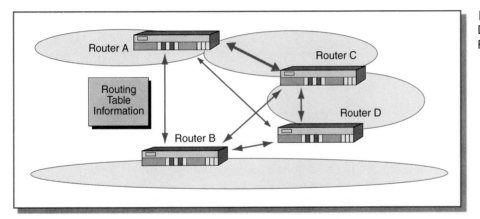

Figure 3.8
Dynamic Routing
Protocols

IP Version 6   Today's Internet Protocol is Version 4. This was the first version of the protocol to be used, and it has been in use on the Internet since 1981. **IPv4** is beginning to show its age. Of most pressing concern, the 32-bit IP source and destination address fields are too small, allowing too few possible IP addresses. Quite simply, we will run out of 32-bit IP addresses in a few years.

128-Bit Addresses   The Internet Engineering Task Force has created a new version of IP, **IP Version 6.**[14] **IPv6** will have 128-bit address fields. This will allow the Internet to grow for many years, even when many people have multiple IP addresses for several computers and even for household appliances like coffee pots.

　IPv6 has a number of other advanced features for security, priority levels (see Chapter 8), and other matters. However, the Internet Engineering Task Force has been working on ways to retrofit many of these advances into IPv4. This has tended to slow the adoption of IPv6. If the IETF even retrofits IPv4 to handle larger addresses, IPv6 may be delayed indefinitely.

TCP/IP versus TCP and IP

One constant source of confusion for students is the fact that *TCP/IP* is a standards architecture, while *TCP* and *IP* are individual standards within that architecture.

Test Your Understanding

Answer Core Review Questions 6–12, Detailed Review Questions 3–6, and Thought Questions 5 and 7.

---

[14] While IPv5 was partially defined, it was never used.

Figure 3.9
Negotiation in the
Point-to-Point
Protocol

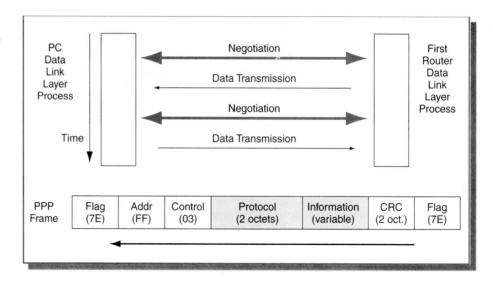

A CLOSER LOOK AT THE DATA LINK LAYER WHEN PPP IS USED

The **data link layer** is for standards to manage the flow of messages (frames) through a single subnet. In this chapter, we have been using a specific subnet consisting of a telephone line and a modem. Such subnets use the **Point-to-Point Protocol (PPP).**

Negotiation   When two data link layer processes using PPP begin to communicate, they do not immediately begin to send data frames. Rather, they engage in negotiations to determine what options they should implement as they communicate. Figure 3.9 shows such a negotiation. In TCP, opening activities are very limited. In PPP, however, there is a rich set of commands for the two data link layer processes to negotiate how data will be delivered. For instance, the two sides may agree to suppress (not transmit) certain fields in the PPP header,[15] thereby reducing transmission overhead. Another option provides for authentication. Only after this initial negotiation phase will data be exchanged.

Negotiations are possible because PPP has a **Protocol** field, as shown in Figure 3.9. This field tells whether the **Information** field contains an internet layer packet for delivery or whether the Information field has supervisory information. If the Information field holds supervisory information, the

---

[15] PPP is based on an older standard, HDLC. PPP inherited the HDLC Address and Control fields, which are not used by PPP. The Address field is given a value of FF hex (11111111), and the Control field is given a value of 03 hex (00000011). The two data link layer processes can agree not to transmit these two fields after the initial negotiation phase.

Protocol field will even tell what type of supervisory information the data field contains.[16]

Negotiation does not have to end with the initial opening phase, as Figure 3.9 shows. The two data link layer processes may also exchange supervisory messages to renegotiate some aspects of the transmission at any time during the transmission.

Unreliable Protocol PPP is an unreliable protocol. The Cyclical Redundancy Check (CRC) field can be used to detect an error in transmission. However, the error is not corrected. The frame simply is discarded.

Test Your Understanding

Answer Core Review Question 13.

KEY POINTS

Chapter 2 introduced standards in the context of layering and encapsulation. It noted that when a layer process creates a message, it passes this message down to the next-lower-layer process for delivery. That process adds a header and perhaps a trailer and passes the message down to the next lower layer.

Details at Each Layer However, we saw in this chapter that more goes on at each layer. There is also supervisory communication to consider and other complexities. We looked at what really happens at the application, transport, internet, and data link layers when you use HTTP, TCP, IP, and PPP, respectively.

Connection-Oriented versus Connectionless Standards Some layer standards are connection oriented, creating a connection between the two processes before beginning and breaking down the connection after the end of the communication. Other layer standards are connectionless, meaning that messages are transmitted without any prior preparation.

Reliable and Unreliable Standards Another key concept is that some standards are reliable, meaning that they do both error detection and error correction. Other standards are unreliable. They do not do error correction and may not even do error detection. Unreliability in a layer standard is not necessarily a bad thing. In fact, it brings substantial benefits—as long as errors that would cause problems are corrected in a higher layer. The trend today is to

---

[16] PPP frames have several other fields besides the Address and Control fields mentioned in the last footnote. The two flag fields, which each have the value 7E hex (01111110), mark the start and end of the frame, eliminating the need for a length field.

have all layer standards, except for the transport layer standard, be unreliable. However, this is only a trend. It is not a universal situation.

REVIEW QUESTIONS

Core Review Questions

1. What is the main standard you use at each layer when you dial into a web-server on the Internet from home using a telephone line and modem?

2. I wish to download an HTML webpage containing three graphics images. **a)** What standard will I use? **b)** How many request–response cycles will be needed for the download? **c)** How many HTTP messages would be sent?

3. **a)** Is HTTP connection oriented or connectionless? **b)** Is HTTP reliable or unreliable? **c)** Why is the answer to the second part of the question good?

4. **a)** Is TCP connection oriented or connectionless? **b)** Is TCP reliable or unreliable? **c)** Why is the answer to the second part of the question good?

5. Explain error correction in TCP.

6. **a)** Is IP connection oriented or connectionless? **b)** Is IP reliable or unreliable? **c)** Why is the answer to the second part of the question good?

7. **a)** Why is hierarchical addressing good? **b)** What are the three parts in IP addresses? **c)** What part(s) does (do) border routers look at to determine whether the destination host is within the network or outside of it? **d)** What part(s) does (do) internal routers look at to determine whether the destination host is within one of the router's subnets?

8. **a)** What do routers look at to determine the size of the network part? **b)** What do routers look at to determine the size of the network plus subnet parts? **c)** What does the subnet mask 255.255.255.0 tell you? **d)** What does 128.171.17.13/24 tell you?

9. **a)** What does a source host do if the destination host is on the source host's subnet? **b)** What does a source host do if the destination host is **not** on the source host's subnet? **c)** What does a router do if the destination address is on one of the router's subnets? **d)** What does a router do if the destination address is **not** on one of the router's subnets? **e)** What does a border router do if the destination address is **not** on the router's network?

10. **a)** In router forwarding tables, what constitutes a match? **b)** What is the longest match rule? **c)** What does a router do if two next-hop routers have the same length of match? **d)** What may a router do if two next-hop routers have the same length of match and the same metric? **e)** What does it mean if the next-hop router field says "local"?

11. **a)** What are dynamic routing protocols? **b)** Why do we need them?

12. **a)** What is the most important improvement in IP version 6? **b)** Why is it important?

13. a) What standard is used at the data link layer when you connect to the Internet from home with a telephone line? **b)** What happens before two processes using this standard exchange data? **c)** Where is supervisory information carried during negotiation? **d)** What field distinguishes between PPP frames carrying data and those carrying supervisory information?

Detailed Review Questions

1. **a)** What are TCP messages called? What are **b)** SYN, **c)** FIN, and **d)** ACK messages?
2. When is UDP a better choice than TCP?
3. What are IP packets officially called in the standard?
4. Why are "network" and "subnet" organizational concepts?
5. **a)** Who assigns the network part? **b)** The subnet part? **c)** The host part?
6. A subnet part is 8 bits long. How many subnets can it represent?

Thought Questions

1. What was the most surprising thing you learned in this chapter?
2. What was the most difficult part of this chapter for you?
3. **a)** Create an HTTP 1.2 HTTP request message to download the file bit.jpg. The file is in the \data\temp directory of webserver voyager.cba.Hawaii.edu. **b)** Give the first line of the HTTP response message if the webserver cannot find the file.
4. HTTP is connectionless and unreliable. How do you think this allowed Berners-Lee, who created the HTTP, to develop the standard very rapidly?
5. **a)** In the router forwarding table shown in Figure 3.7, what will the router do if it receives an IP packet addressed to 172.40.6.47? Explain your answer in detail. **b)** What will the router do if it receives an IP packet addressed to 172.15.12.18? **c)** What will the router do if it receives an IP packet addressed to 172.99.12.187?
6. Based on what you learned in this chapter, answer the president's concerns in the opening vignette for this chapter about using unreliable IP and HTTP protocols.

Case Studies

For case studies, go to the book's website, **http://www.prenhall.com/panko**, and look at the "Supplementary Readings" for this chapter.

Projects

1. **Getting Current.** Go the book's website, **http://www.prenhall.com/panko,** and read the "Errors" page for this chapter to see any reported errors and the "New Information" page for new and expanded information on the material in this chapter.

2. **Internet Exercises.** Go the book's website, **http://www.prenhall.com/panko,** and do the Internet exercises for this chapter.

3. **Client/Server Computing.** Building on the project in Chapter 1, make your client into a browser to be able to download a webpage from a server. Details are available on the Internet exercises page for this chapter at the book's website, **http://www.prenhall.com/panko.**

Chapter 4

Physical Layer Concepts

*I*t began as a nightmare. Then things got really bad.

Glenn Davis was back from one of his many trips. When he came into the office in the morning, his computer seemed slow. In a few minutes, it got even worse. Sometimes, it locked up for several seconds before unfreezing.

Glenn walked down to Chen May-Ling's office. He saw May-Ling and a technician standing by a box with wires coming out of it. They were pulling out wires one at a time and plugging them into a small box.

May-Ling stopped to explain that the "protocol analyzer" program on her PC was reporting a lot of transmission errors. This meant that many messages had to be retransmitted. These retransmissions were literally clogging the network.

To her, this kind of problem indicated bad wiring. Fortunately, all wires from the office's client PCs came into the central box, which May-Ling called a switch. She and her staff were unplugging the wires one at a time to check them with a tester box.

While she was talking to Glenn, her technician yelled out, "Got it!" May-Ling excused herself and walked over to take a look. The tester's meter read, "near-end cross talk." May-Ling ordered her technician to replace the wire with a temporary wire running through the floors and hallways of the office. Later, they would install a new wire properly, running it inconspicuously through the false ceiling. They would also test the other wires in the evening, after most people had left.

May-Ling explained to Glenn that a contractor that normally installed telephone wire had installed this wire (and many others) recently. May-Ling had chosen this kind of company because Paradise Groceries' "Ethernet" LAN uses high-grade telephone wiring. Outsourcing the installation was much cheaper than doing it internally. Unfortunately, the installer had been a little sloppy with this particular wire. You could get away with that sort of thing in telephony, but data wiring at 100 Mbps was unforgiving. Often, as in this case, a single badly installed wire could generate hundreds of dollars in lost time for May-Ling's staff and even more lost time for users. ■

Learning Objectives

By the end of this chapter, you should be able to describe:

- Digital transmission speeds.
- Propagation effects that tend to harm signal reception.
- Types of transmission media, including closed media and radio transmission.
- Basic physical layer transmission concepts, such as serial versus parallel transmission and half-duplex versus full-duplex transmission.

INTRODUCTION

Chapter 1 introduced the Internet. Chapters 2 and 3 looked at the higher-layer standards we use when we access the Internet using a telephone line and modem. This chapter and the next look in more detail at the physical layer standards involved in Internet access.

In this chapter, we will examine transmission theory. In other words, we will look at what happens between the time that a signal begins to propagate down a wire or on radio waves and the time that it reaches its destination.

In the next chapter, we will focus on popular physical-layer alternatives for Internet access today, including modems, ISDN, cable modems, digital subscriber lines, and wireless systems.

TRANSMISSION THEORY

Digital Transmission Speeds

The first question that people ask about their Internet connection is how fast it will run.

Bit Rate As noted in Chapter 1, we measure speed in bits per second. This **bit rate** *is the number of information bits we can transfer in a single second,* with each information bit being a one or a zero.

Baud Rate A related measure of line speed is the **baud rate,** *which is the number of* **clock cycles** *per second—the number of times the line can change per sec-*

ond. Marketers often confuse the two concepts, for instance calling modems that operate at 33.6 kbps "33 kilobaud modems."

However, as discussed in the box "Baud Rates," bit rates and baud rates are only equal in **binary** transmission, in which there are only two line states (for example, two voltages), with one line state representing a zero and the other line state representing a one. Then, a single bit is sent with each line change.

Test Your Understanding

Answer Detailed Review Question 1.

Baud Rates

As noted in the body of this chapter, the *bit rate* measures the rate at which we send actual information, which is almost always encoded as ones and zeros. In contrast, the *baud rate* is the number of clock cycles per second, that is, the number of times per second the **state**—typically, the voltage level—of the transmission line can change. (Between these transition times, the state is constant.)

Figure 4.1 shows a situation in which a line has only two states for each clock cycle: either a high voltage or a low voltage. From Chapter 1, this is *binary* digital communication. A high voltage represents a one, while a low voltage represents a zero. In this case, each clock cycle sends a single bit of content. The bit rate is equal to the baud rate in binary digital communication.

Figure 4.1   Baud Rates and Bit Rates

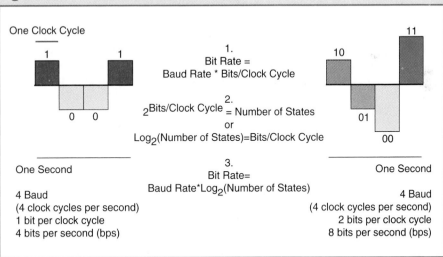

In contrast, Figure 4.1 also shows a situation in which each clock cycle can put the line in any of four states—high, medium high, medium low, and low. We can associate two bits with each state. For instance, high can be 11, medium high can be 10, medium low can be 01, and low can be 00. In this example, each clock cycle transmits two bits. So, in this example the bit rate will be twice the baud rate. There are four clock cycles per second, so the baud rate is four baud (not four

Continued.

bauds or four bauds per second). There are two bits sent per clock cycle, so the bit rate will be eight bits per second. Figure 4.1 gives four equations to compare bit and baud rates. The first is simply that the bit rate is the baud rate times the number of bits sent per clock cycle. In this example, the baud rate is four and the bits sent per clock cycle is two, so the bit rate is four bits/second.

How many bits can we send per baud? As shown in Figure 4.1, if we wish to send N bits per clock cycle, we will need to have 2^N possible states. To send one bit per clock cycle, for instance, we need to have 2^1 (2) possible states. To send two bits per clock cycle, we need to have 2^2 (4) possible states. To send three bits per clock cycle, we need to have 2^3 (8) possible states. Another way to look at this is that the bits per clock cycle is Log_2 of the number of states.

For example, suppose we have eight possible states and a baud rate of 3,000 baud. With eight possible states, we can send three bits per clock cycle ($2^3=8$ or $Log_2(8)=3$). We have 3,000 clock cycles per second (3,000 baud), so our bit rate is 9,000 bps or 9 kbps.

Unfortunately, as noted in the text, marketers often find it easier to say that a device such as a modem can transmit at 33.6 kilobaud. However, such modems really transmit at 33.6 kbps, and their baud rates are far lower (see Module B). This drives some networking teachers crazy, and they insist on accuracy in the use of the term *baud rate*. Others accept the degradation of the term *baud* with resignation.

PROPAGATION EFFECTS IN CLOSED MEDIA

Typically, we send computer signals through a **closed medium,** such as a pair of telephone wires. Because this situation is so common, we will look at it first.

Propagation

If we change the voltage of the medium, this disturbance in the voltage level will **propagate** (travel) down the transmission medium at the speed of electromagnetic radiation in that medium. The effect is similar to throwing a pebble in a quiet lake and watching the ripples spread out from the center. Propagation allows a distant receiver to detect the disturbance and so to hear your transmission.

Unfortunately, propagation is never perfect. There are always **propagation effects** that change the signal as it travels down the medium. Figure 4.2 shows such propagation effects. Propagation effects can make it difficult or impossible for the receiver to identify the line state represented by the disturbance. All propagation effects have the same impact. They make the received signal (disturbance) different from the transmitted signal.

Attenuation

The most obvious propagation effect is **attenuation,** meaning that the signal gets weaker (*attenuates*) as it propagates. Figure 4.2 illustrates this effect. If the signal gets too weak, the receiver will not be able to detect it. For instance, in the EIA/TIA-232 serial ports used in personal computers, a zero is anything between 3 and 15 volts. If the signal begins at 12 volts but weakens to 1 volt, the receiving serial port will not accept it as a zero. The farther a signal travels, the more it will attenuate.

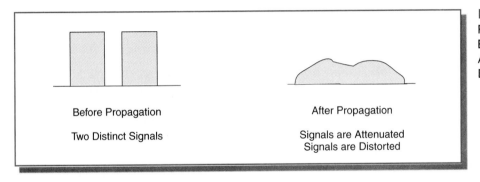

Figure 4.2
Propagation
Effects:
Attenuation and
Distortion

Before Propagation

Two Distinct Signals

After Propagation

Signals are Attenuated
Signals are Distorted

Distortion

Figure 4.2 also illustrates another common propagation effect, **distortion.** As signals travel, they tend to spread out in time. So a nice sharp square wave will tend to become rounded. Worse yet, it will begin to overlap the signals before and after it, making those signals difficult or impossible to distinguish by the receiver.

Noise

A signal is electrical energy. Unless the propagation medium is at absolute zero temperature, its electrons will move around, creating random electrical energy called **noise.** As shown in Figure 4.3, the average noise intensity is called the **noise floor.** Because noise is random, there can be momentary **noise spikes** that will make individual ones and zeros unreadable or that will flip ones to zeros or zeros to ones.

The ratio of signal power to noise power is called the **signal-to-noise ratio (SNR).** If the SNR is very high, then few noise spikes will cause propagation errors. However, if the SNR is low, then quite a few noise spikes will cause errors. (Try listening to a conversation in a noisy restaurant.)

Distance and Noise Propagation Errors Attenuation reduces the signal strength, thus reducing the signal-to-noise ratio. This increases the number

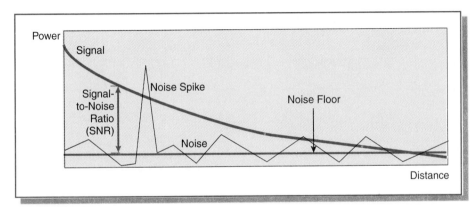

Figure 4.3
Noise and
Attenuation

Power

Signal

Signal-
to-Noise
Ratio
(SNR)

Noise Spike

Noise Floor

Noise

Distance

of errors. So *noise errors increase as propagation distance increases, even if the noise level is constant.*

Transmission Speed and Noise Propagation Errors   In addition, *noise errors increase as transmission speed increases.* If a bit period is very long, say a tenth of a second, then most random noise spikes will be too brief to cause errors, as Figure 4.4 indicates. Noise spike energy plus normal noise energy will be close to the noise floor during that long period.

However, as transmission speed increases, the duration of each bit decreases, and the same noise spikes that averaged out in a longer bit duration will no longer average out. They will be the same duration as a bit, and they will cause errors. *So as transmission speed increases, the number of noise errors also increases, even when the average noise level is constant.*

Interference

Noise is inherent in any transmission medium. In contrast, **interference** is an external signal. The transmission medium, acting like an antenna, will pick up the external signal and convert it into electrical energy, where it will have the same effect as noise. However, whereas noise is relatively constant, apart from brief noise spikes, interference typically comes and goes, making it difficult to diagnose.

Interference and Wire Twisting   One way to reduce cross-talk interference problems is to twist each pair of wires several times per inch. (You need two wires for an electrical communication circuit, just as you need two wires in electrical and telephone connections.) As Figure 4.5 indicates, interference on adjacent halves of each twist will tend to be opposite in direction, adding to the signal in one half of the twist and subtracting from it during the second half of the twist. So interference tends to cancel out over each full twist. This simple approach is surprisingly effective.

Figure 4.4
Transmission
Speed and Noise
Propagation Errors

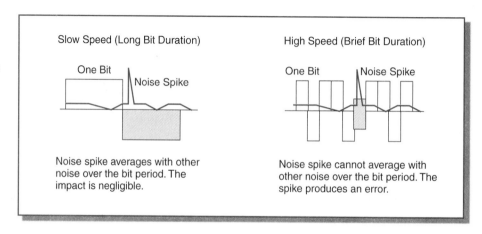

Chapter 4   Physical Layer Concepts

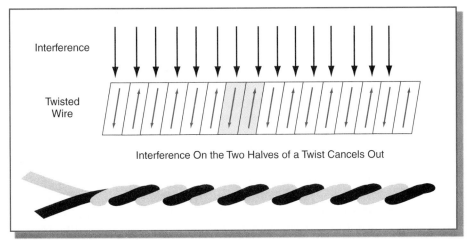

Figure 4.5
Interference
Reduction through
Wire Twisting

Interference

Twisted
Wire

Interference On the Two Halves of a Twist Cancels Out

Termination Problems One source of interference is other wires in a wiring bundle. Figure 4.6 shows that if transmission wires are placed side by side, they will each radiate some of their signal, and the other wire will pick up leaked signal as interference. This is called **cross-talk interference.**

Generally, twisting wires prevents cross-talk interference. However, when the wire bundle is terminated in a connector, each pair must be untwisted to allow the individual wires to be placed in the connector. This untwisting must be limited to about 1.25 cm (half an inch), or there will be **terminal cross talk** near connectors, where the wires that are untwisted to fit into the connector no longer have the interference-fighting benefit of twisting and so interfere with one another. It is very difficult to do connections when you only are allowed to untwist wires 1.25 cm. Consequently, some installers "cheat" and untwist the wires a bit farther. This can create terminal cross-talk problems.

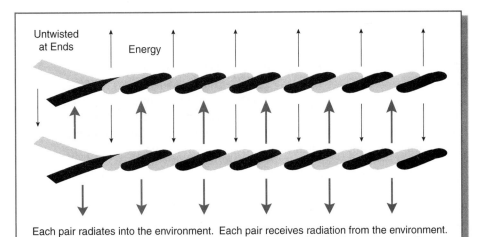

Figure 4.6
Cross-Talk
Interference: A
Termination
Problem

Untwisted
at Ends

Energy

Each pair radiates into the environment. Each pair receives radiation from the environment. Signals in adjacent pairs interfere with one another (cross talk). Twisting each pair helps reduce this cross-talk interference. Cross-talk interference is worst at the ends, where the wires are untwisted. This is terminal cross talk.

The terminal cross-talk problem raises an important point. Although propagation effects may cause problems as a signal travels down the line, termination problems tend to be more common in real installations.

Test Your Understanding

Answer Core Review Question 1, Detailed Review Questions 2–4, and Thought Question 5.

CLOSED MEDIA

We have been speaking about closed transmission media in the abstract. Now we will look at the three specific closed media in common use. The first two are widely used in new networks, while the third is seen almost exclusively in old legacy networks.

Unshielded Twisted Pair (UTP)

The cheapest LAN transmission medium is ordinary copper wire. For a complete electrical circuit, you need a pair of wires. As noted earlier in the chapter, the wires in a pair usually are twisted around each other. Although twisting reduces interference problems, typical data transmission wiring usually does not have any other shielding against electrical interference. So it is called **unshielded twisted pair (UTP).**[1]

RJ-45 Jacks   In home telephone wiring, you have only a single pair of wires. However, as Figure 4.7 illustrates, business telephone wiring usually comes in a multipair bundle. The most common configuration is four pairs (eight wires). This requires a special telephone jack, an **RJ-45 jack,**[2] which is slightly wider than the normal RJ-11 telephone jack used in the home because RJ-45 jacks have to fit eight wires.

Limiting Propagation Distances   In UTP LAN connections, propagation effects are addressed by limiting the maximum distance that UTP wiring can run between network interface cards (NICs) and hubs or switches (see Chapter 1). This distance is 100 meters. Restricting UTP runs to 100 meters ensures that well-installed UTP will not run into significant noise or attenuation problems. Restricting transmission distances is common in media standards as a way of limiting propagation effects.

---

[1] Local area networks occasionally use shielded twisted pair (STP) wiring, in which a metal mesh is wrapped around each twisted pair and in which another metal mesh is wrapped around a multipair bundle. This reduces interference but increases media cost and makes the wiring thick and difficult to lay.

[2] Strictly speaking, the connectors and jacks should be called 8-pin modular connectors and 8-pin modular jacks. "RJ-45" specifically refers to the use of these connectors and jacks for modem access. However, "RJ-45" is used almost universally today for 8-pin connectors and jacks.

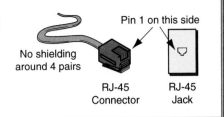

Four pairs (each pair is twisted) are enclosed in insulation. The bundle terminates in an 8-pin RJ-45 connector, which plugs into an RJ-45 jack in the NIC, hub, or switch.

No shielding around 4 pairs

Pin 1 on this side

RJ-45 Connector

RJ-45 Jack

Figure 4.7
Unshielded
Twisted Pair (UTP)
Wire Bundle

Optical Fiber

UTP wiring uses voltage levels to indicate ones and zeros. In contrast, **optical fiber** uses light. In each clock cycle, the transmitter turns light on for a one or off for a zero.

Perfect Internal Reflection   As Figure 4.8 illustrates, when light rays reach the outside of the central glass **core,** they hit a layer of glass **cladding** with a slightly lower index of refraction.[3] The indices of refraction are set so that there is total internal reflection at the boundary—none of the light escapes. Because no light energy escapes, there is very little attenuation. Nor is there interference, because few interference sources operate at light frequencies, and because the outer cladding is wrapped in an opaque covering.

Distortion   The major problem limiting optical fiber propagation distance is distortion. Note, in Figure 4.8, that light rays enter the core at slightly different angles. Over a long enough distance, different rays[4] will travel different distances because they will be internally reflected a different number of times. So light rays from adjacent ones and zeros will begin to overlap.[5]

---

[3] The core varies from 5 microns to 62.5 microns in diameter. The cladding can be as large as 125 to 150 microns in diameter. Most optical fiber in LANs and site networks is 62.5/125 fiber, labeled in terms of its core and cladding diameters.

[4] Figure 4.8 shows light rays emerging from the light source at several angles. Technically speaking, light propagates in fiber only in certain *modes.* Roughly, think of this as restricting light rays to a few angles. If the core is very thin (5 to 8 microns in diameter), only one mode can propagate, so distortion is negligible. This is called *single mode* fiber. (In contrast, fiber with cores of 50 microns to 62.5 microns is called *multimode* fiber.) The thinness of single mode fiber makes it difficult to install and splice. It is used mostly in the telephone network and in WANs, rather than in LANs and site networks. However, as Chapter 8 notes, single mode fiber has been defined for gigabit Ethernet for longer runs, such as those between buildings. Other optical fiber in LANs and site networks is multimode fiber.

[5] To reduce distortion, most multimode (see the previous footnote) optical fiber is graded index fiber, in which the index of refraction in the core decreases from the center to the outer edge. This reduces the difference in distances traveled by light rays entering at different angles (more correctly, as noted in the previous footnote, in different modes), thus reducing distortion.

Figure 4.8
Optical Fiber

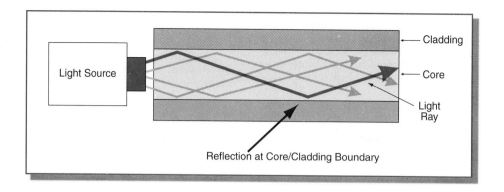

UTP and Optical Fiber: Complementary Uses

In corporations today, there is a strong division of labor between UTP and optical fiber.

UTP from the Desktop to the Nearest Hub or Switch UTP normally is used for the connection between the desktop computer and the nearest hub or switch in a LAN, as Figure 4.9 illustrates. UTP is less expensive than optical fiber and is easier to connect.[6] Even more importantly, UTP is more durable. (Hey, optical fiber is glass!) Because desktop runs often have to lie on the floor, optical fiber links would break frequently.

Fiber Elsewhere Figure 4.9 also shows that for connections other than desktop connections within a LAN or site network—the connections between hubs, switches, and routers—it is becoming normal to use optical fiber. Optical fiber can carry data at very high speeds over distances of a few hundred meters to a few kilometers. In addition, optical fiber does not have to be exposed to work area abuse in longer runs, because it can be laid in conduits, false ceilings, false floors, and other protected environments.

Coaxial Cable

Although UTP and optical fiber now dominate in new LANs, many older LANs still use an older technology, **coaxial cable,** as shown in Figure 4.10.

Good Electrical Characteristics Electrical transmission requires two conductors. In coaxial cable, they are a wire and a cylinder on a common axis. The cylinder, which normally is wire mesh, both shields the cable from external interference and traps the signal within the cylinder, preventing the energy loss that causes attenuation.

---

[6] Splicing optical fiber, while not extremely difficult, requires special splicing and testing equipment. Optical fiber can also come in pre-cut length terminated in SC, ST, or other connectors. The connector must match the jack in the hub, switch, or router.

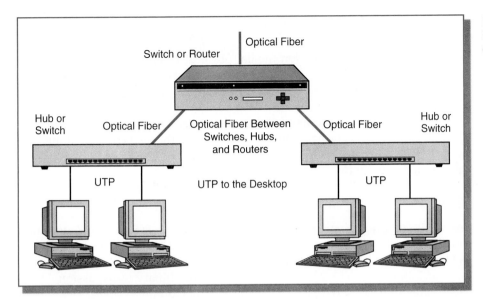

Figure 4.9
Roles of UTP and Optical Fiber

An Obsolete Technology However, UTP today is less expensive than coaxial cable and now offers higher speeds. For really high speeds, in turn, optical fiber offers far more throughput at lower cost. There is no realm of speed in which coaxial cable is still a good choice for new networks. However, coaxial cable is still very common in 10 Mbps legacy LANs (see Module C).

Test Your Understanding

Answer Core Review Question 2.

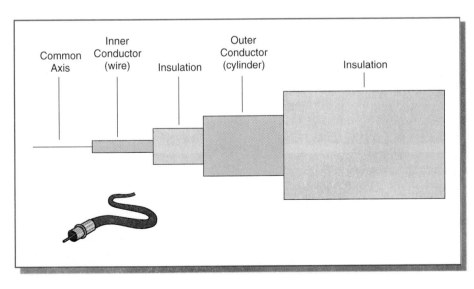

Figure 4.10
Coaxial Cable

EIA/TIA-232 PC SERIAL PORTS

Besides governing transmission media, physical layer standards also govern connector plugs and their operation. On a personal computer, a **port** is a physical **connector plug** plus the electronic circuit needed to send and receive data using this plug.

The most widely used port on PCs for data communications is the **EIA/TIA-232**[7] PC serial port. External modems (discussed in the next chapter) connect to a PC through a serial port. Most PCs come with at least one **EIA/TIA-232 serial port** and usually two.

Binary Electrical Signaling

As Figure 4.11 illustrates, EIA/TIA-232 serial ports have only two states: high and low. The high state is any voltage between 3 and 15 volts, which represents a zero. The low state is any voltage between minus 3 and minus 15 volts. It represents a one. EIA/TIA-232 serial ports, then, use binary transmission. However, other types of serial ports do not use binary communication.

Signaling Speeds

Serial ports are capable of transmitting at multiple speeds. Popular choices are 19.2 kbps, 57.6 kbps, and 115.2 kbps.

Plugs and Pin Assignments

Plugs   As Figure 4.12 shows, there are two possible plugs for serial ports: a 9-pin plug and a 25-pin plug. Modems can work with either because most modems use only 9 pins, and the 9-pin plug's pins match that subset of pins from the original 25-pin standard.

Figure 4.11
Binary Electrical Signaling in EIA/TIA-232 Serial Ports

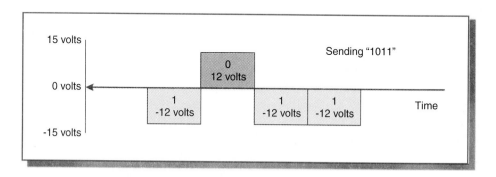

---

[7] The Electronic Industries Association and Telecommunications Industry Association created this standard. There is an equivalent international port designated by three standards: ISO 2100 for the shape of the plug, V.24 for the meanings associated with the pins and for procedures to be followed when signals appear on various pins, and V.28 for electrical signaling.

Actually, current serial ports do not follow the standards strictly. For instance, the standard specifies a maximum transmission speed of 20 kbps, while PC serial ports can operate at 115.2 kbps. Also, the standard only specifies a 25-pin connector, while 9-pin serial ports are common on PCs.

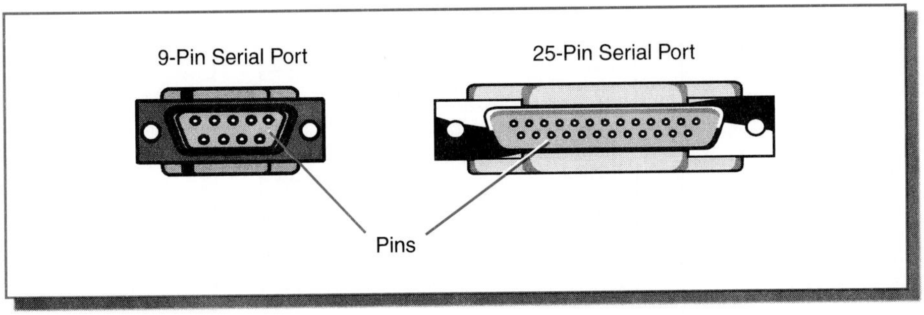

Figure 4.12
EIA/TIA-232 PC
Serial Ports

Pin Assignments for Data Transmission Figure 4.13 shows how the PC serial plug and the serial plug on the modem exchange data.

- When the PC serial port transmits to the modem with a 9-pin plug, it transmits on Pin 3. Pin 5 is an electrical ground that gives a zero reference voltage. It acts as a second pin for all other pins in transmission.
- Going in the other direction, the modem serial port transmits on Pin 2. It also uses Pin 5 as an electrical ground.

Pin Assignments for Supervisory Signaling Other pins are used to govern the transmission. For instance, they allow each site to indicate to the other that it is ready to receive.[8] Other pins allow the modem to tell the PC about line conditions.[9]

Serial Transmission

Sending data through a single wire, one bit at a time, is called **serial** transmission. The bits follow one another in series. This is why EIA/TIA-232 ports are called serial ports. They send signals in each direction on a single pin (plus a ground pin).

Serial Transmission Rates In each clock cycle, one bit is sent along the wire in each direction in a serial port. Figure 4.14 illustrates this process.

Parallel Transmission is Faster In contrast, Figure 4.14 shows that **parallel** transmission uses *several* wires to send information in one direction. If there are eight wires, a parallel system can send eight bits per clock cycle. This obviously moves information eight times faster than sending it at one bit per

---

[8] In other pins, a high voltage indicates "on," while a low voltage indicates "off."

The PC turns on Pin 7 to Request to Send and to indicate that it is Ready for Receiving. The modem replies with Clear to Send by turning on Pin 8. In addition, the modem indicates that it is ready by turning on Pin 6. The PC also indicates that it is ready by turning on Pin 4. In summary, the PC does not send unless Pins 6 and 8 are on. The modem, in turn, does not send unless Pins 4 and 7 are on.

[9] Pin 9 is the Ring Indicator; it is on if the modem hears ringing on the telephone line. Pin 1 is turned on when the modem hears another modem at the other end of the telephone line.

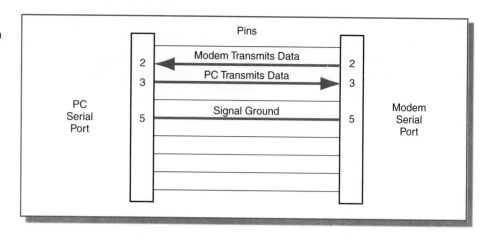

Figure 4.13
Data Transmission between 9-Pin Serial Ports

clock cycle. Parallel transmission is always faster than serial transmission, given comparable clock cycles.

Serial versus Binary   In Figure 4.14, both serial and parallel transmissions are sending one bit at a time. In other words, both are shown as binary. However, in serial and parallel transmission, there can be more than two states per clock cycle. In other words, serial and parallel transmissions are not limited to binary transmission. EIA/TIA-232 serial ports are serial because they transmit only on one pin in each direction, but they are binary because they have only two states—high (3 to 15 volts) and low (minus 3 to minus 15 volts).

Figure 4.14
Serial and Parallel Transmission

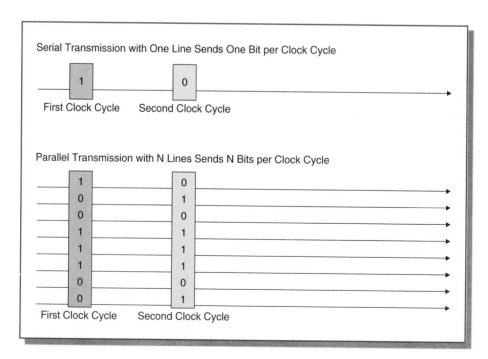

Not Always Eight Pins There is nothing magic about eight wires, by the way. We selected eight wires for our example because PC parallel ports use eight wires. However, many parallel transmission systems use a different number of wires—from as few as four to more than a hundred.[10]

Full-Duplex and Half-Duplex Transmission

One important consideration in any type of port is whether the port will operate in half-duplex or full-duplex mode.

Half-Duplex Transmission If you use a walkie-talkie, only one person can transmit at a time. The other person must wait until the first person has finished talking. Then, this other person can reply. This is called **half-duplex** transmission. As Figure 4.15 shows, in half-duplex transmission, both sides share a single channel. Only one side can transmit at a time.

Full-Duplex Transmission In a telephone conversation, in contrast, both parties can talk at the same time. Although they do not both talk constantly, one side can interrupt the other to ask the other party to slow down, correct an error the other party has made, and so forth. This is **full-duplex** transmission. As Figure 4.15 shows, full-duplex transmission usually requires two channels, one in each direction.[11]

Can *Communicate Simultaneously,* **Not** **Do** Note that full-duplex transmission does not mean that both sides *always are* transmitting at the same time, only that they *can* transmit at the same time. In full-duplex transmission, it is often the case that one side does most of the transmission, while the other side interrupts only as needed. In fact, there often are periods in which neither side transmits.

Full-Duplex Transmission Speeds When channel capacity is given in full-duplex transmission, it usually is given only for a single channel, despite the fact that two channels usually are used, one in each direction. For instance, a 100 kbps full-duplex channel usually consists of two 100 kbps channels, one in each direction.

---

[10] Unfortunately, parallel transmission is good only for short distances. Think about a marching band with several rows of musicians. Now blindfold the band members, so that they cannot see one another. Unless the musicians in each row walk at exactly the same speed, a musician in the second row might end up in the third row or the first row after a short distance. Similarly, different wires have slightly different transmission speeds. After only a few meters, some bits transmitted in different clock cycles will arrive at the same time.

[11] Actually, it is possible to do full-duplex transmission with a single channel. Both sides may transmit simultaneously. Then, each device subtracts what it is sending from what it hears, to get the received signal. This "echo cancellation" approach actually is used in many modems and other network systems.

Figure 4.15
Full-Duplex and
Half-Duplex
Transmission

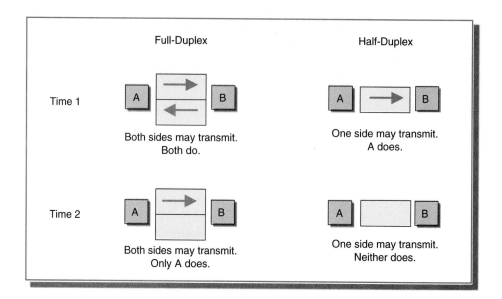

Test Your Understanding

Answer Core Review Questions 3–5 and Thought Questions 1–3.

RADIO PROPAGATION

In the past, **radio propagation** was confined to the microwave towers and satellites of telephone networks. Now, however, some companies have their own satellite networks for data, and we are beginning to see radio local area networks, which allow you to roam with your computer within a building. Wireless Internet access, in turn, will allow us to use the Internet no matter where we are.

Electromagnetic Waves

If an electron oscillates as if on a spring, it will generate **electromagnetic waves,** as Figure 4.16 illustrates. Of course the electromagnetic wave from a single electron will not be very large. However, radio transmitters can cause

Figure 4.16
Electromagnetic
Wave

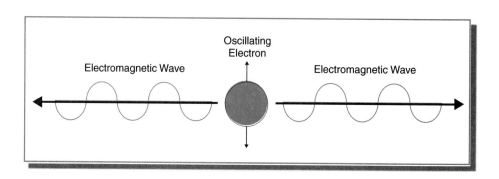

trillions of electrons in an antenna to oscillate in unison. When this happens, we create radio waves strong enough to be received tens of meters or even tens of kilometers away.

Radio Frequencies: Measured in Hertz   The frequency of the electron's oscillation determines the frequency of the radio waves it emits. Radio frequencies are measured in **hertz (Hz).** One hertz is one cycle per second. For higher frequencies, in increasing factors of 1,000, we have *kilohertz (kHz), megahertz (MHz), gigahertz (GHz),* and even *terahertz (THz).*

Frequency Spectrum, Service Bands, and Channels   The range of frequencies from zero hertz to infinity is called the **frequency spectrum.** The spectrum is divided into **service bands** for particular uses, such as cellular telephony bands. As Figure 4.17 shows, these service bands are subdivided into individual **channels.** Individual transmissions are sent in individual channels. Signals in different channels generally do not interfere with one another.

Channel Bandwidth

Each channel has a highest frequency and a lowest frequency. The difference between the two is called the channel's **bandwidth.** For example, if a channel's highest frequency is 12 MHz and its lowest frequency is 10 MHz, then the channel's bandwidth is 2 MHz.

Channel Bandwidth and Maximum Possible Transmission Speed in a Channel   Shannon[12] discovered that there is a relationship between channel bandwidth, noise, and the maximum possible transmission speed within a channel. Equation 3.1 shows this relationship.

$$W = B \, Log_2 \, (1 + S/N) \qquad\qquad \textbf{3.1}$$

Here, W is the maximum possible throughput in bits per second. B is the bandwidth in hertz. S/N is the ratio of signal strength to noise energy strength.

Although having a good signal-to-noise ratio is important, the most important factor limiting the maximum possible transmission speed is the *bandwidth.* Holding noise constant, the maximum possible transmission speed doubles if you double the bandwidth. To use a rough analogy, a thick hose can carry more water than a thin hose. If you want speed in a channel, you need bandwidth.

Note that W is the *maximum possible* transmission speed, not the actual transmission speed. For example, modems were not able to approach the maximum possible speed for telephone lines for many years and are still not quite up to the maximum level.

Telephone Bandwidth and Possible Transmission Speed   In the telephone network, when your signal reaches the first switching office, it is

---

[12] C. Shannon, "A Mathematical Theory of Communication," *Bell System Technical Journal,* July 1948, pp. 379–423; October 1948, pp. 623–656.

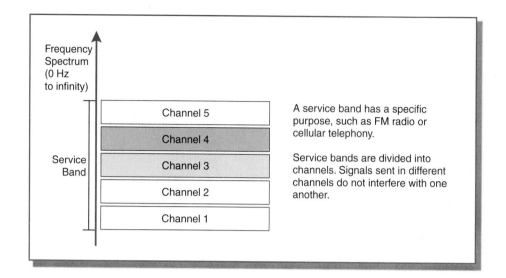

Figure 4.17
Radio Frequency
Bands and
Channels

Frequency
Spectrum
(0 Hz
to infinity)

Service
Band

Channel 5

Channel 4

Channel 3

Channel 2

Channel 1

A service band has a specific
purpose, such as FM radio or
cellular telephony.

Service bands are divided into
channels. Signals sent in different
channels do not interfere with one
another.

passed through a filter, as Figure 4.18 illustrates. The human voice has a broad
range of frequencies, and a young and healthy human ear can hear up to about
20 kHz. However, frequencies below about 300 Hz are filtered out, in order not
to pick up the hum caused by 50 or 60 Hz electrical equipment in the telephone
network. Frequencies above about 3,400 Hz are also filtered out because bandwidth is expensive. The bandwidth is therefore 3,400 Hz minus 300 Hz, or
3,100 Hz.[13] By limiting the telephone bandwidth, the telephone system can
stack more telephone channels into a service band when it uses radio transmission.

Given typical signal-to-noise ratios and a telephone bandwidth, Equation 3.1
indicates that you can transmit at only about 35 kbps over the telephone network. Current modems can transmit up 33.6 kbps, which is very close to the
ultimate limit of telephone networks. (We will see later how so-called 56 kbps
modems avoid this limit by avoiding analog transmission bandwidth filtering.)

Figure 4.18
Telephone
Bandwidth

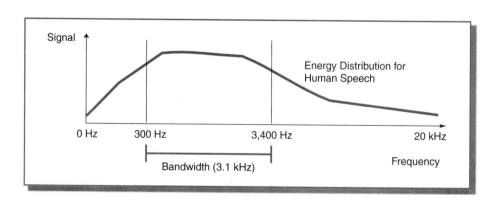

Signal

Energy Distribution for
Human Speech

0 Hz   300 Hz   3,400 Hz   20 kHz

Frequency

Bandwidth (3.1 kHz)

---

[13] Telephone bandwidth varies somewhat among local telephone systems, varying the maximum possible transmission speed as a consequence.

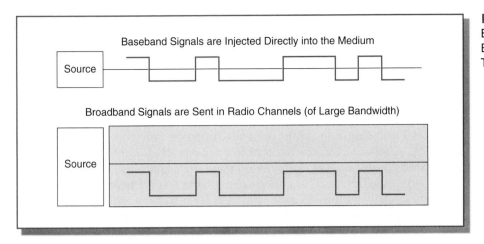

Figure 4.19
Baseband versus
Broadband
Transmission

Baseband and Broadband Transmission

You will frequently hear the terms "baseband" and "broadband" in transmission.

The Technical Distinction   With UTP and optical fiber, we inject the signal directly into the medium.[14] This signal then propagates down the wire. This situation, called **baseband** transmission, is shown in Figure 4.19.

Figure 4.19 also illustrates broadband transmission. In broadband transmission, we send different signals in different channels. We begin with an original signal (called a baseband signal). We modulate this baseband signal so that it will fit into its radio frequency channel. This modulated signal is called the radio frequency (RF) signal. If the channel bandwidth is wide (broad), we call this **broadband** transmission. (If the channel bandwidth is narrow, we call this narrowband transmission.)

The Economic Distinction   There is also an economic distinction between baseband and broadband transmission. In general, baseband transmission is much less expensive because the process of modulating a signal and placing it in a radio channel is quite expensive. In LANs, baseband transmission is dominant for this reason.

Two Uses of the Term "Broadband"   As we have just seen, high bandwidth in a channel means high potential speed, so in radio, "broadband" is synonymous with high speeds.

Although it is not correct technically, there is a growing tendency to refer to *all* high-speed systems as "broadband" systems, even when baseband transmission is used.

---

[14] For wire transmission, we usually change voltage levels to represent different states, say a high voltage for one and a low voltage for zero. For optical fiber, we usually turn the light on or off to represent one or zero.

Test Your Understanding

Answer Core Review Questions 6–8 and Thought Question 4.

KEY POINTS

Chapters 2 and 3 introduced the data link, internet, transport, and application standards needed to use the Internet from home. This chapter looks in more detail at the physical layer, focusing on theoretical concepts. The next chapter focuses on more practical matters, such as the use of telephone lines and modems as well as alternatives for physical layer transmission.

The chapter introduced a number of fundamental transmission concepts that networking professionals have to master when dealing with physical layer standards and processes.

- Transmission speed is measured in both bits per second and baud. The baud rate tells how many clock cycles there are per second.
- Propagation effects in closed transmission media, including attenuation, distortion, noise, interference, the relationship between noise errors and propagation distance, and the relationship between noise errors and transmission speed.
- Wire media, including unshielded twisted pair (UTP) wire, optical fiber, coaxial cable, and the trend toward using UTP to the desktop and optical fiber for longer runs.
- PC serial ports, in order to give the reader an understanding of how connector plugs in general tend to work in terms of pin organization, pin meaning, and electrical signaling.
- Half-duplex versus full-duplex transmission.
- Serial versus parallel transmission.
- Radio transmission, including frequency, channels, bandwidth, and the relationship between channel bandwidth and maximum possible transmission speed.
- Baseband versus broadband transmission, including two uses of the term "broadband."
- Shannon's law and the relationship between maximum possible bit rates and channel bandwidth and noise.

REVIEW QUESTIONS

Core Review Questions

1. Explain the main propagation effects: **a)** attenuation, **b)** distortion, **c)** noise, and **d)** interference. **e)** What is terminal interference?
2. **a)** What are the three main wire transmission media? **b)** Which is used most frequently to the desktop from the nearest hub or switch? Why? **c)** Which is used most frequently between switches and hubs within and

between buildings? Why? **d)** Which is seen mostly in legacy networks? Why?

3. **a)** In EIA/TIA-232 PC serial ports, how many pins are used for data transmission in each direction? **b)** In general, what is the purpose of other pins? **c)** Is transmission digital? **d)** Binary? **e)** What is the speed of a serial port?

4. What is the advantage of parallel transmission compared to serial transmission?

5. Distinguish between half-duplex and full-duplex transmission.

6. **a)** What is the frequency spectrum? **b)** What is a service band? **c)** What is a channel? **d)** A channel has a highest frequency of 50,000 cycles per second and a lowest frequency of 40,000 cycles per second. Express its bandwidth properly.

7. As bandwidth increases in a channel, how does maximum possible transmission speed through that channel change?

8. **a)** What is baseband transmission? **b)** In what two ways is the term "broadband" used? **c)** Which is used more in LANs—baseband or broadband transmission? Why?

Detailed Review Questions

1. Referring to the box, "Baud Rates," **a)** What is the difference between the bit rate and the baud rate? **b)** If a transmission line has a baud rate of 10,000 baud and there are eight possible line states, what is the bit rate? **c)** If you wish to send two bits per line change, how many possible states must you have?

2. **a)** What is the relationship between distance traveled and noise errors if the noise level is constant? Explain. **b)** What is the relationship between bit rate and noise errors if the noise level is constant? Explain.

3. Why is UTP twisted?

4. In general, as <u>noise</u> increases, what happens to the maximum transmission speed in a channel?

Thought Questions

1. Why is EIA/TIA 232 serial port transmission binary?

2. When a teacher is lecturing in class, is this half-duplex transmission or full-duplex transmission? Explain.

3. Full-duplex transmission at 100 kbps requires two 100 kbps channels, one in each direction. However, do we say that this is a 100 kbps system or a 200 kbps system?

4. How can you send two signals at the same time if you are using radio transmission?

5. **a)** In the opening vignette, what problem had May-Ling uncovered? **b)** How did she uncover it? **c)** What would have happened if May-Ling did not have a protocol analyzer program on her PC or a wiring tester?

Case Studies

For case studies, go to the book's website, **http://www.prenhall.com/panko,** and look at the "Supplementary Readings" page for this chapter.

Projects

1. **Getting Current.** Go to the book's website's "New Information" and "Errors" pages for this chapter to get new information since this book went to press and to correct any errors in the text.

2. **Internet Exercises.** Go to the book's website's "Exercises" page for this chapter and do the Internet exercises.

3. Create a one-meter length of UTP wiring, ending at both ends with an RJ-45 terminator. For this, you will need a spool of Category 5 UTP wire, a bag of RJ-45 terminators, a wire-stripping tool, a wire-cutting tool, and a crimping tool for RJ-45.

   When you look at an RJ-45 jack (not an RJ-45 connector on the wire), the pins are numbered 1 through 8 from your left to your right. The table below lists the wire you will place in each slot. There are two common wiring schemes, as shown in the table. Your company or site should select one and be consistent.

   To do the work, place the cable on a table. Use a stripping tool to strip off an inch or two of the covering over the bundle and around each wire pair.

   Lay out the wires as they will go into the holes of the connector, then cut them straight across so that all lengths are exactly the same. Be sure that no more than 1.25 cm (a half inch) of wiring is untwisted after the cut.

   Then push the wires in the appropriate holes. Push the wires as far as they will go, because this is a butt connection, and all wires must reach the tip of the connector. Make sure that some of the covered wiring bundle jacket is inside the connector.

   Crimp the connector to tighten it. Press hard or the connection will not be set. Try pulling the wiring bundle out of the connector with medium pressure to make sure that the crimping worked. If you have a wiring tester, test the connection.

Pin[a]	TIA568A	TIA568B
1	White-Green	White-Orange
2	Green	Orange
3	White-Orange	White-Green
4	Blue	Blue
5	White-Blue	White-Blue
6	Orange	Green
7	White-Brown	White-Brown
8	Brown	Brown

[a]Pin 1 is on the left side of jack when you are facing the jack.

Chapter 5

Modems and Beyond

*A*t home, Glenn Davis has two PCs. There is a Windows 98 computer for the family downstairs and a Windows 95 computer in Glenn's office upstairs. The family got cable modem service for the downstairs PC. As discussed later in this chapter, cable modem service brings downstream (to the home) speeds of as much as 10 Mbps, so many Internet downloads are nearly instantaneous.

Glenn wanted to get cable modem service for the computer in his upstairs office, too. Both machines already had Ethernet network interface cards (see Chapters 1 and 4). Glenn added a second NIC to the downstairs machine, as shown in Figure 5.1. The figure shows that this allowed the downstairs computer to be the family's gateway to high-speed Internet service.

On the downstairs computer, Glenn installed a gateway program, which makes the downstairs computer act as a router. To use the program, Glenn gave each PC a permanent IP address. As Figure 5.1 indicates, the gateway program translates between these internal addresses and the single IP address the cable modem gives to the household, routing incoming packets to the correct computer. This is called network address translation (NAT).

The gateway program also acts as a firewall (see Chapter 10), preventing people on the Internet from getting access to the family's two PCs. This is necessary because the family uses peer–peer PC networking, as discussed in Chapter 6. In this form of networking, users of the upstairs and downstairs machines can access files on each other's disk drives and can print to each other's printer. Without a firewall, people on the Internet also might be able to access their disk files. ■

Figure 5.1
Connecting Two
Windows PCs to a
Cable Modem
Service

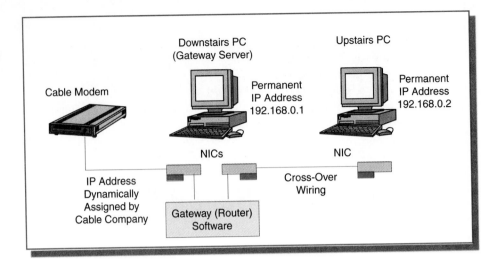

Learning Objectives

By the end of this chapter, you should be able to describe:

- The operation of modems and other translation devices (codecs and DSUs)
- How to evaluate telephone modems compared to ISDN, DSLs, and cable modems

INTRODUCTION

Chapter 1 introduced the Internet. Chapters 2 and 3 looked at the standards we use at the internet, transport, and application layers however we access the Internet. Chapter 4 looked at physical layer propagation in general. In this chapter, we will look at Internet access via telephone lines and modems, plus new alternatives to telephone–modem transmission, including ISDN, cable modems, digital subscriber lines (DSLs), and radio transmission.

MODEMS

In the last chapter, we looked at transmission in terms of abstract principles. Now, we will look at how these principles apply to the transmission and reception of data from home, using a transmission line offered by a telephone company or data carrier. We will begin with modems and then move to faster alternatives to modem transmission.

Modems

Ordinary telephone lines are very useful for low-speed data transmission. Most homes already have a telephone line, so there is no incremental transmission cost in using this line to carry data.

Unfortunately, telephone transmission has a problem. Ordinary telephone technology, created long before digital transmission was economical, uses analog transmission to and from the home. In contrast, computer signals are digital. So there must be a way to translate between them, so that computer signals will travel over analog telephone lines. As we saw in the first chapter, *a modem's job is to transform digital computer signals into an analog form that will travel over an analog telephone line. At the other end, the analog telephone signal is translated back into a digital computer signal.*

Modulation

If you try to transmit a digital signal over the telephone system directly, the digital signal's abrupt voltage changes will be filtered out at the first switching office. So to transmit digital computer data over a telephone line, you must convert it into electrical vibrations. For instance, Figure 5.2 shows **frequency modulation** in which a high-frequency vibration represents a one and a low-frequency vibration represents a zero. The modem jumps between the two frequencies to transmit ones and zeros. To send 1011, you would send high-low-high-high in four consecutive clock cycles.

Converting a digital source signal into an analog transmitted signal is called **modulation.** At the other end, the receiving modem **demodulates** the

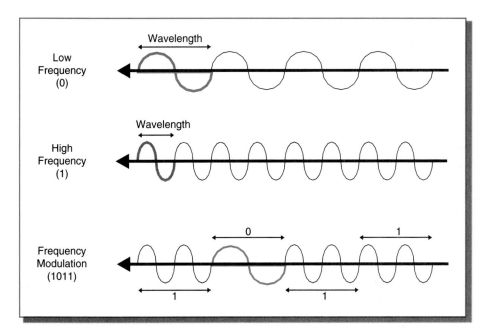

Figure 5.2
Frequency
Modulation

Figure 5.3
Modem Forms

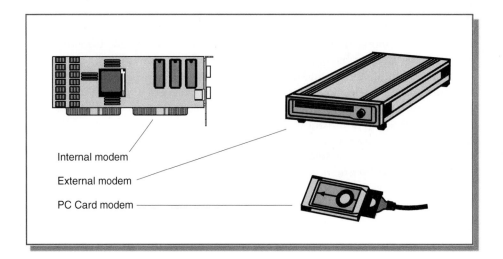

Internal modem

External modem

PC Card modem

transmitted signal back to a digital source signal. The term "modem," then, is a merciful contraction for **modulator/demodulator.**

Modem Forms

Modems come in several different forms. As Figure 5.3 indicates, modems can be printed circuit boards inside the PC systems unit, external boxes, or PC Card modems that stick into the sides of notebook computers. The box "Modem Forms" talks about the relative advantages of these three modem forms. However, no matter how a modem is packaged, modulation works the same way.

Modem Forms

Modems come in three basic forms: (1) external modems, (2) internal modems, and (3) PC Card modems.

External Modems
As shown in Figure 5.3, an **external modem** sits outside the system unit. You connect it to the PC's EIA/TIA-232 serial port with a serial cable. External modems are easy to install because you do not have to open your PC to install it. You merely connect it to a serial port.

However, external modems take up precious desktop real estate. (After all, "desktop" computers are given this name because they tend to take up your entire desktop.) In addition, the serial cable from the modem to the PC and the power cable for the modem add to desktop wiring clutter.

Internal Modems
Second, there are **internal modems.** As shown in Figure 5.3, internal modems are printed circuit boards that sit inside the system unit. They do not need a serial port; they have one built in. Internal modems are attractive because they do not take up valuable desktop real estate.

Continued.

Chapter 5   Modems and Beyond

However, internal modems are somewhat more difficult to install, requiring you to open your PC systems unit to insert the modem board and sometimes to deal with various address settings on the board.

PC Card Modems
Figure 5.3 shows yet another type of modem. This is a **PC card modem**. It is inserted into a **PC card slot** found in most notebook computers. Installation usually is trivial, and the modem does not sit outside the computer, which would add to desktop clutter. Unfortunately, few desktops have such slots. In addition, PC Card modems are more expensive than internal or external modems.

Test Your Understanding
Answer Detailed Review Question 1.

Modem Standards

The International Telecommunications Union–Telecommunications Standards Sector (ITU-T) sets most new modem standards. This is the same standards organization that, along with ISO, manages OSI. As Table 5.1 illustrates, ITU-T has created a number of modem standards.

Speed Standards The most important standards govern modem transmission speed. Most new modems today follow the **V.90** standard, which allows a modem to *receive* at 56 kbps, although it can only *transmit (send)* at 33.6 kbps. However, in the field you will still encounter many older **V.34** modems, which both send and receive at 33.6 kbps and even **V.32 bis** modems (**bis** means second edition), which both send and receive at only 14.4 kbps.

Table 5.1 Modem Standards

Speed Standards		
Name	**Speed**	**Origin**
V.90	56 kbps receiving	ITU-T
V.34	33.6 kbps	ITU-T
V.32 *bis*	14.4 kbps	ITU-T
Error Correction and Data Compression Standards		
Name	**Type**	**Origin**
V.42	Error correction	ITU-T
V.42 *bis*	Data compression	ITU-T
Facsimile Modem Standards		
Name	**Speed**	**Origin**
V.14	14.4 kbps	ITU-T
V.29	9600 bps	ITU-T

The V.90 modem appears to violate the 35 kbps maximum transmission (sending) speed that we saw in the last chapter for telephone transmission. The box, "V.90 Modems: Breaking the 35 kbps Speed Barrier," shows how 56 kbps *reception* speeds are possible. However, when a V.90 modem *sends*, it is still limited to 33.6 kbps.

V.90 Modems: Breaking the 35 kbps Speed Barrier

In the last chapter, we saw that you can only send information at about 35 kbps through a typical 3.1 kHz telephone bandwidth. However, as Figure 5.4 illustrates, the telephone itself is digital internally, with 56 kbps channels for individual telephone calls.

Figure 5.4 V.90 Modem

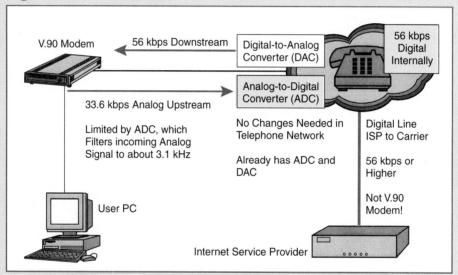

The ADC Limits Transmission Speed

Then where does the 35 kbps limit appear? As Figure 5.4 illustrates, your telephone sends an analog signal up the line to the first switching office of the telephone system. There, a device called an **analog-to-digital converter (ADC)** first filters your signal to 3.1 kHz and then converts the analog telephone signal into a digital signal to travel within the telephone network. Note that it is the ADC that creates the 3.1 kHz bandwidth limitation and therefore the 35 kbps speed limitation.[1]

Why ADCs?

The ADC is needed because the internal telephone system is entirely digital. Once, the telephone system was entirely analog. Over time, however, the internal switches and the trunk lines that

---

[1] Actually, the ADC codec digitizes everything from 0 Hz to 4 kHz rather than just frequencies from 300 Hz to 3,400 Hz. Encoding this wider frequency range reduces potential encoding problems and results in the 64 kbps speeds of digital telephone channels. However, filtering is done before encoding, limiting the range of frequencies passed to the codec to between 300 Hz and 3.4 kHz and therefore limiting actual data transmission to about 35 kbps.

Continued.

connect switches were converted entirely to digital. Today, only the signal on the line to and from your home is still analog.

No ADC, No 35 kbps Speed Limit
When your ISP transmits to a V.90 modem, however, it does not use an analog telephone line to the telephone system. Rather, as Figure 5.4 shows, the ISP uses a digital line. Note that there is no ADC when the ISP uses a digital line because there is no need to convert from analog to digital. Without an ADC, there is no bandwidth filtering and therefore no 35 kbps limit.

Still a 56 kbps Speed Limit
By not going through an ADC, the ISP can make full use of the telephone network's internal 56 kbps digital channels. However, these channels create a very hard speed limit of 56 kbps. V.90 modems are one-time tricks. They will not lead to faster speeds in the future.

DACs are OK
When the 56 kbps signal reaches the last telephone switching office, Figure 5.4 shows that a device called a *digital-to-analog converter (DAC)* translates the digital signal back into an analog signal and sends this analog signal to your telephone and therefore to your modem. However, the DAC does not impose 3.1 kHz bandwidth limitations when it transmits to your home, so your modem can receive at 56 kbps.

Nothing New for V.90
Telephone companies have always had ADCs and DACs to handle ordinary voice calls. In other words, ADCs and DACs were *not* installed by the telephone company for V.90 modem service. Rather, modem vendors merely exploited the 56 kbps capabilities of the telephone system, using digital connections to transmit and DACs to send analog signals at 56 kbps. The telephone company, then, does not have to do anything differently to handle V.90 modems.

Some Problems With V.90 Modems
Unfortunately, there are some problems with V.90 modems at this time, including the fact that not all telephone lines will support these modems. In fact, even good lines often limit you to between 40 and 50 kbps.

Test Your Understanding
Answer Core Review Question 9 and Detailed Review Questions 4–5.

Training   What if there is a 33.6 kbps V.34 modem at one end of a telephone line and a 14.4 kbps V.32 *bis* modem at the other end? Before two modems begin to transmit data, they go through a **training period,** during which they exchange messages to learn what the other modem can do.[2] The faster modem automatically slows down to match the speed of the slower modem. In this case, then, transmission would take place at V.32 *bis* speed, which is only 14.4 kbps.

---

[2] The two modems also check the line by transmitting test data and noting errors. If the error rate is too high, they automatically slow down. (Recall from Chapter 3 that error rates are related to transmission speed for a constant level of noise.)

Error Correction and Compression   Most modems today can do error correction during transmission. This involves retransmitting information that was garbled during transmission. Error correction is governed by the **V.42** standard.

In addition, most modems today can do data compression, using the **V.42 bis** standard. Under ideal circumstances, you can get up to 4:1 compression. So if your modem is transmitting at 33.6 kbps, you can feed it data at a speed of 115.2 kbps, which is the maximum speed of a serial port. Your modem will compress the data down to 33.6 kbps for transmission over the telephone network.

What if a modem that does not do compression is at one end of the line and a modem that does compression is at the other end? During the training period, the modem that can do compression automatically agrees not to compress its data before transmission. Transmission still takes place, although without compression. Error correction is negotiated in the same way.

Facsimile Modem Operation   We have been focusing on data transmission. However, most modems today can also act as **facsimile modems,** transmitting and receiving facsimile images at 14.4 kbps **(V.14)** or at 9,600 bps **(V.29).**

Test Your Understanding

Answer Core Review Questions 1–4, Detailed Review Questions 2–3, and Thought Questions 1–2.

ALTERNATIVES TO ORDINARY MODEMS

Even with a 33.6 kbps modem and compression, downloading webpages can take an excruciatingly long amount of time. For this reason, you would like to have faster transmission speeds.

The Speed Problem

Unfortunately, we cannot expect to get much higher speeds with traditional modems on standard telephone lines. As discussed in the last chapter, an analog telephone line has a theoretical maximum speed of about 35 kbps when we transmit. Modems today are very close to this theoretical transmission limit. The V.90 modem, in turn, is a one-trick pony and will not be able to raise speeds beyond 56 kbps when we receive.

For this reason, some home users of the Internet are turning to higher-speed connections. These higher-speed connections typically are called *broadband* access services. As noted in the last chapter, this use of the term "broadband" is technically incorrect but is also rather common.

The Costs of Faster Access

Unfortunately, these faster alternatives have higher costs.

1. New translator devices are more expensive than voice line modems.

2. You may not be able to use your EIA/TIA-232 serial port and may have to install a faster port.
3. The telephone company or other carrier will charge more for monthly transmission service to connect you to the ISP than they do for voice telephone service.
4. Internet service providers may charge more because you are placing a heavier load on the ISP's network.

Transmission Carriers versus ISPs   When you use a telephone line to reach an Internet service provider (ISP), the telephone line and Internet access services are provided by different companies—the telephone company and the Internet service provider. You pay the telephone company for telephone service, and you pay the ISP separately for Internet access.

The same is true for higher-speed access. You have to pay a carrier for high-speed transmission service to your ISP, and you have to pay the ISP, separately, for Internet access. Although some high-speed services combine transmission and ISP service, not all do.

If you reach the ISP through a high-speed line, by the way, the ISP is likely to charge more because you will be moving more data through its connections.

Modem   You need a modem for voice telephone access to your ISP. You generally do not buy this modem from either the telephone company or from the ISP. Similarly, high-speed transmission services also require devices called modems. Sometimes you buy these from the transmission carrier. Other times, you purchase them separately from a hardware supplier.

Ports for External Connections   Modems for high-speed transmission often are external to the PC. Most external high-speed modems need a higher-speed port than EIA/TIA-232 serial ports, which are limited to 115.2 kbps. For instance, cable modems, which we discuss below, usually require the installation of an Ethernet network interface card (NIC), which can send and receive at 10 Mbps. Other high-speed modems can use **Universal Serial Bus (USB)** ports, which operate at 12 Mbps,[3] or the even faster **Firewire (IEEE-1394)** ports, which operate at 400 Mbps to a few gigabits per second. Of course high-speed modems built into expansion boards do not require external connections.

Test Your Understanding

Answer Core Review Question 9.

ISDN

For guaranteed faster speeds, you need to move beyond your current dial-up voice telephone service. Many transmission carriers now offer a competing

---

[3] A new USB-2 standard, now in development, would offer a speed of about 480 Mbps on USB ports.

Figure 5.5
Integrated
Services Digital
Network (ISDN)

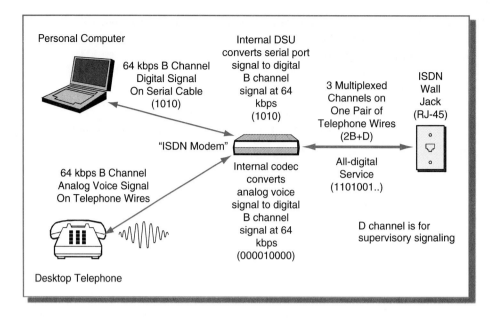

service, called the **Integrated Services Digital Network (ISDN).** Figure 5.5 shows an ISDN connection.

All-Digital, Dial-Up Service

What is not obvious in this picture is that ISDN is a purely digital system. Also not obvious from the figure is that ISDN is a dial-up service. You can dial up any other ISDN subscriber and connect digitally. You can even call ordinary telephone customers because ISDN is interconnected with the public switched telephone network.

ISDN Modem

Figure 5.5 shows that the ISDN line into your home terminates in a device that is usually called an **ISDN modem.** It costs substantially more than an ordinary telephone modem.

2B+D: Multiplexing

The ISDN line coming into your home multiplexes (i.e., mixes) three distinct data channels onto a *single UTP wire pair* running from your home to the first switching office.

Two of these are 64 kbps "B" channels, and one is a 16 kbps "D" channel. For this reason, the service that ISDN brings to the desktop is called **2B+D.**

Bonding

Originally, it was expected that users would use one "B" channel for voice and the other "B" channel for data, while the "D" channel would be used for supervisory signaling.

Most ISPs, however, now support **bonding,** in which the two "B" channels act as a single 128 kbps data channel for Internet access. The "D" channel is still used for supervisory signaling.

Not So Great Expectations

Unfortunately, ISDN service costs about three times as much per month as ordinary telephone service, and most households and remote workers would find this cost prohibitive for ISDN's modest speed gains.

Test Your Understanding

Answer Core Review Questions 5–6.

TRANSLATION DEVICES

Data Service Units (DSUs)

Although the device that connects your computer to the ISDN system is called an "ISDN modem," it really is not a modem at all. Figure 5.6 shows that different data translation devices are needed depending on the type of *device* attached to the transmission line (e.g., computer, telephone) and the type of the *transmission line* being used. For a digital computer device and an analog transmission line, you truly do need a modem.

However, the figure shows that if you have a *digital device* and a *digital transmission line,* as you do in ISDN, then you do not need a modem. Rather, as Figure 5.6 shows, you need a translation device called a **data service unit (DSU).** Figure 5.7 shows that although both the source signal and the digital transmission line are digital, there are different digital formats, involving different signaling rates, different numbers of bits per baud, different voltage levels, and so forth. In your ISDN "modem," there is a DSU to translate between the digital signal from your PC EIA/TIA-232 serial port and the digital transmission format used by the ISDN system's "B" channels.

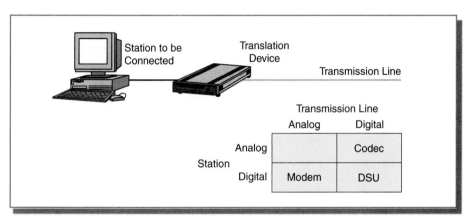

Figure 5.6
Signal Translation
Devices

Figure 5.7
DSU Translates between a Digital Device and a Digital Transmission Line

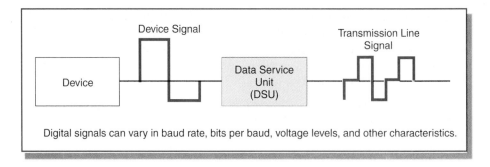

Digital signals can vary in baud rate, bits per baud, voltage levels, and other characteristics.

Codecs

If you tie your telephone into the ISDN "modem," you have another problem. Your *device* (telephone) is *analog,* but the ISDN *transmission line* is *digital.* As Figure 5.8 illustrates, you need a translation device called a **codec.**

Sampling Periods Codecs work through a technique called **sampling.** Figure 5.8 illustrates this process. It shows that a sound signal is nothing more than a loudness level that varies with time. In sampling, each second is divided into many time periods. For voice, there usually are 8,000 sampling periods per second.[4]

Measuring Loudness in Each Sampling Period For each sample, only the loudness level is measured and recorded. Historically, loudness was mea-

Figure 5.8
Codec Translates between an Analog Device and a Digital Transmission Line

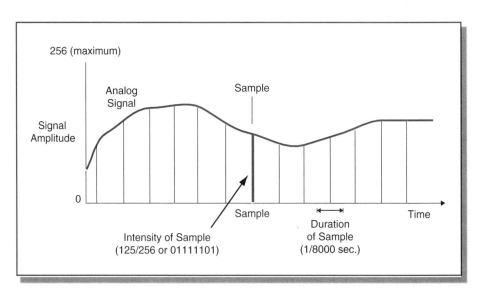

---

[4] The basic rule is that you should sample at twice the highest frequency. According to this rule, 8,000 samples per second would assume a highest frequency of 4 kHz. As discussed in the last chapter, the normal telephone frequency range stops at 3.4 kHz, but as noted in an earlier footnote, treating it as 4 kHz is safer.

sured and then converted into an 8-bit binary number, giving 256 (2^8) possible loudness levels. The loudest possible sound level is given the value 256. Absolute quiet is given the value 0. The human ear cannot easily distinguish differences between adjacent loudness levels if there are 256 levels.

The 64 kbps (or 56 kbps) Data Rate   If we have 8 bits per sample and 8,000 samples per second, then digital voice sampling gives a data stream of 64 kbps. This is why most digital transmission lines operate at multiples of 64 kbps. Another popular speed is 56 kbps, which results when 8 kbps is "stolen" from the channel for supervisory signaling.

Test Your Understanding

Answer Core Review Question 7, Detailed Review Questions 6, 8, and 9, and Thought Question 6.

DIGITAL SUBSCRIBER LINE (DSL) MODEMS

The telephone companies are beginning to offer an even faster service, the **digital subscriber line (DSL).** As in the case of ISDN, digital subscriber lines are entirely digital and are faster than ordinary voice lines. They also are much faster than ISDN, offering transmission speeds of 384 kbps to several megabits per second. (There are several types of DSLs with different speeds and costs.)

ADSL   You must get the proper DSL modem for the particular DSL service your telephone company offers. As Figure 5.9 shows, **ADSL** (*A* is for asymmetric) offers high-speed **downstream** service (to the home) and lower-speed **upstream** service (from the home). This asymmetry is acceptable for Web surfing.

ADSL Speeds   ADSL can offer downstream speeds up to several megabits per second. However, many carriers only offer ADSL downstream speeds of 384 kbps to 640 kbps to reduce costs. ADSL typically gives 64 kbps to 256 kbps upstream service.

G.Lite   The ITU-T has developed a standard for low-speed ADSL. The standard is designated as G.992.2, but it is popularly known as **G.Lite.** G.Lite specifies downstream speeds of up to 1.5 Mbps, although, as just noted, slower downstream speeds often are used.

Pricing in Flux   At the time of this writing, DSL prices are still fluid. However, in the United States, it appears that the *combined price* of residential ISP service plus an ADSL line of about 640 kbps will remain about $50 per month. Business service is likely to cost substantially more but will offer higher speeds (up to 1.5 Mbps and sometimes faster). ISP service will also offer multiple IP addresses so that several computers can share the line. Dataquest

Figure 5.9
G.Lite Asymmetric
Digital Subscriber
Line (ADSL)

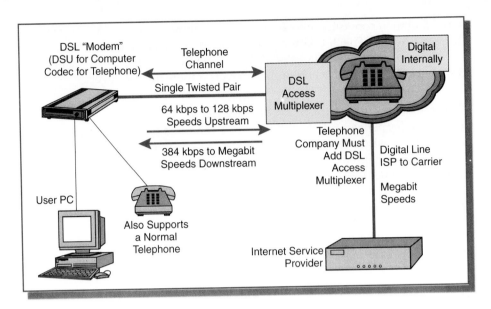

forecasts that DSL modem sales will grow from 2.3 million units in 2000 to 9.8 million units in 2003.[5]

Multiplexed Voice   Figure 5.9 shows that a G.Lite ADSL delivers more than data traffic. It also multiplexes an ordinary full-duplex telephone channel on the pair of wires already coming into the home. This allows you to talk on the telephone at the same time you are surfing the World Wide Web.

DSLAMs   One of the good things about V.90 modems is that the telephone company does not have to install any special equipment. However, as Figure 5.9 indicates, when the telephone company offers DSL service, it has to install **Digital Subscriber Line Access Multiplexers (DSLAMs)** at its end offices. Telephone companies tend to move somewhat slowly, so DSL service is not yet available in many areas.

Test Your Understanding

Answer Detailed Review Question 10 and Thought Question 3.

CABLE MODEMS

Not to be outdone, many cable television companies offer data transmission services at downstream speeds of 10 Mbps, as shown in Figure 5.10. Upstream

[5] Dataquest, "Gartner Group's Dataquest Says Need for Higher Bandwidth Connection Spurs xDSL Equipment Growth," press release, July 26, 1999, "http://gartner5.gartnerweb.com/dq/static/about/press/pr-b9941.html".

speeds, as in ADSL, are much slower, typically 64 kbps to 256 kbps. To use this service, you need a **cable modem.** The cable television company usually operates as both a transmission carrier and an ISP. Most cable companies price their services aggressively, at under $50 per month for both transmission and Internet access. Dataquest forecasts that sales of cable modems will grow from 1.8 million units in 2000 to 5.3 million in 2003.[6]

10 Mbps Shared Downstream Speeds Cable modems offer speeds of up to 10 Mbps downstream and ISDN-like speeds upstream.

However, individual users do not get the full 10 Mbps of downstream speed. Multiple customers share this capacity, so the real throughput for individual customers is somewhat lower. In contrast, ADSL downstream transmission services are not shared, although ADSL downstream speeds normally are far less than 10 Mbps.

Still, sharing should not be a matter of extreme concern. Recall from Chapter 1 that data transmission is bursty, with each user receiving only occasionally. Capacity is only shared among the subscribers actually downloading at a particular moment. For instance, if there are 50 customers sharing the speed, only a few are likely to be downloading at a particular moment. Only if there are 100 or more customers sharing the cable modem service should sharing be a serious concern. Most cable modem services divide their service regions into groups of about 500 households, only some of which will take cable modem service.

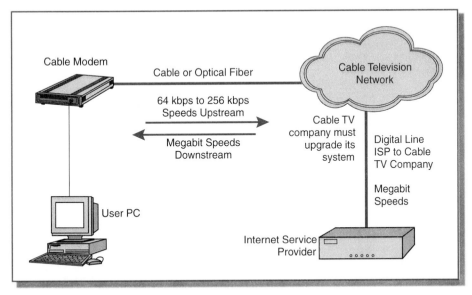

Figure 5.10
Cable Modem

---

[6] Dataquest, "Gartner Group's Dataquest Says Need for Higher Bandwidth Connection Spurs xDSL Equipment Growth," press release, July 26, 1999, "http://gartner5.gartnerweb.com/dq/static/about/press/pr-b9941.html".

Not in All Countries Cable modem service is growing very rapidly in the United States, which is heavily cabled. However, most other countries do not have extensive cable television service to build upon for Internet access.

Mostly Residential Another problem with cable modem service is that it tends to be available mostly in residential areas because that is where most cable television systems have been installed. This limits its usefulness in business offices, which are mostly in commercial areas.

Test Your Understanding

Answer Core Review Question 8, Detailed Review Question 7, and Thought Question 4.

Wireless Internet Access

Mobile computer users also want to link their laptops to the Internet. Today, they need to find a telephone to do this. Figure 5.11 shows an alternative: **wireless Internet access.** Wireless Internet access systems use a radio **transceiver** (transmitter/receiver) in the computer to link it to the wireless Internet access supplier's site. As you might expect, high-speed wireless Internet access is very expensive today.

LEO and MEO Satellites Satellite-based wireless Internet access systems use satellites in relatively low orbits. This places them relatively close to users, so their signals are strong. As Figure 5.11 indicates, users do not need dish antennas. They can use **omnidirectional antennas,** which do not have to be

Figure 5.11
Wireless Internet Access

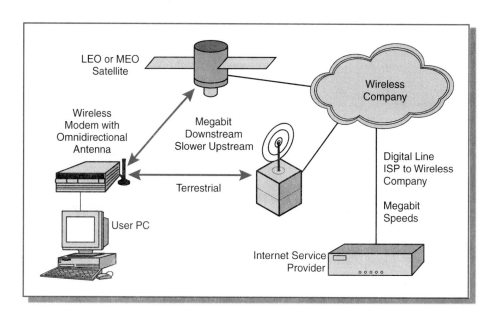

Figure 5.12
LEO and MEO
Satellite Systems

Currently Responsible
LEO or MEO

Small
Omnidirectional
Transceiver

pointed in a specific direction. (Imagine having to bring a dish antenna with you while carrying your notebook computer.)

Some services use **low earth orbit (LEO)** satellites that orbit below the first Van Allen radiation band, which peaks at about 3,000 km (about 1,800 miles). Most **LEOs** orbit at a few hundred miles. Other satellite-based Internet access systems use **medium earth orbit (MEO)** satellites, which orbit above the first Van Allen belt but below the second Van Allen belt, which peaks at about 15,000 km (about 9,000 miles). Most **MEOs** operate at about 10,000 km.

Both LEOs and MEOs remain in sight of a ground receiver for only short periods of time. Consequently, as Figure 5.12 indicates, a user has to be *handed off* constantly from one satellite to another. This is like the reverse of cellular telephony, in which the cellsite antennas remain constant while the subscriber moves. With LEOs and MEOs, users remain constant while the satellite serving them moves. Orbiting higher than LEOs, MEOs stay in sight longer; however, their signals are also weaker because they are farther away.

Radio communication follows an "inverse cube" law. If one satellite is three times farther away than another of comparable signal power, its signal will be only one twenty-seventh as strong.

GEO Satellites   For their trunk lines, telephone companies sometimes use **geosynchronous earth orbit (GEO)** satellites. Orbiting at about 36,000 km (22,300 miles), **GEOs** orbit every 24 hours, making them turn with the earth and therefore making them appear stationary in the sky.

As Figure 5.13 indicates, telephone companies use **dish antennas,** which are highly directional. This allows them to pick up the weak signals from distant GEOs. The narrow beams created by dish antennas allow point-to-point transmission between switching offices, making them ideal for trunk line use.

Figure 5.13 shows the footprint as being very narrow. Large dishes on satellite create narrow footprints. This is fine for point-to-point trunk transmission, in this case providing a point-to-point connection to Earth Station A.

However, if a small dish is used on the satellite, the footprint will be very large. It may encompass an entire country or at least a large geographical region.

Figure 5.13
GEO Satellite
System

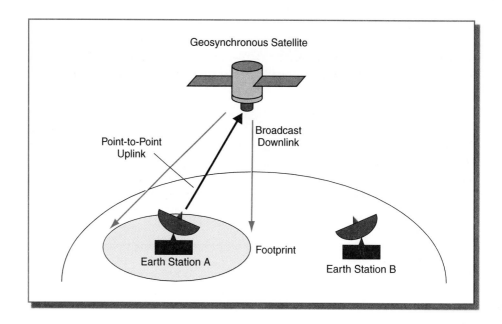

This is how direct broadcast television works. The satellite uses a small dish to broadcast the signal to many receivers in a region. Usually, receivers have small antennas, leading to the name **very small aperture terminal (VSAT)** system. VSATs can also be used for Internet access, although two-way VSAT systems that would allow small stations to send as well as receive are difficult to make.

Test Your Understanding

Answer Detailed Review Question 12 and Thought Question 7.

SMALL OFFICE SERVICE

A small office may have a half dozen or more PCs that need access to the Internet. As discussed in the vignette at the beginning of this chapter, it is possible to share a DSL or cable modem connection to the Internet service provider (ISP). Chapter 6 discusses how to connect several PCs to a high-speed Internet access line.

Most DSL vendors and cable modem vendors do not approve of the approach discussed in the vignette. Instead, they require you to pay more if you have multiple computers sharing the connection. On the positive side, they give each machine its own IP address, so that several PCs do not have to share a single IP address. The network address translation described in the opening vignette is not required.

Test Your Understanding

Answer Detailed Review Question 13 and Thought Question 8.

KEY POINTS

In this chapter, we looked at modem transmission over telephone lines and at newer alternatives that will provide higher speeds, albeit at a higher price.

Analog Telephone Lines and Modems   We focused on modem transmission over ordinary telephone lines because this is the most common form of **small office and home (SOHO)** access today and, given the costs of other alternatives, is likely to dominate in the near future. The chapter discussed modulation, followed by modem forms and modem standards.

The discussion of modem standards emphasized that there are several types of standards for modems, including standards for speed, error correction, compression, and facsimile operation. When two modems connect, they go through a training period that can last for several seconds. During this period they negotiate the highest common denominator for these various standards.

Alternatives to Analog Telephone Lines and Modems   Modems are inexpensive and can use your ordinary telephone line. However, modem speeds cannot increase above V.90 levels, given the nature of telephone transmission. Higher speeds will require new technologies. Fortunately, several of these new technologies are now available or are becoming available. These other technologies also free your home telephone for voice calls.

- With bonding, ISDN can provide 128 kbps transmission and reception speeds.
- The ISDN "modem" really contains DSU and codec circuitry rather than modem circuitry.
- Cable modems usually can download data at 10 Mbps, although this speed is shared.
- Telephone carriers are introducing relatively high-speed digital subscriber lines (DSLs) that offer high kilobit to megabit downstream speeds and, in asymmetric digital subscriber lines (ADSL), slower upstream speeds.
- Wireless access will allow portable computers to use the Internet at any time.

The Cost of Speed   Although these new transmission options are attractive in terms of speed, they are also very costly.

- First, you must have a translation device between your PC (and possibly your telephone line) and the transmission line. This can be a modem, codec, or DSU, but it will probably be called a "modem."
- Second, you must pay a carrier for the high-speed transmission line.
- Third, your ISP, which usually is *not* your carrier (although it can be) probably will charge you more because your higher download speeds (and perhaps upload speeds) will require more ISP resources.
- Fourth, you may need a port faster than a serial port unless your "modem" is built into an expansion board placed inside your PC.

REVIEW QUESTIONS

If an answer has multiple parts, write your answer to each part in a separate paragraph.

Core Review Questions

1. **a)** Define *modulation*. **b)** Define *demodulation*. Do not just say translation between digital and analog or analog and digital. For both modulation and demodulation, characterize whether the transmission line is analog or digital, and whether the device attached to the transmission line is analog or digital.

2. **a)** What is the speed of a V.34 modem? **b)** What are the speeds of a V.90 modem? Be specific.

3. **a)** What is "training" in initial modem communication? **b)** If a V.34 modem tries to communicate with a V.32 *bis* modem, what will happen?

4. To use a V.90 modem, can you use your ordinary home telephone line, or do you need an additional line?

5. **a)** In ISDN, what is 2B+D? **b)** What is the maximum reception speed for ISDN with bonding? **c)** What is the maximum transmission speed with bonding? **d)** To use ISDN, can you use your ordinary home telephone line, or do you need an additional line?

6. How does multiplexing apply to ISDN?

7. **a)** If you have a *digital device* communicating over an *analog transmission line,* what type of translation device do you need, if any? **b)** If you have an *analog device* communicating over a *digital transmission line,* what type of translation device do you need, if any? **c)** If you have a *digital device* communicating over a *digital transmission line,* what type of translation device do you need, if any?

8. **a)** What type of organization offers cable modems? **b)** What type of organization offers digital subscriber lines (DSLs)? **c)** How do cable modems and DSLs compare to 56 kbps V.90 modems in terms of speed and cost?

9. When you move from ordinary telephone modem transmission to a high-speed alternative, what four additional costs may you incur?

Detailed Review Questions

1. Referring to the box "Modem Forms," **a)** Which modem form is easier to install—internal or external? **b)** What is the advantage of internal modems over external modems? **c)** What is the most expensive modem form?

2. **a)** What does V.42 standardize? **b)** What does V.42 *bis* standardize?

3. What are the two standards for facsimile modem speeds?

4. Referring to the box "V.90 Modems: Breaking the 35 kbps Speed Barrier," **a)** What device limits your speed when you transmit over the telephone system? **b)** Where is this device located?

5. Referring to the box "V.90 Modems: Breaking the 35 kbps Speed Barrier,"
   a) In using a V.90 modem, what does the PC user need, *compared to when a V.34 modem is used?* b) What does the ISP need, *compared to when a V.34 modem is used?* c) What does the telephone company need, *compared to when a V.34 modem is used?*

6. a) If you attach a telephone to an "ISDN modem," are you dealing with a modem at all? b) If not, what type of translation device are you really using? c) If you attach a computer to an "ISDN modem," are you dealing with a modem at all? d) If not, what type of translation device(s) are you really using?

7. A cable modem can often give you download speeds of 10 Mbps. Why will you usually not achieve this speed?

8. In codec encoding, what do you measure in each sampling period?

9. A DSU translates between digital formats. What things could be different between two digital formats?

10. a) Distinguish between DSL and ADSL. b) What does the *A* in *ADSL* mean? c) What is G.Lite?

11. When you buy an ISDN, DSL, or cable "modem," what types of ports might you specify?

12. a) What are typical distances for LEO, MEO, and GEO satellites? b) For satellite Internet access, what is the advantage of LEOs and MEOs, compared with GEOs? c) What is the disadvantage?

13. a) If you have six PCs in a branch office, can you connect them all to the Internet with a single DSL? b) Will you pay more for the DSL if you do?

Thought Questions

1. What happens if a modem that follows the V.42 standard tries to communicate with a modem that does not follow the V.42 standard?

2. You and a friend both have PCs with V.90 modems. At what speed can you transfer files between yourselves?

3. Several forms of transmission are asymmetric, with downstream speeds being higher than upstream speeds. a) For what application is this good? b) For what applications do you think asymmetric transmission speeds are not good? (The answer to this part is not in the text.)

4. a) Which is better for downloading, a 10 Mbps cable modem or a 10 Mbps ADSL line? Explain. b) Which is better for downloading, a 10 Mbps cable modem or a 1 Mbps ADSL line? Explain.

5. Besides the speed of your line to the ISP, what determines download speed in World Wide Web access?

6. In encoding, the general rule is that you need to sample at twice the highest frequency. In addition, for each sample, if you store N bits, you can have 2^N loudness levels. a) How many bits per second would you generate if you wanted to encode music? Assume a highest frequency of 20 kHz and 65,536 loudness levels. Assume stereo music, in which you have two channels.

Second, convert this into bytes per second. **b)** How much storage would you require on a disk holding 74 minutes of stereo music? **c)** How does this compare with the storage capacity of a CD-ROM disk of about 650 MB? Remember that one KB is 1,024 bytes and that one MB is 1,024 kilobytes. **d)** Repeat the first two parts using the sampling rate actually used in audio CDs, namely 44,100 samples per second, which is called 44.1 kHz.

7. For satellites of comparable power, relatively how much power will reach the ground if you have a LEO, a MEO, and a GEO? Consider a LEO satellite's power on the ground as equal to 1.0. You will have to make reasonable assumptions about LEO and MEO orbital distances.

8. **a)** In the vignette at the start of the chapter, what problem did Glenn face? **b)** What did he have to add to solve it? **c)** What was the problem with IP addresses, and how was it solved?

Case Studies

For case studies, go to the book's website, **http://www.prenhall.com/panko,** and look at the "Supplementary Readings" for this chapter.

Projects

1. **Getting Current.** Go the book's website's "New Information" and "Errors" pages for this chapter to get new information since this book went to press and to correct any errors in the text.

2. **Internet Exercises.** Go the book's website's "Exercises" page for this chapter and do the Internet exercises.

Chapter 6

A Small PC Network

As noted in the last chapter, Glenn Davis has a Windows 95 computer in his upstairs office. Glenn wanted to use the laser printer on his family's downstairs Windows 98 machine, and he wanted to use files on the downstairs computer's hard drive. He wanted to do this without having to carry floppy disks between the machines or having to wait for someone using the new computer to finish so that he could print or work with a file on the hard drive.

As Figure 6.1 indicates, Glenn got a hub and installed it downstairs. Then he installed a network interface card (NIC) in his upstairs computer. (The new downstairs computer came with a NIC.) Finally, he bought wiring in pre-cut lengths to connect the computers to the hub. The total cost was about $100.

Next, Glenn had to configure Windows on the two computers. This turned out to be a nightmare until his son, David, discovered an obscure help file noting that the IPX/SPX protocol stack is best for connecting Windows 95 machines to Windows 98 machines. Once Glenn installed IPX/SPX, the computers worked perfectly. From his room, Glenn could now print to the laser printer downstairs. In addition, he stored all his files on the new computer so that his files were all in one place. As Chapter 5 noted, he later connected his two computers to his cable modem service. The downstairs machine could also print to the color printer in Glenn's office, as Figure 6.1 indicates.

However, whenever someone working at the downstairs computer shuts the machine down or crashes it, this creates problems for Glenn. Also, when Glenn is using file service (disk drive sharing) or print service, the downstairs machine slows significantly. This kind of peer–peer PC network would not work with many more PCs. We will see in this chapter that most PC networks use dedicated file servers that are not also used as client PCs. ∎

Figure 6.1
A Small Peer–Peer
PC Network

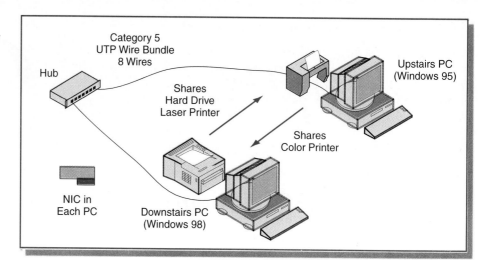

Learning Objectives

After studying this chapter, you should be able to describe:

- How to select the hardware and software needed to build a small PC network on an Ethernet LAN, using hubs or switches.

- Key PC networking services, including file service, print service, remote access service, Internet access, and directory service.

- Steps needed to install a small PC network or an Ethernet LAN.

- Major issues in systems (server) management.

INTRODUCTION

The last four chapters focused on the Internet. In this chapter, we will begin to look at another critical network environment, the PC network. More specifically, in this chapter and the next, we will look at what is needed to create a small PC network with only a few PCs. Chapter 8 looks at larger and more complex site networks, which can serve dozens to thousands of users at a corporate site.

PC Networking for Internet Access

Of course, the PC network is the way that most office workers reach the Internet. Instead of using PPP at the data link layer and modems at the physical layer, the office worker uses the LAN's physical and data link layer standards. Standards at the internet, transport, and application layers are exactly the same, no matter how you reach the Internet. We will look at Internet access for PC network users near the end of this chapter.

PC Networking to Use Internal Servers

On a PC network, however, Internet access is not the only application or even the main application. Client PC users work most of the time with the company's own file servers, print servers, and other types of internal PC network servers. While Internet access is glamorous, PC networking using internal servers handles most processing chores for the typical office worker.

A Small PC Network on an Ethernet LAN

In this chapter, we will focus on small PC networks built on simple Ethernet LANs. Ethernet is by far the most popular LAN technology in business, and PC networking is by far the most common use of LANs.[1]

Figure 6.2 shows the elements of such small PC networks. Figure 6.3 shows a key element of many PC networks—a switch—in more detail.

LAN ELEMENTS: NICs, HUBS, SWITCHES, AND WIRING

In this section, we will look at the LAN elements of small PC networks built on Ethernet LANs. These LAN elements, shown in Figure 6.2 and Figure 6.3, include network interface cards (NICs), a hub or switch, and wiring.

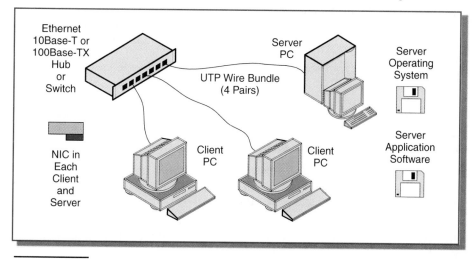

Figure 6.2
Simple PC Network

---

[1] Many textbooks equate "PC network" with "LAN." However, this is inaccurate. A LAN is a single network, so it involves only the physical and data link layers. In contrast, PC networks require all layers to operate successfully, because they require application–application interactions. In a sense, the LAN is the transmission service for a small PC network.

In addition, as we will see in Chapters 8 and 9, PC networks are not limited to single LANs. Enterprise PC networks can span the entire corporation. They can contain thousands of client PCs and dozens of servers spread across multiple sites. Any client PC at any site can reach any server at any other site, as long as it has administrative permission.

Finally, LANs are not limited to PC networking. They also support communication among other types of computers, such as workstations and mainframes.

Figure 6.3
Stackable Switch

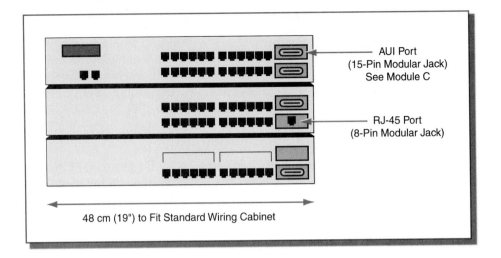

AUI Port
(15-Pin Modular Jack)
See Module C

RJ-45 Port
(8-Pin Modular Jack)

48 cm (19") to Fit Standard Wiring Cabinet

Network Interface Cards (NICs)

To communicate over a telephone line, your PC needs a modem. To communicate over a PC network, your PC instead needs an expansion board called a **network interface card (NIC).**

The NIC handles all subnet communication at the physical and data link layers. The PC, therefore, only needs to implement the internet, transport, and application layers in software.

NICs are readily available in computer stores and cost between $10 and $70 depending on speed (usually 10 Mbps or 100 Mbps), quality, and marketing.

Hubs and Switches

When one station wishes to transmit to another, the sending computer transmits the frame to the Ethernet hub or switch. The hub or switch then sends the frame on to the destination computer. Both hubs and switches do this, but they send the frame on in different ways.

RJ-45 Ports   Although hubs and switches operate differently, both have multiple RJ-45 ports, which we saw in Chapter 4.

Speeds   Another point of similarity is that both Ethernet hubs and switches can operate at one of three speeds.

- A 10Base-T hub or switch sends and receives at 10 Mbps.
- A 100Base-TX[2] hub or switch sends and receives at 100 Mbps.
- A gigabit Ethernet (1000Base-T) hub or switch sends and receives at one gigabit per second. For a small LAN, gigabit Ethernet would be extreme overkill.

---

[2] Why not just 100Base-T? The 802.3 Working Group created three UTP-based 100Base standards: 100Base-TX, 100Base-T4, and 100Base-T2. Only the 100Base-TX standard was accepted by the market.

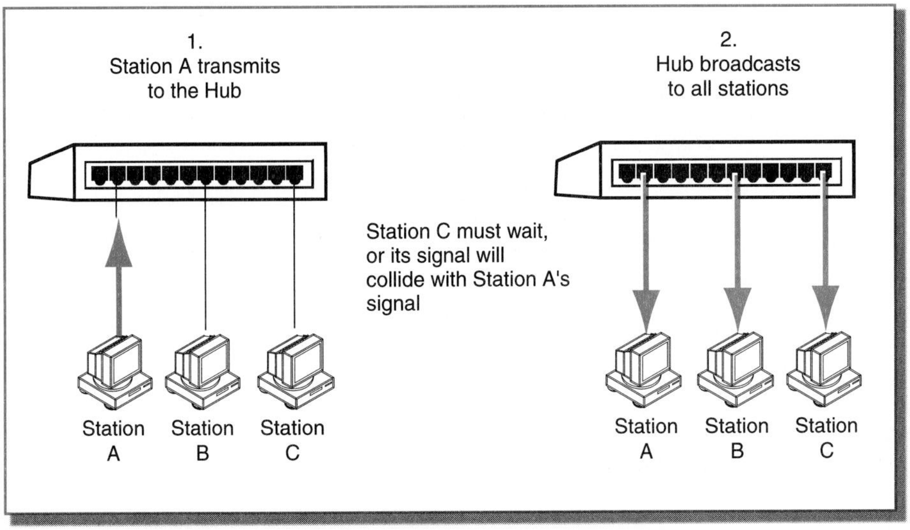

Figure 6.4
Ethernet Hub
Operation

1.
Station A transmits
to the Hub

2.
Hub broadcasts
to all stations

Station C must wait,
or its signal will
collide with Station A's
signal

Station   Station   Station
A   B   C

Station   Station   Station
A   B   C

Naturally, faster hubs and switches cost more than slower ones. In addition, the speeds of NICs must be matched to the speed of the hub or switch.

Hubs

Broadcasting   Figure 6.4 illustrates how hubs operate at any speed. When a station (in this case Station A) transmits a bit to the hub, the hub broadcasts the bit out all ports, to all stations attached to the hub (in this case, Stations A, B, and C).

Broadcasting is very simple. This makes hubs extremely inexpensive. Of course, each receiving station must decide whether each frame is intended for it or is intended for another station. Fortunately, this is not difficult. As we will see in the next chapter, an Ethernet frame has a destination address in its third header field. If the destination address does not match the NIC's own address, the NIC simply discards the frame.

Congestion and Latency   Hubs are fine for small networks. However, as Figure 6.4 illustrates, suppose that Station C wishes to transmit while Station A is sending. In this case, Station C must wait. Otherwise, its bits and those of Station A's transmission would be hopelessly scrambled.

From Chapter 1, this wait is called *latency*. If there are only a few stations on the LAN, waits will be infrequent and brief. However, as the number of stations grows beyond about 100, latency will be quite noticeable to users of 10Base-T hubs. Beyond about 200 stations, latency will be intolerable for 10Base-T hubs. Just as an eight-lane freeway can become stalled during rush hour, hub LANs become "LAN locked" if there are too many stations.

Fortunately, somewhat more expensive 100Base-TX hubs can alleviate this congestion problem. Each transmission takes only one tenth as long, so waits will be less frequent and briefer.

Figure 6.5
Ethernet Switch
Operation

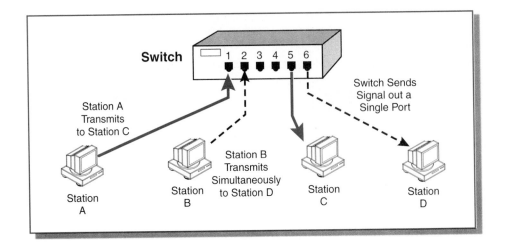

Shared Speed   Although most hubs (and NICs) today operate at 10 Mbps or 100 Mbps, all stations must share this speed because of waiting. If a station can get a sustained 1 Mbps on a 10Base-T hub, it is lucky. A 100Base-TX hub also delivers much less than its rated speed to each NIC.

Switch Operation

Output on a Single Port   As Figure 6.5 illustrates, switches are smarter than hubs. When a switch receives a frame, it does not broadcast the frame out all ports. It only transmits the frame out a single port—the one connected to the receiver. Here, Station A is transmitting to Station C. Station C is on Port 5, so the switch only sends the frame out Port 5.

Multiple Simultaneous Transmissions   What if Station B wishes to transmit to Station D while Station A is sending to Station C? As Figure 6.5 illustrates, this causes no problems because the A–C and B–D transmissions use different pairs of ports. There are no collisions.[3] As long as internal switch capacity is adequate, there is no congestion or latency in a LAN using a single Ethernet switch.

Non-Shared Speed   In addition, the stations do not share the transmission speed of a switch as they do with hubs. With a 10Base-T switch, stations can transmit and receive at a full 10 Mbps. With a 100Base-TX switch, stations can transmit and receive at a full 100 Mbps. In other words, 10Base-T and 100Base-TX switches are much faster than 10Base-T and 100Base-TX hubs.

---

[3] Of course, if two stations are trying to transmit simultaneously to a third station, problems can still occur, although many switches will usually store the frames and deliver them in order. In addition, if a station is receiving, it cannot transmit, although some NICs are "full duplex," allowing even this to happen.

Prices Unfortunately, switches are more expensive than hubs of the same speed. At 10 Mbps, the difference in price is very small, and 10Base-T switches will soon render 10Base-T hubs obsolete. However, for 100Base-TX, the price differential between hubs and switches is still substantial. At gigabit speeds, the price differential is extremely large.

Wiring

We must connect all of the PCs to the hub or switch. Small Ethernet networks use the *unshielded twisted pair (UTP).*

8-Wire UTP Bundles with RJ-45 Connectors Specifically, Ethernet specifies UTP wire bundles with four pairs of wires to connect NICs to the hub or switch. At each end of the wire bundle is an RJ-45 connector, which fits into an RJ-45 jack in the NIC or in a hub or switch. Chapter 4 discussed UTP and RJ-45.

Pre-Cut Wire versus Custom-Cut Wire UTP wiring is readily available in computer stores. You can even buy it in fixed lengths with the connectors already installed, so that you do not have to cut wire.

However, for neater operation, you will wish to get a long spool of wire, cut it to length, and add connectors yourself. The projects for Chapter 4 discuss how to do this.

Category 5 and Enhanced Category 5 Wiring All wiring in stores today follows the **Category 5** quality standard. This is sufficient for both 10 Mbps and 100 Mbps Ethernet. Some wiring is **enhanced Category 5,** which is better if you are thinking of installing gigabit Ethernet. For small LANs, however, gigabit Ethernet is far faster than you will need for quite a long time.

Plenum Wiring Some wire is **plenum** wire, which is specially designed to go through air conditioning ducts and other areas where air flows. In a fire, plenum wire will not give off dangerous toxic fumes. Plenum wire is more expensive to buy. In addition, because it is thicker than regular UTP, it is more difficult to install.

Test Your Understanding

Answer Core Review Questions 1–4 and Detailed Review Questions 1–3.

CLIENT PCS AND SERVERS

Client PCs

The PCs that sit on the desks of ordinary managers, professionals, and clerical workers are **client PCs.** As the name suggests, these client PCs are the *clients* or *customers* of the network, receiving various services from the servers. Even a small PC network will have a half dozen or more client PCs.

When you buy a client PC today, its operating system is already capable of working with servers over a network. No other software is needed to convert a stand-alone PC into a client PC. In terms of hardware, you must add a NIC, but some new PCs even come with NICs today. You also must configure the operating system's communication capabilities to work with file servers.

Servers

Servers provide services to the client PCs. In the peer–peer network shown in Figure 6.1, the PCs are both clients and servers. However, in PC networks with more than two to five PCs, it is important to have **dedicated servers** that are limited to providing service and cannot be used as client PCs. Only one dedicated server appears in Figure 6.2. However, it is common to have about one server for roughly every 10 to 50 client PCs.

Although some servers are high-power computers, such as workstation servers (see Chapter 1), *most servers on a PC network are themselves personal computers*. This is especially true on smaller PC networks. In fact, many PC servers are not even high-end PCs.

Server Operating Systems (SOSs)

You are probably most familiar with operating systems designed for stand-alone PCs and client PCs, such as Windows 3.X, Windows 9.X, Windows NT Workstation,[4] and Windows 2000 Professional (the client version of Windows 2000).

Servers, however, have special needs—most obviously, the ability to communicate with many client PCs simultaneously. Instead of running operating systems designed for client machines, servers run **server operating systems (SOSs)**,[5] which are tailored to server needs.

Novell NetWare   Until the 1990s, Novell **NetWare** dominated the server operating system market. Although NetWare has lost much of its market share, it still provides excellent file and print service. In addition, as Chapter 12 notes, NetWare has the most advanced directory service, which is important except in small organizations. This strong directory service is convincing many medium and large firms to continue using NetWare on many of their new servers.

---

[4] Confusingly, the Windows NT Workstation operating system is used primarily on PCs, rather than on client workstations, which were introduced in Chapter 1. Microsoft chose to use the name *workstation* for all client computers it supports with the client version of Windows NT.

[5] You will sometimes hear the term *network operation system (NOS)*. In the early days, you needed to add special networking software to *both* your servers and your client PCs. This software was called the NOS. Initially, all PCs and servers on a network had to use the client and server versions of the same NOS.

Now, however, we have networks with multiple servers running multiple server operating systems, and there is no need to install special software on the client PCs. The only networking software to be added is the software on the server, so the term *server operating system* has come to dominate in the literature.

Microsoft Windows SOSs Although the most familiar members of the Microsoft Windows operating system family are client operating systems versions, there are also server versions of Windows. Until Windows 2000, these were called **Windows NT Server.** Now, they are versions of **Windows 2000 Server.**

Windows SOSs are growing rapidly in market share. The user interfaces of server versions are very similar to those of client versions, minimizing the need for relearning. Windows SOSs are now dominant in smaller companies and for departmental servers. Microsoft hopes that Windows 2000 Server will make Windows competitive for large enterprise servers.

One problem with Windows has been a lack of reliability. Windows servers tend to crash more frequently than other servers. Microsoft hopes that Windows 2000 Server will reverse this reputation.

UNIX Most of the largest servers today use **UNIX.** UNIX has the high reliability needed for mission-critical applications. It also has the high functionality needed for complex server situations. In addition, most large servers are workstation servers (see Chapter 1), which almost always require UNIX.

On the negative side, UNIX is difficult to learn and use, requiring the hiring of a UNIX staff or extensive retraining for the current staff.

Another problem is that different UNIX vendors produce different versions of UNIX. Different versions have different management software, increasing UNIX's training problems.

LINUX One version of UNIX has gathered a great deal of attention recently. This is LINUX. LINUX is attractive for several reasons:

- LINUX can run on ordinary PCs with Intel or Intel-compatible microprocessors.
- LINUX is free, although it is common to pay about $50 for LINUX in order to get slicker packaging and (modest) technical support.
- LINUX has inherited UNIX's high reliability.

However, LINUX is difficult to learn and use, and the costs of retraining and extra labor time must be compared to the savings from not buying a commercial SOS.

Server Application Software Although server operating systems are expensive, the biggest software cost in PC networks often is the cost of the **application software** installed on servers. It is the application software—such as electronic mail and word processing—not the SOS itself, which provides services to the client PCs.

Fortunately, most SOSs come bundled with some application software. For instance, they always come bundled with file service, print service, and remote access service (RAS), which we discuss later in this chapter.

Test Your Understanding

Answer Core Review Question 5 and Detailed Review Question 4.

Although all layers are important, it is only at the application layer that we get the services that users really want. Everything at every other layer exists merely to support application services.

Servers and Services

In this section, we will use such terms as *file server* and *remote access server* as if they are always separate machines. However, one of the strengths of PC networking is that an organization can decide on the basis of performance, reliability, security, and economics whether to have one server or many.

Using a Single Server   For example, Figure 6.6 shows a single server running all of a small PC network's services. To the server operating system, services are merely application programs. All server operating systems are multitasking operating systems, so running multiple application service programs on a single server presents no inherent problems. Running all applications on a single server is the least expensive solution if you only have a handful of client PCs on your network.

One Application per Server   Figure 6.6 also shows the other extreme—using multiple servers, each running a single application on each server. This approach often is used in the largest networks because it has several advantages:

- **Optimization.** First, it allows the organization to *optimize* each server for that single application. For example, file servers need a great deal of very rapid disk storage. Client/server application servers, in turn, need very fast processors.
- **Reliability.** Second, server specialization enhances *reliability*. Communication service applications crash frequently, so it is good to separate them from other applications.

Figure 6.6
Single Server versus Multiple Servers

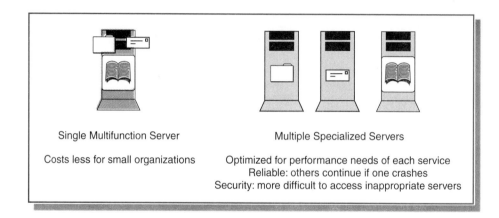

Single Multifunction Server

Costs less for small organizations

Multiple Specialized Servers

Optimized for performance needs of each service
Reliable: others continue if one crashes
Security: more difficult to access inappropriate servers

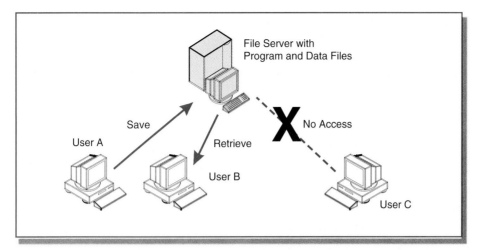

Figure 6.7
Sharing Data and
Application Files
on a File Server

File Server with
Program and Data Files

Save

User A

X No Access

Retrieve

User B

User C

- **Security.** Third, putting separate applications on separate servers also enhances *security*. For instance, most universities use different file servers for faculty and students to prevent students from getting access to testing and grading information.

Hybrid Approaches We have now looked at two extremes—putting all services on one server or having only a single service per server. Most firms take a hybrid approach, using multiple servers but having some of these servers run multiple applications.

Cost *Cost* is a difficult matter to assess. Certainly, a firm with only a handful of client PCs is unlikely to buy several servers. However, in larger PC networks, the benefits of optimizing usually tip the scales to multiple servers.

File Servers

The first type of server on PC networks was the file server. In **file service,** the server acts like a very large hard disk that is shared by many client PCs. Figure 6.7 shows this situation.

Sharing One of the big advantages of file service is file sharing. Figure 6.7 shows that members of a project team might share a directory for the team's work products. In addition, all employees on a PC network might get access to an application program. Of course, access to most files and directories will be available only to some users for security and privacy reasons.

File Server Program Access For network administrators, perhaps the biggest advantage of sharing is the ability to install new programs and software updates only once, on the file server. Previously, new programs and updates had to be installed on each individual PC separately. This was very time consuming and costly.

Programs shared this way, however, can be run only via file server program access. We saw in Chapter 1 that file server program access limits the size of programs because client PCs do not get very large. In addition, these programs usually must be able to fit on most corporate PCs, even older underpowered PCs.

Print Service

Fast laser printers and other good printers are rather expensive for individual client PCs. **Print service** allows a PC network's users to share a few very good printers.

Print Queues on the File Server   As Figure 6.8 illustrates, the print job actually goes first from the client PC to a file server, where it is placed in a **print queue** directory with other jobs waiting to be printed. A **print queue management program** manages the print queues on a file server.

Print Servers   In turn, printers are connected to boxes called **print servers.**[6] These simple boxes basically combine a NIC, a parallel port, some RAM, and just enough intelligence to receive data and commands from the print queue manager program on the file server. This simplicity makes print servers quite inexpensive, allowing us to scatter print servers and printers around the office. A typical print server costs only $100 to $300.

As Figure 6.8 also illustrates, the print server connects to a hub or switch port as well as to the printer. You must be sure to consider print servers when figuring how many ports you will need for a LAN.

Figure 6.8
Print Service

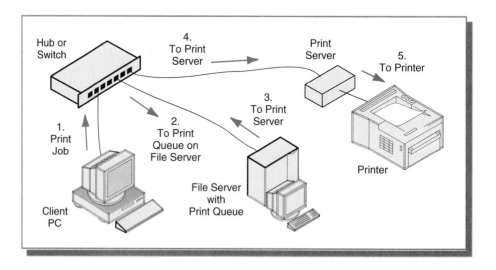

---

[6] It is also possible to attach a printer directly to a file server, eliminating the need for a print server box. However, people do not have to walk far to get their printout, so it is important to distribute printers around the office using print servers.

Balancing Costs While maintaining print queues on the file server instead of on print servers adds complexity to the printing process, it is attractive in terms of costs. The file server already has the hard disk capacity and processing power needed to manage print queues. Placing burdens on the file server allows print servers to be extremely inexpensive so they can be scattered around the office, together with the printers they serve.

No Need for Special Printers Printers do not have to be designed specially to be network printers. The print server feeds them print jobs exactly as a locally attached PC would. Printers do not even know that they are on a network.[7]

Client/Server Application Servers

In Chapter 1, we saw that the limits of file server program access can be overcome through client/server processing. In client/server processing, the heavy work of information retrieval and other tasks is done by the server application program on the server.

Recall from Chapter 1 that client/server processing is platform independent. Because we are talking about PC networking, the client machine will be a PC. However, the server can be a high-end PC, a workstation server, or some other high-end computer. This means that even when employees use client PCs, there can be high scalability in client/server applications.

Remote Access Server (RAS)

If you are at home or traveling, you sometimes need to access files on your organization's internal servers. As Figure 6.9 shows, many PC networks have **remote access servers (RASs),** which allow users to dial into the PC network via modems.

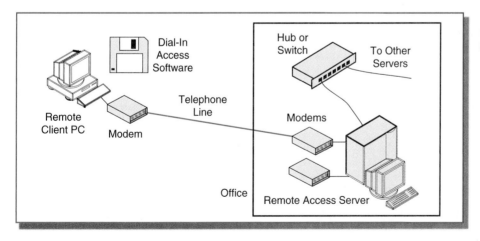

Figure 6.9
Dial-In Access Server

---

[7] Some newer printers, however, have built-in NICs and print server hardware, allowing them to communicate directly with the file server at megabit speeds.

Authentication When the remote user first connects to the remote access server, the server asks the user to type his or her login name and password. The server then compares the login name and password to an approved list. The password **authenticates** the user (confirms the user's identity). The user then is given access to the same resources he or she could use through a client PC connected directly to the hub or switch. Once the user is authenticated, the remote access server basically becomes invisible to the user.

Remote Access Client Software Figure 6.9 shows that the client PC dialing into the network needs **remote access client software** to work with remote access servers and to work with PC network resources after the user has been granted access.

   Although a remote user has access to exactly the same resources as local users, remote access users typically use low-speed telephone lines to reach the network. As a result, remote users do not enjoy the same response time that local users enjoy.

Internet Access via Serial Routers

In previous chapters, we were concerned exclusively with Internet access. In this chapter, we have seen some of the other applications that office workers use. However, we cannot ignore Internet access because it is very important to LAN users as well as to mobile and remote users.

Serial Routers Figure 6.10 shows that a small LAN can give its users access to the Internet through a **serial router.** A simple serial router has two ports: a LAN port with an Ethernet connector to link the router to the LAN, and an outside port that connects the serial router to the external transmission line leading to the ISP. These simple serial routers cost only $1,000 to $3,000.

   The external line can be an ordinary analog telephone line, one of the DSL or cable modem lines we saw in Chapter 5, or one of the leased lines we will see in

Figure 6.10
Internet Access via
Serial Router

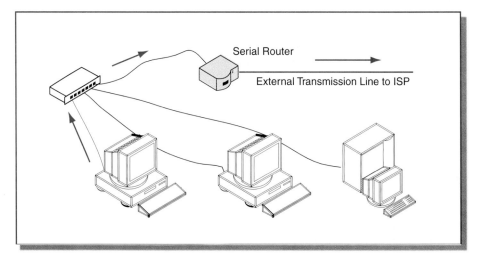

Serial Router

External Transmission Line to ISP

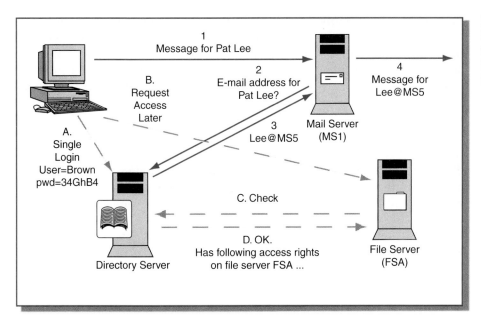

Figure 6.11
Directory Server
for Resource
Lookup and Single
Login

Chapter 9. All of these are point-to-point lines on which serial transmission is used. Hence the name "serial router." In Figure 5.1, we saw that a PC on a very small PC network can act as a router, eliminating the need for a serial router.

Beyond Access   Serial routers provide services beyond access. In the vignette in the previous chapter, we saw network address translation (NAT), which allows multiple PCs to use a single external IP address (or a few such addresses).

In addition, serial routers often provide simple security. In Chapter 10, we will see IP firewalls that restrict access to the internal network by people on the outside.

Directory Servers

In the small PC networks described in this chapter, there are only a handful of servers at most. However, in the larger site networks and enterprise networks discussed in Chapters 8 and 9, there may be dozens or even hundreds of servers. This multiplicity of servers requires a special server to resources spread across the network. This server is called a directory server. Figure 6.11 illustrates the roles of directory servers.

Resource Lookup   One problem with having many servers is that you may not know which server holds a resource you need. For instance, suppose you wish to send Pat Lee e-mail. Unfortunately, you do not know that Pat's mailbox is Lee@MS5.

A directory server has information about all users of all servers. If your mail server (MS1) is directory-enabled, you can just put "Lee" in the *To:* field of your message. As shown in the arrows with numbers in Figure 6.11, MS1 can query the directory server for Pat Lee's e-mail address. The directory server will tell the mail server that Pat Lee's address is Lee@MS5. The mail server will then send it to that address.

Resource look-up is not limited to e-mail addresses. Directories can store information about many resources other than people (e.g., printers, print queues, files). Other servers or user software can query the directory server, allowing users to work with friendly names rather than complex addresses.

Single Login Another benefit of directory servers is **single login,** in which a user only has to login once, when they first start using the network. As Figure 6.11 illustrates, when a user first logs in, they really are logging into the directory server.

Thereafter, when the user seeks access to another server, as shown in the dashed arrows with letters in Figure 6.11, the target server will query the directory server to see if the party sending the message is logged in properly, and has access rights to this particular server.

Users like single login because they do not have to remember separate login names and passwords on many different servers. Systems administrators also like single login because they can store all access rights information at a single point, greatly simplifying the management of access rights.

Test Your Understanding

Answer Core Review Questions 6–10 and Detailed Review Question 5.

Client PC Setup in Windows 98

Suppose you purchase a new PC and wish to install it as a client PC on an existing LAN. This box will discuss how to do this in Windows 98, which currently is the most popular version of Microsoft Windows.

Installing the NIC
In many ways, installing the NIC is the most daunting part of creating a network. Installing the NIC requires you to turn off your PC and open your systems unit, which many people find disturbing. However, once the systems unit is open, installation of the NIC usually is very simple. As Figure 6.12 shows, you will see a main board called a **mother board.** Normally, it will have open **expansion slots.**[8] You simply press the NIC very firmly into any expansion slot it will fit.[9] Usually, there is also a screw to tighten the NIC into the system unit chassis. Now, all you have to do is close up the systems unit. The hardware portion of the NIC installation is finished.

---

[8] There are different types of expansion slots. Your NIC's connector must be matched to one of these types of slots. The most common type of open slot today is the PCI slot.

[9] Before you install your NIC, however, write down its MAC address, which is silk-screened onto the NIC. As discussed in the next chapter, this consists of six pairs of letters or numbers separated by dashes. You may need this information later, and you don't want to open your machine to get it.

Continued.

Figure 6.12   Installing a Network Interface Card (NIC)

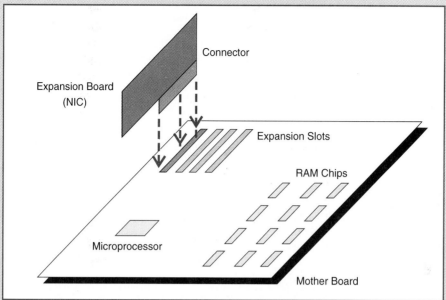

Now close your machine and turn it back on. If all goes well, Windows will recognize the NIC as a new piece of hardware. It will ask you a series of basic questions. Most importantly, you will see a button that says "Have Disk." If your NIC comes with a floppy disk, insert this floppy into the drive and click on the Have Disk button. This disk will install your NIC's device driver software.

If you go to Start, Settings, Control Panel, and then Network, you will see that your NIC has been installed as an adapter. Recall from Chapter 2 that adapters combine the physical and data link layers. NICs implement both of these layers, leaving only the internet, transport, and application layers to be handled in software.

Installing the Appropriate Protocol

Chapter 2 discussed how to add appropriate internet/transport protocol stacks and how to bind them to your adapter.[10] Choose the protocol stacks used by your servers. Usually, this means installing TCP/IP, IPX/SPX, or both.

Installing the Correct Client

To use a server, you must install a client matched to that server. Chapter 2 also discussed how to add the correct client. Again, the server will dictate your choice. Usually, you choose the Microsoft Client for Microsoft Networks or the Microsoft Client for NetWare Networks.

Bindings

As noted in Chapter 2, the client has to be bound to the protocol, and the protocol has to be bound to the adapter. The Properties button for the adapter, protocol, and client usually allow you to see what bindings exist, to set new bindings, and to delete unused bindings. Usually, this is as simple as checking a box by the name of the adapter, protocol, or client to be bound.

Test Your Understanding

Answer Detailed Review Question 6.

---

[10] In the vignette, Glenn wanted to network a Windows 95 to a Windows 98 machine. After much aggravation, he discovered that Windows 95 has a strong preference for IPX/SPX in peer–peer networking with Windows 98 machines.

SYSTEMS ADMINISTRATION: MANAGING A FILE SERVER

We have looked briefly at installing a small PC network. However, it only takes a few days to set up a PC network. The rest of your working life, you do the day-to-day work needed to keep it functioning. Most of this work comes in managing the servers. Historically, this is called **systems management.** (For some reason, it is always written in the plural.)

Access Rights

Perhaps the biggest headache in systems management is assigning **access rights,** which limit what resources users can see and what actions users can take for each resource. Obviously, not everybody should be given the right to view any file in any directory, much less modify or delete any file in any directory. Different SOSs have different access rights, but the following is a list of access rights found in most server operating systems:

- The ability to see a directory or file.
- The ability to get a read-only copy of a file in a directory (a copy that cannot be edited and then saved under the same name).
- The ability to edit and then save a file.
- The ability to create and delete files.
- The ability to create and delete subdirectories.
- The ability to assign access rights in a directory to other users.

Groups

Assigning rights to many users in hundreds or thousands of directories is a potential nightmare. Fortunately, SOSs reduce the workload by allowing the assignment of access rights to **groups.** For instance, suppose that a user is a member of the accounting department. The systems administrator can set up an *accounting group* and add the user to this group. The systems administrator can then assign rights to the accounting group in various directories. This is far less work than assigning rights to individual members of the group in all of these directories. Often, there is a group called something like *Everyone,* to which all users are assigned automatically.

Also, if a user changes departments, he or she can simply be shifted to another group. The user in the example will lose accounting access rights but will gain access rights appropriate for the new group.

Automatic Inheritance

Another way that SOSs reduce the work of assigning access rights is by allowing assigned rights to be **automatically inherited** by lower-level directories.

In Figure 6.13, there is an *applications* directory with *word processing* and *database* directories beneath it. Under the database directory, there are *Oracle* and *QuickDB* directories.

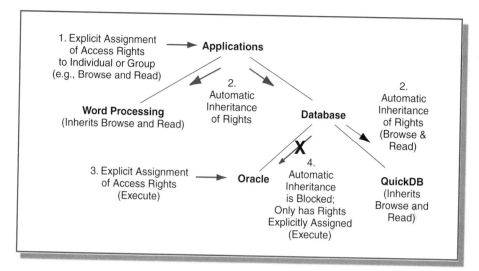

Figure 6.13
Inheritance of
Access Rights

Suppose that the systems administrator assigns a certain set of access rights, "Browse" and "Read," to a user or group in the *applications* directory. Browse allows a user to see files and subdirectories. Read allows a user to open files and view them, although not modify them.

As Figure 6.13 illustrates, the user or group members will automatically inherit the Browse and Read access rights in the word processing and database directories. Inheritance of Browse and Read rights will also flow automatically to lower-level directories, for instance QuickDB.

Blocking Inheritance through Explicit Assignment

What if a systems administrator assigns different access rights, say Execute only, to the user or group in the Oracle directory? As Figure 6.13 shows, this **explicit assignment** of access rights will block the automatic inheritance of Browse and Read rights. No rights will be inherited from the database directory. The only right in this directory will be the one that was specifically assigned by the administrator, Execute. Of course, if there are lower-level directories beneath Oracle, this newly assigned right, Execute, will be inherited by these directories.

To understand automatic inheritance and explicit assignment, think of a situation in which a person dies. The government might have automatic inheritance regulations to determine how to divide the estate. However, if the person leaves a will (which is analogous to explicit assignment), the will takes precedence and blocks all automatic inheritance rules.

Systems Administrators and Omnibus Access Rights

Users normally have very limited access rights. However, the systems administrator often has **omnibus access rights**—total access rights in every directory. This can be very helpful because it allows the systems administrator to fix problems wherever they occur. However, it also means that no file is hidden from the eyes of the systems administrator unless it is encrypted. In addition, systems administrators often can assign these omnibus rights to their assistants. Omnibus access rights are dangerous. However, eliminating them can create serious limitations on the systems administrator's ability to manage the server.

Test Your Understanding

Answer Core Review Questions 11–12 and Thought Question 4.

KEY POINTS

In this chapter, we have looked at a simple PC network consisting of a few client PCs and servers on a single local area network (LAN). Although we will see in Chapter 8 that many PC networks now have thousands of PCs and span multiple corporate sites, it is less confusing to start on a smaller scale. Even on a small scale, PC networking on a LAN is fairly complex.

Elements Figure 6.2 shows the elements of a small PC network on a single LAN. Client PCs receive services from servers. Usually, a stand-alone PC needs only a network interface card (NIC) to become a client PC. Servers require NICs as well. However, servers also require a server operating system (SOS) designed for server operation, plus server application programs.

To link the computers together, we need a hub or switch plus wiring. Switches have better performance than hubs but also cost more. In addition, both hubs and switches come at speeds of 10 Mbps, 100 Mbps, and one gigabit per second. Of course, faster hubs or switches cost more.

Application Layer Services At the application layer, we looked at a number of widely used services, including file service, file server program access, client/server processing, print service, remote access, and Internet access.

Setting Up a Client PC for Networking Chapter 2 discussed how to set up Microsoft Windows for using the Internet. The box "Client PC Setup in Windows 98" shows the similar work needed to set up a client PC to work on a PC network.

Systems (Server) Administration Once a network is installed, the biggest job is managing the servers, a task known as *systems administration*. The systems administrator constantly has to add or drop users, change user rights, back up files, and do other day-to-day chores.

REVIEW QUESTIONS

Core Review Questions

1. **a)** Distinguish between client PCs and servers. **b)** What does a Windows PC need to be a client PC? **c)** What do you have to add to a PC to make it a server? **d)** What are the elements of a LAN to connect the PCs of a PC network? **e)** Compare the major server operating systems.

2. What do NICs do?

3. Explain the difference between 10Base-T, 100Base-TX, and gigabit Ethernet hubs or switches, in terms of both **a)** speed and **b)** cost.

4. **a)** Distinguish between hub and switch operation. **b)** Which can have problems with latency? Why? **c)** Which is more expensive? **d)** Do 10Base-T hubs and switches give equal speed to individual users? Explain.

5. What are the four factors to take into account in deciding how many servers to use to implement a PC network's services?

6. **a)** Does file service allow file sharing by several people? **b)** Can anyone access shared files? **c)** Why does file sharing for programs make software installation easier? **d)** Why is storing program files on a file server limiting?

7. **a)** To what two devices does a print server connect? **b)** Where does a print job go when it leaves the client PC (not counting the hub or switch)? **c)** Do you have to use special printers for print service?

8. **a)** In remote access service, what does the PC network need? **b)** What does the remote PC need?

9. What does a small PC network need to connect to the Internet?

10. What two things do directory servers make easier for users?

11. **a)** What is systems administration? **b)** List the main systems administration tasks mentioned in the book.

12. **a)** What are access rights? **b)** How does the use of groups simplify the assignment of access rights? **c)** How does automatic inheritance simplify the assignment of access rights? **d)** How does explicit assignment modify automatic inheritance?

Detailed Review Questions

1. **a)** Why is peer–peer PC networking attractive? **b)** What are its problems? **c)** What are dedicated servers?

2. What layers of the TCP/IP–OSI hybrid framework do NICs implement?

3. **a)** Explain "Category 5." **b)** Explain "enhanced Category 5." **c)** Explain plenum wiring.

4. Of the major server operating systems, **a)** which is easiest to learn and use? **b)** Which has reliability problems? **c)** Which is cheapest to buy? **d)** Why

may it not be cheapest over time? **e)** Which has the best directory service? **f)** Which are highly reliable? **g)** Which run on workstation servers?

5. Based on Figure 6.11, explain the steps involved **a)** in sending e-mail in a directory-enabled mail system, and **b)** in accessing servers without logging in to each.

6. Referring to the box, "Client PC Setup in Windows 98," what are the steps you go through in setting up a stand-alone PC to be a client PC?

Thought Questions

1. Your organization has 12 employees, each with his or her own stand-alone PC running Windows 98. **a)** List *all* the additional hardware and software you would have to buy to install a simple PC network. Be very sure that you list all the things the organization will have to buy. The organization wishes to use electronic mail, word processing, file sharing, and print sharing with four existing printers. **b)** How many ports on the hub or switch will your organization use? Explain.

2. Using the links at the Internet Exercises for this chapter, cost out the LAN you just specified. For installation labor, assume $125 per client PC or server. You do not have to cost out the application software. Be very specific. Cost out your system **a)** with a 10Base-T hub, **b)** with a 10Base-T switch, **c)** with a 100Base-TX hub, and **d)** with a 100Base-TX switch (if possible). (Note: 10/100 switches or hubs are 100 Mbps switches or hubs. They are more expensive than 10 Mbps switches or hubs.)

3. In the opening vignette, Glenn Davis installed a small peer–peer PC network in his home. **a)** What benefits was he seeking? **b)** Did he get them? **c)** What problems did he run into installing the PC network? **d)** What problems did he run into using the PC network? **e)** Why don't we see more peer–peer PC networks in business?

4. Directory X has Subdirectories Y and Z. The systems administrator assigns user Lee to the group Outer. The administrator assigns Outer the access rights R, S, and T in Directory X. (Don't worry about the meaning of R, S, and T. They are simply types of rights.) The administrator assigns Outer the access rights S, U, and V in Subdirectory Y. **a)** What access rights does user Lee have in Directory X? Explain? **b)** What access rights does user Lee have in Directory Y? Explain. **c)** What access rights does user Lee have in Directory Z? Explain.

5. What access rights would you give the group Everyone in the Shared directory? This directory has subdirectories created for different project teams.

6. What access rights would you give the group Everyone in the Systems directory? This directory contains programs used by the systems administrator.

7. What access rights would you give the group Everybody in the Policies directory, which contains corporate policies? All users should be able to read these policies.

Case Studies

For case studies, go to the book's website, **http://www.prenhall.com/panko,** and look at the "Case Studies" page for this chapter.

Projects

1. **Getting Current.** Go to the book's website's "New Information" and "Errors" pages for this chapter to get new information since this book went to press and to correct any errors in the text.

2. **Internet Exercises.** Go to the book's website's "Exercises" page for this chapter and do the Internet exercises.

3. The chapter's "Internet Exercises" page has you cost out the elements of an Ethernet 802.3 10Base-T LAN, including NICs, hubs, and wiring. Cost out the LAN needed in Thought Question 1.

4. Using the same sources as in the last question, compare the prices of Microsoft Windows NT Server and Novell NetWare for 12 users. Also compare how much you would have to pay if you had 70 users.

5. Prepare a Windows 95 computer or a Windows 98 computer to work with a Windows NT or Novell NetWare file server.

6. Install a NIC in a computer.

Chapter 7

Small Ethernet LANs

*C*hen May-Ling has kept a close watch on the company's LAN since correcting the wiring problems (discussed in the vignette for Chapter 4). She runs her protocol analyzer several times a day to check on the LAN's health. The protocol analyzer examines the frames traveling through the LANs. It collects a few thousand of these frames then stops to analyze them and give May-Ling a statistical picture of what is happening on the LAN.

The protocol analyzer looks at all fields in each frame. It also looks at fields in the internet layer packet being carried by LAN frames and even at fields in the encapsulated transport and application layer frames. This allows May-Ling to know, for instance, what portion of the network traffic is due to file servers and what portion is due to HTTP World Wide Web traffic. (Although Internet use is growing, traffic between client PCs and file servers still dominates LAN traffic.)

May-Ling has been worried about two recent trends. First, she is seeing an increasing number of truncated frames that only include the first few fields instead of all fields. NICs do not have any problem dealing with such frames. NICs merely throw them away. However, truncated frames can be symptomatic of problems.

Second, she notices that one of the NICs on the LAN appears to be "jabbering." This means that it is transmitting a great deal—much more than normal usage could explain. This suggests a malfunctioning NIC. She knows that the NIC address is "01-23-AA-B7-C3-FF." However, she does not know which computer in the network has this NIC. ∎

Learning Objectives

After studying this chapter, you should be able to describe:

- Layering in 802 LAN standards, including the MAC and LLC layers.
- Ethernet LAN technology at the physical and data link layers.
- Distinctions among the terms *topology, media access control method, bus, ring, CSMA/CD,* and *token passing.*
- How client PCs can work with multiple servers using different internet and transport layer protocols.

INTRODUCTION

The main focus of this chapter is Ethernet LAN technology. LANs are extremely important in organizations, handling perhaps 80% of all corporate data traffic. Ethernet, in turn, is the most important LAN technology. Perhaps 80% of all LAN traffic takes place on Ethernet networks.

We will look at Ethernet subnet (single network) standards, beginning with the physical layer. We saw the most important aspects of physical layer operation in the previous chapter. In this chapter, we will focus on more theoretical and more subtle aspects of Ethernet physical layer technology, for instance Ethernet's use of a bus topology. We will then look at Ethernet's data link layer, which, as we will see in the chapter, is subdivided into a media access control (MAC) layer and a logical link control (LLC) layer. In the MAC discussion, we will focus on a media access control process called CSMA/CD.

A box looks at other LAN technologies, including wireless LANs and token-ring networks. Token-ring networks are important in and of themselves. However, we will also use the discussion to underline the distinction between physical layer topology and MAC layer media access control methods.

Ethernet standards end at the data link layer. However, in PC networking, PCs still need to communicate at the internet, transport, and application layers. A box looks at how client PCs can communicate simultaneously with two servers using different internet and transport standards.

ETHERNET AND 802.3

A Brief History of Ethernet and 802.3 Standards

Born at Xerox Ethernet was born in the 1970s at the Xerox Palo Alto Research Center. Later, Xerox worked with Digital Equipment Corporation and Intel in the early 1980s to define the Ethernet I (Version 1.0) and Ethernet II (Version 2.0) standards.[1]

---

[1] Ethernet II data link layer framing is still used in some PC networks, as Module C discusses.

The IEEE 802 LAN MAN Standards Committee   Later, Ethernet standardization was turned over to the **Institute for Electrical and Electronics Engineers (IEEE).** The IEEE formed the **802 LAN MAN Standards Committee**[2] to create LAN standards.

Working Groups, Including the 802.3 Working Group   The 802 Committee created several **working groups** to develop specific standards. The **802.3 Working Group,** for example, creates Ethernet standards. For this reason, we will often call these standards *Ethernet 802.3* standards. In turn, the 802.1 and 802.2 working groups create standards used across all types of 802 LANs, not just Ethernet LANs.

OSI Standards   The IEEE 802 Committee creates LAN standards according to the OSI architecture. After creation, these standards are submitted to ISO and ITU-T for confirmation.[3] Fortunately, ISO and ITU-T have routinely accepted 802 LAN standards and have done so without modification. Vendors usually begin developing products as soon as 802 working groups have finished their work.

802 Layering

Recall that OSI divides subnet (single network) standards into two layers: a physical layer that governs the transmission of individual bits and a data link layer that governs the transmission of messages, called frames, within the subnet.

Subdividing the Data Link Layer   However, as Figure 7.1 illustrates, the 802 LAN MAN Standards Committee subdivided the data link layer into two layers: media access control and logical link control.

Media Access Control (MAC)   In the last chapter, we saw that if two stations transmit at the same time, their signals will collide and will become unreadable. Consequently, it is necessary to control when stations transmit. This is called media access control. It is controlling when a station may access the medium (to transmit). As its name suggests, the **media access control (MAC)** layer implements this function. The MAC layer standard also governs the MAC layer frame. Recall that data link layer messages are called *frames.* The messages at both the MAC and LLC layers are therefore called frames.

Logical Link Control (LLC) Layer   Media access control is only one of the functions that might be needed at the data link layer. Other data link layer functions are implemented at the logical link control (LLC) layer. One

---

[2] A MAN is a metropolitan area network, which spans a single urban area.

[3] Actually, the 802 Committee submits standards to the IEEE Computer Society. Standards next go to the American National Standards Institute and then to ISO.

Figure 7.1
802 LAN
Standards
Layering

Internet Layer		TCP/IP Internet Layer Standards (IP, ARP, etc.)	Other Internet Layer Standards (IPX, etc.)		
Data Link Layer	Logical Link Control Layer	802.2			
	Media Access Control Layer	Ethernet 802.3 MAC Layer Standard			Other MAC Standards (802.5, 802.11, etc.)
Physical Layer		10Base-T	100Base-TX	1000Base-T	Other Physical Layer Standards (802.5, 802.11, etc.)

of these functions is error correction, although this capability is rarely used. Another function of the LLC layer is to designate which next-higher-layer program should receive the contents of the LLC frame's data field. As Figure 7.1 illustrates, IP is not the only possible internet layer protocol that networks can use.

NICs   NICs implement *all* subnet layers: the physical, media access control (MAC), and logical link control (LLC) layers.

Test Your Understanding

Answer Core Review Question 1.

ETHERNET 802.3 PHYSICAL LAYER STANDARDS

Now that we have looked at Ethernet 802.3 standards broadly, we can begin looking at them in more detail, beginning at the physical layer.

The previous chapter described the most important aspects of Ethernet 802.3 physical layer processes. These are the physical layer processes that govern the operation of hubs and switches. This chapter covers the concept of physical layer topology and compares the most popular UTP-based Ethernet 802.3 physical layer standards.

Topology

An important physical layer concept is topology. **Topology** *is the order in which stations receive transmitted bits.* Note that topology is a physical layer concept. Every LAN technology has a characteristic topology governing the order in which stations receive bits.

Figure 7.2 illustrates two common topologies. These are the bus topology used with Ethernet hubs and the switched topology used with Ethernet switches.

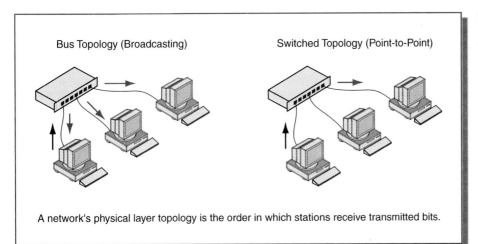

Figure 7.2
Bus and Switched
Topologies

Bus Topology (Broadcasting) Switched Topology (Point-to-Point)

A network's physical layer topology is the order in which stations receive transmitted bits.

Bus Topology for Hubs As Figure 7.2 illustrates, whenever a station transmits to a hub, the hub broadcasts the bit out all ports, to all attached stations. Broadcasting delivers each bit to all stations simultaneously (or nearly so). This is the same way that computer buses transmit microprocessor signals to all attached circuits (almost) simultaneously. Therefore, when all stations receive each transmitted bit simultaneously, this is called a **bus topology.**[4]

Ethernet 802.3 mandates a bus topology at the physical layer when hubs are used. For this reason, Ethernet networks usually are called bus networks. As Module C discusses, broadcasting also was used in Ethernet II and in early versions of Ethernet that did not use hubs. Therefore, these earlier versions of Ethernet 802.3 also had bus topologies.

Switched Topology for Switches Switches changed everything in Ethernet. As Figure 7.2 reminds us, switches do not broadcast bits to all attached stations. Instead, they only send bits out a single port—the port to which the destination host is attached. This is a **switched topology.**

Are Switches Really Ethernet? Since its beginning, Ethernet was called a bus topology because switches came late in the evolution of Ethernet. Many people have even listed bus operation as a defining element of Ethernet. One 802.3 Working Group member even called switching "the Switching Heresy." However, within five or ten years, all new Ethernet 802.3 networks will use switches. So if we define switches as not being Ethernet, we will be defining Ethernet out of existence. Redefining bus operation as embracing switching, in turn, would be worse because of its total violation of the bus topology concept.

---

[4] Some authors describe hubs as having physical star topologies with logical bus topologies. If this is useful, that is good. However, strictly speaking, the topology concept only refers to the logical order in which transmitted bits arrive at the LAN's stations.

Specific UTP Ethernet 802.3 Physical Layer Standards

Since the early 1980s, several physical layer standards for Ethernet have been defined. We will only focus on unshielded twisted pair (UTP) variants that are used in almost all small Ethernet 802.3 LANs, which are the focus of this chapter. (Chapter 5, which deals with more complex site networks, also discusses optical fiber versions of Ethernet.) The similarities and differences between these UTP standards are summarized in Figure 7.3.

Speed   The initial number in an Ethernet 802.3 physical layer standard's name designates its speed. So:

- Ethernet 802.3 **10Base-T** operates at 10 Mbps, while
- Ethernet 802.3 **100Base-TX** operates at 100 Mbps, and
- Ethernet 802.3 **1000Base-T** operates at 1 Gbps.

The 802.3 Working Group is even working on a new physical layer standard that will run at 10 Gbps.

The "Base" in the standards name stands for baseband transmission (discussed in Chapter 4), while T stands for "twisted pair."

Speed Autosensing   A 10Base-T hub or switch can only work with 10Base-T NICs. However, 100Base-TX NICs, hubs, and switches are **autosensing.** They can tell the speed of their communication partner and adjust automatically. Specifically, 100Base-TX NICs, hubs, and switches can drop down to 10Base-T signaling. Gigabit Ethernet (1000Base-T) devices, in turn, can slow to 100Base-TX signaling due to autosensing.

Wiring   We saw in the previous chapter that 100Base-TX requires Category 5 quality wiring, while gigabit Ethernet, although rated for Category 5 wiring

Figure 7.3
Ethernet 802.3
10Base-T,
100Base-TX, and
1000Base-T
Physical Layer
Standards

	10Base-T	100Base-TX	1000Base-T
Speed (Mbps)	10	100	1,000
Autosensing for speed?	No	Yes	Yes
Wire pairs used	2	2	4
Maximum LAN distance span with a single hub or switch (meters)	200	200	200
EIA/TIA-568 Wiring Categories Supported	3, 4, 5	5	5, although enhanced Category 5 is recommended
Congestion with 200 users in a hub network?	Yes	No	No

Note: Shaded areas indicate differences from the basic pattern.

probably should use enhanced Category 5 wiring. As Figure 7.3 shows, Ethernet 802.3 10Base-T also can use less stringent Category 3 or Category 4 wiring.

Both 10Base-T and 100Base-TX[5] only use two pairs in the standard four-pair telephone-wiring bundle. Their NICs transmit on one pair (connected to Pins 1 and 2) and receive on another pair (connected on Pins 3 and 6). Their hubs, in turn, must receive on Pins 1 on 2 and transmit on Pins 3 and 6. The other two pairs, which are connected to Pins 4, 5, 7, and 8, are not used.

In contrast, 1000Base-T uses all eight wires when it transmits or receives.[6] This reduces the number of bits per second sent per wire pair. This reduces the transmission's tendency to cause interference.

Electrical Signaling As Figure 7.4 illustrates, Ethernet 10Base-T uses **Manchester encoding,** in which there is always a transition in the middle of each bit period. The transition in the middle of the time period effectively resynchronizes the sender's clock to the receiver's clock.

A one is encoded as a low voltage in the first half of the bit time period and a high voltage in the second half. Zeros have a high voltage followed by a low voltage. The way to remember this is that ones end high, while zeros end low. The line can change 20 million times per second, so the baud rate is 20 Mbaud.

More specifically, in transmission, Pin 1 is called TD+ and Pin 2 is called TD−. A low voltage is when TD+ is between 2.2 and 2.8 volts *below* the voltage of TD−. A high voltage is when TD+ is between 2.2 and 2.8 volts *above* TD−.

Ethernet 100Base-TX and 1000Base-T use more complex electrical signaling. Business networkers rarely have to get involved with electrical signaling.

Test Your Understanding

Answer Core Review Questions 2–4.

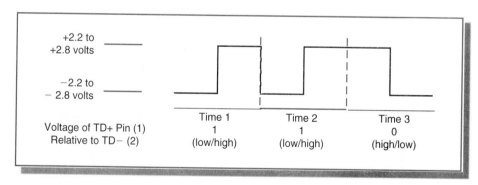

Figure 7.4
Ethernet 10Base-T
Electrical Signaling
(Manchester
Encoding)

---

[5] The 802.3 Working Group also defined the 100Base-T4 standard, which uses all four pairs. However, the marketplace never accepted this standard. It also created a 100Base-T2 standard that used a wire bundle consisting of two pairs. Both were enthusiastically ignored in the marketplace.

[6] When communicating with switches, it can both send and receive simultaneously on all eight wires. It simply subtracts what it is sending from what it is hearing to get the incoming signal.

Having looked at physical layer standards, we will now move up a layer, to Ethernet 802.3 data link layers standards. As we saw in Figure 7.1, the 802.3 LAN MAN Standards Committee divided the data link layer into a media access control (MAC) layer and a logical link control (LLC) layer.

Media Access Control: CSMA/CD

As noted earlier in this chapter, the main job of the **media access control (MAC)** layer is to ensure that only one station at a time can "access the media" to transmit. Note in Figure 7.1 that there are multiple 802.3 Ethernet physical layer standards (e.g., 10Base-T, 100Base-TX); but there is only a single 802.3 Ethernet MAC layer standard.

CSMA/CD

As just noted, the MAC layer has to control when stations may transmit. Ethernet 802.3 uses a media access control method called **Carrier Sense Multiple Access with Collision Detection (CSMA/CD).** Although this name sounds complex, the actual process is quite simple.

Carrier Sense Multiple Access (CSMA) When the transmission of several stations must be controlled, this is called **multiple access.** "Carrier sensing," in turn, means listening to (sensing) the signal (carrier) coming in from the network.

In **carrier sense multiple access (CSMA),**[7] NICs follow two simple rules, as Figure 7.5 illustrates.

- If a NIC does not hear another station sending, it may transmit.
- However, if a NIC does hear another station transmitting, it must wait until no station is transmitting before transmitting.

Figure 7.5
Carrier Sense
Multiple Access
(CSMA) in
Ethernet 802.3
Media Access
Control

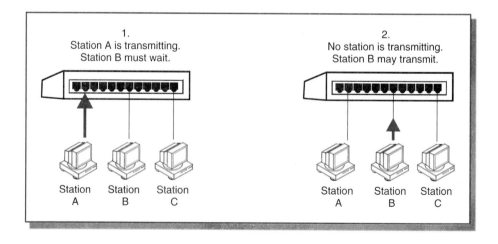

----

[7] Not Carrier Sense *Media* Access.

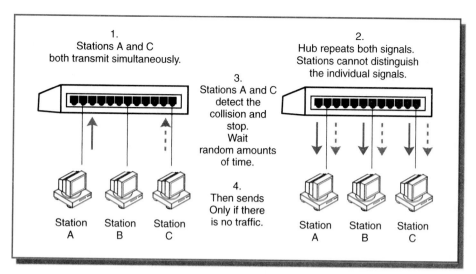

In other words, CSMA simply implements the rule of polite conversation: do not talk if someone else is speaking.

Collision Detection Sometimes, two stations will accidentally begin to transmit at the same time. If they do, their signals become mixed and unreadable. This is called a **collision.** As illustrated in Figure 7.6, *collision detection (CD)* determines what stations will do if they perceive a collision.

- First, all stations involved in the collision must stop and wait a random length of time. The random wait will be different for each station.
- Second, when the wait is over, each station implements CSMA, transmitting if the line is free or waiting if the line is not free.

What if there is another collision? Again, each NIC involved stops and waits a random length of time. This time, however, the random wait is increased. This process of increasing the duration of the random wait continues if there are more collisions. After 16 collisions and random waits, however, the NIC gives up trying to deliver the frame.

CSMA/CD in Perspective[8] CSMA/CD is a very simple media access control method. This makes it very inexpensive to implement. This low cost has allowed Ethernet consistently to beat technologies that were technologically

---

[8] Note that stations do not merely transmit immediately after their random wait. They must first check to see if other stations are transmitting. If other stations are transmitting, the NIC must wait until nobody else is sending.

Note also that CSMA/CD is not merely collision detection. When asked to define CSMA/CD, you must first describe CSMA and then describe CD.

Finally, note that waiting a random amount of time is part of CD, not CSMA. There are only random waits if there is a collision.

superior but more expensive. Ethernet survived and dominated LAN technology by providing good performance at a very good price.

CSMA/CD and Switches Switch operation does not require CSMA/CD. However, switches work with NICs that implement CSMA/CD. There is no broadcasting, so the only time a NIC attached to a switch will hear other traffic is when another NIC is sending a message directly *to that NIC*. This will rarely occur, so the NIC can transmit at almost any time, without waiting.

There is even a standard, **802.3x,** which allows a NIC to transmit even when it is receiving incoming messages. This is useful when a client PC and server are sending many messages back and forth. This is full-duplex operation because both pairs of communicating stations can transmit at the same time. In contrast, CSMA/CD normally allows only one station at a time to transmit, making Ethernet fundamentally half-duplex. Full-duplex operation essentially turns off collision detection, so NICs feel free to transmit at any time. Full-duplex NIC operation can only be used with switches.

The Ethernet 802.3 MAC Layer Frame Format

Figure 7.7 gives the Ethernet 802.3 MAC layer frame format. Messages at the data link layer, including both the MAC and LLC layers, are called frames.

Preamble and Start of Frame Delimiter The first two fields in the Ethernet 802.3 MAC frame are the **Preamble** and **Start of Frame Delimiter (SFD)** fields. The Preamble is 7 octets of the pattern 10101010. The start of frame delimiter is a single octet with the pattern 10101011. Overall, the preamble and start of frame delimiter have a strong repeating pattern that is broken in the last bit to indicate the beginning of the rest of the message.

The preamble and start of frame delimiter allow the sending NIC to give a strong repeating pattern to the receiving NIC, so that the receiving NIC can perfectly synchronize its internal clock to the clock of the sending NIC. This allows the receiving NIC to know exactly where each bit starts and ends.

Destination Address Next comes a 48-bit **destination address** field. Each NIC has a unique 48-bit address when it leaves the factory.[9] This is its **Media Access Control (MAC) address.**

Recall from Chapter 2 that 32-bit IP addresses at the internet layer usually are written in dotted decimal notation, in which the address is broken into four 1-octet segments, each of which is converted to a decimal number.

In contrast, 48-bit Ethernet destination addresses are divided into twelve 4-bit **nibbles.** With 4 bits, there are 16 (2^4) possible combinations for each nibble. So each nibble is given a value from 0 through F, as shown in Table 7.1. This is called **hexadecimal** (Base 16) notation.

---

[9] Each vendor is assigned the first 24 bits and must assign the remaining 24 bits uniquely.

Figure 7.7
Ethernet 802.3
MAC Layer Frame
Formats

Basic 802.3 MAC Frame

Preamble (7 octets)
10101010 . . .
Begins synchronization

Start of frame delimiter (1 octet)
10101011
Ends synchronization
Begins content of frame

Destination address (6 octets)
48 bits expressed in hexadecimal
Example: A1-34-CD-7B-DF hex

Source address (6 octets)
Unique value set at factory

Length (2 octets)
Length of data field in octets
1,500 (decimal) maximum

Data field (variable)
LLC frame

PAD (if needed to bring data field
up to 46 octet minimum)

Frame check sequence (4 octets)

Tagged 802.3 MAC Frame

Preamble (7 octets)
10101010 . . .
Begins synchronization

Start of frame delimiter (1 octet)
10101011
Ends synchronization
Begins content of frame

Destination address (6 octets)
48 bits expressed in hexadecimal
Example: A1-34-CD-7B-DF hex

Source address (6 octets)
Unique value set at factory

Tag protocol ID (2 octets)
1000000100000000
81-00 hex
33,024 decimal
Larger than 1,500, so not a length

Tag control information (2 octets)
Priority level (0 to 7) (3 bits)
VLAN ID (12 bits)

Length (2 octets)
Length of data field in octets
1,500 (decimal) maximum

Data field (variable)
LLC frame

PAD (if needed to bring data field
up to 46 octet minimum)

Frame check sequence (4 octets)

Usually, the hex values are combined with dashes between adjacent pairs. For instance, the network interface card in the author's home computer has the following address:

00-40-D0-0A-09-33 hex

To convert a binary string to hex, divide it into 4-bit nibbles and give each nibble's hex value in that place. So 11110000 is F0, where 1111 is F and 0000 is zero. To convert a hex string to a binary string, give the 4-bit binary representation of the hex digit in the hex digit's place. So 1F is 00011111, where 1 is 0001 and F is 1111.

Source Address   When we send letters, we normally put a return address on our envelopes. The **source address field** serves this function in Ethernet frames. It gives the sending NIC's 48-bit MAC address.

Table 7.1   Hexadecimal Notation

Binary Nibble (Base 2)*	Decimal (Base 10)	Hexadecimal (Base 16)
0000	0	0 hex
0001	1	1 hex
0010	2	2 hex
0011	3	3 hex
0100	4	4 hex
0101	5	5 hex
0110	6	6 hex
0111	7	7 hex
1000	8	8 hex
1001	9	9 hex
1010	10	A hex
1011	11	B hex
1100	12	C hex
1101	13	D hex
1110	14	E hex
1111	15	F hex

* $2^4 = 16$ combinations. For example, A1-34-CD-7B-DF hex begins with 10100001.

Length Field   The length field gives the length of the *data field* (not of the entire frame) in octets. This is a 2-octet field, so there could be values up to 65,536. However, Ethernet data fields are limited to 1,500 octets.[10]

Data Field   The **data** field contains the message of the next higher layer. This is the LLC layer frame, which we will see later.

PAD Field   Ethernet 802.3 frames have a minimum data field size of 46 octets. If there are not enough octets in the LLC layer frame, a **PAD** field consisting of zeros[11] is added after the data field to bring the data field plus the PAD up to 46 octets in length. The receiver ignores the contents of the PAD field.

Frame Check Sequence   The **frame check sequence** field contains a 4-octet check number created by the sender on the basis of the bit patterns in other fields (excluding the Preamble, Start of Frame Delimiter, and Frame Check Sequence Fields).

The receiver recomputes the frame check sequence field value. If the recomputed value matches the value stored in the arriving frame, the NIC knows that there have been no bit errors during transmission. The NIC processes the

---

[10] There is currently a movement to allow larger "Jumbo Frames," at least in gigabit Ethernet. These frames would have as many as 9,000 octets of data (six times as much data as the current standard allows).

[11] RFC 894.

frame. However, if an error is detected, the NIC discards the frame. This is error detection but not error correction.

Tag Fields Ethernet is a best-effort service. It tries to deliver frames but offers no guarantees of timely delivery. If congestion increases, there will be substantial delay (latency) in frame delivery. The 801 Working Group is now extending all LAN standards to include priority information so that high-priority frames will be able to get through first. Figure 7.7 illustrates the tag fields created for priority and other purposes. The **802.1Q** standard governs the overall structure. The **802.1p** standard specifically governs priority levels.[12]

Tag Protocol Identifier (TPID) Field The first field is the Tag Protocol Identifier (TPID) field. This 2-octet field essentially tells the receiver that the frame is tagged. Its value is set to 81-00 hex. How can a hub or switch tell that a frame is tagged?

- The hub or switch looks at the 2 octets following the source address field. If the value in these 2 octets is 1,500 or less, then this must be a length field.
- In contrast, if the hub or switch sees 81-00 hex (33,024 decimal) in the 2 octets following the source address field, it will know that this is a Tag Protocol Identifier field and that this frame is tagged.

Tag Control Information (TCI) Field The next field is the **Tag Control Information (TCI)** field. This field has three parts:

- **User Priority.** These three bits contain the priority field. Three bits give eight (2^3) possible priority levels. The 802.1p standard defines how these priority levels should be assigned by senders and interpreted by receivers. For larger values on this 0-to-7 priority scale, the hub or switch should give the frame higher priority. The 802.1 Working Group is now working on more precise meanings for these eight priority levels.
- **Canonical Form Indicator (CFI).** In Ethernet 802.3, this one-bit field is zero unless the frame encapsulates an 802.5 Token-Ring Network frame with a routing information field. This is almost never the case.
- **VLAN Identifier (VID).** In Chapter 8, we will discuss virtual LANs (VLANs). The VID field defines up to 4,096 (2^{12}) possible VLANs, although the value 0 is reserved to indicate that the frame is not tagged for VLAN purposes.

Processing an Ethernet 802.3 Frame

The NIC handles both the physical layer and the MAC layer. So far, we have been looking at what happens on the *sending* NIC. This section describes what the MAC layer process on the *receiving* NIC does when it gets an Ethernet 802.3 MAC layer frame from the NIC's physical layer process.

---

[12] A capital letter, such as Q, indicates a major change in the standard. A lower-case letter, such as p, indicates a minor revision.

Preamble and Start of Frame Delimiters   The NIC reads the Preamble and Start of Frame Delimiter, synchronizing its clock with the clock of the sender.

Destination Address   The NIC reads the MAC destination address and compares the destination address with its own MAC address. If the two do not match, the NIC stops processing the frame and discards it. Otherwise, the NIC continues to process the frame.

Source Address, Length Field, Data Field, and PAD   The NIC reads the next three fields (four if a PAD is present). It stores the Source Address, Length Field, and Data Field values in memory for later use.

Frame Check Sequence   As noted earlier, the NIC recomputes the Frame Check Sequence value and compares this with the value transmitted in the Frame Check Sequence field. The NIC then discards the frame or continues.

Passing the Frame to the Next Higher Layer   Finally, the NIC passes the data field up to the next-higher-layer process. As Figure 7.1 shows, this is the logical link control layer process on the NIC.

Logical Link Control (LLC) Layer

The **logical link control (LLC)** layer has two jobs.

Interface to the Next-Higher Layer   The first is to provide a uniform interface to the next-higher layer, interacting with the appropriate internet layer process (which is not always IP). As Figure 7.1 shows, there is only a single LLC standard, **802.2,** no matter what MAC standard is in use. To the next-higher layer, all 802 LANs look exactly the same, because a process cannot look below the process in the layer directly beneath it. Internet layer standards only have to deal with the 802.2 LLC standard.

Optional Error Correction   In addition, the 802.2 LLC standard offers the option of error correction. However, this option is almost never used in practice. The common practice, as noted in the Chapter 3, is to make all layers unreliable except for the layer directly beneath the application layer.

LLC Framing   Network administrators do not deal with LLC layer matters. However, LLC framing is discussed in Module C.

Other Physical and Data Link Layer LAN Standards

Although Ethernet is the most popular family of OSI LAN standards, some other OSI LAN families are also used in organizations. The box "Other LAN Standards" looks briefly at two of these standards: 802.11 wireless network standards and token-ring network standards in general.

Test Your Understanding

Answer Core Review Questions 5–7, Detailed Review Question 1, and Thought Question 3.

Other LAN Standards

Ethernet is not the only LAN standard. However, the market shares of other LAN standards are extremely low. We will look at two other LAN standards. We will begin with 802.11 wireless LAN standards, which are rarely used today, but show promise for future growth. We will then look at token-ring standards that have seen some use but that have been hampered by high cost due to the inherent complexity of token-ring operation. The next chapter discusses ATM.

802.11 Wireless LAN Standards

An **802.11** wireless LAN allows us to take notebook computers, personal digital assistants, and other mobile computers with us when we work anywhere in a building.

Access Points

As Figure 7.8 illustrates, mobile devices communicate via radio or infrared light with **access point** units located on walls or ceilings. These access points connect mobile devices with one another and usually with the company's main wired LAN as well.

Figure 7.8　　802.11 Wireless LAN

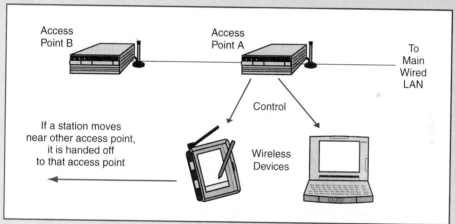

Slow Initial Acceptance

Acceptance of 802.11 standards has been slow. The initial 802.11 standards operated at only 1 or 2 megabits per second, and wireless NICs have been very expensive. In addition, unless many wireless stations are implemented at once, the cost per station is extremely high. In comparison, benefits are fairly intangible.

Increased Speed

Fortunately, higher speeds are coming. An 11 Mbps version has already been standardized, and products are beginning to appear. Even higher speeds will come in the future. This should make 802.11 LANs much more attractive.

Continued.

Bluetooth

A non-802 short-range wireless standard, **Bluetooth,** is also under development. However, while 802.11 is good for large corporate wireless LANs, Bluetooth is best for home LANs and to connect cellular telephones and other pieces of consumer equipment together. The initial version of Bluetooth was very limited in speed, in distance, and in the number of devices that could be connected. Future versions should relax these restrictions somewhat, but Bluetooth is likely to remain a low-cost, limited-ability wireless technology.

Token-Ring Networks

Several Ethernet competitors are **token-ring networks,** which are very different from Ethernet CSMA/CD-bus networks. In this box, we will focus on the key differences between token-ring technology and CSMA/CD-bus technology. Module C discusses specific token-ring networks in somewhat more detail.

Physical Layer Ring Topology

We saw earlier that a network technology's **topology** describes the order in which stations receive transmitted bits. Ethernet uses a **bus topology,** which is characterized by *broadcasting.* One station transmits, and this transmission is broadcast to all other stations. All stations receive the bit at (almost) the same time.

In contrast, Figure 7.9 shows that token-ring network stations connect to boxes called **access units,** which are connected in a **ring** (loop). Signals travel around the ring in one direction, so there is only a single possible path between any two access units on the ring. Token-ring networks use a physical layer **ring topology.**

Figure 7.9   Bus versus Ring Topology at the Physical Layer

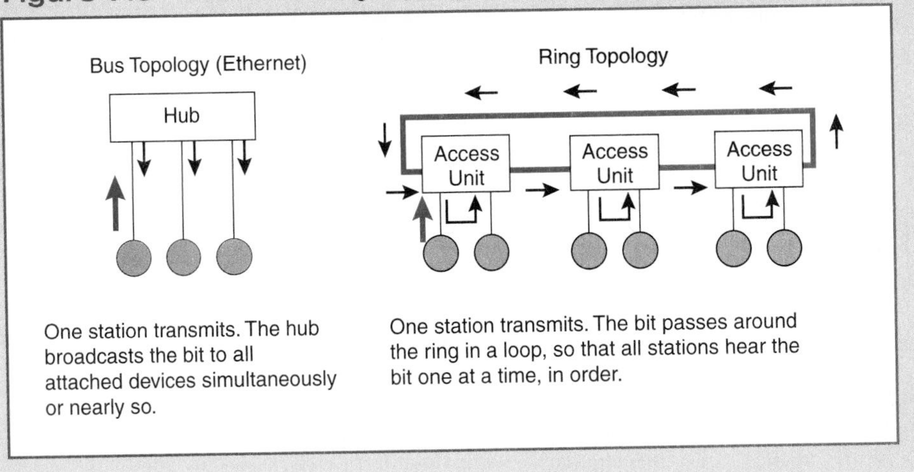

One station transmits. The hub broadcasts the bit to all attached devices simultaneously or nearly so.

One station transmits. The bit passes around the ring in a loop, so that all stations hear the bit one at a time, in order.

Token Passing at the Media Access Control Layer

Figure 7.10 shows that whereas Ethernet uses CSMA/CD at the MAC layer for media access control, token-ring networks use **token passing** at the MAC layer to determine when each station may transmit.

A special frame called a **token** circulates when no station is transmitting. A station may transmit only when it has captured the token. Otherwise, it must wait. This ensures that only one station may transmit at a time.

Continued.

Figure 7.10   CSMA/CD versus Token Passing at the Media Access Control Layer

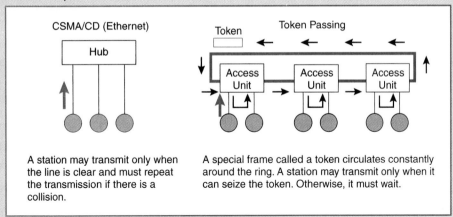

CSMA/CD (Ethernet)

Hub

A station may transmit only when the line is clear and must repeat the transmission if there is a collision.

Token Passing

Token

Access Unit   Access Unit   Access Unit

A special frame called a token circulates constantly around the ring. A station may transmit only when it can seize the token. Otherwise, it must wait.

802.2 at the Logical Link Control Layer

Like all other LANs, token-ring networks are designed to use 802.2 as the logical link control layer standard.

Perspectives on Token-Ring Networks

In many ways, token-ring network technology is superior to 802.3 Ethernet technology. However, most firms find Ethernet sufficient for their needs. Token passing, although offering some advantages over CSMA/CD, is also more complex, and this has led to high-priced products. On LANs, neither the 802.5 Token-Ring Networks nor the FDDI token-ring networks discussed in Module C have enjoyed large market shares.

CSMA/CD–Bus versus Token-Ring Networks

To recap what we have seen:

- At the *physical layer,* Ethernet uses a bus topology while token-ring networks use a ring topology.
- At the *media access control* layer, Ethernet uses CSMA/CD for access control, while token-ring networks use token passing.
- At the *logical link control layer,* all LANs use 802.2.

Test Your Understanding

Answer Core Review Questions 8 and 9 and Detailed Review Question 2.

Figure 7.11
Layering in
Popular Standards
Architectures

	TCP/IP	OSI	IPX/SPX		NetBEUI
Application	Various	Application	Other	NCP	Various
		Presentation			
		Session			
Transport	TCP, UDP	Various	SPX		NetBEUI
Internet	IP, etc.	Various	IPX		None
LLC	802.2	802.2	802.2		802.2
MAC	802.3	802.3	802.3		802.3
Physical	100Base-TX	100Base-TX	100Base-TX		100Base-TX

Note: Assumes an Ethernet 802.3 100Base-TX network.

INTERNET AND TRANSPORT LAYER STANDARDS

Client PCs have to communicate with servers at all layers. LANs merely implement the subnet layers: the physical, media access control, and logical link control layers. Client PCs and servers also have to communicate at the internet and transport layers, as well as at the application layer.

Most servers today use TCP/IP standards at their internet and transport layers. These include UNIX and LINUX servers, Microsoft NT/2000 servers, and newer Novell NetWare servers. In such cases, PCs can use the same TCP/IP internet and transport layer software that they use to connect to the Internet.

Figure 7.12
Simultaneous
Connection to
TCP/IP and
IPX/SPX Servers

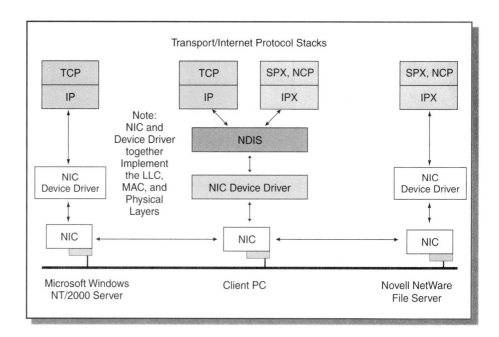

Multiple SOS Internet and Transport Standards

However, not all server operating systems use TCP/IP standards at the internet and transport layers. For example, Novell NetWare servers traditionally used IPX/SPX standards at these layers. Apple Macintosh servers, in turn, traditionally used AppleTalk standards at these layers. Small networks might even have their servers use the NetBEUI standard at the transport layer. NetBEUI is very fast, but very limited. For instance, NetBEUI has no internet layer and cannot be used easily where internetting is present. Figure 7.11 shows how some popular standards architectures are similar and different in terms of layering.

Note that *all* architectures use 802 standards at the physical, MAC, and LLC layers. This is why all of them can send frames through the same LAN simultaneously. All 802.2 LLC frames look the same, regardless of their content.

Simultaneous Communication with Servers Using Different Internet and Transport Standards

What happens if a client PC needs to communicate simultaneously with two servers that use different internet and transport standards? As Figure 7.12 illustrates, this causes no problems. Client PCs have no problem communicating simultaneously with multiple servers using different internet and transport layer standards. The box "Multiprotocol Server Connections" provides more detail on this process.

Test Your Understanding

Answer Core Review Question 10 and Detailed Review Question 3.

Multiprotocol Server Connections

Multiple Protocol Stacks
Protocol stacks are two or more layers from a single standards architecture. Client PCs can run multiple internet/transport protocol stacks simultaneously. In Figure 7.12, the client PC would use its TCP/IP protocol stack to communicate with the Microsoft Windows 2000 server while using its IPX/SPX protocol stack to communicate simultaneously with the Novell NetWare server.

Network Driver Interface Specification (NDIS)
However, there is a problem with running multiple protocol stacks. NICs only expect to work with a *single* protocol stack, and protocol stacks expect to work with a NIC to which they have exclusive access. To multiplex transmissions for several protocol stacks to and from a single NIC, Windows adds a layer of software called the **Network Driver Interface Specification (NDIS).**[13] This software layer is installed automatically. NDIS acts like a traffic cop to ensure fair access to the NIC and to route each incoming packet to the correct protocol stack.

---
[13] Novell NetWare has a similar standard, ODI.

Continued.

The NIC implements the physical, MAC, and LLC layers. So NDIS is a layer added *between* the logical link control layer and the internet layer. Such added layers are called "bumps in the stack."

NIC Device Driver
Figure 7.12 shows one more layer of software on the client PC. This is the NIC device driver. Most pieces of hardware that can be installed on a personal computer, including NICs, come with a related piece of software called a **device driver.** Higher-level software actually talks to the device driver instead of directly to the hardware, as Figure 7.12 indicates. Software can be changed more readily than hardware, so device drivers can be updated if errors are found in the device driver or to add new functionality. For network interface cards, the device driver sits between the NDIS software and the NIC hardware, as Figure 7.12 illustrates.

Earlier in this chapter, we noted that NICs handle the LLC, MAC, and physical layers. Speaking more correctly, we can say that the NIC and device driver *together* handle the LLC, MAC, and physical layers.

Test Your Understanding
Answer Detailed Review Question 4.

KEY POINTS

In this chapter, we focused on small Ethernet 802.3 LANs. Although we will see in the next two chapters that many PC networks now have thousands of PCs and span multiple corporate sites, it is less confusing to start on a smaller scale. Even on a small scale, PC networking on a LAN is fairly complex.

Ethernet LAN Technology   We looked in some depth at LAN technology, at the OSI physical and data link layers. The IEEE 802 LAN MAN Standards Committee sets most LAN standards. The 802.3 Working Group sets Ethernet standards today.

At the *physical layer*, we discussed the concept of network topology and looked at Ethernet standards that use UTP wiring with hubs and switches, including 802.3 10Base-T, 100Base-TX, gigabit Ethernet, and the developing standard for 10 Gbps Ethernet.

At the *media access control layer*, Ethernet uses Carrier Sense Multiple Access with Collision Detection (CSMA/CD) to ensure that two stations will rarely transmit at the same time and will respond appropriately if they do transmit simultaneously. We then looked at MAC layer framing. We briefly discussed the logical link control (LLC) layer's two roles of adding functionality (including optional error correction, which is rarely used) and providing a uniform interface to the next higher layer, the internet layer.

Other LAN Technologies   The box "Other LAN Standards" looked briefly at 802.11 wireless networks and token-ring networks. At the *physical layer*, token-ring networks use a ring topology, rather than the bus (broadcasting) topology of Ethernet hub networks. At the *MAC layer*, token-ring networks use token passing for media access control, rather than the CSMA/CD access control method used on Ethernet networks. All LANs use 802.2 at the LLC layer.

The Internet and Transport Layers Above the logical link control layer, we have the internet and transport layers. Different server operating systems use different standards at these layers. Fortunately, a client PC can use multiple sets of internet and transport layer protocols simultaneously to communicate with different types of servers.

REVIEW QUESTIONS

Core Review Questions

1. **a)** List, from bottom to top, the standards layers you encounter in a small PC network. Do not say "data link layer." List one layer per line. **b)** Which layers are subnet layers? **c)** Which layers are implemented by the NIC?

2. **a)** What is a topology? **b)** What topology does a hub use? **c)** What is the characteristic of this topology? **d)** What topology does a switch use? **e)** What is the characteristic of this topology?

3. Compare 10Base-T, 100Base-TX, and 1000Base-T in terms of **a)** speed, **b)** the ability to do autosensing, **c)** how many pairs are used to send and receive, **d)** UTP wiring categories supported, and **e)** maximum distance span with a single hub or switch. **f)** What does "Cat 5" mean? **g)** "Enhanced Cat 5"?

4. **a)** How does Ethernet 802.3 10Base-T represent a one? **b)** Why does it do this instead of representing a one as a simple high or low voltage?

5. **a)** What is media access control? **b)** At what layer is it implemented? **c)** Explain CSMA/CD in detail.

6. **a)** Make a table naming each of the fields in the basic Ethernet 802.3 MAC layer frame and giving each field's length (in octets) and purpose. **b)** What does the receiving NIC do if it detects an error? **c)** What are the two tag fields? **d)** What does the first of these fields define? **e)** What does the second of these fields define?

7. **a)** What is the single logical link control layer standard for all IEEE 802 LANs? **b)** Can it provide error correction? **c)** Is this ability widely used? **d)** What is its function other than error control?

8. Referring to the box, "Other LAN Standards," **a)** What 802 Working Group creates wireless LAN standards? **b)** Why has use of these standards been limited to date? **c)** What is the speed of the most recent 802 wireless standard? **d)** Compare 802.11 wireless standards with Bluetooth.

9. Referring to the box, "Other LAN Standards," **a)** Compare Ethernet and token-ring networks in terms of physical layer topology. **b)** Compare them in terms of MAC layer media access control. **c)** Compare them in terms of LLC layer standards.

10. Can a client PC communicate with both an IPX/SPX server and a TCP/IP server at the same time?

Detailed Review Questions

1. **a)** Does every NIC have a unique 802.3 MAC layer address when it comes from the factory? **b)** What is the minimum size of 802.3 MAC layer data fields (including the PAD)? **c)** What is the maximum size of MAC data fields? **d)** What is in the data field of a typical MAC layer frame?

2. **a)** At what layers will IPX/SPX and TCP/IP web servers use the same standards if they are on the same LAN? **b)** At what layers will they use different standards?

3. **a)** What does NDIS do? **b)** What are the processes above and below NDIS? **c)** What is a NIC device driver? **d)** Why are device drivers used? **e)** What are the standards layer above the NIC device driver? **f)** What process or processes (hardware or software) implement(s) all of the LAN subnet layers?

Thought Questions

1. Create a flow chart for CSMA/CD.

2. Referring to Table 7.1, **a)** Convert the following binary number to hexadecimal: 0001, 1001, 11100111, and 1. **b)** Convert the following hexadecimal values to binary: 00-00-00 hex, 03 hex, and AA hex. **c)** (A tough one that will not be penalized if you cannot answer it.) What types of games use Base 13? How do they handle the values 11, 12, and 13?

3. Referring to the opening vignette, **a)** What does a protocol analyzer do? **b)** What problem could the incomplete frames be indicating? **c)** Why is a jabbering NIC bad? **d)** How could May-Ling avoid problems like her inability to find the computer with the jabbering NIC?

Case Studies

For case studies, go to the book's website, **http://www.prenhall.com/panko,** and look at the "Case Studies" page for this chapter.

Projects

1. **Getting Current.** Go to the book's website's "New Information" and "Errors" pages for this chapter to get new information since this book went to press and to correct any errors in the text.

2. **Internet Exercises.** Go to the book's website's "Exercises" page for this chapter and do the Internet exercises.

3. Search the Internet for protocol analyzers you can use on your own PC. Download a demo version of one of them. Install it on a LAN machine. Collect a data sample. Write a report summarizing your main findings.

Chapter 8

Larger Site Networks

*C*laire Cunningham is the IS director for a large clothing manufacturing facility. The company selected Ethernet early. As demand grew, the plant's site network went from 10Base-T hubs plus routers to Ethernet switching. They still have a single router, but its main job is to connect the plant to the Internet and to the firm's other sites.

The center of the site network today is Claire's new gigabit Ethernet switch. As Figure 8.1 illustrates, this core campus switch is about the size of a narrow refrigerator. Unlike most smaller switches, which simply are boxes resembling the hubs we saw in the last chapter, the gigabit Ethernet switch is a **chassis switch.** There is a central "backplane" that connects the switch's multiple subnet interfaces.

Switch Subnet interfaces come clustered in modules that plug into the face of the chassis. There are many possible modules for Claire to install, including modules with a dozen 10Base-T ports, modules with eight 10/100 Mbps ports, and modules with five gigabit Ethernet

Figure 8.1 Large Switch

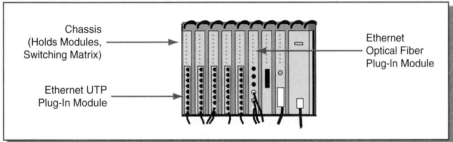

Chassis
(Holds Modules,
Switching Matrix)

Ethernet UTP
Plug-In Module

Ethernet
Optical Fiber
Plug-In Module

ports. There is even an ATM module, which Claire will not use because the company has no ATM switches at the site. The switch can take several modules, so Claire has great flexibility in selecting (and changing) the switch's interfaces.

Much of the site's traffic flows through this central gigabit Ethernet switch. This gives Claire a central point from which to monitor and control the network. Unfortunately, the switch is also a potential single point of failure. If the gigabit Ethernet switch fails, Claire will be visited by several vice presidents, who will explain in detail how much their operations lost during the outage. ■

Learning Objectives

After studying this chapter, you should be able to describe:

- Large Ethernet switched site networks in some detail
- Basic considerations in selecting ATM switched networks
- Congestion, latency, and remedies
- The site roles of Routers, Layer 3 switches, and Layer 4 switches

INTRODUCTION

Chapters 6 and 7 introduced small Ethernet (802.3) networks. In these networks, which use only a single hub or switch, UTP limits stations to being within 100 meters of the hub or switch. Consequently, the farthest stations can only be 200 meters apart, as Figure 8.2 indicates. This is fine for small buildings, but it is not enough for large buildings, university campuses, and industrial parks.

In this chapter, we will look at larger **site networks** for individual corporate, government, or educational sites. We will look at the following technologies:

- Ethernet networks with multiple hubs, which suffer from distance limitations.
- Ethernet switched networks, which do not suffer from the distance limitations of Ethernet hub networks and which are fast and fairly inexpensive.
- ATM switched networks, which offer excellent quality of service (QoS) guarantees but which are very complex and expensive.
- Routers, which bring the sophistication of routing to individual sites, albeit at high cost.
- Layer 3 switches, which bring many of the benefits of switching to IP forwarding, and Layer 4 switches, which do switching based on application.

Modern site networks are "switch rich." Ethernet switches dominate site network technology, and the use of Layer 3 switches is spreading rapidly.

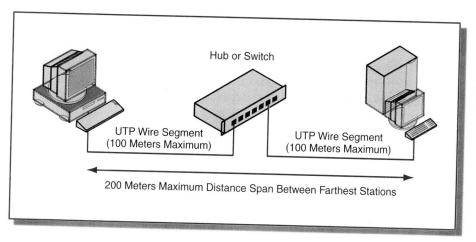

Figure 8.2
200-Meter (m) Maximum Distance Span with One Hub or Switch and UTP

Hub or Switch

UTP Wire Segment (100 Meters Maximum)

UTP Wire Segment (100 Meters Maximum)

200 Meters Maximum Distance Span Between Farthest Stations

Hubs, in contrast, have severe distance limitations. ATM switches and routers are extremely expensive to buy and manage and are used primarily in certain types of situations, most notably when voice is being transmitted. Our discussion in this chapter will mirror real-world use patterns.

LARGER ETHERNET HUB NETWORKS

In the last two chapters, we looked at Ethernet LANs having only a single hub or switch. We have just noted that this creates a maximum distance span of only 200 meters for UTP connections to the desktop.

Multiple Hubs with 10Base-T Can we lengthen the maximum distance span by placing multiple hubs between the most distant stations? The answer is "sort of." As Figure 8.3 shows, 10Base-T allows multihub networks.[1] Theoretically, the farthest stations can be separated by as much as 500 meters if UTP wiring is used exclusively. If we put in some optical fiber, even longer theoretical distance spans are possible.[2]

However, *at 10 Mbps, the number of stations within the distance spanned by the multihub network is much more important than the maximum theoretical distance span.* To avoid unacceptable congestion, 10Base-T hub networks should be limited to about 100 stations. Even with a 200-meter span, we may have more computers than 10Base-T can serve. Therefore, even if we use multiple hubs, we cannot use very many of them. Still, the ability to have a LAN with two or

---

[1] There cannot be a loop among the hubs, or bits would circulate endlessly around the loop. In a later section on Ethernet switched networks, we also will see a "no loops" rule, but we will see two ways to get around this rule sometimes. The same approaches could also be applied to multihub 10Base-T networks.

[2] The farthest stations can only be five UTP and/or optical fiber segments (four hubs) apart. Violating this rule can greatly degrade the network's capacity. Although the network would not stop functioning completely, violating the maximum distance span rule is a very bad idea because it can lead to severe performance degradation.

Figure 8.3
Multiple Hubs in
10Base-T

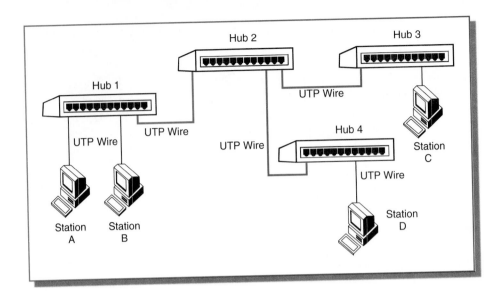

three 10Base-T hubs sometimes is useful as a way to extend a 10Base-T LAN's distance span slightly.[3]

Multiple Hubs in 100Base-TX and Gigabit Ethernet At higher speeds, using multiple Ethernet hubs to increase distance is not possible at all. The 100Base-TX standard allows two hubs in most circumstances, but these hubs must be located in the same place, so there is no increase in distance span. Gigabit Ethernet cannot use multiple hubs to increase its distance span, either. For both 100Base-TX and gigabit Ethernet hubs, connecting stations using UTP limits distances to 200 meters, as Figure 8.2 shows.

Test Your Understanding

Answer Core Review Question 1 and Detailed Review Question 1.

ETHERNET SWITCHED NETWORKS

Ethernet switching is now the most common tool for site networking and is growing rapidly in prominence.

No Maximum Distance Span with Ethernet Switches

We have just seen that with *hub*-based Ethernet, there are strong limitations on the maximum distance span of a network. These limitations, by the way, result

---

[3] Some 10Base-T hubs have an RJ-45 port marked with an X. This is an uplink port. If you wish to connect two 10Base-T hubs, run an ordinary UTP wire bundle between the uplink port on one hub and a normal port (not another uplink port) on the other hub.

from the need for the farthest two stations to be able to detect collisions from one another.[4]

No Limit on Maximum Distance Spans With switched Ethernet, however, there are no collisions, so there is no need to worry about collision detection by the farthest two stations. Therefore, there is no maximum distance span for switched Ethernet networks. Even the largest sites can be served with Ethernet switches.

Limits on Distances Between Pairs of Switches Although there is no maximum distance span for the *entire network* with Ethernet switches, there still are distance limitations *between pairs of switches*. As Table 8.1 indicates, when UTP is used, this limit is only 100 meters. Optical fiber allows longer distances between pairs of switches, as Table 8.1 also shows. However, there are still limitations on the maximum distance between *pairs of switches*, even when fiber is used.

No Limit on the Number of Switches Between Stations What is *not* limited in switched networks, then, is the *number of switches between the farthest two stations*, as Figure 8.4 indicates. Two stations can be 5, 10, or even 100 switches apart. Therefore, there is no limitation on overall network size.

Ethernet Switch Hierarchies and Single Possible Paths

As Figure 8.5 illustrates, Ethernet switches must be arranged in a **hierarchy,** with no loops among the switches. Otherwise, frames would circulate endlessly around the loop. In a hierarchy, there is only a single possible path among stations. To see this, trace several end-to-end paths through Figure 8.5.

Mixing Switches of Different Capacities in Hierarchies As Figure 8.5 indicates, a site might have a central gigabit Ethernet **campus switch,** each building might have a 100Base-TX **building switch,** and offices might have 10Base-T **workgroup switches** that give each employee 10 Mbps to his or her desktop. Of course, switches in the hierarchy must be carefully sized according to the particular organization's current and anticipated traffic patterns. The gigabit—100Base-TX—10Base-T hierarchy in this example is only one possibility. Sometimes, in fact, the bottom of the hierarchy is not a switch but rather a hub, to take advantage of the lower costs of hubs.

---

[4] Suppose the two most distant stations transmit simultaneously to destination stations in the middle of the LAN. Their signals will collide in the middle of the LAN, so receivers in the middle will not be able to read the frames. If the network is not too large, the two end stations will also hear the collision before they finish transmitting. As discussed in Chapter 7, both end stations will stop, wait, and then retransmit the frames when the line is clear. However, if the end stations are too far apart, they will both finish sending before the signal from the other end station reaches them. They will not realize that a collision has occurred, so they will not resend the frames.

Table 8.1 Switch–Switch Distance Limits in Ethernet 802.3 Networks

Standard	Speed	Maximum Segment Length	Medium
UTP			
10Base-T	10 Mbps	100 m	4-pair Category 3, 4, or 5
100Base-TX	100 Mbps	100 m	4-pair Category 5
1000Base-T	1,000 Mbps	100 m	4-pair Category 5; 4-pair enhanced Category 5 is preferred
Optical Fiber			
10Base-F[a]	10 Mbps	1–2 km[a]	62.5/125 micron multimode, 850 nm[b]
100Base-FX	100 Mbps	412 m	62.5/125 micron multimode, 1,300 nm, half-duplex operation
100Base-FX	100 Mbps	2 km[a]	62.5/125 micron multimode, 1,300 nm, full-duplex operation
1000Base-SX	1,000 Mbps	220–275 m[c]	62.5/125 micron multimode, 850 nm
1000Base-LX	1,000 Mbps	550 m	62.5/125 micron multimode, 1,300 nm
1000Base-LX	1,000 Mbps	5 km	9/125 micron single mode, 1,300 nm
Other Media			
10Base5	10 Mbps	500 m	Thick coaxial cable (see Module C)
10Base2	10 Mbps	185 m	Thin coaxial cable (see Module C)

Notes:

[a]Several 10 Mbps fiber standards were defined.

[b]Core is 62.5 microns. Cladding is 125 microns. Multimode fiber is thick and, therefore, less difficult to install than very thin and fragile single mode fiber. However, signals in multimode fiber and cannot travel as far. See Module B for more on fiber technology.

[c]Distance depends on quality of the optical fiber. Most U.S. fiber falls at the lower end of the quality range, but new fiber usually implements newer and higher quality standards.

Vulnerability and Remedies Restricting switches to being organized in a hierarchy with only one possible path between any pair of end stations makes Ethernet switched networks vulnerable to **single points of failure.** If a switch fails, or if a link between two switches fails, then the network will be broken into two or more separate networks whose stations cannot communicate with one another.

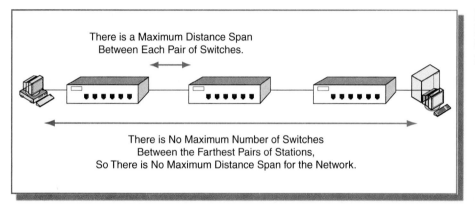

Figure 8.4
Distance Spans in
Switched Ethernet
Networks

802.1D Spanning Tree Standard   The 802 Committee has developed two ways to reduce this vulnerability. First, the **802.1D Spanning Tree** standard automatically disables accidental loops by closing the ports that connect them. This permits a crude form of backup by allowing the firm to install additional links between some switches. The switches make these extra links active when an active link fails. The switches then automatically reconfigure themselves into a loop-free hierarchy. However, adjustment is slow when failures occur, and it is very difficult to know which extra links to install to provide protection for failures.

Link Aggregation Protocol Standard   Another tool to reduce vulnerability is the **Link Aggregation Protocol (LAP)** standard. This standard allows you to connect a single pair of switches with multiple UTP or fiber links. For instance, two switches might be connected using three 100Base-TX links, giving an

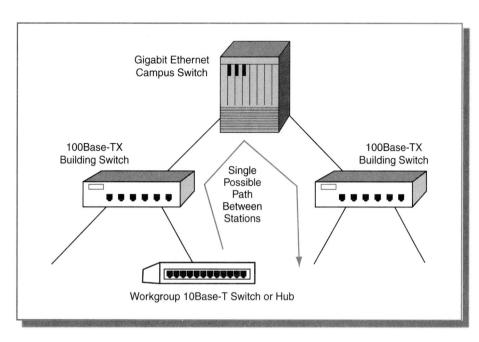

Figure 8.5
Ethernet Switch
Hierarchy

aggregate capacity of 300 Mbps. If one link fails, operation will continue at reduced (200 Mbps) capacity. However, if a switch fails, or if a conduit through which multiple links run is severed, there will still be complete disruption.

Ethernet Switching: High Speeds and Low Prices

As just noted, Ethernet has a hierarchical organization of switches. This results in there being only a *single possible path* between any two stations. Having only a single possible path between any two stations radically simplifies switch forwarding decisions. As Figure 8.6 indicates, Ethernet **switch forwarding tables** are very simple. For each MAC address, there is one and only one port number. The switch merely reads the MAC destination address in the frame to be switched, looks up the corresponding port number, and forwards the frame out that port.

Speed and Low Prices This switch forwarding table is far simpler than the router forwarding table shown in Chapter 3. With a router forwarding table, the destination IP address has to be compared with *every* entry in the router forwarding table, and, if there are differences in match length or metrics, these factors must be taken into account. In contrast, the switch has to find only the *one* match in the table to the destination MAC address, and this lookup can be done very quickly. This simplicity allows Ethernet switches to be much *faster* than routers. This simplicity also makes switches much *less expensive* than routers. "Faster and less expensive" is a good recipe for success.

The box "More on Ethernet Switching" provides more detail on Ethernet switches and their operation.

Test Your Understanding

Answer Core Review Question 2 and Detailed Review Question 2.

Figure 8.6
Ethernet Switch
Forwarding Table

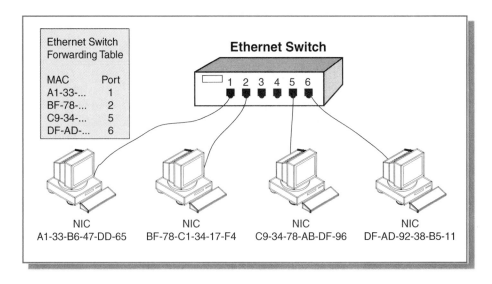

Chapter 8   Larger Site Networks

More on Ethernet Switching

ETHERNET SWITCH LEARNING

Figure 8.6 shows a typical Ethernet switch forwarding table. How are such tables created? One way is for the network administrator *manually* to enter all MAC addresses and port numbers. However, this is impractical for large networks because of their sheer size and also because stations will be added and dropped constantly, making manual table editing a perpetual chore. Instead, most organizations allow their switches to *learn* the associations between ports and MAC addresses, as shown in Figure 8.7.

Figure 8.7 Ethernet Switch Learning: Initial Broadcasting

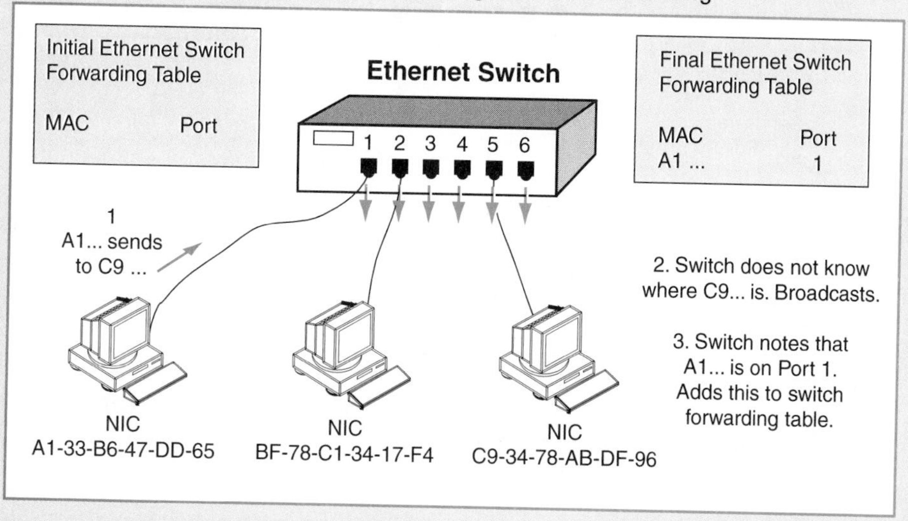

Initial Ethernet Switch Forwarding Table

MAC   Port

Ethernet Switch

1 2 3 4 5 6

Final Ethernet Switch Forwarding Table

MAC   Port
A1 ...   1

1
A1... sends to C9 ...

2. Switch does not know where C9... is. Broadcasts.

3. Switch notes that A1... is on Port 1. Adds this to switch forwarding table.

NIC
A1-33-B6-47-DD-65

NIC
BF-78-C1-34-17-F4

NIC
C9-34-78-AB-DF-96

Initial Broadcasting

When an Ethernet switch is turned on, its switch forwarding table is completely empty. Under these circumstances, Figure 8.7 shows that Ethernet switches must act like hubs, broadcasting every incoming frame out every port. In other words, we pay switch prices but only get hub operation in terms of congestion control.

Broadcasting but Learning

Fortunately, Ethernet switches learn very quickly. For instance, Figure 8.7 shows Station Ax (A1-33-B6-47-DD-65) on Port 1 transmitting to Station Cx (C9-34-78-AB-DF-96) on Port 5.

When the switch receives the frame, it sees Station Cx's MAC address in the destination address field. The switch forwarding table is empty, so there is no entry for C9-34-78-AB-DF-9G. The switch must broadcast the frame out all attached ports. The NICs in all stations must process the frame to determine whether or not the frame is intended for them.

However, the frame contains Station Ax's MAC address in the *source* address field, as discussed in Chapter 7. While processing the frame, the Ethernet switch reads the source address field. From this, it learns that Station Ax is attached to Port 1. It places this entry into its switch forwarding table as shown in Figure 8.7.

Continued.

Learning from Responses

Station Cx is likely to respond to Station Ax's frame. Now, the switch knows that Station Ax is attached to Port 1, so as Figure 8.8 illustrates, the switch only sends the frame out Port 1. The switch is beginning to act like a switch.

Figure 8.8 Ethernet Switch Learning: Acting Like a Switch

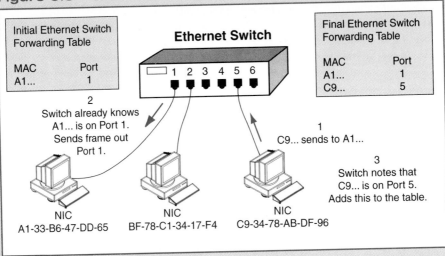

In addition, Station Cx has placed its MAC address in the source address field of the frame. Now, the switch can add Station Cx's MAC address to the switch forwarding table as Figure 8.8 shows.

Working as a Switch

Station Ax and Station Cx are likely to continue sending many frames back and forth. Now the switch has their MAC addresses in its switch forwarding table, so there is no need for further broadcasting. Overall, only a few frames in any exchange typically are broadcast.

Forgetting

What happens if stations are dropped, disconnected, or have their NICs changed? Then the switch forwarding table will contain incorrect information. To eliminate obsolete information, switches erase their switch forwarding tables every few minutes. They must then rebuild their switch forwarding tables from scratch.

Learning for Hierarchical Switches

What if another Ethernet switch, rather than a single station, is attached to a port, as shown in Figure 8.9? This creates no problems for switch learning.

Suppose that the lower-level switch is attached to Port 1 of the higher-level switch. Now, the frames from stations Dx, Ex, and Fx (we again name stations after the first hex digit in their MAC address) that are physically attached to the lower-level switch may enter the higher-level switch through Port 1. The higher-level switch merely adds each new MAC source address it sees to the switch forwarding table, associating that MAC address with Port 1. Whenever frames arrive at the higher-level switch for Stations Dx, Ex, or Fx, the switch merely sends the frame back out on Port 1.

Continued.

Chapter 8   Larger Site Networks

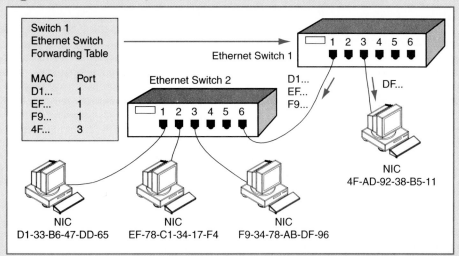

Figure 8.9 Learning in an Ethernet Switched Hierarchy

Switch 1
Ethernet Switch
Forwarding Table

MAC	Port
D1...	1
EF...	1
F9...	1
4F...	3

Ethernet Switch 1

Ethernet Switch 2

D1...
EF...
F9...

DF...

NIC
4F-AD-92-38-B5-11

NIC
D1-33-B6-47-DD-65

NIC
EF-78-C1-34-17-F4

NIC
F9-34-78-AB-DF-96

Note what the higher-level Ethernet switch does *not* learn from this process. It does not learn that there is a switch between itself and Stations Dx, Ex, and Fx! Ethernet switch forwarding tables do not include any information about the organization of switches in their network—only MAC addresses.

PURCHASING AN ETHERNET SWITCH

Hubs are hubs. The only things you have to worry about when buying a hub are the number, speeds, and types (RJ-45, etc.) of ports you want on the hub. However, purchasing an Ethernet switch is quite complex.

Switching Matrix Throughput

As Figure 8.10 illustrates, a switch has a **switching matrix** that connects input ports to output ports. (Of course, in UTP, the RJ-45 port is both an input port and an output port.)

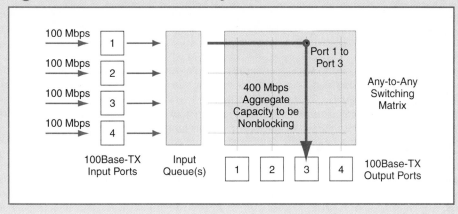

Figure 8.10 Ethernet Switch Organization

100 Mbps → 1 →
100 Mbps → 2 →
100 Mbps → 3 →
100 Mbps → 4 →

100Base-TX
Input Ports

Input
Queue(s)

Port 1 to
Port 3

400 Mbps
Aggregate
Capacity to be
Nonblocking

Any-to-Any
Switching
Matrix

1 2 3 4

100Base-TX
Output Ports

Continued.

A critical consideration in Ethernet switch selection is the switching matrix's **aggregate throughput.** Suppose you have a 24-port 100Base-TX switch. In the worst case, all ports may receive data simultaneously at 100 Mbps each. This would require the switching matrix to have an aggregate throughput of 2.4 Gbps (24 times 100 Mbps).

Switches that can handle even their highest possible input load are called **nonblocking.** The aggregate capacities of most switches are not fully nonblocking because it is not likely that all ports will be receiving simultaneously. However, if a switching matrix's aggregate throughput is too far below nonblocking capacity, frames may have to wait for transmission sometimes, and latency will result.[5]

Switching matrix throughput is especially important for switches high in the hierarchy, such as campus switches (see Figure 8.5). Each port will carry traffic to and from many individual stations, so it is common to find most ports sending and receiving at any given moment.

Number of Possible MAC Addresses in the Switch Forwarding Table

Another consideration in Ethernet switch purchasing is the maximum size of the switch forwarding table, specifically the number of MAC address–port pairs it can store. Switches must broadcast to any address not in their address table, as we saw earlier in this box. Large campus switches may have to store port numbers for thousands of MAC addresses.

Queue Size(s)

If too many frames arrive at the switch simultaneously, the matrix may have to store some frames temporarily in a **queue** (buffer). If a queue is too small, some frames will be lost during temporary congestion. Often, a switch has several waiting queues for different ports or different priorities.

Reliability Through Redundancy

Switch failures can incapacitate dozens or even hundreds of users. Ways to improve switch reliability include having redundant switching matrices, redundant power supplies, and even redundant cooling fans.

Manageability

As discussed in Chapter 12, a company is likely to have many switches, and it would like to be able to manage all of them from a single network control center. The center's network management program must be able to ask each switch for information and must also be able to issue commands to switches (say, to shut down a port that appears to be malfunctioning). The switch's management functions must be compatible with the company's network management standards, as discussed in Chapter 12.

VIRTUAL LANS (VLANS)

The Need for Broadcasting

Ethernet switches are designed to send traffic out a single port once they know a destination MAC address. This assumes **unicasting,** in which the message is intended for only a single destination address.

Some processes, however, *require* the **broadcasting** of frames to all stations. For example, some servers periodically broadcast advertisement messages to notify clients of their presence. Such messages *must* go to all stations.

---

[5] Kevin Tolly has suggested that top-level switches have an aggregate throughput at least 75% of the maximum load and that no switch is acceptable at any level if it has an aggregate throughput less than 25% of the maximum load. Tolly, Kevin, "Exploding the Price-per-Port Fallacy," *Network World,* 9/22/98. HTTP://www.nwfusion.com/forum/0921tolly.html.

Continued.

Note that "broadcasting" is used in two ways in Ethernet networks. First, it can denote what the sender wishes to do (send a message to all stations). Second, it can denote what hubs always do. Hubs broadcast both unicast and broadcast messages.

Ethernet switches turn off single-port delivery when they encounter a broadcast frame (in Ethernet, a broadcast frame has all ones in its destination address field). Instead, switches send the frame out all ports. Server advertisements and other broadcast messages are no problem in small switched site networks. However, they would cripple capacity if they had to be delivered to all stations attached to all switches in very large switched site networks.

VLANs

Ethernet switches resolve the conflicting needs for broadcasting and broadcast limitation by creating logical groups consisting of servers and the clients they serve. These groups are called **virtual LANs** or **VLANs**. When a server broadcasts, only its VLAN clients hear it. This greatly reduces broadcast traffic.

VLANs Sharing a Single Switch

As Figure 8.11 illustrates, the members of different VLANs may even share a single switch. In the figure, both the marketing and accounting department VLANs have clients and a server attached to a single switch. Yet the switch will allow traffic to flow only between VLAN members.[6]

Figure 8.11   Virtual Local Area Networks (VLANs)

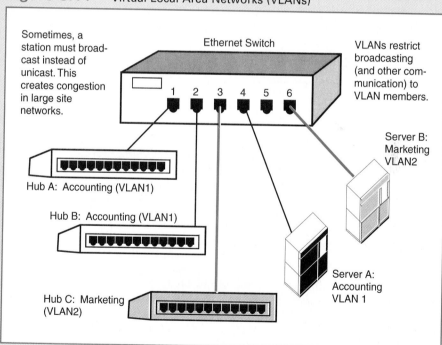

Sometimes, a station must broadcast instead of unicast. This creates congestion in large site networks.

VLANs restrict broadcasting (and other communication) to VLAN members.

Ethernet Switch

Hub A: Accounting (VLAN1)

Hub B: Accounting (VLAN1)

Hub C: Marketing (VLAN2)

Server B: Marketing VLAN2

Server A: Accounting VLAN 1

---

[6] This example bases VLANs on organizational roles. VLANs can also be based on applications, internet layer protocols, or other things that groups of users have in common.

Unfortunately, VLANs have not been standardized in the past, so vendor interoperability has been poor. However, as Chapter 7 noted, the new Tag Control Information field allows the specification of 12-bit VLAN ID (**VID**) numbers in a standardized way. (Switches will base switching on these VLAN ID numbers instead of destination addresses.) Hopefully, this will lead to vendor interoperability in VLANs.

STORE-AND-FORWARD VERSUS CUT-THROUGH SWITCHING

Recall from Chapter 7 that an Ethernet frame contains multiple fields and that the data field alone can be as large as 1,500 octets long.

Store-and-Forward Ethernet Switches

As Figure 8.12 illustrates, some switches wait until they have received the *entire frame* before sending it out. This allows them to check each frame for errors and to discard incorrect frames. This is called **store-and-forward** switching. Although it prevents the propagation of incorrect frames, it also introduces a slight delay for each frame it processes.

Figure 8.12   Store-and-Forward Versus Cut-Through Ethernet Switches

Preamble	Ending Points for Processing
Start of Frame Delimiter	
Destination Address	Cut-Through Based on MAC Destination Address
Source Address	
Tag Fields if Present	Cut-Through for Priority or VLANs
Length	
Data (and Perhaps PAD)	Cut-Through at 46 KB of Data (Not a Runt)
Cyclical Redundancy Check	Store-and-Forward Processing Ends Here

Cut-Through Ethernet Switches

In contrast, **cut-through** Ethernet switches examine only *some fields* in a frame before sending the frame back out. Obviously, as shown in Figure 8.12, they must at least read the destination address, in order to know what port to use to send the frame back out. This requires reading the preamble, start of frame delimiter, and destination address, for a total of only 14 octets.

VLANs and priority also require the reading of tag fields if they are used. Some cut-through switches, in the "extreme" case, wait for 46 octets of data because a smaller frame would be illegal. By examining only a few dozen octets, cut-through switches have less latency than store-and-forward switches, which typically have to examine hundreds or thousands of octets.

Mixed Switches

Some switches provide the best of both worlds. They begin forwarding using cut-through approaches. However, they sample some frames to determine error rates. If error rates are too high, they switch to store-and-forward processing unless they are forbidden to do so—for instance, if voice is being processed and cannot tolerate the delay.

Continued.

INTELLIGENT SWITCHED NETWORK ORGANIZATION

Not all patterns for assigning stations to Ethernet switches are equally effective at reducing latency compared with hubs.

Bad Switch Organization

For instance, the first station assignment pattern shown in Figure 8.13 has all client PCs using a single server. If we are using a 10Base-T switch, then the link between the switch and the server will be a bottleneck through which all traffic must pass. There is little or no performance gain compared with using a hub.

Figure 8.13   Good and Bad Ethernet Switch Layouts

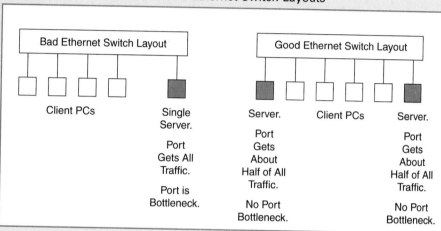

Good Switch Organization

Figure 8.13 also illustrates a good assignation of stations to a switch. Here, different applications are placed on different servers, so that not all server traffic goes to any one server. Now there is no single bottleneck, and multiple conversations between clients and servers can take place simultaneously.[7]

Test Your Understanding

Answer Detailed Review Questions 3–7 and Thought Question 3.

---

[7] Another solution would be to use a switch that has a faster port for the server link (some 10Base-T switches can be purchased with one or two 100Base-TX ports, for instance). Also, in most servers it is possible to install several NICs and connect each NIC to a different switch port. As long as the server has the capacity to keep up with the load, switching will improve throughput.

Congestion, Latency, Overprovisioning Capacity, Priority, and Quality of Service (QoS)

Congestion and Latency

In large site networks, congestion can be a serious problem. As Figure 8.14 illustrates, a brief **traffic peak** may exceed the capacity of switches or trunk lines between switches. This brings temporary **congestion**—the presence of more traffic than the network can handle at that time.

When temporary congestion occurs, switches have to hold frames for a while before sending them out again. This delay is called **latency,** as we saw in Chapter 1. Switches may even have to *discard* some frames if their queue capacity is exceeded. Of course, frame loss results in upper-layer retransmissions for error correction, which further increases traffic and, therefore, congestion.

Overprovisioning Capacity

One response to temporary congestion is to **overprovision capacity,** that is, to install far more trunk line and switching capacity than will be needed during normal traffic loads, as Figure 8.14 illustrates. Overprovisioning will prevent congestion in all but the largest traffic peaks.

The Wastefulness of Overprovisioned Capacity Unfortunately, providing overprovisioned capacity wastes network capacity. Most of the time, overprovisioned capacity is not needed. We would like to be able to reduce our network's capacity without creating unacceptable latency during occasional traffic peaks.

The Cost Effectiveness of Overprovisioned Capacity However, given the economics of networking today, overprovisioning capacity, although wasteful, *usually is the least expensive way to reduce latency problems.* This may change in the future, as the costs of switching logic fall, so that we can provide the more sophisticated remedies to latency reduction we will see in this section. For now, however, overprovisioning capacity usually is the right choice.

Priority

Not all traffic is equally sensitive to latency. For instance, some traffic, such as e-mail, is tolerant of latency. It seldom matters whether e-mail delivery takes a few microseconds, a few seconds, or even a few minutes. In contrast, other traffic is highly **latency-intolerant.** If we are having a voice conversation over a network, even a delay of a quarter second (250 milliseconds [ms]) can disrupt normal turn taking in conversations.

Priority for Latency-Intolerant Traffic This varying tolerance to latency suggests that we should give **priority** (preference) to latency-intolerant traffic.

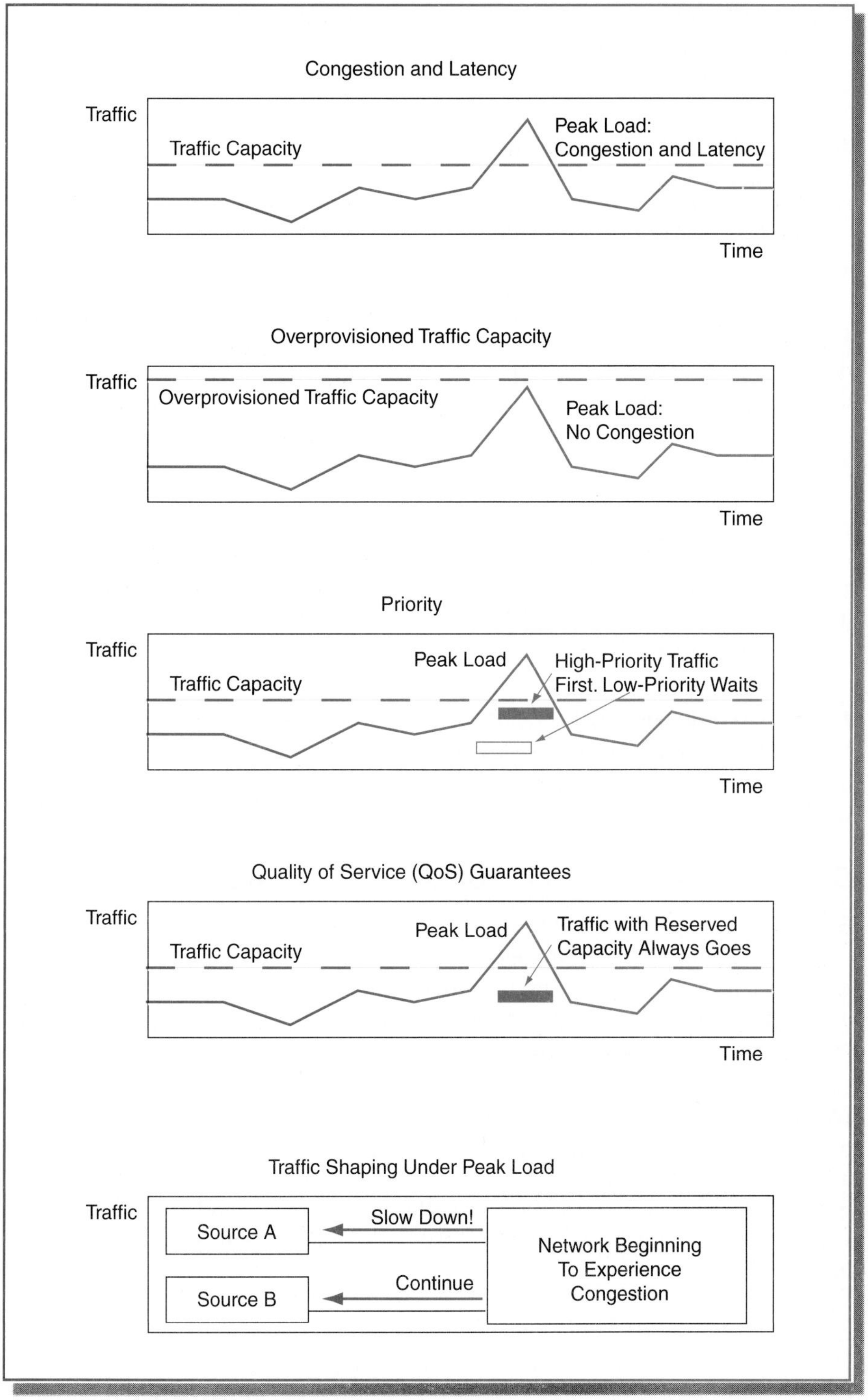

Congestion and Latency

Traffic

Traffic Capacity

Peak Load:
Congestion and Latency

Time

Overprovisioned Traffic Capacity

Traffic

Overprovisioned Traffic Capacity

Peak Load:
No Congestion

Time

Priority

Traffic

Traffic Capacity

Peak Load

High-Priority Traffic
First. Low-Priority Waits

Time

Quality of Service (QoS) Guarantees

Traffic

Traffic Capacity

Peak Load

Traffic with Reserved
Capacity Always Goes

Time

Traffic Shaping Under Peak Load

Traffic

Source A

Slow Down!

Network Beginning
To Experience
Congestion

Source B

Continue

Figure 8.14
Temporary
Congestion and
Remedies

As Figure 8.14 shows, if high-priority and low-priority frames arrive at a switch at the same time, the switch should send high-priority frames out first. Low-priority traffic may even be stopped entirely during brief traffic peaks.

An Illusion, but a Good One   Priority gives the illusion of latency reduction for latency-intolerant users. However, priority *does not reduce overall latency*. It only *allocates latency* to different classes of traffic. If there is adequate capacity, this will pose no problems, because high-priority users will benefit, and users of latency-tolerant applications will not care.[8]

Priority in 802 LANs   As noted in Chapter 7, the Tag Control Information field being added to 802 MAC layer frames will have a three-bit **priority** subfield. This gives 8 (2^3) possible priority levels. The 802.1 Working Group is now working on the definitions of these eight priority levels, so that they can be applied uniformly across LAN vendors.

Priority in IP   Although we have been focusing on switches, we also have problems with congestion and latency in routers. The Internet Engineering Task Force is developing a **Differentiated Services (diffserv)** complex of standards to establish priority for both IP Version 4 and IP Version 6, so that routers can implement priority-based router forwarding decisions.

Harmonizing Ethernet and IP Priority Schemes   The IETF and the 802 Committee plan to harmonize their prioritization approaches. This will allow integrated priority treatment from the time a message leaves the source host until the time it reaches the destination host.

Quality of Service (QoS) Guarantees for Latency

By themselves, Ethernet and IP merely do their best to deliver frames and packets. Priority adds some intelligence to what they do by giving special treatment to latency-intolerant traffic. Full **quality of service (QoS)** does more. It offers *quantitative guarantees* for various service parameters. For example, there may be a QoS guarantee of a **maximum latency** of 50 ms 99.9% of the time.

Dedicated (Reserved) Capacity   As Figure 8.14 illustrates, QoS guarantees for latency require that capacity be **dedicated (reserved)** on each switch along the way and on each trunk line as well. If this sounds like circuit switching, which we saw in Chapter 1, it certainly is similar, and the same disadvantages occur. For bursty traffic, reserved capacity will be wasted during long silences.

---

[8] However, if there is too little capacity in the network, latency will increase so much for low-priority applications that it will become intolerable. In addition, if too many frames are delayed, the switch's queue capacity will be exceeded, and some frames will have to be discarded. Priority is not a magical cure for inadequate capacity. It is only a way to deal with temporary congestion caused by traffic peaks.

However, capacity for only *some* traffic must be reserved, because not all traffic needs a high quality of service. Remaining switch capacity can be allocated as needed to traffic with less exacting needs.

Overall, however, maintaining QoS guarantees is quite expensive. Overprovisioning capacity may be good enough, and, if not, priority may be all that is needed for adequate service.

QoS in ATM   Ethernet does not offer QoS latency guarantees. Nor does it plan to offer them. However, Ethernet's main switching competitor for site networks, ATM, does offer QoS guarantees for both latency and exact timing. We will see ATM in the next section.

Traffic Shaping

The latency control techniques we have looked at so far help the network cope with temporarily high levels of traffic *already in* the network. Another approach shown in Figure 8.14 is to limit traffic *entering* the network during peak periods, based on some criteria, such as priority. This is called **traffic shaping.** The term "shaping" reflects the fact that restrictions should be based on policy guidelines about what specific types of traffic should be reduced during peak periods.

In the telephone system, if you try to make a call on an extremely busy day, such as Christmas, you may not be able to place the call, although once you do, you will not be interrupted. Overall, traffic shaping similarly rations capacity but reduces the problems caused by the loss of frames during peak periods.

For example, in the next chapter, we will see that Frame Relay and ATM networks often guarantee a certain level of traffic throughput but allow faster temporary bursts. As Chapter 9 also discusses, Frame Relay switches have a way to tell stations that congestion is appearing in the network. When this happens, stations should restrict their traffic to the guaranteed level. If they fail to do so, switches can enforce the restriction themselves.

Test Your Understanding

Answer Core Review Question 3 and Detailed Review Question 8.

ATM SWITCHED NETWORKS

Although Ethernet dominates site networking today, many organizations use **asynchronous transfer mode (ATM)** for some or all of their site networking.

Like switched Ethernet, ATM is a switched technology. However, ATM is much more sophisticated than Ethernet. Unfortunately, the complexity created by this sophistication makes ATM switches very expensive. ATM's complexity also requires intensive staff training and extensive ongoing management labor, making operating costs very high.

Cells

In one area, however, namely the basic organization of frames, ATM is much simpler than Ethernet. Whereas Ethernet uses variable-length frames whose data fields can range from 46 to 1500 octets, ATM uses fixed-length frames called **cells.** As Figure 8.15 indicates, each ATM cell has 5 octets of header and 48 octets of **payload** (data), for a total length of exactly 53 octets.

Advantages of Fixed Length   Fixed length allows ATM cells to be processed very efficiently. Fields are always in exactly the same position in each frame. Consequently, ATM switches do not have to do complex calculations based on length fields to determine how much RAM to set aside to hold various fields. In addition, predictability allows some processing to be done in parallel in hardware, speeding the processing of each cell.

Advantages of Brief Length   Why are cells so short? The answer is that brief length can reduce the latency at each switch. If an incoming cell must be held until an outgoing cell is finished being sent out a port, the short length of cells means that the wait will be very brief. Reducing latency at each switch was a key design goal in ATM, which was always intended to carry latency-intolerant voice.

Disadvantage of Brief Length   Brief length does have one problem, namely high overhead. **Overhead** is defined as all bits other than data bits, that

Figure 8.15
ATM Cell

Bit 1	Bit 2	Bit 3	Bit 4	Bit 5	Bit 6	Bit 7	Bit 8
Virtual Path Identifier							
Virtual Path Identifier				Virtual Channel Identifier			
Virtual Channel Identifier							
Virtual Channel Identifier				Payload Type		Reserved	Cell Loss Priority
Header Error Check							
Payload (48 Octets)							

There is a slightly different cell structure for the network–network interface (NNI), shown here, between the switches of different carriers and the cell structure for the user–network interface (UNI) between the customer premises and the ATM carrier. (The terminology was created for wide area networking, which is in the next chapter.) The first eight bits of the UNI cell header form a generic flow control field whose use has not been standardized to date. This reduces the length of the virtual path identifier to 8 bits.

In the Payload Type field, if the middle bit is set to 1, the cell has experienced congestion. This is used in traffic shaping.

For the Cell Loss Priority bit, a zero indicates a cell being sent within the committed information rate. A 1 indicates transmission faster than the committed information rate, and the cell will be discarded first if there is congestion.

is, all header and trailer bits. ATM has 5 overhead octets (the header) for every 48 octets of data, giving an overhead of about 10%. As discussed in Module E, ATM has other sources of overhead as well. In general, ATM does not make efficient use of transmission capacity.

Virtual Circuits

As Figure 8.16 illustrates, ATM switches can be organized in a mesh. Theoretically, this allows alternative routes between any two end stations. However, once communication begins, ATM restricts all traffic between two end stations to a single path called a **virtual circuit.**

Virtual Circuits and Switch Forwarding Tables With Ethernet switches, we saw that a switch forwarding table holds each station's MAC address and the port associated with that MAC address. When a frame arrives for a MAC address, the switch sends the frame out the corresponding port.

In ATM, the switch forwarding table again has two entries. Now, however, they are a <u>virtual circuit number</u> and a <u>port</u> associated with that virtual circuit number. The address field in an ATM cell (see Figure 8.15) really gives the virtual circuit number for the cell rather than a destination address.[9] The ATM switch merely reads the virtual circuit number, looks at the ATM switch forwarding table, and sends the cell out the indicated port.

ATM Virtual Circuit Details As shown in Figure 8.16, ATM has a hierarchical naming system for virtual circuits. At the higher level, there is the

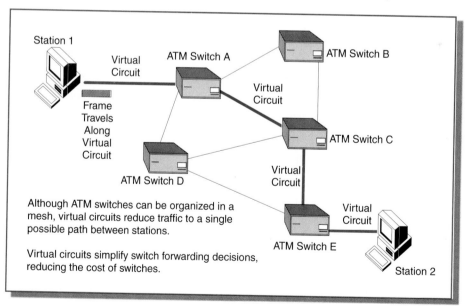

Figure 8.16
Virtual Circuits in ATM

Station 1

Virtual Circuit

ATM Switch A

ATM Switch B

Virtual Circuit

Frame Travels Along Virtual Circuit

ATM Switch C

ATM Switch D

Virtual Circuit

Although ATM switches can be organized in a mesh, virtual circuits reduce traffic to a single possible path between stations.

Virtual circuits simplify switch forwarding decisions, reducing the cost of switches.

Virtual Circuit

ATM Switch E

Station 2

---

[9] Each ATM node also has a unique 20-octet hierarchical address. However, this address is used only in setting up virtual circuits and restoring them in case of disruptions. It is not used in ATM switch forwarding decisions.

virtual path identifier (VPI). At the lower and more specific layer, there is the **virtual channel identifier (VCI).** In intersite transmission, the virtual path identifier can be used to designate a particular site. The virtual channel identifier, in turn, can then be used to designate a particular station at that site. We saw in Chapter 3 how hierarchical addressing makes message delivery more efficient. For instance, between sites, switches might only have entries for virtual path identifiers, forwarding all frames with the same VPI the same way without even looking at VCIs.

ATM Service Classes and Categories

ATM is attractive because it offers different quality of service support levels for different service categories. Not all traffic has the exacting requirements of voice communication, and traffic with less exacting requirements can be handled without full capacity reservation.

ITU-T and the ATM Forum   As Figure 8.17 illustrates, ITU-T has defined four **classes** of service, A, B, C, and D. Extending these classes, the **ATM Forum,** an industry vendor and user group, defines specific **service categories** that are more detailed than the class descriptions. Switches usually are based on the ATM Forum service categories.

Class A (CBR)   **Class A** offers exact timing and fixed guaranteed bandwidth. This is why the ATM Forum called its corresponding service category **constant bit rate (CBR).** CBR is ideal for voice and video traffic. In many ways,

Figure 8.17
ATM ITU-T
Service Classes
and ATM Forum
Service Categories

ITU-T Class of Service	Class A	Class B	Class C	Class D
Exact timing (almost no jitter)	Yes	Yes	No	No
Bit rate	Constant	Variable	Variable	Variable
Connection oriented (CONS) or connectionless (CNLS)	CONS	CONS	CONS	CNLS
Example	Telephony	Video-conferencing with varying motion	Connection-oriented data transmission, which is very rare	CNLS data transmission, especially IP
ATM Forum Service Categories	Constant bit rate (CBR)	Variable bit rate–real time (VBR-RT)	Variable bit rate–not real time (VBR-NRT)	Available bit rate (ABR) Unspecified bit rate (UBR) Guaranteed frame rate (GFR)

it is the heart of ATM networking. All switches implement CBR. Otherwise, why use ATM?

Class D (ABR, UBR, and GFR)   Of course, ATM has to carry a great deal of data traffic, typically IP data traffic or LAN–LAN data traffic. Obviously good service definitions are needed for data traffic. However, although ITU-T placed such traffic in **Class D,** the ATM Forum has struggled to create useful service categories for bursty data traffic.

Initially, the ATM Forum defined **available bit rate (ABR),** which was designed to provide low cell loss rates. However, ABR proved difficult to implement and was not widely supported.

Next, the Forum defined **unspecified bit rate (UBR).** This was simpler, but there were no protections at all for UBR traffic. In case of high congestion, UBR traffic would be almost shut down. Although UBR is far from perfect, it is widely implemented on ATM switches.

Most recently, the ATM Forum has defined the **guaranteed frame rate (GFR)** service category for data traffic. Like UBR, GFR is simple and fast. Whereas UBR may completely stop data traffic during periods of high congestion, GFR implements "fairness," so that data traffic can continue at a reduced rate.

This lack of good standards for handling data has been a serious impediment to ATM.

Classes B and C   **Class B** and **Class C** both deal with variable bit rate traffic whose demand for traffic capacity may vary over time. The main difference is that Class B is connection-oriented and reduces latency, which is why the ATM Forum called this service **variable bit rate–real time (VBR-RT).** It is good for traffic such as videoconferencing, in which more capacity is briefly needed to avoid image degradation if there is sudden movement in the picture.

For connection-oriented service that wishes to have variable traffic capacity, there is Class C service or **variable bit rate–not real time (VBR-NRT).** This can be used for data traffic, although Class D solutions are far more common.

In general, Class B and Class C are not widely implemented on ATM switches, but support is increasing for VBR-RT.

Service Category QoS Parameters   Our characterizations of various service categories have been rather general. In practice, specific parameters must be set to define service category QoS exactly. These parameters include the following:

- *Peak cell rate.* The fastest allowed burst speed.
- *Maximum burst size.* The number of cells that can be sent at the peak cell rate.
- *Sustainable cell rate (SCR).* The rate that is always allowed.
- *Cell delay variation tolerance (CDVT).* The possible deviation from exact timing in cell delivery.
- *Cell loss ratio.* The percentage of cells lost during transmission.

Test Your Understanding

Answer Core Review Question 5 and Detailed Review Question 9.

ROUTERS, LAYER 3 SWITCHES, AND LAYER 4 SWITCHES IN SITE NETWORKS

Routers

We looked at routers extensively in Chapter 3, although we focused only on IP processing on routers. In reality, most routers are **multiprotocol routers** that can handle IP packets, IPX packets, AppleTalk packets, SNA Internet layer messages, and other types of packets simultaneously. This alone makes routers very expensive.

Traditionally: Routers and LANs   Early site networks had only two types of devices, as shown in Figure 8.18. First, there were hub-based Ethernet LANs. Second, there were routers. Each LAN would be a subnet, and routers would connect these subnets. There often was a hierarchy of routers, with central routers having higher capacity.

Pushing Routers to the Edge of the Network   Because of the complexity of router forwarding decisions, routers are much more expensive than switches and also are slower. As shown in Figure 8.19, the switch explosion has pushed routers to the edges of site networks. Switches, rather than routers, usually connect individual LANs today. In fact, it is increasingly common to see switches go all the way to the desktop, eliminating hubs completely.

We still need routers at the edges of our site networks. Routers are much more intelligent than switches at managing transmission lines. This is crucial

Figure 8.18
Traditional LAN-Router Site Network

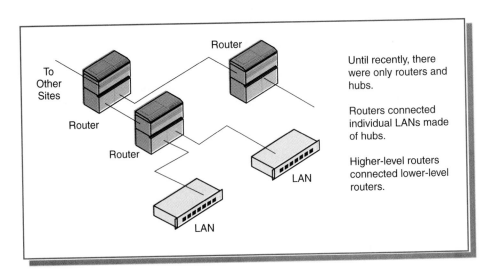

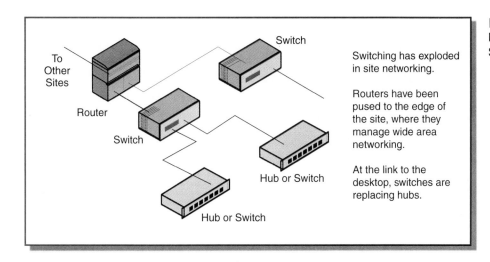

Figure 8.19
Router at Edge of
Site Network

Switch

To
Other
Sites

Switching has exploded
in site networking.

Routers have been
pused to the edge of
the site, where they
manage wide area
networking.

Router

At the link to the
desktop, switches are
replacing hubs.

Switch

Hub or Switch

Hub or Switch

for communication between a corporation's sites because long-distance transmission is very expensive on a per-bit basis compared with LAN and site network transmission.

Layer 3 Switches

As Figure 8.20 shows, some switches are called **Layer 3 switches.** Traditional Ethernet and ATM switches are Layer 2 (data link layer) devices that work on the basis of MAC addresses or ATM virtual circuit numbers. They manage transmission *within a single subnet.*

IP Operation In contrast, Layer 3 (internet layer) switches operate at layer 3, the internet layer. They forward IP packets on the basis of the IP destination addresses, just as Layer 2 switches forward frames based on Ethernet MAC addresses or ATM virtual circuit numbers.

High Speeds and Low Prices Most importantly, Layer 3 switches offer IP-based switching at layer 2 switching speeds and prices. As a consequence, their use has been growing explosively. Unfortunately, it is difficult to talk about Layer 3 switch technology compared with router technology because different Layer 3 switches use different technologies to cut cost and increase speed.[10] In addition, many innovations introduced in Layer 3 switches are now being adopted in router designs, further blurring the technical difference

---

[10] One characteristic of almost all Layer 3 switches is that they do not make separate full router forwarding decisions for each IP packet that arrives, as traditional routers do. Rather, a Layer 3 switch remembers the decisions it makes for various destination addresses, so that when a new IP packet arrives, it simply forwards the new packet according to the previous forwarding decision it made for the packet's destination address instead of making another full router forwarding decision. Of course, technology abhors a distinction; so many routers now act similarly. MultiProtocol Label Switching (MPLS) will be one way to standardize the removal of individual packet decision making by creating what are in effect virtual circuits for routers.

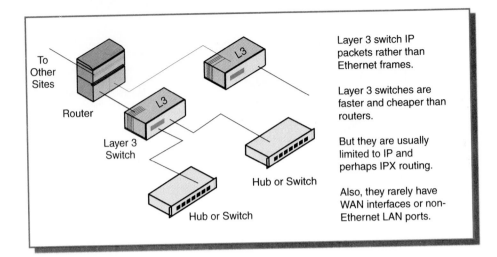

Figure 8.20
Router and Layer 3 Switches

Layer 3 switch IP packets rather than Ethernet frames.

Layer 3 switches are faster and cheaper than routers.

But they are usually limited to IP and perhaps IPX routing.

Also, they rarely have WAN interfaces or non-Ethernet LAN ports.

To Other Sites

Router

Layer 3 Switch

Hub or Switch

Hub or Switch

between routers and Layer 3 switches. It is best to think about the distinction between routers and Layer 3 switches not in terms of technologies but in terms of faster speeds, lower prices, and the limitations we will see next.

Limitations of Layer 3 Switch Protocol Support

Limited Layer 3 Protocol Support   Layer 3 switches have not replaced routers everywhere in site networks. First, they are not full multiprotocol routers. Most handle only IP, and the rest usually add only IPX. They do not handle the other protocols used in corporations, such as AppleTalk and SNA, so not all sites can use them at all or can only use them to replace some routers.

Limited Layer 2 Protocol Support: Not for WAN Use   Second, they normally support only one or at best a few data link layer protocols. For instance, they normally have only Ethernet ports. Most seriously, they rarely have ports for the wide area transmission lines and networks we will see in the next chapter. Consequently, as Figure 8.20 illustrates, although Layer 3 switches have pushed slower and more expensive routers to the edges of site networks, routers are still thriving for connections to the outside world.

Layer 4 Switches

In the hybrid TCP/IP–OSI architecture, the fourth layer is the transport layer. As Figure 2.2 illustrates, the TCP header begins with 16-bit *port numbers* that identify the application layer process that sent the data in the TCP segment's data field and that should receive the data. For instance, 80 is the **well-known** (commonly used) TCP port number for HTTP. UDP also begins with 16-bit source and destination port numbers.

Layer 4 switches read port numbers in TCP and UDP messages encapsulated within IP packets. This allows them to do such things as setting priority levels for IP packets based on the application indicated by the port number. They also can discard IP packets if port numbers indicate forbidden applications.

Test Your Understanding

Answer Core Review Question 6.

KEY POINTS

Ethernet Hub Networks   At the beginning of the chapter, we saw that Ethernet hub networks operating at 100 Mbps, or a gigabit per second, are limited to 200 meters in total distance. A 10Base-T hub network can only be somewhat larger in practice. Overall, Ethernet hub networks cannot span large sites.

Ethernet Switched Networks

We saw that Ethernet switched networks have no maximum distance span. Although there are maximum possible distances between *pairs of switches,* there is no limit on *how many switches* there may be between the farthest two stations. We saw that Ethernet switches must be arranged in a hierarchy, limiting transmission to a single possible path. As a consequence, each Ethernet switch has a simple switch forwarding table that allows it to make fast decisions for each frame. On the negative side, Ethernet switched networks do not have alternative routes to deal with failures, and the Spanning Tree and Link Aggregation Protocols provide only some failure protection. The box in this chapter discussed how switches learn MAC address–port number associations automatically, the key purchasing considerations for Ethernet switches, virtual LANs (VLANs), store-and-forward versus cut-through switching, and good and bad network designs using Ethernet switches.

Latency Reduction   We looked at several ways to reduce latency resulting from temporary congestion caused by traffic peaks. We saw that overprovisioning capacity—installing more capacity than you normally need—is wasteful but usually is the most inexpensive way to reduce temporary latency. Priority lets latency-intolerant frames to go through first, reducing at least apparent latency. Full quality of service (QoS) handles latency very well but is expensive to implement. Traffic Shaping controls the amount of traffic *coming into* the network, in order to prevent congestion in the first place.

ATM   We looked briefly at ATM networks. We saw that ATM uses fixed-length frames, called cells, which are only 53 octets long. We saw that ATM headers have virtual circuit numbers instead of destination addresses and that ATM switches make switch forwarding decisions based on virtual circuit numbers. We also noted that ATM offers several ITU-T service classes and ATM Forum service categories with varying QoS guarantees.

Routers, Layer 3 Switches, and Layer 4 Switches   We noted that although routers have been pushed to the edges of site networks by lower-cost switches, routers are still used to connect sites to other sites. In addition, we saw that new devices called Layer 3 switches can do switch forwarding on the basis of IP addresses at speeds and costs comparable to those of traditional Layer 2 LAN switches (Ethernet and ATM switches). However, Layer 3 switches usually only support IP and perhaps IPX, usually only support Ethernet, and they usually do not have wide area connectivity ports. Therefore, Layer 3 switches cannot replace all routers. Layer 4 switches can make forwarding decisions on the basis of the type of application data being carried by a packet.

REVIEW QUESTIONS

For questions with multiple parts, write the answer to each part in a separate line or paragraph.

Core Review Questions

1. **a)** What limits distance in a 10Base-T hub network? **b)** 100Base-TX hub network? **c)** Gigabit Ethernet hub network?

2. **a)** How are groups of Ethernet switches organized? **b)** How many possible routes are there between any two stations? **c)** How does this make switch forwarding fast and inexpensive? **d)** What disadvantages does Ethernet switching have? **e)** What standards reduce these problems?

3. **a)** What is a traffic peak? **b)** What problems does it create? **c)** Why is over-provisioning capacity good? **d)** Why is overprovisioning capacity bad? **e)** What does priority apparently do? **f)** What does priority really do? **g)** Why is full QoS for throughput good? **h)** Why is it bad? **i)** What is traffic shaping? **j)** Why is it good and bad? **k)** What usually is the least expensive way today to deal with temporary traffic congestion caused by traffic peaks?

4. **a)** What are ATM frames called? **b)** How long is an ATM header? **c)** How long is an ATM data field? **d)** Why are ATM frames so small? **e)** Describe overhead in ATM. **f)** Describe what ATM switches look at in switch forwarding decisions.

5. **a)** Distinguish between ITU-T service classes and ATM Forum service categories. **b)** What are the two most widely implemented ATM traffic classes? **c)** For what type of traffic is each good? **d)** What ATM Forum service category corresponds to Class A? **e)** What does it guarantee? **f)** What ATM Forum service category is most widely implemented today for Class D? **g)** What is the weakness of this service category? **h)** What new service category is being implemented for Class D? **i)** What is its advantage?

6. **a)** Describe the traditional role of routers in site networks. **b)** How is the site network role of routers changing because of switches? **c)** What are Layer 3 switches? **d)** Why are Layer 3 switches so attractive? **e)** What are their limits? **f)** How do Layer 4 switches work? **g)** Why are they good?

Detailed Review Questions

1. **a)** In Figure 8.3, list the hubs a bit will go through to get from Station A to Station D. **b)** How many hubs are there between A and D? **c)** How many UTP segments? **d)** List the hubs along the single path between other pairs of stations.

2. **a)** What were the three levels of switches in the Ethernet switch hierarchy shown in Figure 8.5? **b)** Do all site networks use this arrangement?

3. Referring to the box, "More on Ethernet Switching," **a)** In a single sentence, how are MAC address–port associations created in Ethernet switch forwarding tables? **b)** After a switch has had its memory wiped, what does a switch do the first time a frame arrives? **c)** What does a switch learn when this happens? **d)** Why is an Ethernet switch's forwarding table erased frequently? **e)** In a network with many switches, what is the only thing an individual switch knows?

4. Referring to the box, "More on Ethernet Switching," **a)** Briefly describe the switch evaluation criteria. **b)** What is a nonblocking switch? **c)** What kind of switches must store many MAC address–port associations? **d)** A switch has four gigabit Ethernet ports. What aggregate switch matrix capacity is needed to give nonblocking capacity? **e)** To give 80% of nonblocking capacity? Show your calculations.

5. Referring to the box, "More on Ethernet Switching," **a)** Distinguish between unicasting and broadcasting. **b)** What is a VLAN? **c)** Why do we need VLANs? **d)** Describe VLAN standardization.

6. Referring to the box, "More on Ethernet Switching," **a)** Describe the technical difference between store-and-forward switch operation and cut-through switch operation. **b)** Describe their relative advantages.

7. Referring to the box, "More on Ethernet Switching," critique the statement, "Switches always reduce congestion relative to hubs."

8. **a)** How is priority being standardized in Ethernet? **b)** How is priority being standardized in IP?

9. **a)** Describe ATM Class B and Class C and their related ATM Forum service categories. **b)** Explain why GFR is promising in Class D.

Thought Questions

1. What was the most surprising thing you learned in this chapter?

2. What was the most difficult part of this chapter for you?

3. An Ethernet switch has just had its switch forwarding table erased. On Port 6, it receives a frame from a station with the MAC address 01-AA-03-B4-55-C3 to address 02-CC-D2-FF-34-6A. **a)** What will the switch do with the frame? Explain your reasoning in detail. **b)** What will the switch forwarding table look like afterward? The station with address 02-CC-D2-FF-34-6A immediately replies to 01-AA-03-B4-55-C3. **c)** What does the switch do with the frame? Explain your reasoning in detail. **d)** What will the switch forwarding table look like afterward?

4. If you are using ATM exclusively for data traffic, will there be any advantage over using Ethernet with 802.1p priority? Explain.

5. In the vignette at the start of this chapter, Claire Cunningham has a core campus switch. Describe its organization. How does this bring flexibility?

Case Studies

For case studies, go to the book's website, **http://www.prenhall.com/panko,** and look at the "Case Studies" page for this chapter.

Projects

1. **Getting Current.** Go to the book's website's "New Information" and "Errors" pages for this chapter to get new information since this book went to press and to correct any errors in the text.

2. **Internet Exercises.** Go to the book's website's "Exercises" page for this chapter and do the Internet exercises.

Chapter 9

Wide Area Networking

*P*aradise Groceries has several operations on different islands in the state of Hawaii. In the past, Paradise Groceries installed a mesh of point-to-point transmission lines, called *leased lines,* among its various sites. It then added its own switching. Now, it has to manage all of this on an ongoing basis. Chen May-Ling, the network administrator, has to have a small but expensive staff to maintain this network based on leased lines.

May-Ling is now working on a plan to get out of the business of operating a leased line network. She is considering Frame Relay service, which will offer comparable performance without the need for a large internal staff. The Frame Relay carrier will handle all switching and maintenance concerns. May-Ling will have to add a printed circuit board to each site's router, so that it can talk to the Frame Relay's first switch. She will also need a leased line from each site to the carrier switch nearest that site, but this will be much less trouble and expense than maintaining a full mesh network of leased lines. If fact, the Frame Relay vendor can handle the leased lines itself, charging a modest fee to manage those lines. Best of all, the Frame Relay carrier offers service level agreements (SLA) that guarantee various performance parameters.

On the negative side, May-Ling is discovering that the purchasing of Frame Relay service is very complex. In addition, a colleague in another firm has told her that most of their router problems have come from setting up Frame Relay interfaces on those routers.

The president of Paradise Groceries, Lehua Akana, has heard that Paradise Groceries might be able to save money by sending data between sites over the Internet rather than using leased lines or Frame Relay. She has asked May-Ling to check into that possibility. ∎

Learning Objectives

After studying this chapter, you should be able to describe:

- Carriers, rights of way, tariffs, and deregulation
- Wide area networks that use point-to-point digital leased lines
- The relative advantages of various public switched data networks (PSDNs)
- Frame Relay's frame organization and the pricing of Frame Relay service
- The concept of Internet-based virtual private networks (VPNs)

INTRODUCTION

In this book, we began with Internet access and LANs because most readers already work in these network environments. This allowed us to present basic theory (and practical information) in a familiar context. Now, however, we must begin to move into areas that are new to most readers. In this chapter, we will look at **wide area networks (WANs),** which link a corporation's sites together and which may link one firm's sites to those of its customers and suppliers.

Beyond the Customer Premises In site networking, you own the land and the buildings and can select any technology you wish to use. Of course, if you own something, it is your job to maintain it, and this certainly is true in site networking.

Carriers and Rights of Way In wide area networking, however, you cannot simply lay wires between your sites or between your sites and those of other organizations. (Imagine how you would feel if a neighbor started running wires through your yard.) You lack the required **rights of way,** that is, permissions to lay wires in public areas. Instead, you must use the services of a carrier. **Carriers** transport data and voice traffic between customer premises, charging a price for their services. ("Customer premises" is always spelled with a plural.) The government gives carriers rights of way to lay wires where they need to do so. In addition, the government usually gave carriers **monopoly** status within their service realm.

Regulation and Deregulation In return for receiving rights of way and monopoly status, carriers must work under government rate and service **regulation.** One element of this regulation is a requirement to offer tariffs for most services. **Tariffs** specify two things: a detailed description of the service to be offered and the pricing of the service. Tariffs are published to prevent secret deal making by public monopolies.

One important aspect of many tariffs is the inclusion of **service level agreements (SLAs),** which guarantee specific service performance levels. If the carrier fails to meet these SLAs, the user organization can demand penalties.

Many governments are now **deregulating** much of their telecommunications infrastructure. This involves the removal or weakening of regulations that gave carriers protected monopoly status. Deregulation allows competitors to enter the market. Even deregulated carriers often offer SLAs.

Leased Line Networking In this chapter, we will look first at *leased line networking.* Leased lines are point-to-point circuits that offer high-speed communication at a relatively low cost per bit transmitted. Unfortunately, leased line networks are expensive to design, create, and maintain.

Public Switched Data Networks (PSDNs) We will look next at newer *public switched data networks (PSDNs).* PSDNs eliminate the need to design, implement, and operate complex leased line networks to link a large company's many sites. A PSDN customer merely gets one leased line from each site to the PSDN's nearest access point. PSDN carriers do all the rest of the work, including switching and maintenance. Although leased line networks are widely used and will continue to be widely used, leased line use is decreasing, whereas PSDN use is growing explosively.

Public switched data networks are single networks (subnets), and subnet standards are produced within the OSI model. Specifically, the ITU-T sets PSDN standards, including ISDN, X.25, Frame Relay, and ATM. These standards, being subnet standards, only involve the physical and data link layers.[1]

Virtual Private Networks (VPNs) Companies are also beginning to look at the Internet as a way to link their sites together. We will look at *virtual private network (VPN)* technology, which allows us to communicate among sites, over the Internet, with high security. VPNs are promising, but their use is limited and will continue to be limited for several years.

The High Cost of Long-Distance Communication One thing to keep in mind is that although local and site networking is relatively inexpensive on the basis of cost per bit transmitted, wide area networks have much a much higher cost per bit transmitted. Consequently, whereas LAN speeds tend to be measured in hundreds of megabits per second and even gigabits per second, most long-distance data transmission takes place at speeds of about 56 kbps to a few megabits per second.

Test Your Understanding

Answer Core Review Question 1.

---

[1] X.25 actually was viewed as an OSI Layer 3 (Network) standard, but Frame Relay and ATM, which use similar technology, are broadly viewed as operating at only the lowest two layers.

Leased Lines Are Circuits

To connect their sites, companies traditionally used **leased lines.** In Chapter 1, we noted that voice telephone circuits pass through multiple switches and trunk lines between two customers. We also saw that transmission capacity is reserved all along the circuit. Leased lines are the same, although they operate at much higher speeds.

Leased Lines Are Dedicated Point-to-Point Circuits Although telephone circuits are disconnected at the end of each call, leased lines provide **dedicated** connections that are available 24 hours a day, seven days a week.

Reduced Price Leased lines provide point-to-point connections between two sites. Why would companies wish to use transmission circuits that are limited to only two points? The answer is, "To save money." A leased line essentially is a way for carriers to give volume discounts on high-traffic routes.

Multisite Leased Line Networks As Figure 9.1 indicates, many companies now create multisite networks to link LAN users through meshes of leased lines. They then add switching at each site to link any user at one site to any resource at any other site.

Figure 9.1
Multisite Leased
Line Network

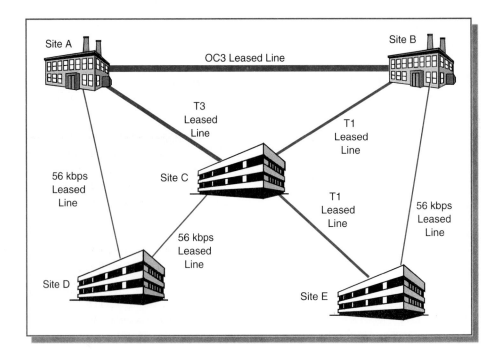

Table 9.1   Popular Leased Line Speeds

Line	Speed
Analog Voice Grade Lines	
Leased Telephone Line	Up to about 35 kbps using modems
North American Digital Hierarchy	
56 kbps (DS0)	56 kbps (sometimes 64 kbps)
T1 (DS1)	1.544 Mbps
Fractional T1	128 kbps, 256 kbps, 384 kbps, etc.
T3 (DS3)	44.7 Mbps
CEPT Multiplexing Hierarchy	
64 kbps	64 kbps
E1	2.048 Mbps
E3	34.4 Mbps
SONET/SDH[a]	
OC3/STM1	156 Mbps
OC12/STM4	622 Mbps
OC48/STM16	2.5 Gbps
OC192/STM64	10 Gbps
HDSL[b]	
Single Pair	768 kbps
Two-Pair	1.544 Mbps
HDSL2,[b] Single Pair	1.544 Mbps

Notes:

[a]Speeds are multiples of 51.84 Mbps. OCx is the SONET designation. STMx is the SDH designation.

[b]HDSL and HDSL2 use voice grade copper instead of data grade copper.

Leased Line Speeds   The first leased lines were slow analog leased lines—essentially point-to-point telephone connections. However, almost all leased lines in use today are digital leased lines. Table 9.1 describes these digital leased lines. Leased line standards, by the way, are physical layer standards. Circuits in general involve only the physical layer.

56-kbps Digital Leased Lines   The most popular leased lines, in terms of number of circuits, are 56 kbps leased lines. These lines are relatively slow, but they are also inexpensive. As discussed in Chapter 4, when you digitize a telephone signal, you generate a bit stream of 64 kbps. Carriers often "steal" 8 kbps for supervisory signaling, leaving 56 kbps. The 56 kbps leased line technology was first created by telephone companies to carry digitized voice calls.

Although these lines are called 56 kbps leased or private lines, they are also called **DS0** lines because DS0 is their signaling format.

T1 Lines   Carriers eventually added faster leased lines.[2] For example, in North America and many other parts of the world, the **T1** line operates at 1.544 Mbps. T1 signaling is designated by **DS1.** Although 56 kbps leased lines dominate in terms of the number of lines in use, T1 lines dominate in terms of revenues. There are fewer of them, but they cost five times as much as a 56 kbps leased line or even more.

Fractional T1 Lines   There is a large difference in speed between 56 kbps and 1.544 Mbps. For users with intermediate requirements, some carriers supply **fractional T1** lines that operate at speeds such as 128 kbps, 256 kbps, or 384 kbps.

T3 Lines   The next step is the **T3** line, which operates at 44.7 Mbps. This is a large jump in capacity, and only large firms need such lines.[3] Its signaling is designated as **DS3.**

CEPT Multiplexing Hierarchy: E1 and E3   In Europe and many other parts of the world, there is a different hierarchy of leased line speeds. This is the CEPT multiplexing hierarchy. (CEPT is the Council of European Postal and Telecommunications authorities. It is the coordinating group for European telecommunications.) Instead of a T1 line, there is an **E1** line operating at 2.048 Mbps. Instead of a T3 line, there is an **E3** line operating at 34.4 Mbps.

SONET/SDH   For higher speeds, the world's telecommunications authorities offer a technology that is called **Synchronous Optical Network (SONET)** in the United States and **Synchronous Digital Hierarchy (SDH)** in Europe. The two standards are almost identical and interoperate fairly easily, so we will simply call them SONET/SDH.

SONET/SDH operates at multiples of 51.84 Mbps. The four most common leased line speeds offered to SONET/SDH subscribers are 156 Mbps, 622 Mbps, 2.5 Gbps, and 10 Gbps. As demand grows, faster speeds will be offered.

As Figure 9.2 illustrates, SONET/SDH uses a dual ring. In normal operation, only one ring is used. However, if there is a break in a trunk line between switches, the ring is wrapped, as Figure 9.2 also illustrates. Note that there is still a closed ring among the switches after wrapping, so service can continue without interruption. This ring physical layer topology is important because the most common reason for disruptions in wide area networks is the accidental breakage of underground transmission lines during unrelated construction projects.

---

[2] These were created to multiplex several 64 kbps voice channels on trunk lines between switches. For instance, the T1 line was created to multiplex twenty-four 64 kbps voice channels, as discussed in Module B. However, T1 lines often are used simply as fat pipes for data transmission.

[3] T2 speeds are defined but are rarely offered by carriers.

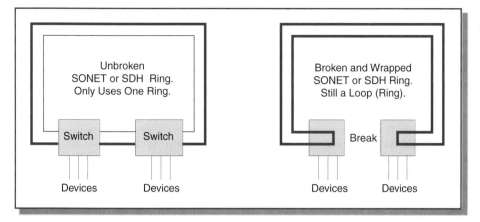

Figure 9.2
SONET/SDH
Double Ring

Digital Subscriber Lines (DSLs)   Chapter 7 introduced digital subscriber lines (DSLs) in the context of Internet access. DSLs use a single pair of copper wires running to the customer premises. Low-end digital leased lines, including 56 kbps, T1, E1, and fractional T1 lines, also use copper wires. However, as Figure 9.3 shows, low-speed leased lines use **data grade copper,** which is specially **conditioned** for transmission quality and which uses *two* pairs of wires—one pair for transmission in each direction.

In contrast, DSLs use the ordinary **voice grade copper** wires installed for telephone service. These are single pairs, and they are not subjected to special installation or quality conditioning. Telephone experts cringe at the thought of sending megabit data over voice grade copper, but new transmission technology now makes this possible, although only for some existing lines.

In Chapter 7, we focused on *asymmetric DSLs (ADSLs)*, which have high downstream speeds but low upstream speeds. These are good for Internet access when webservice is the key application.

However, there are several other types of DSL under development. Companies will soon be replacing at least some of their expensive T1 leased lines with less expensive **high-speed DSLs (HDSLs)** that offer 768 kbps (half a T1's speed) over a single pair of wires. Two pairs provide full T1 speeds. About 20% of all "T1" lines installed recently actually use HDSL for the

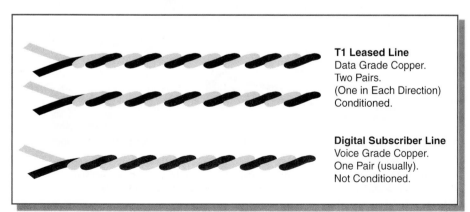

T1 Leased Line
Data Grade Copper.
Two Pairs.
(One in Each Direction)
Conditioned.

Digital Subscriber Line
Voice Grade Copper.
One Pair (usually).
Not Conditioned.

Figure 9.3
Traditional Copper
Leased Line
Versus Digital
Subscriber Line

customer premises connection.[4] The newer HDSL2 standard will even carry full T1 speed over a single pair.

Test Your Understanding

Answer Core Review Questions 2 and 3 and Detailed Review Questions 1 and 2.

PUBLIC SWITCHED DATA NETWORKS (PSDNs)

Although leased line networks are useful, they require user organizations to plan their lease line mesh, provide all switching functions, and perform ongoing management and maintenance work. This means high labor costs.

PSDNs and Their Advantages

Figure 9.4 shows that **public switched data networks (PSDNs)** are much simpler to use.

The PSDN Cloud The actual PSDN is portrayed as a cloud to indicate that the user organization does not have to know what is going on inside the PSDN. All switching, management, and maintenance tasks are handled by the PSDN.

Access Device At the user's site, the user needs an **access device,** which is likely to be a router. The type of access device varies by PSDN technology. The access device implements the physical layer standard required by the leased access line discussed next. At the data link layer, the access device must imple-

Figure 9.4
Public Switched
Data Network
(PSDN)

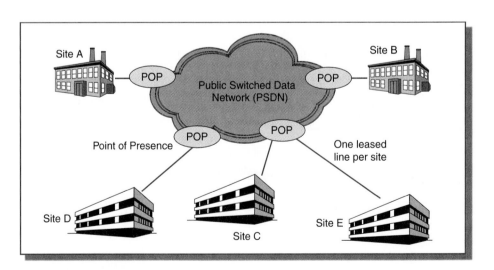

[4] Kentrox Corporation, *High-Speed Access for Business: An Overview of HDSL Applications,* undated. HTTP://www.kentrox.com/solutions/cellworx/wp/high_speed_access/business.htm. Accessed 9/17/99.

ment the appropriate data link layer protocol, which usually is Frame Relay or ATM.

Leased Access Line to the Point of Presence (POP)   The user organization also needs a single leased line from the access device to the PSDN's **point of presence (POP).** A POP is a place to which a user organization must lease a line to connect to the PSDN.

Note that there is no need to plan and pay for a complex mesh of leased lines. For instance, if you have 10 sites, you only need 10 leased lines if you use a PSDN. In contrast, with a mesh of leased lines connecting all sites, you need 45 leased lines[5] if there is a connection between each site and every other site.

Note also that PSDNs do not eliminate the need for leased lines. The company still needs one leased line per site.

Note finally that the company may have to lease the access line from the local telephone carrier rather than from the PSDN. This cost must be added to the service price charged by the public switched data network carrier.

Perspective   Overall, PSDNs are *simpler to use* than networks of leased lines. Thanks to vigorous price competition, PSDNs also tend to be *less expensive* than comparable meshes of leased lines when labor costs are considered. Many organizations are dismantling their traditional leased line networks and replacing them with PSDN service, although leased line networks will continue to be important for many years.

PSDN Characteristics

As Table 9.2 illustrates, there are several PSDN services. We can compare them in terms of a number of general characteristics.

Circuit Switching Versus Packet Switching   As noted in Chapter 1, data networks normally use packet switching, which allows packets from many conversations to share expensive long-distance transmission lines. For data transmission, packet switching's multiplexing of traffic from many conversations onto trunk lines to *reduce transmission line costs* normally is decisive in corporate PSDN selection. As Table 9.2 shows, only the ISDN is circuit switched.

Really Frame Switched Data Networks   Although the term "packet switched" is used to describe services in Table 9.2, the most popular services, Frame Relay and ATM, operate at the data link and physical layers only. Consequently, their messages should be called *frames,* rather than *packets.* The very name "Frame Relay" attests to this fact. However, in wide-area networking, the expression "packet switched" is almost universally used, so we will use it too.

---

[5] For a full mesh of leased lines, if you have N sites, you need N(N-1)/2 leased lines. Although companies rarely have a full mesh, they usually have far more leased lines than they would with a PSDN.

Table 9.2 PSDN Services and Characteristics

Service	Typical Speeds	Circuit or Packet Switched[a]	Reliable or Unreliable[b]	Virtual Circuits?[b]	Relative Price
ISDN	Two 64 kbps B channels	Circuit	Unreliable	No	Moderate
X.25	9,600 bps to 64 kbps	Packet	Reliable	Yes	Low
Frame Relay	56 kbps to about 40 Mbps	Packet	Unreliable	Yes	Low
ATM	1 Mbps to about 156 Mbps	Packet	Unreliable	Yes	High

Notes:
[a]Packet switching allows multiplexing, which reduces transmission line costs for bursty data.
[b]Unreliability eliminates error-checking work on switches. Virtual circuits restrict transmission to a single possible path, reducing switch forwarding work. Both reduce the work that switches must do and, therefore, the cost of switches, which are the most expensive components in PSDNs.

Reliable Versus Unreliable Service Chapter 3 noted that some standards are reliable, whereas others are unreliable. Reliable PSDNs do error detection and correction. This is a costly pair of tasks requiring complex calculations for error detection and many processing cycles to handle retransmissions for error correction. In addition, error detection and correction must be done at *each and every hop between switches*. Unreliable services, in contrast, let a higher-layer process catch any transmission error. This greatly *reduces the costs of switches*. As Table 9.2 illustrates, only the first packet switched network, X.25, was reliable. Again, reducing the cost of switches is decisive.

Virtual Circuits As discussed in the last chapter, ATM can arrange its switches in a mesh, potentially creating alternative routes between end stations. However, ATM requires all traffic between end stations to go over a single route across the switches. This route is called a *virtual circuit*. Table 9.2 shows that all packet switched PSDNs use virtual circuits.

With alternative routing, switches would have to do much more work, just as routers do. Virtual circuits, by taking away complex choice, allow switches to handle data very efficiently and so to *reduce the cost of switches*. Note, in Table 9.2, that *all* packet switched services use virtual circuits. Again, economics are decisive.

Reducing the Cost of Transmission Lines and Switches Do you see a pattern developing? Cost is almost always decisive. Packet switching *reduces transmission line costs*. Usually, however, switching costs are far more expensive than transmission line costs. Both virtual circuits and unreliable service *reduce the cost of switches* by reducing the processing that switches must do per packet.

PSDN Services

Table 9.2 shows how the common public switched data network standards vary along the dimensions we have just seen. The table also shows typical speed ranges and relative prices.

Integrated Services Digital Network (ISDN)   Chapter 5 introduced ISDN. Table 9.2 shows that ISDN is different from other PSDNs in one critical way: it alone is circuit switched. This means that congestion will not occur. However, this does not make up for ISDN's slow speed of only 128 kbps even with bonding. In addition, circuit switching is expensive for data transmission, and ISDN is expensive for the speeds it brings. ISDN once seemed to hold promise, but it has achieved only limited use.

Unlike other services, ISDN uses dial-up connections instead of dedicated (always active) connections. This means that you pay for ISDN service only when you actually use it. However, most organizations need dedicated connections to the outside world.

X.25   The early success of the ARPANET led several private companies to create commercial packet switched data networks in the 1970s. Commercial packet switched networks soon adopted a common subnet standard, which was later ratified by the ITU-T as **X.25.**

X.25 was very slow. Its highest speed usually was only 56 kbps, and X.25 service often ran at 9,600 bps or less. This was not a problem when X.25 was created because the dominant use was terminal–host communication, for which such speeds were adequate. However, X.25 is now too slow for most corporate needs and, therefore, is a declining service. However, there are still many X.25 legacy connections, especially in countries with substandard telecommunications infrastructure and in Europe. Many exceed the traditional 56 kbps speed limit of X.25.

Among the services in Table 9.2, only X.25 is a reliable service. X.25 was made reliable because early transmission lines were less reliable than they are today, so the network had to compensate. Unfortunately, reliable service makes X.25 expensive for the speed it brings.

Frame Relay   Most **Frame Relay** vendors offer speeds of 56 kbps to about 40 Mbps. Note that these speeds correspond to the use of 56 kbps and T3 leased access lines. Intermediate speeds require the use of one or more T1 access lines.

Frame Relay is the most popular public switched data network today.[6] Although its speed is not blindingly fast, *its speed range matches the speed range of greatest corporate demand today, 56 kbps to a few megabits per second.* In fact, although Frame Relay goes up to about 40 Mbps, most demand lies at lower speeds.

---

[6] *PC Week,* "Frame Relay and ATM: High Stakes," 10/5/99, p. 17. Based on worldwide service and equipment revenue. Data were from the Vertical Systems Group.

In addition, competition among Frame Relay carriers has driven prices to very attractive levels. It may even be cheaper to connect two sites with Frame Relay than with a leased line. The relative simplicity of Frame Relay compared with ATM also accounts for its popularity.

ATM Chapter 8 noted that **asynchronous transfer mode (ATM)** switching offers extremely high speeds. Most ATM PSDN vendors offer speeds of 1 Mbps to 156 Mbps, with higher speeds coming. This requires access lines ranging from T1 through OC3. In addition, ATM offers quality of service (QoS) guarantees, including maximum latency and exact timing (see Chapter 1). ATM is a "Ferrari" service. Unfortunately, Ferraris are expensive, and so is ATM.

In local area networking, ATM has limited attractiveness because Ethernet offers comparable speeds at much lower prices. For WAN use, in turn, although ATM overlaps much of Frame Relay's speed range, Frame Relay is economically more attractive at lower speeds. ATM's main customers are firms that need higher WAN speeds. Lower ATM speeds are used primarily to connect a few smaller sites in such WANs.

For high-speed WANs, however, ATM is the only service that carriers offer today or that is under ITU-T development.[7] It is generally believed that, as corporate needs for high-speed, long-distance transmission grow, companies will move from Frame Relay to ATM for more and more of their corporate wide area networking needs.

Frame Relay–ATM Cooperation Frame Relay and ATM seem to be competitors. However, they generally are used at different speed ranges, so they really are complementary. In fact, most PSDN carriers offer both services. This allows them to serve the full range of corporate WAN needs. Some carriers even integrate their networks, allowing firms to use Frame Relay connections to lower-speed sites and ATM connections to higher-speed sites.

PSDNs Versus Meshes of Leased Lines

Figure 9.1 showed an organization that has constructed a mesh of leased lines to serve its many sites. Larger firms have built such networks and are comfortable with them. However, these companies are also concerned with the relatively high cost of leased line networks and the need for the firm to provide its own switching, management, and maintenance.

Traditional Leased Line Placement As Figure 9.5 illustrates, PSDN vendors normally make their services look a good deal like the network manager's

---

[7] However, some carriers may begin to offer IP over SONET, which will carry IP packets directly over physical-layer SONET/SDH connections, using PPP at the data link layer. In addition, there are efforts to create point-to-point connections based on the emerging 10 Gbps Ethernet standard, which will use optical fiber at the data link layer. This may be an economical alternative to OC192 SONET lines.

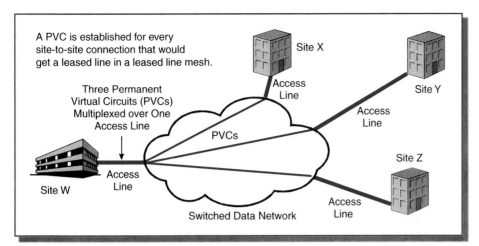

Figure 9.5
PSDN Similarities
to a Mesh of
Leased Lines

normal image of networks of leased lines. In leased line meshes, there often is a leased line running from each site to each other site.[8]

Virtual Circuit Placement Similarly, the PSDN customer normally sets up a virtual circuit between each pair of sites, as Figure 9.5 illustrates. These typically are **permanent virtual circuits (PVCs),** which are set up manually when a company subscribes first to the PSDN, and which usually change only when sites change. *The PVCs are created wherever the company previously had a leased line between the sites, so PVCs take the place of leased lines in the network manager's imagery.*

Access Line Speed Versus PVC Speed Note that there usually are full-duplex PVC connections from each site to several other sites. However, there is only one leased line from each site. This means that multiple PVCs have to be multiplexed over the leased access line. Therefore, it is important for the leased access line to be fast enough to serve these PVCs. If a site has fifteen 64-kbps PVCs to multiplex, this will require a leased access line with at least 840 kbps of capacity. From Table 9.1, this would require a T1 line.

Frame Relay's Frame Structure

Because of the dominance of Frame Relay, we should understand its basic operation. In Chapter 8, we saw the organization of ATM cells, which are fixed-length frames. The organization of these cells was fairly simple. A hierarchical virtual circuit number took up most of the 5-octet header. As Figure 9.6 illustrates, the Frame Relay frame is more complex.

---

[8] Often, some possible connections are left open because it is less expensive to reach some sites through intermediate sites than to have a full mesh.

Figure 9.6
Frame Relay
Frame
Organization

Overall Frame				
Flag 01111110	Address (2-4 octets) Shown Below	Information (variable)	FCS (2 octets)	Flag 01111110

4-Octet Address Field

Bit 1	2	3	4	5	6	7	Bit 8
Data Link Control Indicator (6 bits)						C/R 0/1	AE 0
Data Link Control Indicator (4 bits)				FECN	BECN	DE	AE 0
Data Link Control Indicator (7 bits)							AE 0
Data Link Control Indicator (7 bits)							AE 1

Notes:
AE = Address Extension bit.
BECN = Backward Explicit Congestion Notification bit.
C/R = Command/Response bit.
DE = Discard Eligible bit.
FCS = Frame Control Sequence.
FECN = Forward Explicit Congestion Notification bit.

Information Field The size of the Frame Relay information field is not fixed, unlike ATM's constant 48-octet data field size that we saw in the last chapter. Larger data fields minimize the overhead caused by the header and trailer fields, so Frame Relay has much lower overhead than ATM.

Flags The frame begins and ends with 1-octet **flag** fields, each of which has the value 01111110.[9] This eliminates the need for a size field.

Frame Check Sequence The **frame check sequence (FCS)** field allows each switch to check for errors. If the switch finds such an error, it merely discards the frame. There is no automatic retransmission, so Frame Relay is not reliable. This keeps its switching costs low.

Address Field The **address field** is fairly complex. There are three alternatives for Frame Relay's variable-length address field. These alternatives are two, three, and four octets long, respectively. Figure 9.6 shows the longest alternative.

Addressing (DLCI) The **data link control identifier (DLCI)** field identifies a specific virtual circuit. In the 4-octet address option, it has a total of 24 bits. This allows 1,024 (2^{24}) virtual circuits to be identified.

---

[9] What if the pattern 011111110 appears somewhere in the data being delivered? There is a process called "bit stuffing" that adds another "1" in the octet where the reserved 01111110 pattern appears.

Note that the DLCI does not give the address of the destination computer. Rather, it identifies the virtual circuit to which the frame belongs. This is similar to ATM addressing, which we saw in Chapter 8.

Address Extension Bit   The **address extension (AE)** bit is set to one if the octet it ends is the last octet in the address field. Otherwise, it is set to zero. For instance, if there are only two octets in the address field, the AE bit in the first octet is zero, and the AE bit in the second octet is one. The last two rows of the address field shown in Figure 9.6 would not exist.

Congestion Control   Three address fields are used for a crude form of congestion control in Frame Relay. These are the discard eligible, backward explicit congestion notification, and forward explicit congestion notification fields.

Discard Eligible   Some Frame Relay networks offer two speeds to customers. The lower rate—the **committed information rate (CIR)**—is guaranteed, although not completely. The higher rate—the **available bit rate (ABR)**—is for bursts at speeds above the CIR.

For transmissions within the CIR, the **discard eligible (DE)** bit is set to zero. For frames going faster than the CIR, the discard eligible bit is set to one. If frames must be discarded because of congestion, the Frame Relay carrier will first discard frames with the discard eligible set to one. Transmitting at the ABR is like flying standby.

Explicit Congestion Notification Fields   Although discarding frames relieves congestion, this is a drastic solution. As noted in Chapter 8, traffic shaping tells stations to reduce their speeds to avoid congestion. In Frame Relay there are two 1-bit explicit **congestion notification** fields. A switch detecting congestion sets one of these fields (makes its value one). The receiving station will see the explicit congestion notification field and act appropriately.

- The **Backward Explicit Congestion Notification (BECN)** field is set to tell the *station that receives the frame* to slow down when it transmits. This is easy to implement.
- The **Forward Explicit Congestion Notification (FECN)** field is more complex. If a station receives this notification in an incoming frame, *it should tell its communication partner at the other end* of the Frame Relay network to slow down.

Command/Response   The **command/response (C/R)** field is application-specific and is rarely used.

Frame Relay Pricing

It is important for networking professionals to know how to purchase PSDN service, especially Frame Relay service. Figure 9.7 shows the main pricing elements in Frame Relay service. We have already seen some of them. (ATM pricing is similar but more complex, thanks in large part to QoS considerations.)

Frame Relay Access Device (FRAD)   First, the company needs a **Frame Relay access device (FRAD).** Often a router, the FRAD connects the Frame

Figure 9.7
Pricing Elements
in Frame Relay
Service

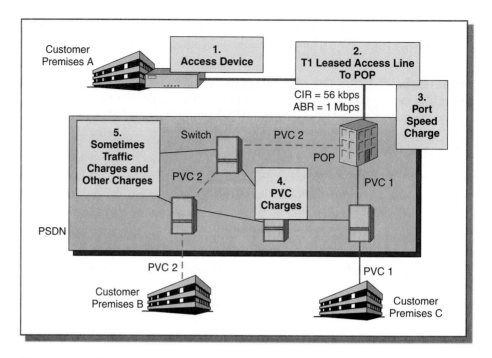

Relay network to the customer's internal network. The FRAD will have an interface offering a physical layer suited to the leased access line and a data link layer that implements Frame Relay.

FRADs usually are purchased from an equipment vendor, although the Frame Relay carrier may supply, install, and manage them for a fee.

Leased Access Line As just noted, the **leased access line** to the point of presence (POP) must be fast enough to serve all of the permanent virtual circuits it will multiplex.

Leased lines are expensive, so the location of the nearest POP is an important consideration in Frame Relay carrier selection. Some carriers have very few POPs, and their customers must use expensive, long-distance access lines to connect some or all sites to these carriers.

Often, you must get the leased access line from the local telephone company, rather than from the Frame Relay vendor. This can be problematic because, if there are technical difficulties, the leased access line carrier and the PSDN carrier may point fingers at one another as being the cause of the problem. *Leased access lines fees* often are billed at a flat monthly rate.

Port Speed At the POP, your leased access line connects to a **port** on the PSDN switch. Common **port speeds** are 56 kbps and 1 Mbps, although faster port speeds may be available. The cost of a port typically depends on its speed. *The port fee usually is the largest single element in Frame Relay pricing.*

It is important for the leased access line speed to be at least as fast as the port speed, to prevent wasting expensive port capacity. For instance, for a port operating at 1 Mbps, you would need a T1 line (1.544 Mbps).

Cost per PVC There will be a *monthly fee per permanent virtual circuit.* The price usually depends on the speed of the PVC.

Committed and Available Bit Rates As noted earlier in this chapter, some Frame Relay vendors offer two rates, namely a committed information rate (CIR) and an available bit rate (ABR). The maximum burst speed is the available bit rate. If CIR and ABR are offered for PVCs, ports, or both, pricing will reflect both speeds. Leased access lines must be fast enough to handle available bit rates.

Other Considerations Frame Relay carriers vary in their approaches to pricing. This makes it very difficult to compare the offerings of competing services. The variables we have just seen usually are the main service parameters, but there can be others.

- Usually, vendors do not charge per bit sent. However, some do build per-bit **traffic charges** into their pricing systems.
- A growing number of Frame Relay vendors offer **switched virtual circuits (SVCs),** which are established on a call-by-call basis. These are costly to set up and drop after use because setup and teardown require a considerable amount of switch processing time, so there is a charge per SVC creation. Some services now offer **soft PVCs** that generally are permanent but are changed as needed if there are service disruptions.
- Most PSDN carriers offer managed Frame Relay service, which provides detailed performance and error information, usually for less than $100 per month per site.
- Finally, there usually are substantial initial **set-up charges** to install a Frame Relay access device, a leased line, a port connection, or a PVC.

Test Your Understanding

Answer Core Review Questions 4–10, Detailed Review Questions 3–8, and Thought Questions 2–6.

VIRTUAL PRIVATE NETWORKS (VPNs)

In many companies, all sites are already connected to the Internet. These Internet connections are already being paid for, so why not use the Internet for site-to-site transmission instead of using a commercial PSDN? When companies implement their site-to-site communication via the Internet, they are said to have **virtual private networks (VPNs).**[10] Figure 9.8 illustrates a VPN.

---

[10] Some authors extend the concept of VPNs to include the use of public switched data networks with added security, as well as the use of the Internet with added security.

Figure 9.8
Virtual Private
Network (VPN)

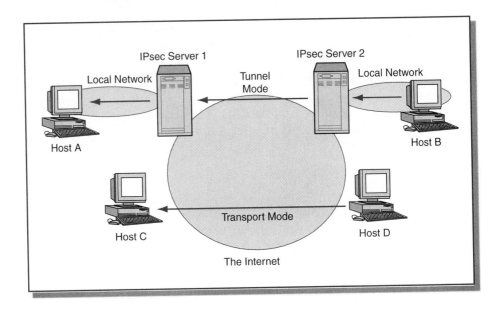

Problems with VPNs

Although the use of relatively inexpensive Internet connections for site-to-site transmission is attractive, there are two serious problems with using the Internet.

Congestion The most obvious problem with the Internet is congestion. For residential use, slowdowns are annoying. For business use, slowdowns are crippling.

Security Another problem with the Internet is its lack of security. The Internet, created in the early 1980s, was designed in a more benign era when security was not a major concern. TCP, IP, and other standards were never created to be secure.

Solving Problems with VPNs

Although congestion and security are formidable problems, firms have begun to attack them.

Security For security, the Internet Engineering Task Force (IETF) is developing a set of internet layer security standards collectively called **IPsec** (IP Security). As Figure 9.8 illustrates, IPsec offers two forms of security, called *modes of operation.*

The simplest mode is **transport mode,** in which two hosts have end-to-end security across the Internet. The two end stations (Hosts C and D in Figure 9.8) handle all security. No other devices need to be involved.

In **tunnel mode,** there is an **IPsec server** at each site. When Host B in Figure 9.8 transmits, the IPsec security server at its site (IPsec Server 2) intercepts the packet and sends the packet securely across the Internet to the IPsec server at the other site. There, IPsec Server 1 passes the packet over the local network to Host A. In tunnel mode, the two end hosts (Host A and Host B) do not have to worry about IPsec security. The servers do all the work. IPsec security is transparent to the two hosts.

The two modes can even be combined. Host A and Host B can establish an end-to-end transport mode connection. A tunnel mode connection can then further protect packets between the two IPsec servers. Tunnel mode provides some protections that transport mode does not. The transport mode connection, in turn, protects packets within the local networks, which tunnel mode security does not.

Although current IPsec standards are fairly good—and products based on IPsec standards exist—there are still missing features in the standard, and existing products have imperfect interoperability. Widespread use is not likely to begin until IPsec standards and products are more mature and until products are more interoperable. Module F discusses IPsec in more detail.

Congestion Congestion control requires an understanding of Internet congestion problems. As Figure 9.9 indicates, each site must connect to an Internet service provider (ISP). ISPs usually are connected via the Internet backbone. Generally speaking, the ISPs are not congested. Rather, *the Internet backbone is the source of most congestion*. When Site A sends to Site B, the packets are likely to be slowed down in the Internet backbone.

To avoid congestion, it is necessary to *avoid the Internet backbone*. In Figure 9.9, Site A and Site C avoid the congestion of the Internet backbone by connecting to the same ISP. To connect sites within a firm, it is easy to use a single ISP because several ISPs offer nationwide or even worldwide service. Connecting to the ISP's access node in each city allows sites to communicate via transmission lines and routers owned by the ISP. A growing number of ISPs offer service level agreements (SLAs), which offer various quality of service (QoS) guarantees such as maximum latency.[11]

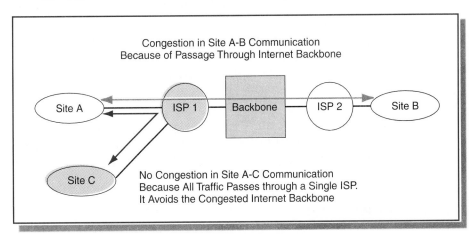

Figure 9.9
Using a Single Internet Service Provider (ISP)

---

[11] Some ISPs "peer" even with other ISPs, connecting to each other directly, without going through the Internet backbone and offering end-to-end service level agreements for traffic across through both ISP systems.

Test Your Understanding

Answer Core Review Question 11 and Detailed Review Question 8.

KEY POINTS

Carriers, Regulation, and Deregulation When you move beyond your customer premises, you must use the services of carriers, which have rights of way to install wires and radio transmission facilities where needed. Carriers usually file tariffs, which specify the services they offer and the prices of these services. There is a general trend toward deregulating carrier services.

Leased Line Networks Leased lines are dedicated point-to-point circuits between sites. By leasing these circuits and then adding switching and management, companies can create wide area networks to link all their sites together. Leased line speeds range from 56 kbps to a few gigabits per second, but *the range of greatest corporate demand is 56 kbps to a few megabits per second.*

Public Switched Data Networks Leased line networks are expensive to plan, create, and maintain because the organization must supply all switching and perform all the other labor needed to get their leased lines to act as a complete network. In contrast, public switched data networks (PSDNs) make life easier for corporate networking staffs by handling most planning, switching, and maintenance functions. Overall, PSDNs are less expensive than leased line meshes in most circumstances and their use is increasing explosively, whereas the use of leased line networking is shrinking.

The most popular public switched data network is Frame Relay, which offers speeds in the range of greatest corporate demand (56 kbps to a few megabits per second). As the demand for higher speeds grows, companies are expected to turn increasingly to ATM. In this chapter, we looked at the complexities of Frame Relay pricing, which includes FRAD charges, leased access line charges, port charges, PVC charges, and sometimes other charges as well.

Virtual Private Networks Virtual private networks (VPNs) use the Internet for site-to-site transmission. However, companies add security through IPsec servers and sometimes send all communication through a single ISP in order to avoid the congested Internet backbone.

REVIEW QUESTIONS

For questions with multiple parts, write the answer to each question in a separate line or paragraph.

Core Review Questions

1. **a)** Why do we need carriers in wide area networking? **b)** What is deregulation? **c)** Why is it being done? **d)** What two things does a tariff describe?

2. **a)** What are leased lines? **b)** How can companies build WANs to link their sites using leased lines? **c)** What is undesirable about WANs created using leased lines? **d)** What is the slowest North American digital leased line? **e)** What is the designation for its signaling? **f)** What is the speed of a T1 leased line? **g)** What is the designation for its signaling?

3. **a)** What is the speed of an E1 leased line? **b)** What standards govern the fastest leased lines? **c)** In the future, how will DSL change things at low speeds?

4. **a)** Spell out "PSDN." **b)** Why are PSDNs attractive to corporations for site-to-site wide area networking, compared with networks of leased lines? **c)** Why is the PSDN network usually shown as a cloud? **d)** Do PSDNs eliminate the need for leased lines? Explain. **e)** Do PSDNs use fewer leased lines than networks of leased lines?

5. **a)** Are most PSDNs reliable or unreliable? **b)** Do most packet switched PSDNs use virtual circuits? **c)** What specific single benefit do the answers in a) and b) bring? If you mention cost, be sure to mention the cost of specific things.

6. **a)** Do most PSDNs use packet switching or circuit switching? **b)** What benefit does this most widely used type of switching bring? If you mention cost, be sure to mention the cost of specific things (trunk lines, switches, etc.).

7. **a)** What is the most popular PSDN service? **b)** Why is it the most popular?

8. **a)** What is the fastest PSDN? **b)** As the need for speed increases, why are most user organizations likely to adopt this service?

9. **a)** Is the length of a Frame Relay frame fixed or variable? **b)** Why does this reduce overhead? **c)** Is the address field of a Frame Relay frame fixed or variable? **d)** Does the address field contain a destination address or a virtual circuit number? **e)** What is the virtual circuit number called? **f)** Briefly, in what two ways does Frame Relay implement congestion control?

10. **a)** Make a table showing the main cost components in Frame Relay pricing and to what organization each is paid.

11. **a)** What is a virtual private network (VPN)? **b)** What two problems must it overcome? **c)** How does it overcome them?

Detailed Review Questions

1. Give the speeds of the following leased lines: **a)** Fractional T1, **b)** T3, **c)** E3, and **d)** the slowest four SONET/SDH leased lines. **e)** What is the designation for T3's signaling?

2. Why should SONET/SDH be very reliable?

3. Briefly characterize **a)** ISDN, **b)** X.25, **c)** Frame Relay, and **d)** ATM.

4. Why should today's packet switched PSDNs really be called frame-switched PSDNs?

5. What in PSDN service corresponds to individual leased lines in leased line wide area networking?

6. In detail, in what two ways does Frame Relay implement congestion control?

7. **a)** Distinguish between committed information rates and available bit rates in Frame Relay pricing. **b)** Which of these two rates should guide the selection of leased access line speed?

8. Distinguish between transport mode and tunnel mode in IPsec.

Thought Questions

1. What was the most surprising thing you learned in this chapter?

2. What was the most difficult part of this chapter for you?

3. You have a Frame Relay port speed of 800 kbps. What kind of leased access line will you get? Justify your choice.

4. You have 10 PVCs of 56 kbps each. **a)** What speed leased line will you use? **b)** What port speed will you need? Choices for this part of the question are 56 kbps, 128 kbps, 256 kbps, 384 kbps, 1 Mbps, 2 Mbps, and 40 Mbps.

5. **a)** Redraw the address field in Figure 9.6 to be a 3-octet address field. **b)** How many DLCI bits will there be? **c)** Redraw the address field in Figure 9.6 to be a 2-octet address field. **d)** How many DLCI bits will there be?

6. **a)** If a new PSDN were defined, do you think it would it be packet switched or circuit switched? Justify your answer. **b)** Would it be reliable or unreliable? Justify your answer. **c)** Would it offer alternative routes or constrain transmissions to virtual circuits? Justify your answer.

7. In the vignette at the beginning of this chapter, **a)** why did Ms. Chen wish to change the way the company linked its sites? **b)** What concerns did she have? **c)** What would you tell her boss about moving to a VPN?

Case Studies

For case studies, go to the book's website, **http://www.prenhall.com/panko**, and look at the "Case Studies" page for this chapter.

Projects

1. **Getting Current.** Go to the book's website's "New Information" and "Errors" pages for this chapter to get new information since this book went to press and to correct any errors in the text.

2. **Internet Exercises.** Go to the book's website's "Exercises" page for this chapter and do the Internet exercises.

Chapter 10

Security

$\mathcal{J}$ohn Crais, the general manager of Claire Cunningham's manufacturing site, frequently works at home. When he does, he accesses the corporate network via the Internet. Claire has long been concerned about home access through the Internet. She recently gave John an intrusion detection program. Its job is to tell him when someone is trying to attack the computer.

When John installed the program, he was startled to find frequent Internet attacks. He noted these attacks and brought his list to Claire. After looking over the list, Claire said that all were relatively innocuous "scanning" attacks that looked for TCP and UDP ports on which the user's PC will accept application messages. However, these scanning attacks can be preludes to more direct attacks. If hackers find vulnerable ports, they may be able to crash John's system or even take it over, read his files, access the corporate network in his name, and erase his hard disk drive.

Claire went on to explain that many Internet intruders today have automated hacker software that allows them to direct scanning attacks at large numbers of user PCs and servers very quickly. Other hacker software allows even unsophisticated hackers to implement dangerous hacks once weaknesses are found. She referred to most intruders as "script kiddies" because of their young age and their reliance on hacker software. However, she warned that the Internet has quite a few more sophisticated hackers as well.

Claire gave John a "personal firewall" program to install on his machine. This program could stop most Internet hacks. John installed the personal firewall program. Every few weeks, however, he has to upgrade his program's database to deal with newly discovered hacks. ∎

INTRODUCTION

When the Internet was born, little thought was given to security. In those benign times, hacking was infrequent and, by today's standards, very mild. Internal corporate networks also had little security. As noted in Chapters 6 and 7, for instance, Ethernet hubs broadcast all bits to all stations. Ethernet relies on the integrity of station owners not to read messages that are addressed to others.

Today, however, security incidents are on the rise everywhere. **Hackers** frequently break into corporate, government, and even military systems. The Computer Emergency Response Team (CERT) Coordination Center, which monitors serious security incidents on the Internet, handled only 132 incidents in 1989. In contrast, in the first half of 1999 alone, it handled over 4,000 incidents.[1] Most disturbingly, modern Internet hackers have automated hacking programs that allow even unsophisticated hackers to wreak havoc with corporate networks and computers. However, although Internet hackers have received wide press coverage, internal corporate break-ins by employees and ex-employees are still the biggest security problems in organizations.

In this chapter, we will look first at the individual elements of security, especially encryption and authentication. We will then see how these elements are combined into complete integrated security systems. We will finish with discussions of Internet firewalls and other security issues.

ENCRYPTION

The most basic building block of security is **encryption,** which scrambles a message before transmission, so that an interceptor cannot read the message as it flows over the network. However, the receiver knows how to **decrypt** (descramble) the encrypted message, making it readable again.

---

[1] CERT Coordination Center, CERT/CC Statistics 1988-1999, Carnegie-Mellon University, http://www.cert.org/stats/cert_stats.html, as of October 1999.

Encryption provides **privacy,** which is also called **confidentiality.** Both terms mean that messages can be transmitted without fear of their being read by adversaries. If you are transmitting your credit card number over a network, or if a bank is transmitting an electronic transaction, privacy (confidentiality) is critical. Later in this chapter, we will see that encryption is also used to achieve other security goals.

The Encryption Process

We have spoken vaguely of encryption as "scrambling" and of decryption as "descrambling." Figure 10.1 looks more closely at encryption and introduces more precise terminology.

Plaintext and Ciphertext Before a message is encrypted, it is called **plaintext.** In Figure 10.1, the plaintext message is "Transfer $5,000." We need to encrypt this plaintext before transmission and, after transmission, decrypt the transmission back to the original plaintext.

You should be aware that the word "plaintext" is somewhat misleading. Although "plaintext" suggests that encryption only works with text messages, such as "Transfer $5,000," it can work with *any* type of data, including graphics, video, and database information. Whatever is to be encrypted is called the plaintext.

After a plaintext message is encrypted, we call the stream of bits that encryption generates the **ciphertext.** We show ciphertext as a random stream of ones and zeros in Figure 10.1. This is exactly how an interceptor would see it. We send ciphertext through the network rather than plaintext.

Encryption: Methodology and Key

Figure 10.1 also looks more closely at encryption. It shows that there are two elements in encryption: an **encryption method** and a **key.** The encryption method specifies the mathematical process that will be used in the encryption.

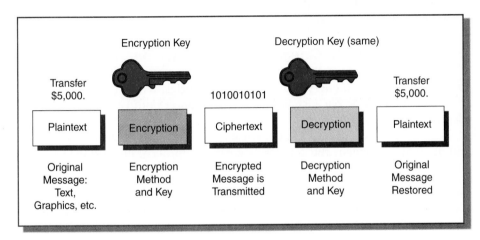

Figure 10.1
Symmetric Key Encryption

In practice, it is very difficult to keep the method secret. Methods are easy to identify because there are only a few encryption methods in use. Furthermore, we would not want to have to change methods every time someone discovered our method, because this would be very expensive.

Fortunately, each encryption method uses a special string of bits called a **key.** Different key values will give different results with the same encryption method. To maintain secrecy, it is necessary to keep only the key secret, not the encryption method itself.

Exhaustive Search and Key Length   Even if you keep your key secret, adversaries may discover it through **exhaustive search,** in which they simply try all possible keys. For instance, if your key is only two bits long, there are only four possibilities: 00, 01, 10, and 11. Only two tries, on average, would be needed to decrypt your message.

To make exhaustive search too expensive to be useful, it is necessary to use long keys. A key is nothing more than a string of ones and zeros. In general, if there are N bits in the key, there will be 2^N possible keys. For instance, if we have a key length of 8 bits, there will be 256 possible keys. A key length of 16 bits gives 65,536 possible keys. On average, exhaustive search will need to try half of the possible keys to be successful.

Thanks to the high speeds of computers today, exhaustive search is quite effective. Key lengths of 40 and even 56 bits can now be cracked fairly quickly, although at a high cost that would make the stealing of consumer credit card numbers economically silly. However, for bank transfers, cracking keys with 40 or 56 bits is or will soon be economically attractive. Encryption with keys that have fewer than about 100 bits is called **weak encryption.**

Companies must use **strong encryption,** which means key lengths of at least 100 bits today. As computer speeds increase in the next few years, even 512 bits may soon be considered weak.[2] Some forms of encryption already use keys of 512 to 4,096 bits.

However, strong encryption comes at a price. Encryption and decryption are complex processes. If encryption is done in software, calculations using long key lengths will cause encryption to use up much of your computer's total processing power. Key length must be chosen to balance risks, user resources, and the resources of adversaries.

Encryption Method Categories and Encryption Algorithms   As Figure 10.2 illustrates, there are many encryption methods. In general, these methods fall into two **encryption method categories,** which are *symmetric key encryption* and *public key encryption.* We will look at both categories in some depth.

Within these two categories, there are numerous specific **encryption algorithms** that implement the category's general approach. For instance, under

---

[2] Harrison, Ann, "Bankers Anticipate Code-Breaking Machine," *Computerworld,* 5/18/99. http://www.computerworld.com/home/print.nsf/all/990517A63A.

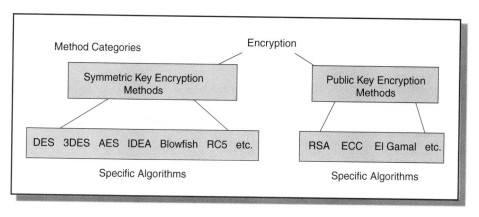

Figure 10.2
Encryption
Categories and
Algorithms

symmetric key encryption, there are the DES, 3DES, AES, IDEA, Blowfish, and RC5 algorithms. Under public key encryption, common algorithms include RSA, elliptical curve cryptosystem (ECC), and El Gamal.

Symmetric Key Encryption

We will look first at symmetric key encryption, which is the simplest form of encryption. Figure 10.1 specifically illustrates symmetric key encryption.

The Process

Figure 10.1 shows that **symmetric key encryption** has a *single key* that is used by both communication partners.

- When Party A sends to Party B, Party A encrypts with the single symmetric key and Party B decrypts with the same key.
- When Party B transmits to Party A, in turn, Party B encrypts with the single symmetric key and Party A decrypts with the same key.

This is called symmetric key encryption because the encryption process is symmetrical: the same key both encrypts and decrypts.

The Key Distribution Problem with Symmetric Key Encryption

One problem with symmetric key encryption is that both parties must keep the symmetric key secret. Anyone else learning the key can intercept messages and read them. Getting the key secretly to both parties can be quite difficult. We will look at general key distribution later in this chapter.

Key distribution is a special problem in symmetric key encryption because *each pair* of partners needs a different key, as Figure 10.3 illustrates. If there are N users, each of which may need to communicate with every other user, then N*(N – 1)/2 symmetric keys would be needed. For only 100 users, this would mean 4,950 keys!

DES   There are many specific symmetric key encryption algorithms. Probably the most widely used is the **data encryption standard (DES),** which

Figure 10.3
Key Distribution
for Symmetric
Keys

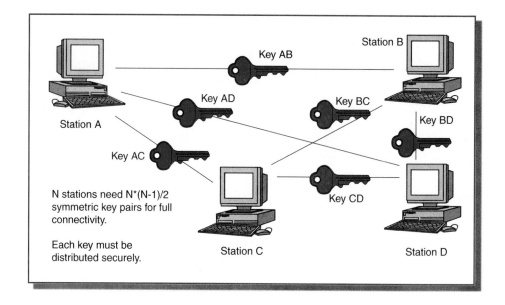

was created in the 1970s by IBM for the U.S. **National Institute for Standards and Technology (NIST).**

DES breaks the plaintext into chunks of 64 bits. It then encrypts each chunk of plaintext using a 64-bit key. However, it is proper to say that DES uses a 56-bit key, because 8 of the key bits are redundant (can be computed from the other 56), to check for incorrect keys. At the other end, each 64-bit chunk is decrypted back to plaintext.

Triple DES (3DES)   With a key length of only 56 bits, DES is no longer considered adequate for applications such as electronic funds transfer. However, it is probably quite safe for consumer Internet credit card purchases, where it does not pay for someone to use thousands of dollars of computer time to steal your credit card number.

Many security systems now use a stronger variant of DES called **Triple DES** or **3DES.** As the name suggests, 3DES involves applying the DES algorithm three times instead of once. However, this has to be done with more than one key to be successful.

Normally, the algorithm is applied three times to a block of 64 bits with a different key each time. This gives an effective key length of 168 bits (3 times 56). Sometimes, only two keys are involved in the three applications of DES.[3] This gives an effective key length of 112 bits.

---

[3] The sending process encrypts with the first key, *decrypts* (not a typographical error) with the second key and encrypts again with the first key. The receiver decrypts with the first key, *encrypts* (that's right) with the second key, and decrypts again with the first key. Decryption and encryption are opposite processes. It is often possible to send information securely by decryption to scramble the message and encryption to recover it.

Other Symmetric Key Encryption Algorithms   DES and 3DES are not the only symmetric key encryption algorithms. In fact, NIST is currently selecting among candidates for a new-generation **advanced encryption system (AES),** which will use much larger keys. There also are several other symmetric key encryption algorithms in use today, including Blowfish, IDEA (International Data Encryption Algorithm), and RC5.

Public Key Encryption

Symmetric key encryption is one of two popular encryption method categories. The other is **public key encryption,** which Figure 10.4 illustrates. Recall that in symmetric key encryption, both parties use a single key to encrypt and decrypt. In contrast, in public key encryption, when one party sends to another, there are *two* keys: the *receiver's public key* and the *receiver's private key.* Note also that both of these keys are those of the *receiver,* not of the sender. In this case, the receiver is Party A.

Public Key   First, there is the receiver's **public key.** As its name suggests, a public key is not secret. Party A can send this key to Parties B, C, and D over nonsecure connections. If someone intercepts Party A's public key, this will do them no good.

As Figure 10.4 shows, everyone encrypts messages to Party A with Party A's (the receiver's) public key. This scrambles the message into ciphertext so that unauthorized parties cannot read the message.

Private Key   Second, there is the receiver's **private key.** As Figure 10.4 illustrates, when the ciphertext arrives, Party A decrypts the message with its own **private key.** Party A can then read the plaintext message. As the name of this

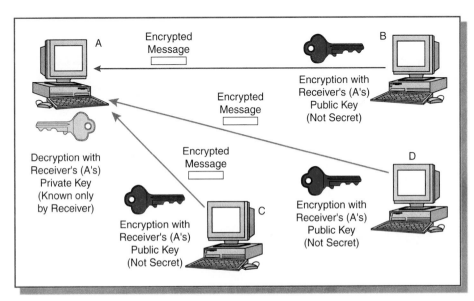

Figure 10.4
Public Key
Encryption

key suggests, Party A keeps its private key secret. Only Party A should know its private key.

The Sender Cannot Decrypt After Encrypting Now return briefly to the sender, Party B. After encrypting the plaintext message with Party A's public key, Party B cannot decrypt the ciphertext afterward. Quite simply, the sender does not have the receiver's private key, and only the receiver's private key can decrypt the ciphertext after the message is encrypted with the receiver's public key. Once a message is encrypted with public key encryption, only the receiver can decrypt it. Of course, anyone stealing the receiver's private key also can decrypt it, so it is critical to keep private keys secret.

Two-Way Public Key Encryption We saw earlier in this chapter that symmetric key encryption uses a single key when two parties communicate, regardless of who is encrypting or decrypting. Figure 10.5 illustrates this situation.

In contrast, in public key encryption, there are *four* keys in two-way communication. As Figure 10.5 also shows, each party has its own private and public key. Each party *encrypts with other party's public key* to send a message. Each party *decrypts with its own private key* when it receives a message.

Public Key Distribution We saw that symmetric key distribution has problems. First, there must be a unique symmetric key for each pair of communicating partners. Second, this key must be delivered securely. In contrast, as Figure 10.6 illustrates, public key distribution is much simpler. For N communicating partners, there are only N public keys—one for each party, not one

Figure 10.5
Two-Way Communication with Symmetric Key and Public Key Encryption

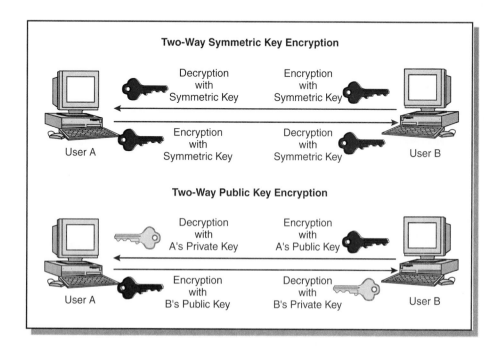

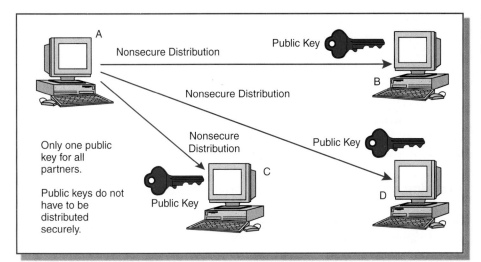

Figure 10.6
Public Key
Distribution

for each pair. For N users, only N private key–public keys pairs are needed, not N*(N – 1)/2.

Each party, furthermore, can distribute its public key to all other partners over nonsecure links. Of course, N private keys must be distributed securely, but these often come embedded in hardware or software when a computer or application program is delivered.

The Problem of Speed One true problem with public key encryption and decryption is that they are about a hundred times slower than symmetric key encryption and decryption. Part of this speed disadvantage is the inherent complexity of public key encryption and decryption. In addition, public key encryption uses much larger keys (usually 150 to a few thousand bits) than symmetric key encryption (usually 40 to 200 bits). This also increases processing time.

Public key encryption cannot encrypt and decrypt long messages fast enough for most purposes. As a consequence, public key encryption is only used to encrypt brief messages. Later on, we will see two uses of encrypting short messages with public key encryption: digital signatures and symmetric key distribution.

Message Limit Based on Key Size There is another factor limiting the size of messages that can be encrypted with public key encryption. Most public key encryption algorithms are limited mathematically to encrypting messages smaller than or equal to the size of the public key. Public keys often are fairly long, for instance 1,024 bits or longer. However, while this is long for a key, it is short for a message.

Common Public Key Algorithms Recall, from Figure 10.2, that public key encryption is an encryption method *category*. Specific products must use specific public key encryption *algorithms*.

RSA   The most popular public key encryption algorithm is **RSA,** which is owned by RSA Security. RSA is widely used in commercial public key encryption. RSA should be even more popular because RSA's patent protection ended in 2000. RSA is now in the public domain and can be incorporated in systems without the payment of royalties. RSA typically uses keys of 1,024 bits or more.

Elliptical Curve Cryptosystems   Another set of algorithms uses elliptical curve encryption, which can use much smaller keys than RSA to give comparable security,[4] reducing encryption and decryption processing time.

Cracking the Private Key Computation Problem   The process of generating public key–private key pairs is based on certain mathematical operations. *Computing a private key if you know its corresponding public key* appears to be extremely difficult to do, so that only exhaustive search can find private keys. However, there is no proof that finding the private key can be solved only through exhaustive search. One of the great nightmares in security is that someone will find a fast way to compute private keys from known public keys. This would make all private keys immediately vulnerable. New technologies now in research labs may in fact make fast private key computation possible in the next few years, requiring us to use ever-larger keys.

Test Your Understanding

Answer Core Review Questions 1–4, Detailed Review Questions 1–3, and Thought Question 3.

AUTHENTICATION

One purpose of encryption is to prevent anyone who intercepts a message from being able to read the message. Encryption brings *confidentiality,* which is also called *privacy.* In contrast, **authentication** has a different purpose, namely *to prove the sender's identity.* If we get a message claiming to be from someone, we want to be certain it is not really coming from someone else.

Forms of Authentication

There are many forms of authentication. We will look briefly at four and then look in more detail at public key authentication. *All forms of authentication require senders to demonstrate that they have something or know something that only the true party should have or know.*

Passwords   In the simplest case, the true party might have a **password.** However, passwords offer only a weak form of authentication. Many people

---

[4] ECC with a 160-bit key gives security comparable to RSA with a 1,024-bit key. Randall K. Nichols, *ICSA Guide to Cryptosystems,* McGraw-Hill, 1999, p. 248.

select passwords that are common words. There are only a few thousand common words, so exhaustive search becomes almost trivial.

If users are given long and meaningless passwords, in turn, they either write them down or have their computer remember them (allowing anyone using their computer to pose as them).

Users must be required to create relatively long passwords with at least 8 characters. They must also be required to place a numerical digit somewhere in the password and, if possible, to insert a change in case. An example would be "triV7ial." This makes exhaustive search through common words useless.

Of course, having a good password is worthless if the user has his or her computer remember important passwords so that anyone walking up to their computer can impersonate them. Often, elaborate security schemes are guarded by nonsecure passwords or by passwords that are rendered useless by user actions.

Authentication Cards Automated teller machines use **authentication cards** that contain coded information. Users swipe them through a card reader slot and usually type a password as well. Computers also are beginning to use authentication cards. These cards are safer than passwords alone, unless users write their passwords on their authentication cards.

Biometrics **Biometric authentication** measures body dimensions. *Fingerprint analyzers* are inexpensive and fairly good. At the other extreme, *iris analyzers,* which look at the iris in one of your eyes, are much more precise but also much more expensive. Currently, biometric products suffer from a lack of vendor interoperability because there are no effective standards.

Public Key Authentication Recall that private keys must be kept secret. Therefore, *if a person or other entity can demonstrate possession of their private key, the person or entity will be authenticated.* Of course, if a person or other entity loses the secrecy of the private key, then others easily can impersonate the person or entity. Many communication partners already have private keys, so public key authentication is very popular.

Public Key Challenge–Response Authentication

Figure 10.7 illustrates one basic way to implement public key authentication. This is **public key challenge–response authentication.** In this form of authentication there is a **verifier,** which wishes to authenticate the identity of its communication partner, the **applicant.**

Challenge Message First, the verifier creates a short plaintext message called the **challenge message.** The challenge message has to be short because it will be encrypted with public key encryption, which is good only for short messages. The verifier sends this plaintext to the applicant.

Figure 10.7
Public Key
Challenge–
Response
Authentication

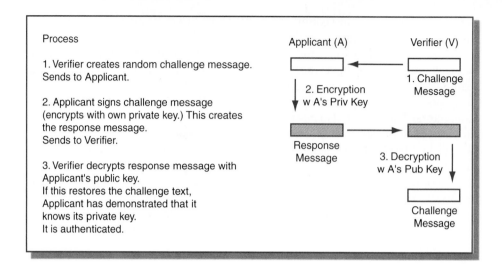

Response Message   Second, the applicant encrypts the challenge message with the applicant's *own private key*. This creates the **response message.** The applicant sends this response message back to the verifier.[5]

Authentication   Third, the verifier attempts to decrypt the response message using the applicant's known public key. If the public key successfully decrypts the response message back to the original challenge message, then the applicant holds the private key of the person or entity the applicant claims to be. Only the authentic person should know this private key. The applicant is authenticated.

Encrypting with the Private Key?   Note that encryption does not always have to go in the usual direction. In public key encryption algorithms, it is possible to encrypt with the private key and decrypt with the public key.

Public Key Encryption for Privacy and Authenticity   Note that to use public key encryption *for privacy (confidentiality), the sender encrypts with the public key of the receiver.* In contrast, *for authentication, the sender encrypts with the sender's private key.* One way to remember this is that each partner needs to know only its own private key and the public key of its partner.

Public Key Authentication Through Digital Signatures

Although challenge–response authentication is good, it only authenticates the user once or at best occasionally during a working session. We also would like to be able to authenticate *each message* that an applicant sends. **Digital signatures** allow us to do that. Figure 10.8 illustrates how digital signatures work.

---

[5] Of course, it may also encrypt the response text message, say with the verifier's public key.

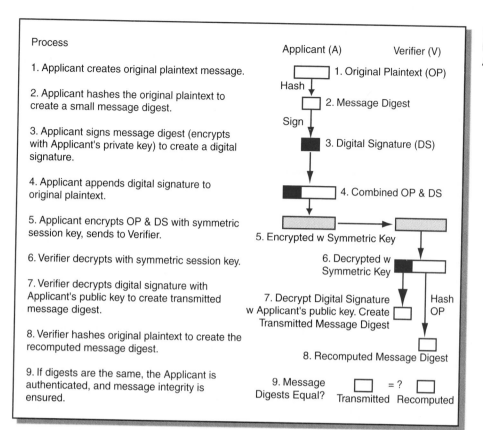

Figure 10.8
Digital Signature
Authentication

Process

1. Applicant creates original plaintext message.

2. Applicant hashes the original plaintext to create a small message digest.

3. Applicant signs message digest (encrypts with Applicant's private key) to create a digital signature.

4. Applicant appends digital signature to original plaintext.

5. Applicant encrypts OP & DS with symmetric session key, sends to Verifier.

6. Verifier decrypts with symmetric session key.

7. Verifier decrypts digital signature with Applicant's public key to create transmitted message digest.

8. Verifier hashes original plaintext to create the recomputed message digest.

9. If digests are the same, the Applicant is authenticated, and message integrity is ensured.

Applicant (A)   Verifier (V)

1. Original Plaintext (OP)
Hash
2. Message Digest
Sign
3. Digital Signature (DS)

4. Combined OP & DS

5. Encrypted w Symmetric Key

6. Decrypted w Symmetric Key

7. Decrypt Digital Signature w Applicant's public key. Create Transmitted Message Digest   Hash OP

8. Recomputed Message Digest

9. Message Digests Equal?   = ?   Transmitted   Recomputed

Limits of Public Key Encryption   Although public key encryption has many virtues, we noted earlier that it is incredibly processing-intensive, requiring about a hundred times as many CPU cycles per message as symmetric key encryption. This means that, in practice, public key encryption and authentication can only be used with small messages. Unfortunately, many messages are very long.

Creating a Message Digest with Hashing   Public key encryption and authentication are too expensive to apply to long messages; however, they are economical for the brief values created by hashing. **Hashing** *takes a message of any length and computes a small bit string of fixed length.* The two most popular hashing algorithms, **MD5** and the **Secure Hash Algorithm 1 (SHA-1),** create hashes that are 128 bits and 160 bits long respectively, no matter how long the original message is.

Hashing is not encryption because hashing is *not reversible.* There is nothing like decryption that could get back the long original message from the brief hash. Nor is hashing a form of compression, because there is nothing like decompression. Hashing is a one-way function.

As Figure 10.8 illustrates, the applicant hashes the long original plaintext message, which results in a brief **message digest.**

Signing the Message Digest to Create the Digital Signature   The applicant then **signs** the message digest, meaning that he or she encrypts the message digest with the applicant's own private key. The resulting ciphertext is called a **digital signature.**

Message Digest Versus Digital Signature   Note that there is an important difference between the *message digest* and the *digital signature*. The message digest is merely a hash of the original plaintext message. It is not encrypted. (Encryption can be undone by decryption, but there is no way to recreate a whole message from its brief hashed value.) The digital signature, in turn, is the encrypted form of the message digest. The message digest is plaintext, whereas the digital signature is ciphertext.

Sending the Message   To transmit the message, the applicant adds the digital signature to the original plaintext and sends the combined message to the receiver.

Usually, this combined message is encrypted with symmetric key encryption, which is fast enough for large messages. This symmetric key encryption is not for authentication purposes. It is done so that an interceptor will not be able to read the original plaintext message to which the digital signature is added.

Keep in mind that sending the original plaintext message securely is the applicant's ultimate goal. Authentication is only done so that the receiver (the verifier) will accept the message. Encrypting the combined original plaintext and digital signature is critical for the ultimate goal.

Receiving the Message   The verifier first decrypts the combined message if it has been encrypted with symmetric key encryption.

Verifying the Digital Signature   Next, the verifier decrypts the digital signature with the applicant's nonsecret public key, restoring the message digest. We will call this the **transmitted message digest.**

To verify the transmitted message digest, the verifier uses the same hashing algorithm that the applicant used and applies this hashing algorithm to the transmitted original plaintext message. No key is necessary because hashing usually does not use keys. Applying the same hashing algorithm to the same string of bits always gives the same output. This step gives what we will call the **recomputed message digest.**

Authentication   If the transmitted and recomputed message digests match, then the sender has proven that they hold their own private key. Only the authentic person should know this private key. The message is authenticated.

Integrity   Digital signatures do more than authenticate the message. One security threat is that someone will intercept a message en route, change it, and then send it on again. For instance, Jones might intercept a message saying

"Credit Smith's account with $100" and change it to "Credit Jones' account with $1,000,000."

However, if a change is made, the transmitted and recomputed message digests will not match. The receiver (the verifier) will know that there has been a transmission error, that the sender is an impostor, or that an adversary has changed the message. All three are bad. It will discard the message.

When the receiver can detect changes made to the message en route, we have **message integrity.** Integrity can be as important as authentication. It is an important by-product of digital signatures.

Test Your Understanding

Answer Core Review Questions 5 and 6, Detailed Review Questions 4–6, and Thought Question 6.

DIGITAL CERTIFICATES AND PUBLIC KEY INFRASTRUCTURE (PKI)

The Problem of Trusting Public Keys

Unfortunately, public key encryption can be used deceptively. For instance, in Figure 10.9, an *impostor* claims to be a certain *true person* in an effort to deceive the *verifier.*

First, the impostor sends its own (the impostor's) public key to the verifier. In the delivery message, the impostor says, in effect, "Hi. I'm the true person. Here is my public key." The verifier now incorrectly believes that it has the true person's public key, although it really holds the impostor's public key. This is the critical deception. Everything else is easy.

When the impostor sends messages with digital signatures using its own private key, the public key that the verifier holds will wrongly "authenticate" the digital signature as being that of the true person.

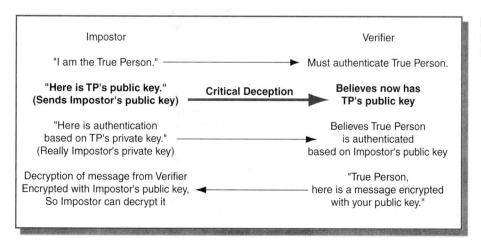

Figure 10.9
Public Key
Deception

For encryption, the verifier will encrypt messages with the public key it has received and send the encrypted messages to the impostor, believing that it is sending these messages to the true person. The impostor can decrypt these messages with its own private key.

In other words, if a verifier does not independently verify an applicant's public key, impersonation can succeed easily and completely.

The Need for a Trusted Third Party and Digital Certificates

Thanks to the threat just discussed, public key encryption is useless unless you can independently verify the true party's public key through a trusted third party. Digital certificates make this possible.

Note that digital certificates by themselves do not authenticate an applicant. They merely provide the true public key for a certain person, program, or hardware device. They make public key encryption and authentication possible without the possibility of deception.

X.509 Digital Certificates Digital certificates normally follow the ITU-T **X.509** standard. As Figure 10.10 shows, an X.509 digital certificate has multiple fields.[6] Some fields identify the certificate authority. Other fields give the digital certificate's expiration date, the name of the issuee, and—this is the critical thing—the issuee's public key. The digital certificate, then, gives the verifier

Figure 10.10
Simplified X.509
Digital Certificate

Field	Description
Version Number	The version of X.509 governing this certificate.
Serial Number	The certificate authority assigns a unique serial number to each of its digital certificates. Used to check certificate revocation lists and for other purposes.
Issuer	The name of the certificate authority.
Valid Period	Time limit for the certificate's validity. Should not be accepted after that time.
Subject	The name of the person, organization, or process to which the certificate is issued.
Public Key of Subject	The subject's public key, which should be used in authentication.
Public Key Algorithm of Subject	The subject's algorithm for public key encryption (RSA, elliptical curve, and so forth).
Signature Algorithm Identifier	The certificate authority's digital signal algorithm.
Digital Signature of the Certificate Authority	The certificate authority's digital signature verifying that it created the certificate and that the certificate has not been altered.[a]

[a]The certificate authority's public key must be learned independently.

---

[6] For clarity, the figure shows only some X.509 fields and uses simplified field naming.

independent third-party proof that a certain public key really does belong to a certain person, organization, computer, or piece of software.

Trusting a Third Party: Certificate Authorities   Obviously, the verifier in authentication must trust the party issuing the certificate, so digital certificates must be issued by trusted third parties called **certificate authorities (CAs).** If the certificate authority is fraudulent, we have a serious problem.

Unfortunately, there is no government regulation of certificate authorities. Any organization, including an organized crime front organization, can become a CA. Although a few public CAs are well known, and although most browsers will accept their certificates, there is no guarantee of even their legitimacy.

Tamper-Proofing Digital Certificates   What prevents an impostor from tampering with the digital certificate by leaving the issuee's name unchanged but typing its own public key in the public key field? This would give an attack like the one shown in Figure 10.9.

The answer is that the certificate authority adds its own digital signature to the certificate, signed by the CA's own private key, as shown in Figure 10.10. As noted earlier, digital signatures give message integrity. If an impostor tampers with the digital certificate, then when the verifier tests the certificate's digital signature with the certificate authority's well-known public key, the authentication will fail. The modification will be detected.

Verifying Digital Certificates with Certificate Revocation Lists (CRLs)
Note in Figure 10.10 that each digital certificate has an expiration date. After that time, it can no longer be used to authenticate the applicant. This date cannot be changed or the certificate authority's digital signature will not work.

In addition, the certificate authority may cancel a digital certificate before its expiration date, for instance, if the issuee engages in fraud. If this happens, checking the expiration date is not enough. As Figure 10.11 illustrates in Steps 6 and 7, the verifier also must check with the certificate authority to be sure that the certificate has not been revoked.

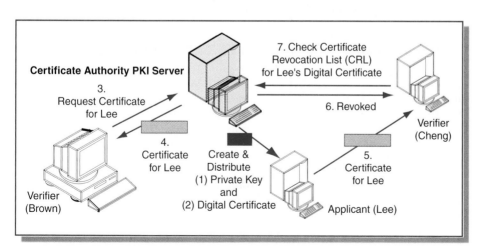

Figure 10.11
Public Key
Infrastructure (PKI)

More specifically, as Figure 10.11 illustrates, the verifier must check the certificate authority's **certificate revocation list (CRL).** Only after the verifier has done so should it accept the public key of the applicant. Unfortunately, many verifiers fail to do this and so accept digital certificates that have been revoked for misbehavior.

Obtaining Digital Certificates   How can a verifier obtain digital certificates? As Figure 10.11 illustrates, there are two basic ways to do this.

- First, the verifier can get the applicant's digital certificate from the certificate authority (Steps 3 and 4 in Figure 10.11). The CA will not send the certificate if it has been revoked.
- Alternatively, the applicant may send the verifier the digital certificate once, usually at the beginning of a communication session (Step 5). Of course, this applicant-supplied certificate must be checked against the certificate authority's CRL (Steps 6 and 7).

Public Key Infrastructures (PKIs)

Certificate authorities are so crucial that security experts now talk about **public key infrastructures (PKIs)** that manage public keys, private keys, and digital certificates. Figure 10.11 illustrates a PKI.

Key Management and Authentication   A certificate authority provides digital certificates and CRLs. A PKI must do even more. It must allow a company or group of companies to specify:

- First, a selected list of trusted certificate authorities and their public keys.
- Second, procedures for requesting and getting digital certificates using secure transmission.
- Third, procedures for checking certificate revocation lists.
- Fourth, procedures for creating public–private key pairs and distributing private keys (Step 1 in Figure 10.11) and digital certificates (Step 2) to individual people, programs, and devices. Private key distribution is very difficult because it must be done securely.

Lack of Standards in PKI Processes   Another problem is that each organization that provides PKI services has a different set of processes for distributing keys and doing other PKI activities. Although basic encryption and authentication algorithms are well standardized, PKIs do many other things. The IETF's emerging **PKIX** standard may change this situation, but for now it is necessary to use a single source for comprehensive PKI services.

Internal PKIs   The lack of certificate authority regulation and of PKI standards is a serious problem for electronic commerce; however, it is less of a problem for internal corporate use. Companies can act as their own certificate authorities and can select a single vendor's PKI toolkit for internal needs.

Chapter 10 Security

Test Your Understanding

Answer Core Review Questions 7–9, Detailed Review Question 7, and Thought Questions 4 and 5.

INTEGRATED SECURITY SYSTEMS

So far, we have only looked at the elements of secure communication. However, if two processes on different computers are to communicate smoothly, we need to implement several forms of security, and we need a process for doing this systematically and automatically. **Integrated security systems (ISSs)** implement this broad spectrum of activities automatically, as Figure 10.12 illustrates.

Secure Sockets Layer (SSL)

In Figure 10.12, the integrated security system is **secure sockets layer (SSL),** which secures most electronic commerce transactions. Every time your browser issues an *https://* command (Step 1 in Figure 10.12), it begins an SSL session. SSL is a relatively simple integrated security system, and this simplicity makes it relatively easy to understand. Module F discusses the more elaborate IPsec (IP security) integrated security system used to protect virtual private network (VPN) communication, which was introduced in Chapter 9. It also discusses the Kerberos integrated security system, which Microsoft servers tend to use for security.

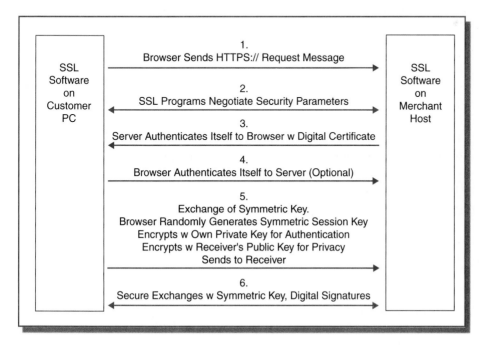

Figure 10.12
Integrated Security System (ISS): Secure Sockets Layer (SSL)

SSL was created by Netscape but now is standardized by the IETF under the name *Transport Layer Security (TLS)*. However, we will use the term "SSL," because "TLS" is not used commonly.

Negotiation   As we have noted repeatedly, there usually are several alternative algorithms for encryption, authentication, and other needs. SSL supports several alternative algorithms for its various functions. The SSL processes on the two machines must first negotiate which specific algorithms they will use, as shown in Step 2 of Figure 10.12. All integrated security systems begin with such a negotiation phase.[7]

Authentication   Next (Step 3), the webserver authenticates itself to the browser user, using a public key challenge–response process (discussed earlier in this chapter) and a digital certificate. However, the browser does not have to authenticate itself (Step 4) and rarely does. This is a sore point for electronic commerce companies, because customer fraud is fairly widespread.[8]

Symmetric Session Key Exchange   Next, the SSL processes exchange a symmetric key to be used in subsequent communication. As Figure 10.12 notes (Step 5), the user SSL process randomly generates a symmetric key. This is called a **session key** because it will be used only during the current conversation between the browser and webserver.

The user SSL process then encrypts the session key with its own private key, ensuring authenticity. It then sends the encrypted session key to the webserver SSL process in a message further encrypted with the webserver SSL process's public key, ensuring confidentiality. The webserver SSL process decrypts the message with its own private key, authenticates the PC user using the PC user's public key, and accepts the session key. Public key encryption is used in session key exchange because session keys are short, so encrypting and decrypting session keys is not too burdensome.[9]

Ongoing Symmetric Key Encryption with Digital Signatures   From that point on (Step 6), the two SSL processes encrypt and decrypt with the session key using (fast) symmetric encryption. However, they do add digital signatures to each message to ensure message-by-message authentication and integrity.

Test Your Understanding

Answer Core Review Question 10 and Detailed Review Question 8.

---

[7] In SSL, the browser proposes a list of specific algorithms to be used. The webserver SSL process presents the algorithms it will use based on the browser's proposal and its own capabilities. The browser can refuse the connection if the webserver's choices are not acceptable.

[8] Morgan, Cynthia, "Web Merchants Stung by Credit-Card Fraud," *Computerworld*, 3/11/99. http://www.computerworld.com/home/print.nsf/all/9903089532.

[9] We should say that it is not *extremely* burdensome. However, using SSL does place a fairly heavy load on servers as a result of public key encryption.

We have discussed only some of the most important security issues facing corporations today. There are several other important security issues to consider.

Multilayer Security

Security can be applied at any layer. Often, as Figure 10.13 illustrates, integrated security systems are implemented at several layers. Old and established security algorithms have a nasty record of having hackers discover security problems after years of effective use. If security is employed at multiple layers, a single breakdown in an algorithm will not compromise security. On the negative side, each layer of security produces delays and increases costs.

Firewalls

Connecting a corporate network to the Internet is inherently dangerous. Hackers may use the Internet to send messages to your internal computers. **Denial of service attacks** may crash your computers, cause them to slow down, or fill up their disk capacity. Worse yet, hackers may be able to log into your computers as **root users,** enabling them to view and destroy all files.

Packet Filter Firewalls   As Figure 10.14 illustrates, a **firewall** intercepts each packet and decides whether to let the packet get into the network. Figure 10.14 shows a **packet filter firewall,** which bases its decisions on the contents of fields in IP packets. For instance, if the source address in an incoming packet is the address of a computer known to be *inside* the firewall, the packet filter firewall will reject the packet. Packet filter firewalls can be attacked fairly easily, but they form a good first line of defense, and packet filter firewall software is built into most routers. Packet filter firewalls can be viewed as security speed bumps for modestly sophisticated hacks.

Packet filter firewalls look at all IP header fields and at the headers of TCP segments and UDP datagrams within IP packets. As noted in Figure 2.2, the first fields in TCP segments (and, by the way, in UDP datagrams) are 16-bit source and destination *port numbers,* which designate applications that send and receive messages. Many port numbers are "well known," meaning that

Layer	Example
Application	Application-specific (for instance, passwords for a database program)
Transport	SSL (TLS)
Internet	IPsec
Data Link	Point-to-Point Tunneling Protocol, Layer 2 Tunneling Protocol
Physical	Physical locks on computers

Figure 10.13
Multilayer Security

Figure 10.14
Packet Filter
Firewall

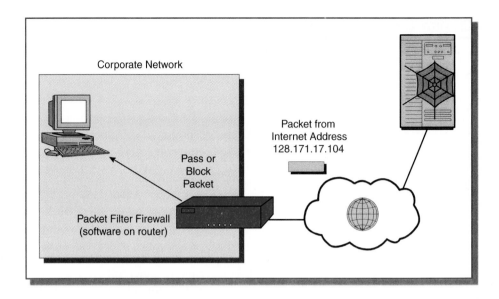

their use is applied consistently. For instance, 80 is the well-known port number for HTTP. Packet filter firewalls may allow IP packets with data going to certain port numbers to go through while denying access to IP packets with data going to other port numbers.

Application (Proxy) Firewalls Figure 10.15 illustrates a more sophisticated firewall called an **application firewall.** As the name suggests, this firewall bases admission on certain application-specific rules. For instance, if the application firewall receives an HTTP response message from a webserver that has not just been sent an HTTP request message, it denies the packet. In addition, application firewalls can filter out viruses and such potentially malicious content as Active-X controls and Java programs.

Figure 10.15
Application (Proxy)
Firewall

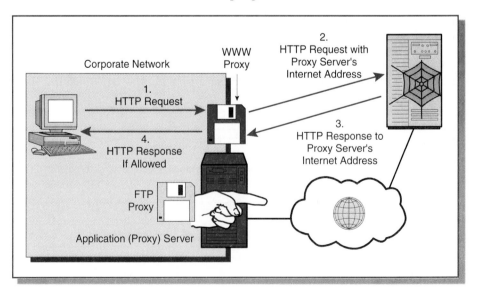

Problems with Application Firewalls Unfortunately, not all applications have predictable behavior that can be used to build application firewall modules. Database applications are particularly difficult to protect with application firewalls.

In addition, because application firewalls do a great deal of work, they can be fairly slow. Total network performance will suffer if the application firewall falls behind in its work.

Proxy Service Application firewalls are also called **proxy firewalls.** A proxy is someone who acts on behalf of another. When a client PC sends an IP packet to a server outside the firewall (Step 1 in Figure 10.15), the proxy firewall intercepts the packet and sends it on to the server, putting the proxy firewall's IP address in the source address field of the IP packet (Step 2).

The external server therefore sends IP packets back to the proxy server instead of directly to the client PC (Step 3). This allows the proxy server to do its job of checking the application data before sending it on to the client PC (Step 4).[10]

In addition, the outside world sees only the IP address of the proxy firewall, never the IP address of the internal client PC. This prevents a snooper from learning about an organization's internal IP addresses by observing traffic.

Firewall Setup Unfortunately, all types of firewalls require the organization to create complex if-then-else statements called filtering rules. These filtering rules dictate packet acceptance or rejection. The complexity of filtering rules (they often consist of nested if-then-else statements with many terms) and the fact that the order of comparisons is crucial result in many packet filter firewalls being set up incorrectly.

Total Security

We have focused primarily on network security in this chapter because this is a networking textbook. However, for total security, it is also important to control computer security and application security, and it is also important to manage user behavior, as Figure 10.16 illustrates.

Server Security Although strong network security is helpful, adversaries will, from time to time, reach your computers. If your computers are not secure, then adversaries will be able to break into them or crash them.[11]

Obviously, servers are prime candidates for attack. Unfortunately, most server operating systems have **known security weaknesses.**[12] When such weaknesses are discovered, operating system vendors offer fixes, called

---

[10] Unfortunately, client PCs have to be specially configured to work with proxy firewalls. Fortunately, newer versions of Windows can handle this through TCP/IP properties setup.

[11] Hackers call companies that only implement firewalls and not internal security "crunchy on the outside but chewy on the inside."

[12] Johnston, Margaret, "Known Vulnerabilities are No. 1 Hack Exploit," *IDG.NET,* 12/16/99, http://nwfusion.com/news/1999/1216anklebite.html.

Figure 10.16
Total Security

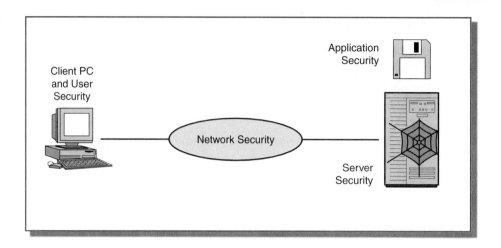

patches, usually on the Internet. However, downloading these patches on all servers is very expensive and time consuming. Many companies fall behind or do not install patches at all. This allows even unsophisticated hackers to break into critical servers using software that automatically detects and exploits known security weaknesses.

Client PC Security   Client PCs and other client machines also have known security weaknesses, and users seldom download security patches or install them properly if they do download these patches.

More importantly, however, users normally use no passwords on their PCs or use passwords that are easy to guess. Even million-bit private keys do no good if the adversary gets control of the user's client PC and its software because of poor user PC security. Once in control of the client PC, the adversary effectively has control over the user's private key and other keys.

Application Software Security   Some application software implements little or no application layer security, making it highly vulnerable. In addition, application software may contain viruses that can spread and damage the computer. It is important to configure application layer security well and to filter incoming messages, especially e-mail messages, for viruses.

Managing Users   Often the simplest way to get a user's password is simply to ask them, say by calling on the telephone and pretending to be a member of the firms' technical staff. Tricking users into giving out passwords and other sensitive information is called **social engineering.**

In addition, users can bypass security in many other ways, for instance, by moving sensitive files from secure machines to nonsecure machines. Most viruses, in turn, propagate with the help of inappropriate user behavior. Users must be educated in the need for security and in what they should do or should not do.

Intrusion Detection

When adversaries attack, we need **intrusion detection** systems that detect when an attack is under way and notify an administrator. The administrator may then take steps to thwart the attack. In fact, the intrusion detection system may take steps to thwart the attack itself.

Limiting Hacker Intrusion Time   It is important to detect intrusions. Otherwise, hackers will simply keep trying different attacks until they find one that succeeds. Intrusion detection allows a company to realize that an attack is underway and to limit the time that the hacker has to attack the system.

Assessing Security Risks   Intrusion detection is also important in helping a company assess the security dangers facing it. Many companies that install intrusion detection systems are amazed by the number of times their systems are attacked. They often find that outsiders are already breaking into their systems and are reading sensitive files.

Audit Logs   Intrusion detection systems keep an **audit log** giving the details of an attack. It is critical to maintain this audit log if the company wishes to take legal measures against attackers. If a serious attack is mounted, and if the FBI or another law enforcement agency is contacted, one of their first concerns will be protecting evidence, including audit logs (but not only these logs). Without this hard evidence, prosecution is very difficult.

Trust

In many secure systems, one system will trust another, as Figure 10.17 illustrates. Typically, trust is established only after authentication. Once **trust** is established, however, the trusting system will accept messages from the trusted system with at most minimal checks. As Figure 10.17 also shows, trust may be inherited. If System A trusts System B, and if System B trusts System C, then System A may trust System C.

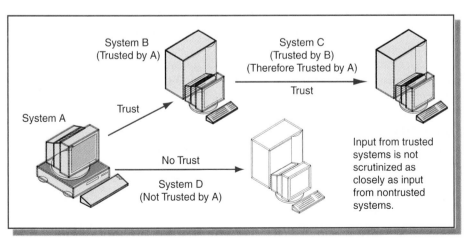

Figure 10.17
Trust
Relationships

In various forms, trust is widely used in security. Once trust is established, the cost of security work is reduced. However, if an attacker can take over a trusted system, it will be able to gain entry to trusting systems very easily. Trusted systems, such as the PKI server shown in Figure 10.11, must be protected very carefully. For instance, each server has a password called a supervisory or root password. This password should be very long and complex.

Test Your Understanding

Answer Core Review Questions 11–13 and Detailed Review Questions 9 and 10.

KEY POINTS

Encryption   Encryption uses a method and a key to convert plaintext to ciphertext and ciphertext back to plaintext. The key must be kept secret. To be secure, keys must be quite long.

The two general categories of encryption are symmetric key encryption and public key encryption. The former has greater key distribution problems but is faster and can be used for long messages. Both categories are used widely, often in conjunction with one another. Within these two categories, there are many specific algorithms, such as DES and RSA.

Authentication   In authentication, the sender is required to prove his or her identity. In public key authentication, the sender proves that it knows its private key, which only the sender should know. This can be done through challenge–response processes and digital signatures, in conjunction with digital certificates. Digital certificates by themselves do not authenticate a person or process. They merely verify that a particular public key belongs to a particular user. Public key authentication, key distribution, and related activities require the creation of public key infrastructures (PKIs).

Integrated Security Systems (ISSs)   Encryption and authentication are merely elements in integrated security systems, which provide fully secure communication. Usually, ISSs begin with a negotiation phase, implement authentication, distribute session keys, and communicate with symmetric key encryption and perhaps digital signatures. Usually, all of this takes place automatically, without the user's awareness.

Other Security Matters   We discussed other policy matters, including multilayer security, packet filter and application (proxy) firewalls, total security, intrusion detection, and trust.

REVIEW QUESTIONS

For questions with multiple parts, write the answer to each part in a separate line or paragraph.

Core Review Questions

1. **a)** In a single sentence, explain encryption. **b)** In encryption, the original message is called the _____. **c)** The encrypted message is called the _____. **d)** Encryption requires a(n) _____ and a(n) _____. **e)** What must be kept secret? **f)** Describe exhaustive search. **g)** What does the threat of exhaustive search require an organization to do?

2. **a)** In two-way communication using symmetric key encryption between two parties, how many keys are required? **b)** Describe the symmetric key distribution problem.

3. Using public key encryption, Party A sends a message to Party B. **a)** What key does Party A use to encrypt? (Don't say "the public key.") **b)** What key does Party B use to decrypt? (Don't say "the private key.")

4. **a)** In two-way communication using public key encryption between two parties, how many keys are required? **b)** Describe why the distribution of public keys is easy. **c)** What is the chief problem of public key encryption?

5. **a)** In authentication in general, what is the applicant attempting to prove? **b)** What, more specifically, is the applicant attempting to prove in public key authentication?

6. **a)** Describe public key challenge–response authentication. **b)** Does it authenticate subsequent messages?

7. **a)** What benefits does a digital signature provide? **b)** Distinguish between message digests and digital signatures. **c)** Which provides message-by-message authentication? Digital signatures, challenge-response authentication, or both? **d)** What two benefits do digital signatures provide?

8. **a)** What is the standard for digital certificates? **b)** What does a digital certificate prove?

9. **a)** What are the main jobs of Public Key Infrastructures (PKIs)? **b)** What is holding back the use of PKIs?

10. **a)** What are the main steps in a conversation using an integrated security system (ISS)? **b)** How much is the user involved in these steps?

11. What is the role of a firewall?

12. **a)** What, besides network security, is needed for total security? **b)** What is social engineering?

13. Why is intrusion detection important for security?

Detailed Review Questions

1. Explain the operation of **a)** DES and **b)** 168-bit 3DES symmetric key encryption processes. **c)** How will AES be better?

2. Compare RSA and the Elliptical Curve Cryptosystem in terms of required key length.

3. What fear do security experts have about public key encryption?

4. **a)** Why is biometric authentication good? **b)** What is holding back biometric authentication? **c)** Why are authentication cards good? **d)** What is the danger of using authentication cards?

5. **a)** What is hashing? **b)** Contrast hashing to encryption. **c)** Contrast hashing to compression.

6. Describe the process of digital signature authentication.

7. **a)** What danger do digital certificates address? **b)** Why does changing a digital certificate do an adversary no good? **c)** What are certificate authorities? **d)** What is the problem with certificate authorities?

8. Describe the operation of the Secure Sockets Layer (SSL) integrated security system.

9. **a)** What is multilayer security? **b)** Why is multilayer security good?

10. **a)** Distinguish between packet filter firewalls and application firewalls in terms of what they examine. **b)** Which type of firewall offers more sophisticated protection? **c)** What are the weaknesses of application firewalls? **d)** How does proxy service prevent an adversary from learning about your internal network?

Thought Questions

1. What was the most surprising thing you learned in this chapter?

2. What was the most difficult part of this chapter for you?

3. Why are symmetric key encryption and public key encryption not really competitors?

4. What do you think the results would be if a certificate authority's private key was compromised?

5. What do you think the results might be if the PKI server's supervisory or root password was stolen? Be specific.

6. If public key encryption was not prohibitively expensive, how do you think we would probably do authentication for long messages?

7. What principles does the John Crais vignette at the beginning of this chapter embody?

Case Studies

For case studies, go to the book's website, **http://www.prenhall.com/panko,** and look at the "Case Studies" page for this chapter.

Projects

1. **Getting Current.** Go to the book's website's "New Information" and "Errors" pages for this chapter to get new information since this book went to press and to correct any errors in the text.

2. **Internet Exercises.** Go to the book's website's "Exercises" page for this chapter and do the Internet exercises.

3. **VeriSign.** VeriSign **(http://www.verisign.com)** is a leading public certificate authority. Visit its website and describe the steps needed to get a personal digital certificate for yourself. Be sure to include the price.

Chapter 11

Networked Applications

Glenn Davis, ever ready to try new innovations, installed a new e-mail client program on his notebook computer. His old client had worked fairly well, allowing him to download his e-mail from anywhere he could dial into the Internet. However, the new client allowed him to create complex pages with boldface, italics, other text formatting, and even graphics. The pages he could create looked almost exactly like webpages.

When he began sending these fancy messages, however, he was immediately deluged with complaints. Several of his fellow employees complained about receiving garbage messages that looked as if they were filled with alien symbols.

Glenn was also initially attracted by the program's ability to send and receive word processing files as attachments. This would allow him to jot down brief progress reports, ship them to his secretary Jaime, and look over the changes Jaime made to make his prose look better. It would also allow him to get Excel files containing new product information and even graphics files to show his customers. However, when Glenn began sending and receiving attachments, he often found that they could not be read.

Although Glenn had problems with e-mail, not everything else was working out badly. Most importantly, he could use his browser to access shipping schedules for various types of fruit sold by his company, Paradise Groceries. Previously, he had been told that it would take years of programming to recreate the database in a form his computer could access, but here Glenn was, accessing this internal data through his browser.

To reduce long-distance calling costs, Glenn even has a telephone headset attached to his notebook. Glenn dials into the Internet and tells his notebook to make a voice connection. He is then connected with his sales office. The application saves a lot of money, but the sound quality is terrible, and it seems as if everybody pauses before they speak. ■

Learning Objectives

After studying this chapter, you should be able to describe:

* Web-enabled database access using application servers
* Internet electronic mail standards
* IP telephony and voice–data convergence

INTRODUCTION

Some years ago, the president of a tool manufacturing company told his board of directors, "Last year, we sold ten million drills that nobody wanted." He explained to his stunned audience that buyers really wanted *holes*. Tools, he explained, are costly and difficult to use. They are merely tolerated, not desired, and they are tolerated at all only because users need them to meet their real goals.

The Primacy of Applications   This book focuses primarily on how to move messages between application programs on different machines. However, it is the applications themselves that users want—applications that can reach out to other applications on other machines, hopefully with a minimum of cost and user involvement. Networking is merely a tool for supporting such networked applications.

Many Networked Application Standards   There are many networked application standards, and more will be appearing each year. Soon, there may be far more application standards than any other type of networking standards.

In this chapter, we will look at only three clusters of networked application standards. The applications in this chapter were selected both because of their inherent importance and also because they illustrate characteristics commonly found in networked application standards.

Web-Enabled Database Access   First, we will look at *web-enabled database access,* which can mate the newest in World Wide Web technology with old "back end" mainframe and server applications. A box in this section looks in more detail at IBM mainframe computers.

Internet E-Mail Second, we will look at Internet electronic mail standards. E-mail, of course, is one of the most popular networked applications. Looking at e-mail standards will help you understand that most application "standards" really are clusters of several standards.

IP Telephony for Voice–Data Convergence Third, we will look at *IP telephony.* Corporations today have to support separate networks for data and voice. IP telephony offers the prospect of *voice–data convergence,* in which both forms of traffic travel over a single network. IP telephony is one of the hottest topics in corporate networking today, and even the most traditional carriers are planning to offer IP telephone services.

WEB-ENABLED DATABASE ACCESS

Although the World Wide Web is one of the youngest Internet applications, it is probably the most widely used. Offering attractive graphical content, the simplicity of linking, and the universality of URL addressing, the Web connects users to resources throughout the world.

The Roles of Application Servers

As Figure 11.1 illustrates, the Web can also be a doorway to non-HTTP applications. Nearly every corporate and residential user has a browser on his or her computer, but not everyone has mail clients, database clients, or other types of application-specific client programs. As Figure 11.1 illustrates, a webserver can be used to translate between the formats of browser programs and those of other application programs.

Here, the webserver is called an **application server.** This is an inexact term used in several different ways in the networking literature, but it generally means that the server does some of the processing. We will see what this means for **web-enabled database** applications.

The term "database server" is deliberately vague. It may be a client/server database server or a mainframe computer. Application servers can work with

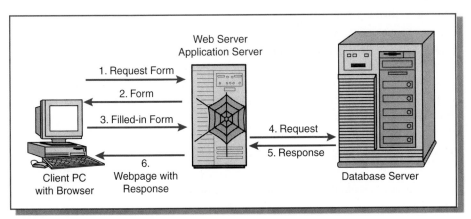

Figure 11.1
Web-Enabled
Database Retrieval

either in the same general way. Of course, there are technical differences at the detailed level.

The Process

Figure 11.1 shows the process by which the application server mediates between the browser user and the database server.

Getting the Form   In a web-enabled database application, the user fills in an HTML form describing the information he or she wishes to receive. Figure 11.1 shows that the user begins the process by typing a form's URL (Step 1). The application server then sends this form to the user (2).

Submitting the Form   The user fills in the form and returns the form to the application server, usually by hitting something like a "submit" button (3). The data in this form go back in an HTTP request message, such as the following:

GET cgi-bin/bogo.exe?last=Lee&first=Pat

A question mark separates the name of the program that should receive the input from the input data. Each piece of input data has a variable name, an equal sign, and the data to be passed. Variables are separated by ampersands. The program, *bogo.exe*, processes the input and often passes the input data to another program, such as a database program.[1]

Sending a Request to the Database Server   Next, the application server extracts information from the form and creates a database request. The application server sends this database request message to the database server (4). The database server does not know that the request is coming from an application server. The application server impersonates a user and sends the request message to the database server just as an ordinary user would.

The Database Server Replies   The database server retrieves the requested information and sends it back in the response format it uses to send responses directly to users (5).

Completing the Loop   The application server extracts the information from the database server's response message. The application server then creates a new webpage containing the information in the database response message. The application server sends this webpage to the browser user (6). The transaction is now finished.

---

[1] Here, we again use the GET keyword. It is also possible to use the POST keyword. The syntax of the rest of the command is slightly different when POST is used.

Transparency

Note that the browser has no idea that information is coming from a database server. The browser merely sees the application server as an ordinary webserver.

In addition, the database server has no idea that it is communicating with an application server. As noted above, it receives normal user requests and sends back normal user responses.

Overall, application servers are **transparent** to both browsers and database servers.

Standards

Of course, the application server uses HTTP to deal with the browser user. All webserver programs come with this capability. We also need a standardized way for the webserver program to communicate with the database program or with an intermediary program.

CGI and Intermediary Programs Many application servers rely on a standardized way to pass information received from a webserver application program to another application program on the same computer. This is the **Common Gateway Interface (CGI),** as Figure 11.2 shows.

CGI is a standardized way for a webserver program to pass input data to other programs. Here, the data are passed to a program called *bogo.exe* in the *cgi-bin* directory. It is common to require programs that use CGI to run in a single directory in order to prevent unwanted access to programs in other directories. The name "cgi-bin" is used frequently for this directory.

As Figure 11.2 illustrates, CGI often is used to pass data to an **intermediary program** rather than to the ultimate database application. This intermediary program can be written in a wide variety of languages. Its job is to take the CGI output and put it into a form acceptable to the database server. This frees the webserver application program from needing to know how to do this translation. It is the intermediary program, in other words, that implements transparency.

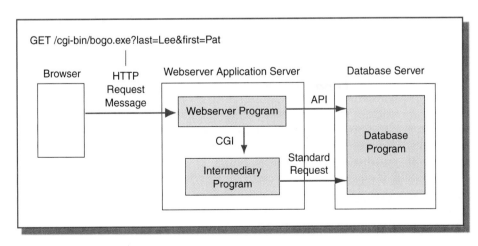

Figure 11.2
CGI and APIs

When the database server replies, it is the intermediary program's job to pass the response back to the webserver program. Before it does so, however, it creates the webpage that the webserver program will pass to the browser.

Intermediary programs, then, allow the webserver application program to do nothing more than it normally does for ordinary webservice, other than passing output to the CGI intermediary program named in the HTTP request message and receiving back webpages to pass onto the browser.

APIs Unfortunately, CGI is a low-performance standard. It is inadequate for high-speed electronic commerce sites. As Figure 11.2 shows, most database applications have a set of proprietary **application program interfaces (APIs)** that provide a standardized method for them to exchange data with other programs, in this case webserver programs. These APIs are far faster than CGI.

However, each database vendor has different proprietary APIs. The webserver application program must know the specific APIs of the specific database application program on the database server. Most webserver application programs only know some vendor-specific APIs for database and other applications.

Other Approaches

There are other ways for browsers to work with database servers. For instance, the webpage that the application server initially downloads may be more than a simple form. It may contain a program written in Java, Active-X, or a scripting language such as Perl or Javascript. This program, running on the user's PC, may be able to interact directly with database servers.

Mainframes

As noted earlier in this chapter, the "database server" mentioned in the preceding discussion might be one of the client/server database servers introduced in Chapter 1. However, it is also likely to be a **mainframe computer.** Mainframes can serve several hundred terminal users at the same time.

Perhaps 70% of all central corporate data resides on mainframe computers. Although there has been a long-term movement to *downsize* mainframe applications (rewrite them to run on PCs or workstation servers), mainframes still are very important and will remain so for many years. Quite simply, for high-volume transaction processing with high reliability, mainframes still have no equal as application development and execution environments. The box entitled "Mainframes" provides more information on these large terminal–host systems that normally use SNA instead of TCP/IP.

Test Your Understanding

Answer Core Review Questions 1–3.

Mainframes

Given the continuing importance of mainframes, is important for you to understand how mainframe terminal–host systems are organized. We will focus on IBM mainframe systems. IBM dominates the mainframe market. In addition, most competitors use the same general hardware organization. Their products are called "plug compatible machines."

BASIC ELEMENTS

3270 Terminals

As Figure 11.3 illustrates, IBM mainframe users work at terminals. These are high-performance terminals that can send and receive up to 2 Mbps and that usually offer color and graphics, although not a full graphical user interface. These terminals are known generically as **3270 terminals**. There are many models of 3270 terminals.

Figure 11.3   Mainframe Terminal–Host System

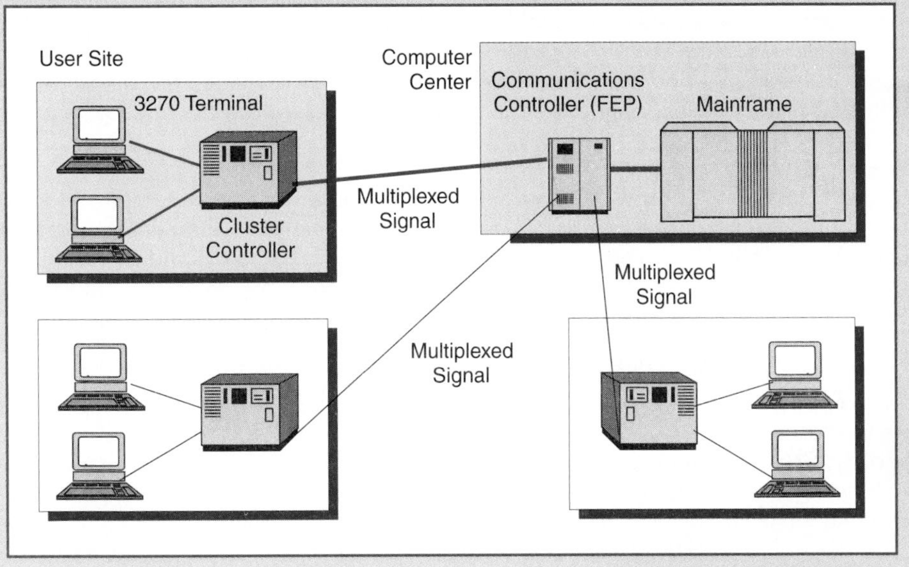

Cluster Controller

Terminal users often work in groups. For instance, in a travel agency, there may be anywhere from three to a few dozen travel agents working in the same office area. As Figure 11.3 illustrates, an IBM mainframe system places a small computer called a **cluster controller** in each group office. The cluster controller has two functions. First, it multiplexes the traffic of terminals and printers over a single transmission line to the mainframe site.

The second function of the cluster controller is to provide processing power for light text editing to terminal users. The mainframe usually sends screens that resemble forms. The cluster controller acts as a local host, allowing terminal users to type and edit information on the screen without the need for mainframe processing.

Cluster controllers provide rapid response times for simple text editing operations because there is no waiting for the mainframe to respond.

Continued.

Cluster controllers also reduce traffic on the network because text editing does not require transmissions between the terminal and the mainframe. Multiplexing further reduces the cost of long-distance communication.

Finally, cluster controllers free the mainframe from mundane text editing work, allowing the expensive mainframe to focus on complex file and database processing, for which its high costs are justified.

Application Servers and IBM Mainframes

Application servers are not part of IBM mainframe systems per se. However, we should note how they interact with IBM mainframe systems. Application servers can operate as 3270 terminals, in which case the cluster controller will think that it is working with a terminal. Alternatively, application servers can operate as combined 3270 terminals and cluster controllers. The latter approach allows them to deal directly with the communications controller discussed next.

Communications Controller

At the mainframe site, a computer called a **communications controller** (sometimes called a **front-end processor**) sits between the cluster controllers and the mainframe. The communications controller works with the cluster controllers to multiplex transmissions, in order to reduce transmission costs. In addition, the communications controller manages the details of communication with cluster controllers, freeing the mainframe to focus on file and database processing.

Mainframe

Typically, applications on **mainframe** computers deal with large files or databases. Mainframes, therefore, require extensive processing power. However, because of the need to deal with large files and databases, mainframes also need ultrafast disk access for reads and writes. In contrast to *supercomputers,* which emphasize high processing performance, mainframes focus on disk access performance because this is the critical factor in most mainframe business applications.

Systems Network Architecture (SNA)

IBM mainframes generally do not use TCP/IP for networking (although they can). Instead, they normally use **Systems Network Architecture (SNA).** Designed for business applications needing high reliability, SNA chooses the certainty of centralized control rather than peer–peer openness. SNA also has quality of service features needed for real-time terminal–host interactions in production environments, where delay is intolerable and reliability is critical.

Layering in SNA

In general, as Figure 11.4 shows, the layers of SNA are very similar to those of OSI (see Chapter 1), although SNA has no application layer. This should not be a surprise, because OSI creators drew on the SNA architecture, which predated OSI.

However, because of deep differences in philosophy between the two architectures, *individual standards* in SNA and OSI tend to be extremely different. In particular, classic SNA focuses on centralized control over each connection through **System Services Control Point (SSCP)** software on the mainframe. In contrast, OSI was designed for peer–peer connections without centralized control.

The exception to differences between OSI and SNA standards comes at the physical and data link layers, where SNA uses OSI standards.

Continued.

Chapter 11 Networked Applications

Figure 11.4   SNA and OSI

OSI	SNA
Application	Not Applicable
Presentation	Network Addressable Unit (NAU) Services (data formatting, programming interfaces)
Session	Data Flow Control (flow control within a session)
Transport	Transmission Control (controls sequence numbers)
Network	Path Control
Data Link	Data Link
Physical	Physical

Beyond Classic SNA

In recent years, SNA has begun to move away from the master–slave orientation of classic SNA. *Advanced Peer-to-Peer Networking (APPN)* allows processes to communicate without first getting permission from the System Services Control Point. In turn, *High-Performance Routing (HPR)* allows SNA to work much more effectively with routers. However, IBM mainframe systems continue to focus on the highly intensive management of connections in order to achieve high levels of reliability and latency control.

Network Addressable Units (NAUs)

Any standards architecture describes how to connect various kinds of entities. In SNA, these entities are called **network addressable units (NAUs).** This makes sense, because these are hardware or software *units* that can be *addressed* by other units via the *network.* Figure 11.5 shows how SNA links its NAUs.

Path Control Network

The **path control network** is the transmission system in SNA. It consists of the subnet and internet layer transmission systems that link nodes.

Physical Units

Physical units (PUs) are NAUs that *do not deal directly with end users,* including cluster controllers, communications controllers, and mainframes.

Logical Units

In contrast, **logical units** do deal directly with end users. The term "logical" may sound like software, but it refers both to software (connections to application programs on the mainframe) and also to hardware (terminals).

Connecting Terminals via TCP/IP

Although SNA is important, most corporations are moving toward TCP/IP support. The Telnet standard allows PC users to work with simple host computers. There is also a **TN3270E** standard that emulates a 3270 terminal on an ordinary PC. As Figure 11.6 illustrates, the PC must have a TN3270E client program. This allows it to communicate, using TCP/IP, with a TN3270E server. That server then attaches to the mainframe.

Continued.

Figure 11.5 End Users, Network Addressable Units, and the Path Control Network in SNA

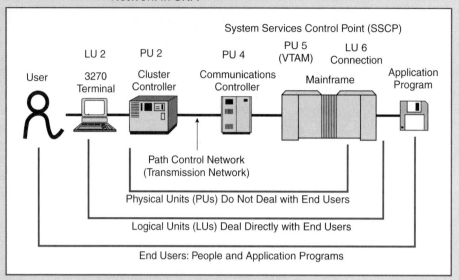

In addition, as Figure 11.6 also shows, cluster controllers can communicate with communications controllers over a router-based internet. SNA messages are encapsulated within IP packets, a process called **data link switching (DLSw).**

Test Your Understanding
Answer Detailed Review Question 1.

Figure 11.6 TN3270E and DLSw Mainframe Communication

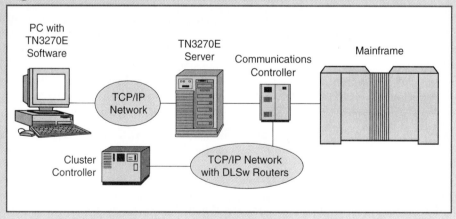

Electronic mail has long been used in industry. There are many proprietary electronic mail programs still in use, but most companies seem to be moving toward adopting **Internet electronic mail (e-mail) standards.** Figure 11.7 shows the main standards that govern Internet e-mail.

Communication Between Mail Hosts: SMTP

The core TCP/IP mail standard for the transmission of messages between mail hosts is the **Simple Mail Transfer Protocol (SMTP),** as shown in Figure 11.7.

SMTP Delivery Typically, a client sends a message to his or her own mail host, as discussed below. That mail host delivers the message to the receiver's mail host or to an intermediary mail host for delivery to the receiver's mail host. *Transmission between mail hosts is always governed by SMTP.*

A Complex Protocol Despite its name, SMTP is a fairly complex protocol, as illustrated in the sample transaction shown in Figure 11.8. Before sending the message, the sending SMTP process first asks the receiving SMTP process for permission to send the message. To get this permission, the sending process sends the mail address of the message's author and the mail address of each receiver. This information allows SMTP mail hosts to be selective about what mail they accept for delivery.

TCP Encapsulation SMTP messages are encapsulated in TCP segments. This gives SMTP the benefit of reliable delivery.

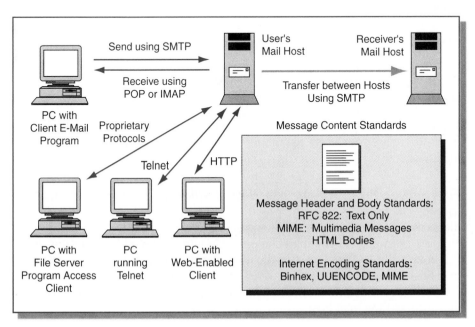

Figure 11.7
Internet Electronic
Mail Standards

Figure 11.8
A Simple Message
Transfer Protocol
Message Transfer

Actor	Command	Comment
Receiving SMTP Process	220 Mail.Panko.Com Ready	When a TCP connection is opened, the receiver signals that it is ready.
Sending SMTP Process	HELO Voyager.cba.Hawaii.edu	Sender asks to begin sending a message. Gives own identity.
Receiver	250 Mail.Panko.Com	Receiver signals that it is ready to begin receiving a message.
Sender	MAIL FROM: Panko@ voyager.cba.Hawaii.edu	Sender identifies the sender (mail author, not SMTP process).
Receiver	250 OK	Accepts author. However, may reject mail from others.
Sender	RCPT TO: Ray@Panko.com	Identifies first mail recipient.
Receiver	250 OK	Accepts first recipient.
Sender	RCPT TO: Lee@Panko.com	Identifies second mail recipient.
Receiver	550 No such user here	Does not accept second recipient. However will deliver to first recipient.
Sender	DATA	Message will follow.
Receiver	354 Start mail input; end with <CRLF>.<CRLF>	Gives permission to send message.
Sender	*When in the course. . .*	The message. Multiple lines of text. Ends with line containing only a single period: <CRLF>.<CRLF>
Receiver	250 OK	Receiver accepts message.
Sender	QUIT	Requests termination of session.
Receiver	221 Mail.Panko.Com Service closing transmission channel	End of transaction.

Communication Between the E-Mail Client and the Mail Host

Typically, the user works at a PC to send and receive mail. As Figure 11.7 illustrates, there are four ways for the user's client PC to interact with the user's mail host.

File Server Program Access E-Mail Clients   Early mail clients had users on the same LANs as their mail hosts. In this case, it was possible to use file server program access for message retrieval (and other operations), as Figure 11.7 indicates. The mail client first would be downloaded to the client PC from a file server. This downloaded client would then interact with the mail host, using proprietary protocols. The proprietary nature of this approach generally meant that the mail client had to be purchased from the same vendor that supplied the mail host.

Internet Mail Clients Today, however, mail clients are seldom on the same LAN as their mail host. Today, many e-mail clients are Internet mail clients, which can be located anywhere on the Internet. They can reach their mail host via the Internet. This allows the user to be located anywhere in the world. It also allows the user to connect to any mail server in the world.

SMTP We saw earlier that SMTP governs the transmission of messages from one mail host to another. Internet mail clients also use SMTP to send messages from the user's Internet mail client to the user's mail host.

Receiving Mail SMTP governs message *sending*. It does not govern how users *retrieve* messages from their mailboxes. Figure 11.7 shows that there are two main standards that an Internet mail client can use to retrieve messages from a mail host using the Internet for transmission. These standards allow a client to ask for messages and sometimes to do limited housekeeping chores on the mailbox on the mail host.

POP The simpler of the two retrieval protocols is the **Post Office Protocol (POP)** shown in Figure 11.7. POP can download some or all new mail to the user's client program, where the user can read the mail at his or her leisure. The user can also delete messages on the mail host. A sample POP interaction is shown as Figure 11.9.

IMAP Although POP has been very popular, it is difficult for POP users to download messages selectively. POP only gives the length of the message in bytes. In contrast, the **Internet Message Access Protocol (IMAP)** gives the user detailed information about each message, including the author's e-mail address and the message's subject. This allows informed message downloading. IMAP also allows you to do quite a few housekeeping chores on your mailbox. However, IMAP is not as widely used as POP.

Telnet

Initially, Internet users worked at terminals, especially the simple VT100 terminals discussed in Module H. These terminals are text-only and offer no graphical user interface. **Telnet** software allows a PC to emulate one of those terminals. Telnet software is built into every PC. (On a Wintel machine, look for it in the Windows directory or a subdirectory.) Most mail hosts support Telnet access as an ugly lowest common denominator access method.

Web-Based E-Mail

Although Internet mail clients are very useful, not everybody has one on their PC. Also, when you are traveling, using a computer in a computer lab, or using a computer in a café with an Internet connection, the computers you encounter may not have Internet e-mail client programs. If they do have such programs, they may not have a familiar mail client program. Furthermore, the owners of

Figure 11.9
Post Office
Protocol (POP)
Transfer

Actor	Command	Comment
Server	+OK POP3 server ready	When TCP connection is established, POP server sends a greeting. Standard version is POP3.
Client	USER Panko	Identifies user mailbox.
Server	+OK name is valid mailbox	Accepts user name.
Client	PASS *password*	User sends password.[a]
Server	+OK Panko's mailbox has two messages (980 octets)	Accepts password.
Client	STAT	Requests information on waiting messages.
Server	+OK 2 980	There are two waiting messages. Their total length is 980 octets.
Client	LIST	Asks server to list message lengths.
Server	+OK 2 messages (980 octets) 1 320 2 660	Shows lengths of messages.
Client	RETR 1	Asks for first message.
Server	+OK 320 octets *entire message*	Server downloads the message.
Client	DELE 1	Client asks that message 1 be deleted.
Server	+OK 1 deleted	Confirms deletion.
Client	QUIT	Requests termination of session.
Server	+OK POP server signing off (1 message left)	Confirms termination.

[a]Password is sent in the clear. POP also offers a more secure authentication approach, APOP, in which the password is not sent in the clear.

these machines may not be happy if you change their client mail program settings. Although Telnet might be available, it is ugly and difficult to use.

To solve this problem, some companies have created **web-based e-mail.** To use these systems, all you need is a browser, and browsers are available on almost every computer connected to the Internet. Like regular e-mail programs, web-based e-mail systems allow you to read mail, send mail, and do housekeeping chores, all via HTTP, as shown in Figure 11.7.

Message Structure

So far, we have been concerned with message *transmission and reception*. However, the *structure* of messages also needs to be standardized so that the mail client can display incoming messages.

RFC 822 Text-Only Messages The standard for text-only messages on the Internet is **RFC 822.** This standard specifies that a message must have two parts: a header and a body. The header must contain specific fields, such as *date, to, from,* and *subject.* Other header fields are optional. Each header field has a keyword, a colon (:), the content of the field, and a CRLF (carriage return and line feed). This rigid all-text header structure allows a mail program to search for messages from a specific e-mail address, sort messages by author name or date, and do many other things to make message handling easier. The body contains free-form text.

RFC 822 is limited to 7-bit ASCII text, in which each byte represents one keyboard character and in which only the seven least significant (rightmost) bits of the byte can be used.[2] Module H discusses 7-bit ASCII in more detail. According to David Crocker, an author of RFC 822, this limit was needed because RFC 822 was created for the original ARPANET, which could only guarantee 7-bit ASCII transmission. Packets whose data fields contained information in the eighth bit often failed to reach the destination host or were scrambled during transmission. Later, the Internet continued this restriction.

MIME The IETF, however, has defined ways to put information other than text into both the message body and the message header. Collectively, these standards are referred to as **Multipurpose Internet Mail Extensions (MIME).** The IETF has added many MIME extensions since creating the MIME framework in 1993. However, MIME has never become popular as a way to create multimedia messages.

HTML Body Parts The popularity of the World Wide Web has led several mail vendors to offer HTML formatting in the body of the message. Note that this is not just for web-based mail systems but for all mail systems regardless of how clients communicate with hosts. Internet mail clients and client server systems can also send and receive e-mail messages with HTML bodies. (Telnet mail systems, however, cannot use HTML bodies.)

HTML bodies are attractive because the technology to render complex web-pages onscreen is well understood by programmers and is familiar to users. However, the standardization of HTML body parts is poor, so mail clients may have problems reading HTML bodies created by clients from different vendors. Worse yet, when messages with HTML in the body are sent to users of text-only or text-plus-MIME mail systems, these users will see all of the tags used in HTML instead of the formatting these tags were designed to convey.

Internet Encoding for Attachments

As just noted, a peculiarity of the Internet is that it will transmit only 7-bit ASCII. Typical "binary" PC data files, however, such as word processing and

---

[2] The eighth bit is assumed to be a parity bit, which supports crude error detection. Parity only works at very slow speeds, where noise, interference, and other factors rarely change more than 1 bit. At higher speeds, however, errors tend to change multiple bits. As discussed in Module H, this makes parity ineffective.

Figure 11.10
Internet Encoding
for E-Mail
Attachments

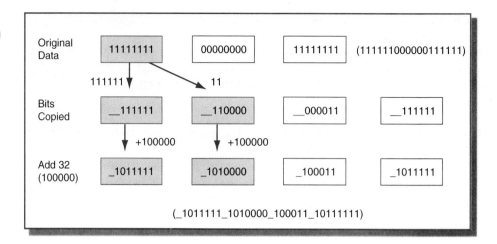

spreadsheet files, use all 8 bits. So if you transmit a binary attachment, it will not travel through the Internet unless you first alter it through **Internet encoding,** as Figure 11.10 illustrates. Internet encoding takes your document and converts it into a 7-bit form that can travel through the Internet.

A Sample Internet Encoding Process

Figure 11.10 gives an example of Internet encoding. Note that this is only an example, not a description of a specific Internet encoding standard.

Here, blocks of 3 data bytes (24 bits) can be sent in blocks of 4 attachment bytes (32 bits). Specifically, the first attachment byte carries bits 1 through 6 of the first data byte. The next attachment byte carries bits 7 through 8 of the first data byte plus bits 1 through 4 of the second data byte. This process continues for the next 2 bytes. At the end of this step, the first 2 bits are free in each attachment byte.

Next, because the first 32 ASCII codes (0 through 31) are supervisory control characters that are also forbidden on the Internet, the binary value for 32 (00100000) is added to each attachment byte. This may create a carry into the seventh bit. After this is done, there are no forbidden control characters, and the most significant (farthest left) bit is still free.[3]

Note again that this is only one possible Internet attachment encoding technique.

Diversity in Internet Encoding Processes

Unfortunately, there are several incompatible Internet encoding methods in common use, including Binhex, UUENCODE, and several versions of MIME, which was noted earlier in this chapter. Fortunately, most mail programs today can work with attachments encoded in **Basic MIME.**

Before you send someone an attachment, then, you must know which Internet encoding standards your mail program and the receiver's mail pro-

---

[3] During transmission, the bit order in the byte is reversed. Consequently, the unused bit becomes the seventh bit transmitted, as required by Internet rules.

gram support. This will allow you to identify an Internet encoding standard your mail clients both support.

Application File Format   Before transmission, you also must agree with your communication partner on an **application file format** for the attachment. For instance, suppose that I am using the latest version of Word for Windows and the other party is using an older version of WordPerfect. Before I send the other party an attachment, I will have to save my file to an older version of Word for Windows (which the receiver probably can import) or export my document to a version of WordPerfect that is the receiver's version of Word Perfect or an earlier version. (All well-written programs can read files created in their earlier versions.)

Viruses   Although attachments are very useful, they have become an excellent way to spread viruses. Even data files, such as word processing documents, may contain **macro viruses,** which are executed by the data file's application program when attachments are opened. A good rule is never to open an attachment unless you trust the source and have a good antivirus program whose virus list has been updated very recently. Note that trusting the source does not mean that you think the sender is a good person; good people who do not know that they have picked up a virus spread most viruses. Trusting the source means that the source has a good history of checking their system frequently with updated antivirus programs. Some newer e-mail viruses can even strike without the user opening an attachment.

Test Your Understanding

Answer Core Review Questions 4–7 and Detailed Review Questions 2 and 3.

IP TELEPHONY

IP telephony is the transmission of voice as IP packets through a packet-switched network, such as the Internet. IP telephony began as a toy service for residential users to make low-quality, inexpensive long-distance and international telephone calls over the Internet. However, these crude early offerings should not be taken as an indicator of where IP telephony will go in the future.

Reducing Costs

To understand why companies are excited by IP telephony, you have to understand that it is common for corporations to spend 2% or more of their total revenues on telephone service. The prospect of reducing this cost is highly compelling.

The Wastefulness of 64-kbps Voice Encoding   As discussed in Chapter 3, it has been traditional to encode human speech as a 64 kbps data

Figure 11.11
IP Telephony

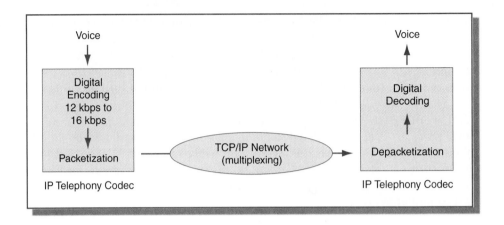

stream. However, newer forms of encoding can reduce the number of bits needed to send human voice to between 12 kbps and 16 kbps with only a slight loss in sound quality. Figure 11.11 shows that low-bit-rate encoding is the first step in IP telephony. It slashes the number of packets that must be sent.

The Wastefulness of Circuit Switching As noted in Chapter 1, the Public Switched Telephone Network has always been *circuit switched.* Circuit switching allocates dedicated capacity for each call. If you do not use your bandwidth, you still pay for it.

In contrast, as Figure 11.11 illustrates, after the codec compresses the human voice, an IP telephony system **packetizes** the voice stream and sends the stream over a packet-switched computer network. As discussed in Chapter 1, packet switching multiplexes the traffic of many conversations onto shared transmission lines, reducing transmission costs.

Voice–Data Convergence **Voice–data convergence,** which is handling both voice and data on a single network, has long been a goal of information systems. With IP telephony, that goal may be realized in the future. Many organizations have already implemented corporate-wide IP networks for data. If voice could also be sent over these IP networks, the labor cost savings from running only a single network could be impressive compared with maintaining separate networks for data and voice.

The Cost Picture Overall, IP telephony holds the promise of saving money three ways: by generating only 12 kbps to 16 kbps of data per voice channel, by multiplexing packets, and by requiring only the labor needed to run a single network.

Dealing with Latency

Although the potential economic benefits of IP telephony are persuasive, networking professionals pale at the prospect of sending voice over IP.

The Sensitivity of Voice to Delay When you speak to someone over the telephone, it only takes a few milliseconds (thousandths of a second) for your voice to reach the other person. This speed of transmission lets people talk back and forth as if talking face to face. However, the Internet often has latencies of 200 to 500 milliseconds (ms). A delay of about a fifth of a second (200 ms) makes conversation difficult. When you think the other side has paused, you begin to talk; but the pause was merely a delay, and as you begin to talk, you hear the other person's voice. Both sides become confused and stop speaking. A delay of about 500 ms makes conversation nearly impossible.

The Sensitivity of Voice to Jitter In addition, circuit switching delivers voice in a steady stream, whereas packet switching creates the possibility of **jitter**—variability in latency. Sometimes, adjacent packets are delivered immediately after one another. At other times, there can be significant delays between packets. This is called jitter because it literally sounds as if the other party is sitting on a vibrating machine.

IP, Latency, and Jitter As discussed in Chapter 3, classic IP can offer no guarantee of either short latency or constant latency. Although priority and other improvements are being retrofitted to IP, it will be several years before these improvements are common.

However, problems of latency and delay primarily are due to the Internet backbone, as Chapter 9 discussed. Chapter 9 also discussed a way to reduce congestion—simply avoiding the Internet backbone by connecting all sites to a single ISP.

A related approach is not to use the Internet at all but rather to send IP telephony traffic over a Frame Relay or ATM network. As noted in Chapter 9, it is common for PSDNs to offer service level agreements that guarantee low latency and jitter.

The Evolution of Corporate IP Telephony

Corporate IP telephony will not come overnight. Nor will it arrive fully functional. There are likely to be at least two stages in the evolution of corporate IP telephony.

Using IP Telephony to Interconnect PBXs As Figure 11.12 illustrates, the first stage in IP telephony will be to use IP only for transmissions between **private branch exchanges (PBXs).** With PBXs, each site effectively has its own internal telephone network, with the PBX acting as a central switch. In addition, PBXs at multiple sites can act together, so that a phone in one site can call a phone in any other site.

Traditionally, companies have used leased lines to connect their PBXs at different sites. Leased lines are dedicated circuits, so they offer guaranteed transmission speed and low latency. However, leased lines are expensive.

Figure 11.12
IP Telephony through Private Branch Exchange (PBX) Connections

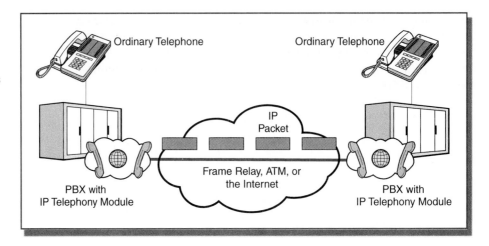

To work with leased lines, PBXs needed DSUs[4] with leased line interfaces. As Figure 11.12 illustrates, many PBXs can now be provisioned with DSUs that have **IP interfaces** that allow the PBXs to send and receive over the Internet, through a single ISP, or over a PSDN. The other aspects of the PBX network do not have to change at all, making the interconnection of PBXs through IP telephony an easy upgrade.

Computer-Telephone Integration (CTI) Although PBX-based IP telephony is simple to implement, it does not allow a company to do anything new. It would be better to bring IP telephony all the way to the user's desktop. This way, telephone applications could be integrated with traditional computer applications. The integration of voice applications and traditional computer applications is called **computer-telephone integration (CTI).** It would make IP telephony more than just a cost-saving innovation.

For instance, a user might only have a single electronic in-box that would contain a user's e-mail and voice messages. To give another example, if a client called and spoke with one representative and then had to be transferred to another representative, the information collected by the first representative could be transferred along with the call.

Unfortunately, there is no agreement on how to bring IP telephony to the desktop. If we send IP packets through traditional LANs and site networks, will the upgrades that would be needed to implement priority or full quality of service make the cost of IP telephony unattractive? Thanks to such uncertainties, desktop-to-desktop IP telephony and attendant CTI applications are not likely to be common in the near future, except for companies using proprietary products.

Standards IP telephony is based primarily on the ITU-T **H.323** standards created for videoconferencing over IP networks. H.323 specifies how voice sig-

---

[4] Most PBX systems are digital, with codecs built into the telephone handset on each desk. Therefore, a DSU is needed to connect a digital PBX with a digital leased line or with a digital IP connection.

nals can be encoded. It also has specifications for setting up conversations, maintaining them, and closing them. However, these capabilities are still rudimentary. In a very encouraging trend, the IETF and ITU-T, which have long been rivals in creating standards, have agreed to work together on IP telephony standards.

Questions About IP Telephony

Although IP telephony now appears to be attractive, there are still unsettled questions.

The Price of Traditional Telephone Service One of the most important issues is price. IP telephony has been seen as a way to reduce expensive long-distance and international calling. However, long-distance prices have been falling dramatically in recent years, thanks to improved long-distance and international technology and also thanks simply to competition. Will IP telephony really save money compared with increasingly less expensive circuit switched telephony?

Reliability Another key issue is reliability. The telephone system is far more reliable than any computer network.[5] Telephone outages are rare, and outages lasting more than a few minutes result in very surprised (and very upset) users. Unless cost savings are very substantial, companies will not be willing to take the risk of losing telephone service with any frequency.

Test Your Understanding

Answer Core Review Question 8 and Detailed Review Question 4.

KEY POINTS

Web-Enabled Database Applications

The first part of this chapter examined web-enabled database applications, in which a webserver used as an application server mediates between a browser user and a database server, typically via CGI or a proprietary API. The box in this chapter discussed IBM mainframe terminal–host systems. Web enabling is not limited to database applications. There is a growing trend toward giving users of e-mail and other applications access via a browser and an application server.

Electronic Mail The next part of this chapter dealt with standards for Internet electronic mail (e-mail). E-mail requires quite a few standards. One

---

[5] Telephony is 99.999% reliable. This amounts to only 5 hours of downtime per year. In contrast, IP is only about 99% reliable, meaning a downtime of 88 hours per year. Erica Shroeder, "Please, Sir, might I have another '9'?" *PC Week*, 3/22/99.

standard is SMTP for sending mail between mail hosts. For communication between the user and the mail host, there are proprietary file server program access approaches, Telnet, Internet mail clients that use SMTP and POP or IMAP, and web-based mail systems that use HTTP. For the content of messages, there are RFC 822 for text messages, MIME, and HTML body parts. For attachments, there are Internet encoding standards—including Binhex, UUENCODE, Basic MIME, and other versions of MIME—and application file format standards.

IP Telephony The distinction between voice and data communication is being eroded by IP telephony, which uses IP networks to carry voice (and video) as well as data. IP telephony promises large cost savings, but falling general telephone costs require a very sharp look at real costs. There are also latency and related concerns. In addition, although PBX–PBX IP telephony is easy to implement, bringing IP telephony to the desktop and integrating it with computer applications, that is, computer–telephone integration (CTI), will require a great deal of new technology. It may be some time before we have full voice–data convergence.

REVIEW QUESTIONS

Core Review Questions

1. A CGI-compliant program called *big.exe* is in the */etc/webpages/test* directory on webserver *ntl.cba.hawaii.edu*. Create an HTTP request message using HTTP 4.0 (which does not exist yet). The request will pass two variables, First and Second, whose values are Apples and Oranges, respectively.

2. **a)** Briefly describe the main steps in web-enabled database access using an application server. **b)** Why is this process called transparent?

3. **a)** What are the roles of CGI and intermediate programs in web-enabled database applications? **b)** Why are proprietary APIs better that CGI? **c)** Why are proprietary APIs worse?

4. What is/are the main standard(s) for sending e-mail between mail hosts? (In this question, spell out all standard names the first time you use them.)

5. What are the main ways for mail clients to communicate with the user's mail host?

6. **a)** What is/are the main standard(s) for mail bodies? **b)** Distinguish between web-enabled e-mail and HTML body parts.

7. **a)** What does Internet encoding do? **b)** Before you send someone an attachment, what should you agree upon with the recipient?

8. **a)** What is IP telephony? **b)** How can IP telephony save money? **c)** Why may these cost savings not be reached? **d)** Describe latency and jitter problems in IP telephony. **e)** Describe how these latency problems can be alleviated. **f)** Explain PBX–PBX IP telephony.

Detailed Review Questions

1. Referring to the box, "Mainframes," **a)** Name the main hardware elements in mainframe computer systems. **b)** How does this arrangement improve response time? **c)** How does this arrangement reduce transmission costs? **d)** How does this arrangement free the mainframe to concentrate on high-value work? **e)** How do the layers of SNA compare to those of OSI? **f)** What is an NAU? **g)** Distinguish between the two forms of NAUs. **h)** Explain TN3270E in terms of its purpose and how it works. **i)** Explain DLSw in terms of its purpose and how it works.

2. **a)** Describe the steps involved in sending a message via SMTP. **b)** Describe the steps involved in retrieving a message via POP. **c)** How would Figure 11.9 change if the mail client had downloaded the second message?

3. Compare RFC 822 message bodies and MIME message bodies.

4. **a)** What standards bodies are developing IP telephony standards? **b)** Are they coordinating their work? **c)** What is the main standard for IP telephony today?

Thought Questions

1. What was the most surprising thing you learned in this chapter?

2. What was the most difficult part of this chapter for you?

3. In the opening vignette, Glenn had several problems regarding e-mail and his voice-over-the-Internet system. **a)** Explain why each of these problems occurred, one answer per paragraph. **b)** Which application was working well? **c)** How did it probably work?

Case Studies

For case studies, go to the book's website, **http://www.prenhall.com/panko,** and look at the "Case Studies" page for this chapter.

Projects

1. **Getting Current.** Go to the book's website's "New Information" and "Errors" pages for this chapter to get new information since this book went to press and to correct any errors in the text.

2. **Internet Exercises.** Go to the book's website's "Exercises" page for this chapter and do the Internet exercises.

Chapter 12

Looking Forward

*C*hen May-Ling is considering the adoption of a wireless LAN standard for her company. She has been following 802.11 products. Their prices have fallen consistently, but she is somewhat worried about their maturity. She also has been reading about a new wireless technology for buildings, called "Bluetooth." This standard, created by an industry consortium instead of by a standards agency, may produce very inexpensive wireless networking. May-Ling wonders if she can implement both and, if not, which she should choose. She would also like her wireless notebooks to be able to keep in touch with servers when the user is out of the office. ∎

Learning Objectives

After studying this chapter, you should be able to describe:

- Budgeting, product selection, and procurement
- Systems administration (server management)
- Centralized management
- New technologies, including wireless computing, ubiquitous computing, network object-oriented programming, and The Next Big Thing, whatever it may be

INTRODUCTION

It is always good to end by looking forward. In this last chapter, we will look at concepts and trends that will be increasingly important in the future.

THE MATTER OF MONEY

When computer scientists and electrical engineers take networking courses in business schools, they often have a difficult time adjusting to the need to select the least expensive technology that meets user needs. For instance, when I ask classes to design a PC network for 10 PCs, I sometimes get solutions that require an ATM switch, which would be prohibitively expensive to buy and maintain. Even business students often say, "Get the best technology you can afford," as if budget should drive selection instead of needs. In business schools, we expect better.

Exploding Demand, Stagnant Budgets

It is obvious to every user that demand for networking is exploding. We want more applications over ever-greater distances and using ever-higher speeds. Needs are growing by perhaps 20% to 40% annually in most firms.

At the same time, budgets are not growing nearly as quickly. Most networking budgets are either stagnant or are growing about 5% to 10% per year. To meet exploding user needs, it is important for network managers to be extremely prudent about the cost of whatever they select.

Measuring Costs

Total Purchase Costs   For instance, we must look at the **total purchase cost of network products.** Just as PCs are sold as collections of components, most network products, such as switches and routers, come as collections of hardware and software components. A **fully configured** switch or router often costs far more than the "base price" listed in catalogs. When comparing products from different vendors, it is critical to compare fully configured products.

Initial Installation Costs   Also, there typically are substantial costs associated with **initial installation.** Some vendors, especially carriers, charge one-time **setup fees.** A company's *internal labor costs* associated with installation also must be considered. These include the costs of the information systems staff's labor and the labor costs of end users. End-user labor costs may rise dramatically during installation periods because of training and disruption. In general, labor costs may be far higher than hardware, software, and transmission costs.

Ongoing Costs   Of course there also are ongoing costs. These may come in the form of hardware or software upgrades over the life of the product selected. There also are ongoing labor costs to manage the network product. Ongoing costs may be far larger than initial costs.

Ongoing costs are especially high for new technologies that are not yet **mature.** It may take several years for products based on new technologies to become easy to install and use. Immature products often lack utilities that allow easy management, requiring a great deal of expensive management work. It is a good idea to avoid new "bleeding edge" technologies if possible.

The Timing of Costs and Benefits When evaluating business investments, businesses normally use **discounted cash flow analysis,** as shown in Figure 12.1. Money not spent could be used for other productive projects, so there is an "opportunity cost" of using money. Most businesses have "hurdle rates" of about 20%. If a new system cannot earn a 20% return on investment over its lifetime, it should not be purchased.

As Figure 12.1 illustrates, discounted cash flow analysis looks at an investment over its entire life. Each year, there will be costs and benefits. Both costs and benefits are discounted by the hurdle rate. In the first year, there is no time discount. In the second year, money could have been invested at 20%, so both cost and benefit values are divided by 120%. In the second year, values are divided by the square of 120%, that is, 144%. In general, discounting is done at the rate of $(1+i)^n$, where i is the hurdle rate and n is the number of years. Dividing costs and benefits by the discounting factor gives the **present value** for that year's figures.

The **net present value (NPV)** *of the investment,* which companies use to compare the investment with alternative possible investments, is the sum of the present values for the individual years.

One way to improve the value of an investment is to start obtaining benefits as rapidly as possible. Once, it was common to invest money for two to five years in development before achieving any benefits. Obviously, it helps the net present value to start getting at least some benefits as rapidly as possible. Psychologically, too, it enhances a project's acceptance if it can start producing some benefits rapidly.

	Year 1	Year 2	Year 3	Year 4	Year 5
Benefits	$1,500	$4,000	$3,000	$2,000	$1,500
Costs	$3,000	$1,000	$1,000	$1,000	$1,000
Discount Factor	1.00	1.20	1.44	1.73	2.07
Discounted Benefits	$1,500	$3,333	$2,083	$1,157	$723
Discounted Costs	$3,000	$833	$694	$579	$482
Present Value	−$1,500	$2,500	$1,389	$579	$241
Net Present Value = $3,209					

Figure 12.1
Discounted Cash Flow Analysis

Procurement

Procuring (purchasing) products is a constant headache for network administrators. They need to get the best value for every dollar they spend.

User Needs The first step, of course, is to understand **user needs.** Although this can be very difficult to do, it must be done as well as possible. Otherwise, there would be no way to evaluate different alternatives or to be sure that a selected product will be useful to real users.

Request for Proposals (RFP) The next step is to issue a **request for proposals (RFP).** An RFP is a document that invites vendors to bid on a project. The RFP lays out exactly what will be required. Writing an RFP is critical; if disagreements arise later about the scope of the work to be done, the wording of the RFP will determine who is correct. An RFP is a legal document.

Leaving something major out of an RFP will bring major headaches later. Although the contractor may agree to do additional work, the purchasing organization will not have any negotiating leverage. The price will be much higher than it would be if the additional work had been included in the RFP in the first place.

Evaluating Proposals with Multicriteria Decision Making In most cases, several vendors will submit **proposals** in response to the RFP. In **lowest-price** decision making, the proposal with the lowest price that is fully compliant with the RFP would be selected.

However, things are rarely that simple. Most companies use **multicriteria decision making,** in which each submission is compared against several criteria, as shown in Figure 12.2.

For each criterion, each proposal is given a **rating,** perhaps on a scale of 1 to 10 with 10 being high.

In addition, each criterion is given a **weight** to indicate its relative importance in selection. The weight might be 1 to 5 or something else. This rating for each criterion will be multiplied by the weight.

If the criteria and weights were selected carefully, and if all proposals were rated well, then the sum of the **rating–weight products** should give an overall **proposal value.** The proposal with the highest value would win.[1]

Negotiation, Monitoring, and Renegotiating Often, if a firm can narrow its choice to two or three vendors, it can go into a second negotiation phase in which it attempts to extract a slightly better deal than the one presented in the proposal. This is the **final and best offer.**

After a contract is awarded, the buyer needs to monitor the performance of the vendor or their product carefully. There is not much point is selecting a vendor based on specific criteria if these criteria are not enforced.

---

[1] If the selection method is published in the RFP, by the way, it must be followed or losing proposers may file grievances with the purchasing company or with the courts.

Figure 12.2
Multicriteria
Decision Making

Criterion	Weight	Product A	Product B	Product C
Price	5	9	8	7
Features	5	7	8	9
Installation	3	6	4	8
Maturity	4	6	6	6
Total		122	116	128

Total for Product A is given by (5*9)+(5*7)+(3*6)+(4*6)=122

Test Your Understanding

Answer Core Review Questions 1–3, Detailed Review Question 1, and Thought Questions 1–3.

SERVER MANAGEMENT (SYSTEMS ADMINISTRATION)

If you ask the manager of a network what technical part of his or her job takes up the most time, you may be surprised to hear the manager talk about the management of servers, which is known for historical reasons as **systems administration.** For better or worse, systems administration usually falls under the networking department, and it is extremely time consuming.

Types of Servers   For small to medium-size servers, most companies use standard PCs running a server operating system (SOS) such as Microsoft Windows NT/2000 Server, Novell NetWare, or LINUX. For large servers, most companies turn to workstation servers running UNIX.

Symmetric Multiprocessing (SMP)   Purchasing a specific server within the PC or workstation category, however, is rather complex. Servers often have multiple microprocessors for faster performance. (This is called **symmetric multiprocessing** or **SMP.**) Although an eight-processor SMP server is not eight times faster than a single-processor server, the gain in speed often is impressive.

RAID   Servers also tend to use **RAID** disk drives. "RAID" stands for "redundant array of inexpensive (or independent) drives." As Figure 12.3 illustrates, instead of writing to and reading from a single disk drive, RAID controllers read and write to several drives simultaneously.

Data is written in **parallel** to all of the drives. We saw in Chapter 4 that parallel transmission is *faster* than serial transmission. A RAID array of inexpensive drives tends to be much faster than a single disk drive of the same total cost.

Figure 12.3
RAID Disk Drive

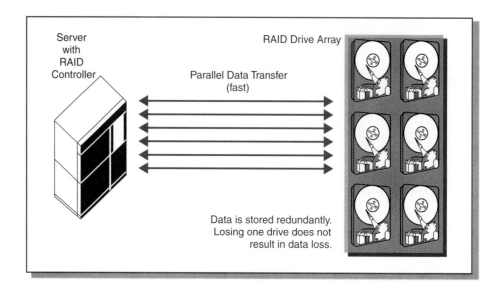

In addition, data are written **redundantly,**[2] across all drives. If one drive fails, files can still be recovered fully. In other words, RAID drives offer high *reliability.* Some RAID arrays even use hot-swappable drives. If one drive in the array fails, it can be removed and replaced without having to shut down the computer.

Server Farms When you go to the website of a large electronic commerce retailer, the URL you type has a specific host name. However, as Figure 12.4 illustrates, that "host" probably is a group of servers called a **server farm.** Quite simply, even UNIX workstation servers cannot be large enough to serve the processing requirements of large sites. In fact, it may be cheaper to use a server farm running many inexpensive PC servers than to use a server farm running a few large UNIX workstation servers.

Figure 12.4 illustrates a process called **load balancing.** In this process, a switch or router sends individual requests to individual servers on the basis of their speed, the current workload, and other factors. Load balancing is practical today. Load balancing switches and routers can also route requests to servers depending upon the application (in Figure 12.4, HTTP or FTP).

Server clustering is the next step in creating server farms. In server clustering, the group of servers acting together distributes the workload among themselves, instead of sharing work under the load balancing control of a switch or router. Server clustering is less mature than load balancing but is potentially faster.

Server farms bring scalability, that is, the ability to grow. As demand grows, you can simply add more servers. Increased speed is the main reason for server farms.

---

[2] There are different levels of RAID, beginning with Level 0. Not all levels offer redundancy to avoid data loss.

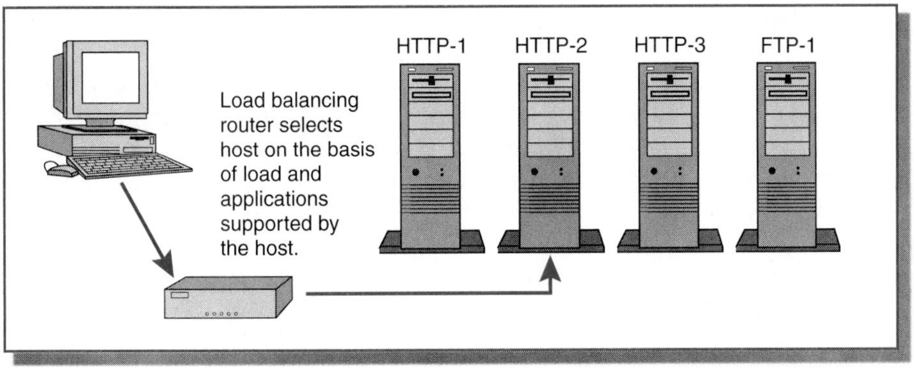

Figure 12.4
Server Farm

Server farms also bring reliability. If a single server fails, others will continue running. However, the servers probably will be set up similarly. It is not uncommon for the same software problem to crash all of a server farm's servers simultaneously.

Server Configuration   When new servers are installed, the installer must go through a process called **server configuration.** This is a complex process that requires taking certain actions in certain sequences and setting parameters within a range of alternatives. Being able to install a Windows NT, Novell NetWare, UNIX, or LINUX server is a valuable skill that requires both knowledge of specific actions and also a broad understanding of hardware installation, software installation, networking protocols, security, and other matters, so that parameters can be set intelligently.

Ongoing Work   Systems administration does not end when a server is installed. The most time-consuming ongoing process is **assigning rights** to individual users and groups in various directories on the server (see Chapter 6). Every user must be assigned rights in every directory the user should be able to use. These assignments are likely to change over time.

Another constant chore is adding new software and software upgrades to servers. A server's SOS and application programs are upgraded constantly. This is done to install both new versions with higher functionality and patches (fixes) for various pieces of software, say to preventing security exploits based on known weaknesses (see Chapter 10).

An extremely crucial chore is **backup.** Servers often hold mission-critical corporate data or data for dozens or hundreds of users. The nightly backup of all data to tape or to other archival media is important in such situations. Failure to do regular backups can only be described as professional malpractice.

Test Your Understanding

Answer Core Review Question 4 and Detailed Review Questions 2 and 3.

So far, we have been looking at current concerns that almost all network administrators must face daily. Now, we will begin looking at longer-term trends. One important trend is a move toward **centralized management.** In its ultimate form, a network administrator would sit at a PC or workstation and diagnose any problem in the network, fix problems remotely, gather data on network performance, fine-tune network performance, control security across the network, and take other global actions. Although this fully centralized control is only an ideal, companies are moving toward it because of the growing complexity of networks.

Network Management Systems

Figure 12.5 illustrates a **network management system** to support centralized control of a network.

Manager The network administrator works at a central PC or client workstation. This computer runs a program called the network management software, or, simply, the **manager.**

Managed Nodes The manager manages many **managed nodes,** including printers, hubs, switches, routers, application programs, and other pieces of hardware and software.

Managed nodes have pieces of software (and sometimes hardware) called network management agents, or, simply, **agents.** In sports and entertainment, an agent acts on behalf of a person. Similarly, agents communicate with the manager on behalf of the managed nodes. In other words, the managed node does not communicate with the manager directly, but only through its agent.

Figure 12.5
Network
Management
System Based on
SNMP

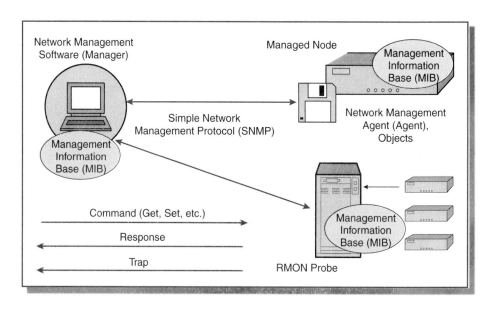

One specialized type of managed node is the **RMON probe** (Remote Monitoring). This may be a stand-alone device or software running on a switch or router. An RMON probe collects data on network traffic instead of information about the RMON probe itself. The manager can poll the RMON probe to get summarized information about the distribution of packet sizes, the number of various types of errors, the number of packets processed, and so forth.

Objects More specifically, the manager, through the agent, manages **objects** on the managed node. For instance, one object might be a port on a switch. A particular switch might have several **instances** of this object (several ports). The manager should be able to get information about each port and even tell the switch to disable the port.

SNMP offers many types of very specific objects. For example, a manager can ask a file server agent for information about a specific print queue. Or, the manager could ask a host computer running TCP about its maximum segment size (see Module A). SNMP objects, in other words, are far more finely grained than "printer" or "switch."

Management Information Base (MIB) In a database, you have a *schema* that describes the design of the database, that is, the specific types of information it contains. Similarly, network management requires a **management information base (MIB)** specification that defines what objects can exist and also the specific characteristics of each object.

Besides the *schema*, there is also the *database itself*, which contains actual data in the form dictated by the schema. Unfortunately, this is also called the management information base, so you must be careful when hearing the term "MIB" to determine whether it means the design or the data itself.

Adding further confusion, there is a MIB on each managed node that contains information about that node's objects, and there is also a MIB on the manager's computer to hold data collected from many objects.

Network Management Protocols

We need standards to govern communication between the manager and the agent. The most popular network management standard is the IETF's **Simple Network Management Protocol (SNMP).** SNMP governs both the MIB schema and manager–agent communications.

Requests and Responses Normally, SNMP communication between the manager and agents works through **request–response cycles.** The manager sends a request. The agent sends a response confirming that the request has been met, delivering requested data, or saying that an error has occurred and that the agent cannot comply with the request.

There are two basic types of requests. **Get** requests ask the agent to retrieve certain information and return this information to the manager. In contrast, **set** requests ask the agent to set a parameter on the managed node. For instance, a set request may ask an agent to set the status of Port 2 on a switch to "on." This causes the device to turn on the port. Although it seems odd, setting an object value causes devices to change their behavior to match the setting. (If you are familiar with object-oriented programming, this approach should be familiar.)

Traps Agents do not always wait for requests to send information. If they detect a condition that they think a manager should know about, they can send a **trap** message to the manager, as Figure 12.5 illustrates. For instance, if a switch detects that a transmission line to which a certain port is connected appears to have failed, it might notify the manager of this situation.

Other Network Management Protocols SNMP is not the only network management protocol in common use today, although it is the most widely used. A growing number of managers can speak to multiple types of agents using different network management protocols, including different MIB designs.

Directory Servers

Chapter 6 introduced directory servers in the context of PC networks, where they provide single login and resource lookup for users. However, directory servers are increasingly becoming the core tool for the idea of central management. The **directory server** is becoming a place to store all central information for a company.

Hierarchical Structure Directory servers store information about objects. These objects are defined hierarchically. For example, Figure 12.6 shows how an organization might store data on its employees. The *organization (O)* is divided into smaller *organizational units (OUs)*[3] and then into specific employees. Information kept about specific employees would include their names, e-mail addresses, network passwords, physical locations, and other pertinent information. The OSI **X.500** standard specifies directory structure rules.

LDAP Various computers on the network must be able to send queries to the directory server and to send updated information. To facilitate this, we need a standardized **directory access protocol** to specify how outside devices will communicate with the directory server. The most common standard for directory access is the **Lightweight Directory Access Protocol (LDAP).** Managed by the IETF, this standard's simplicity and good functionality have made it broadly available, with more directory servers adopting it every year.

Directory Services Markup Language (DSML) As discussed in Chapter 11, webservers can become application servers to link users with database servers and other resources. We would like a standard for webserver application servers to interact with LDAP directory servers. The **Directory**

---

[3] There can be several levels of organizational units.

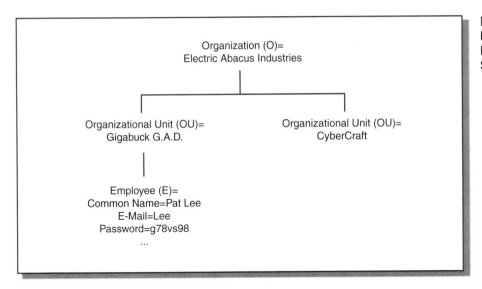

Figure 12.6
Hierarchical Directory Object Structure

Organization (O)=
Electric Abacus Industries

Organizational Unit (OU)=
Gigabuck G.A.D.

Organizational Unit (OU)=
CyberCraft

Employee (E)=
Common Name=Pat Lee
E-Mail=Lee
Password=g78vs98
...

Services Markup Language (DSML) standard is designed to allow this. In fact, a DSML webserver can combine data from two or more directory servers and present integrated results to browser users.

Directory Server Products Although standards are good, we need good directory products that implement these standards and provide full directory server functionality. To date, the leader in directory server products is Novell, with its **NetWare Directory Services (NDS)** product. Initially available only for use on Novell NetWare file servers, NDS is now available on Windows NT/2000 server and UNIX computers. Microsoft has **Active Directory,** which was only released in 2000 and is not as mature.

Converging Boxes

Today, we have many different types of boxes for security, including firewalls, remote access servers, and IPsec servers. We also have several types of boxes for forwarding packets, including switches and routers.

Comprehensive Relay Devices However, security and forwarding are not mutually exclusive activities. In fact, they both involve examining the packet. In the future, we may see **comprehensive relay devices,** as shown in Figure 12.7. These comprehensive relay devices will forward packets to their proper destination but only if the packets meet security requirements.

Multilayer Packet Analysis Comprehensive relay devices may examine a packet at several layers, looking at the headers (and trailers) at the data link, internet, transport, and application layers. At the application layer, they may also check the data field of the packet for viruses and other unauthorized content. This will allow highly intelligent forwarding and security.

Figure 12.7
Integrated
Transmission
Network

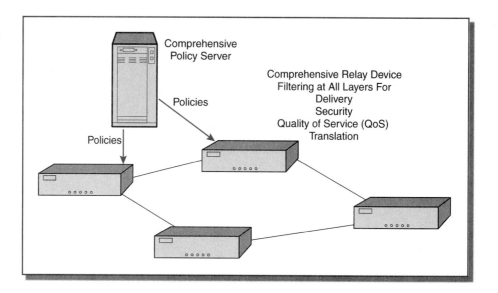

Comprehensive Policy Server

Policies

Comprehensive Relay Device Filtering at All Layers For
Delivery
Security
Quality of Service (QoS)
Translation

Policies

***Reducing Costs and Integrated Forwarding-Security Decision
Making*** Using comprehensive relay devices can be much less expensive
than having many separate devices for forwarding and security. In addition, it
will allow firms to treat forwarding and security in a highly integrated way.

Functionality and Processor Load Concerns On the negative side, initial comprehensive relay devices may not have the functionality available in
"best-of-breed" switches, routers, firewalls, and other discrete forwarding or
security devices. Also, filtering at multiple levels requires many processing
cycles. Purchasers must be sure that comprehensive relay devices can keep up
with traffic processing requirements.

Policy-Based Networking

Figure 12.7 shows that the comprehensive relay devices will get their operating parameters from a centralized **comprehensive policy server.** This will give
uniformity across all comprehensive relay devices. This will thwart an
intruder who is trying to gain access to many devices in an attempt to contact
a device on which security has not been configured properly. It will also allow
very fast response to new threats because the comprehensive policy server can
send changes to all comprehensive relay devices simultaneously.

Policy-based management, however, does not have to wait for comprehensive relay devices. Many security and forwarding devices are now developed
with the ability to work with a policy server designed to provide specific policies relevant to specific types of devices (switches, firewalls, servers, and so
forth). Vendors are now exploring the new **Common Open Policy Service
(COPS)** standard to allow their systems to interact.

Test Your Understanding

Answer Core Review Questions 5–7, Detailed Review Questions 4–6, and Thought Question 4.

NEW TECHNOLOGIES

It is very difficult to appreciate how fast things change on the Internet. It has been said that the Internet "lives in dog years." In other words, change happens about seven times faster on the Internet than it does in traditional business. At the time of this writing, the World Wide Web is so pervasive that it is difficult to believe that it is only about five years old. What will the Internet (and corporate networking) be like in another five or ten years? At great risk of having this last part of the book be read aloud in the future to mock the author, here are a few predictions.

Wireless Communication

Today, we are like early divers who had to work in bulky diving suits, tied to their ships with long umbilical cords for air. Our desktop computers come in basically a single size, and even notebooks have only modest variety. To use a network with both, you have to connect to a physical wire.

Today, when most people dive, they wear lightweight scuba gear that lets them roam freely with no links to the topside world. In the same way, we will soon be able to keep in touch with our networks without physical attachments, and we will be able to use new devices that look very little like personal computers.

802.11 We already know how to connect mobile devices to networks. As discussed in a box in Chapter 7, the 802.11 wireless LAN standard will allow us to carry our notebook computers and new devices throughout our corporate buildings without ever losing touch with the company's servers or the Internet. Falling prices and faster technology should soon make 802.11 fairly attractive.

Bluetooth The one point of confusion in wireless LANs is that another standard, called **Bluetooth,** offers wireless LAN service at a much lower price. However, Bluetooth really is only for **personal networking.** It can link only a few devices, and these devices have to be within a few meters of one another. It is not a full wireless LAN protocol for corporate sites. Bluetooth is good for such things as linking notebooks to nearby printers and linking small lightweight headsets to nearby cellular telephones. Unfortunately, 802.11 and Bluetooth use the same frequency range and may interfere with one another. Corporations may have to decide between them unless new frequency bands are opened.

High-Speed Metropolitan Networking What will happen when an office worker takes his or her notebook outside, into the community? Wireless communication is available there now, but its speeds are only modem speeds and its cost is high. For knowledge workers used to megabit speeds, such slow speeds are likely to be very unattractive. In addition, although high-speed wireless metropolitan area networking (citywide networking) is coming, it may be coming in the form of multiple standards.

Too Many Standards Too much of anything is a bad thing, and that is doubly true for standards. Are users likely to implement three or more wireless standards in their computers for personal, building, and metropolitan areas? Until the standards picture is clarified, wireless prospects will continue to be limited.

Increased Bandwidth One key to the wireless revolution will be the ability to support high capacity. As Chapter 5 indicates, to get high speeds in radio communication, you need wide bandwidth for each user.

Bandwidth at useful frequency ranges (about 500 MHz to a few gigahertz)[4] has been very limited, restricting the number of possible users. However, more bandwidth is being made available in this range for wireless networking, cellular telephony, and other office-related needs.

Cellular Systems Another way to get more effective bandwidth is to divide an area (office, building, or metropolitan area) into separate areas called **cells,** as Figure 12.8 illustrates. Each cell has a cellsite, which is a radio transceiver (transmitter/receiver). Users are served by the nearest cellsite, based on the strength of the user's signals.

Suppose that someone in Cell E is transmitting on Channel 47. Users in adjacent cells (B, C, D, F, H, and I) cannot use this channel, or their signals will interfere with the user in Cell E. However, radio energy drops off rapidly with distance. Users who have a cell between them and Cell E can reuse Channel 47. For instance, Cell G users can communicate on Channel 47.[5]

In general, if there are N cells in a large system, channels can be reused N/7 times on average. For instance, cellular telephony normally has 20 to 100 cells in a city. This allows it to reuse its channels between 3 and 14 times within the city. The multiplication of effective bandwidth through channel reuse will be a major key to wireless technology.

Prospects Overall, the prospects for wireless data service are good, and if standards issues can be resolved, rapidly falling prices should bring an explo-

---

[4] At lower frequencies, there is little bandwidth (see Module B). At higher frequencies, signals do not pass through walls or bend around objects, making anything other than line-of-site reception possible. Government agencies have been forcing line-of-sight microwave radio systems that carriers use for trunk line communication to vacate frequencies in the low-gigahertz region and move to higher frequencies. This will provide more spectrum for mobile device applications.

[5] Of course, if they do, then Cell K cannot use Channel 47.

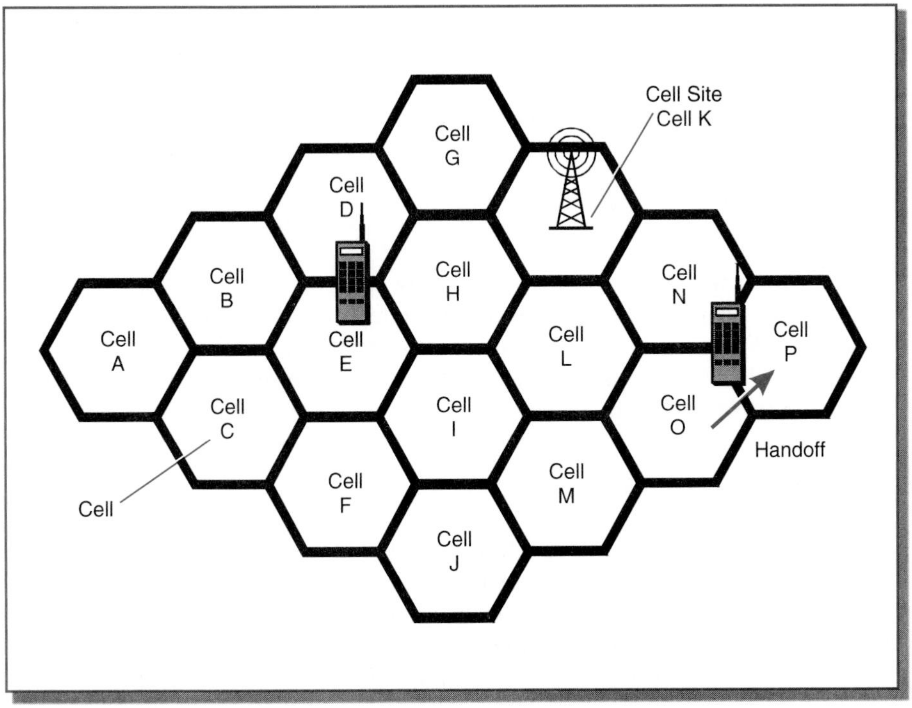

Figure 12.8
Cellular Radio
System

Cell Site
Cell K

Cell G
Cell D
Cell B
Cell A
Cell E
Cell C
Cell
Cell H
Cell N
Cell P
Cell L
Cell I
Cell O
Cell F
Cell M
Cell J
Handoff

sion in mobility. At first, users will do the same tasks they now do at their desktops on the move, such as create documents and handle e-mail. However, whenever a radically new way to get information to people appears, as in the form of high-speed Internet access through ADSLs and cable modems, people use their systems differently, not simply more.

Really Personal Computers

Personal computers come in only two sizes today. First, there are desktop computers. They are called desktop computers because they use up your entire desktop. Notebook computers are smaller, but they are still fairly large. If you put one in your briefcase, you have little room for anything else. If you take a trip, a notebook can give you a serious case of "jet lug."

Personal Digital Assistants (PDAs) and Beyond   We can get a glimpse of the future by looking at today's hand-held **personal digital assistants (PDAs),** such as the Palm Pilot. These devices today are extremely slow and limited and can be used for only very simple applications, such as keeping appointments.

However, as processing speeds and memory increase, hand-held devices will soon have today's desktop processing power and even more. They will also have wireless communication. These new capabilities will allow them to take on new applications, most of which we probably cannot even imagine today. For instance, with wireless communication, your PDA may announce your presence as you walk around, perhaps even unlocking and opening doors as you approach them and turning on the lights in the rooms you enter.

Output Limitations Of course, a problem with hand-held devices is the user interface. Even palm-size devices have very small displays. The device that most people use today for wireless communication, the cellular telephone, has an even smaller screen. Unless information is reformatted, it will not fit on such displays.

For cellular telephones, vendors are now creating standards for a **Wireless Application Protocol (WAP)** that cellular telephones will use to receive webpages. WAP is designed to work at low speeds and high latency.

For WAP, the webpage must be formatted in the **Wireless Markup Language (WML),** which is designed to present information on tiny cellphone displays. It remains to be seen how much web information will be reformatted this way.

Input Input is also a problem that must be considered. Typing will have to be severely limited as a means of input. Script writing with a stylus is one option, although error rates are unacceptably high today. Voice input may become feasible as processing power increases, but again there are error problems, especially when users communicate "in the wild," that is, on the street and in noisy restaurants. The high ambient noise in such locations can cause voice input errors to skyrocket.

Networked Object-Oriented Processing (NOOP)

Today, we are concerned with computers communicating with one another. This is a problem because there are many computers in use. However, the number of computers in use today pales before the number of devices that may communicate in the future. At home, our oven, coffee maker,[6] and other devices may wish to talk to one another. At work, machine tools, locks, and many small office machines may also become intelligent and wish to communicate.

Object-Oriented Processing In fact, it may not just be devices that communicate. One trend in programming today is **object-oriented programming (OOP),** in which programs are broken into small self-contained **objects** that contain both logic and associated data. Objects work together by sending messages to one another.

NOOP In Chapter 1, we saw that client/server processing works by having *two* programs on *two* computers work together. In **networked object-oriented**

---

[6] IETF RFC 2324, Hyper Text Coffee Pot Control Protocol (HTCPCP/1.0), actually specifies a protocol for the remote control of coffee makers. The protocol argues that "there is a strong, dark, rich requirement for a protocol designed espressoly [sic] for the brewing of coffee." The protocol does not support the brewing of decaffeinated coffee, giving the explanation, "Why bother?" Although this was a spoof protocol introduced on April 1, 1998 (April Fools Day), we may eventually implement such small device protocols.

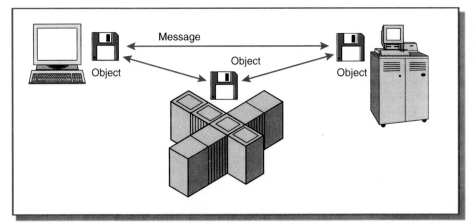

Figure 12.9
Networked Object-Oriented Processing

processing (NOOP), the work to accomplish a task can be achieved by *many* objects working on *many* computers, with message-based communication across computers being used to coordinate their work. Figure 12.9 illustrates this approach.

Capacity Exploitation It will be possible to send objects to machines with temporary excess capacity, so that computers will be loaded more evenly. Today, most computer capacity is wasted on desktop machines.

New Ways to Interact More broadly, NOOP will open new ways for programmers to create programs and to interface with programs that others have written. It may bring an explosion in networked applications.

Standards: DCOM versus CORBA Problems with standards must be considered. Support in the industry has been solidifying behind Microsoft's **Distributed Component Object Model (DCOM)** and a consortium's **Common Object Request Broker Architecture (CORBA).** The two approaches are incompatible, although there are efforts to bridge them.

NOOP Security One critical need in NOOP is excellent security. The speed with which objects may travel from machine to machine and communicate with thousands or millions of other objects could create **flash viruses** that would make today's e-mail viruses seem tame by comparison.

The Changing Internet

Finally, everybody expects the Internet to become even more important than it is today. However, it is important to note that we will not simply be getting more of the same. Tomorrow's Internet will be much less congested as ISPs catch up on their building programs. (We are already seeing less congestion than we saw in earlier years.) It is likely to become a **business-class Internet** with the speed and reliability needed for business processing. However, there are concerns that two or even more loosely connected Internets eventually may develop, appealing to different segments of the user population, with basic residential-class Internet service perhaps not being much better than it is today.

We also know that tomorrow's Internet will be far *faster* than the Internet of today. There is already a glut of high-speed, long-distance optical fiber capacity, and fiber building programs are continuing without abatement. Today, users marvel at sustained download speeds of a megabit per second or more. In a few years, we will be able to bring gigabit download speeds to the desktop. It will no longer be even slightly inconvenient to retrieve huge graphics files or watch full-motion, full-quality video. Although we can only speculate about what users will do with that capacity, we know from experience that when users get new capabilities, they are endlessly inventive.

The Next Big Thing

In the mid-1990s, the World Wide Web exploded onto the Internet. Within a year or two, it was already widespread and allowed us to do new things. It was the ultimate "killer app." Information technology has a tendency to surprise us with such breakthroughs every few years, and so do corporate networks. Since the PC invasion of the early 1980s, we have gone through a long series of shocks. Thanks to the growth of networking, the number of such shocks actually is increasing. Although not all breakthroughs have the impact of the World Wide Web or the introduction of desktop computing, they are cumulatively making deep changes in the way we work.

Test Your Understanding

Answer Core Review Questions 8–11 and Detailed Review Questions 7–10.

KEY POINTS

Money   Although user demand for networking is exploding, networking budgets are not. Network managers have to be extremely smart about the investments they make. They have to master the good budgeting and procurement practices already used in other parts of the firm.

Servers (Systems Administration)   A few years ago, servers were seen as lying outside the scope of network management. Today, systems administration—the management of servers—has become one of the most time-consuming and important aspects of network management. This is particularly true for large electronic commerce sites, where firms literally live or die by their server speed and reliability.

Centralized Management   We can now build networks much larger than we can manage. When faults occur, they may cause a problem with much of a network, and it may take hours simply to find the problem. In addition, companies must have central policies to control quality of service, security, and other service considerations uniformly. We are entering a more disciplined era of network management, with network management systems, directory servers, and other devices that support centralized management.

New Technology We can already anticipate several aspects of new technology, including an expected wireless revolution; the evolution of "ubiquitous computing," in which a vast array of devices are intelligent and need to communicate; networked object-oriented programming; and a much faster and more reliable "business-class" Internet.

REVIEW QUESTIONS

Core Review Questions

1. **a)** Why is "always selecting the best technology" not a good idea? **b)** Why is "choosing the best technology your budget can afford" not a good idea? **c)** What should guide selection if not technology alone or budget alone?

2. **a)** Name the key cost measurement considerations mentioned in the chapter. **b)** Distinguish between total purchase costs and installation costs.

3. **a)** What is an RFP? **b)** What is the purpose of a proposal? **c)** Why do we need multicriteria decision making?

4. **a)** What is server management called? **b)** What is a server farm? **c)** What benefits does it bring? **d)** What is server configuration? **e)** Why is it difficult?

5. **a)** Why do we need network management systems? **b)** In a network management system, what does the manager manage? **c)** With what does the manager communicate? **d)** What is an object? **e)** What is a management information base (MIB)? **f)** What is SNMP? **g)** What does each type of message do in SNMP? **h)** What program (manager or agent) sends each type of message?

6. **a)** Why do we need directory servers? **b)** How is information organized in a directory server? **c)** What does a directory access protocol standardize? **d)** What is the most important directory access protocol?

7. **a)** What is the situation today in wireless standards? **b)** Why does wireless data communication need wide bandwidth? **c)** Why may wide bandwidth not be a problem for wireless data transmission in the future?

8. **a)** Why may small hand-held devices take on broader roles in the future? **b)** What are the user interface problems with such devices?

9. Briefly explain networked object-oriented programming (NOOP).

10. How is tomorrow's Internet likely to be different from today's Internet?

Detailed Review Questions

1. When is the best time for negotiation?

2. **a)** What is symmetric multiprocessing? **b)** What benefit does it bring? **c)** In a single sentence, describe RAID (do not just spell out the name). **d)** What benefits does it bring?

3. List some ongoing systems administration tasks for servers.

4. **a)** What is an RMON probe? **b)** Are there other network management system standards besides SNMP?

5. **a)** What new standard for communication between webserver application servers and LDAP directory servers will allow browser users to access directory server data? **b)** What is the most mature directory server product for PC networks today? **c)** What is the Microsoft entry into this market?

6. **a)** Why would comprehensive relay devices be good? **b)** What problems may they have? **c)** Why are policy servers good?

7. What standard allows policy-based products from different vendors to interoperate?

8. In Figure 12.8, Channel 47 is used in Cell E. Come up with a list of all cells that can use Channel 47. Remember that you cannot assign the same channel in adjacent cells. Note: there are several possible solutions.

9. Compare 802.11 and Bluetooth.

10. **a)** Briefly describe WAP. **b)** Why is it attractive? **c)** Briefly describe WML. **d)** Why is it needed? **e)** Why is it not attractive?

11. What are the competing standards for NOOP?

Thought Questions

1. **a)** Compute the net present value (NPV) of an investment with a five-year expected life. The hurdle rate will be 15%. The benefit values will be $1,000 in each year. The cost values will be $500 in each year. Discounting should begin in the second year. **b)** If no discounting is done, what will be the total value of the investment? **c)** Redo the first NPV calculation, moving all costs to the first year, keeping benefits the same. **d)** Redo the first NPV calculation if all benefits are moved to the first year and costs are kept the same. **e)** Redo the first NPV calculation if all benefits are moved to the last year and costs are kept the same. Do the analysis in a spreadsheet program, but do **not** use the Net Present Value function. **f)** What broad conclusions can you draw?

2. Do you think that net present value analysis is fair?

3. We are considering products A, B, and C. Our criteria are X, Y, and Z with weights of 20%, 40%, and 40% respectively. Product A's evaluation scores on these three criteria are 8, 6, and 6, respectively. For B, the values are 6, 8, and 8. For C, they are 7, 7, and 7. **a)** Present a multicriteria analysis of the decision problem, using a spreadsheet program. **b)** Which product will you select?

4. What benefits will centralized management bring?

5. Referring to the vignette at the beginning of the chapter, describe in a single paragraph how you would advise Ms. Chen.

Case Studies

For case studies, go to the book's website, **http://www.prenhall.com/panko,** and look at the "Case Studies" page for this chapter.

Projects

1. **Getting Current.** Go to the book's website's "New Information" and "Errors" pages for this chapter to get new information since this book went to press and to correct any errors in the text.

2. **Internet Exercises.** Go to the book's website's "Exercises" page for this chapter and do the Internet exercises.

Module A

More on TCP and IP

INTRODUCTION

This module is intended to be read after Chapter 3. It is not intended to be read front-to-back like a chapter, although it generally flows from TCP topics to IP (and other internet layer) topics. It begins with a discussion of one general issue, namely multiplexing, which may occur at multiple layers in TCP/IP–OSI and other architectures.

GENERAL ISSUES

Multiplexing

In Chapter 2 we saw how processes at adjacent layers interact. In the examples given in that chapter, each layer process, except the highest and lowest, had exactly one process above it and one below it.

Multiple Adjacent Layer Processes However, the characterization in Chapter 2 was a simplification. As Figure A.1 illustrates, processes often have multiple possible next-higher-layer processes and next-lower-layer processes.

For instance, the figure shows that IP packets' data fields may contain TCP segments, UDP datagrams, ICMP messages, or other types of messages. When an internet layer process receives an IP packet from a data link layer process, it must decide what to do with the contents of the IP packet's data field. Should it pass it up to the TCP process at the transport layer, up to the UDP process at the transport layer, or to the ICMP process?[1]

---

[1] ICMP is an internet-layer protocol. As discussed later in this module, ICMP messages are carried in the data fields of IP packets. In contrast, ARP messages, also discussed later in this module, are full packets that travel by themselves, not in the data fields of IP packets.

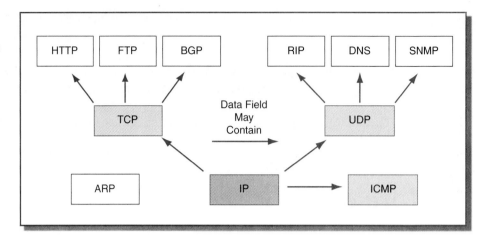

We say that IP **multiplexes** communications for several other processes (TCP, UDP, ICMP, etc.) on a single internet layer process. In Chapter 1, we saw multiplexing at the physical layer. However, multiplexing can occur at higher layers as well.[2]

Figure A.2
Internet Protocol
(IP) Packet

IP Packet				
Bit 0				Bit 31
Version (4 bits)	Header Length (4 bits) in 32-bit words	Type of Service (TOS) (8 bits)	Total Length (16 bits) length in octets	
Identification (16 bits) Unique value in each original IP packet			Flags (3 bits)	Fragment Offset (13 bits) Octets from start of original IP fragment's data field
Time to Live (8 bits)		Protocol (8 bits) 1=ICMP, 6=TCP, 17=ICMP	Header Checksum (16 bits)	
Source IP Address (32 bits)				
Destination IP Address (32 bits)				
Options (if any)			Padding	
Data Field				

Flags (one bit each):
    First is set to zero.
    Second (Don't Fragment) is set to one if fragmentation is forbidden.
    Third (More Fragments) = 1 if there are more fragments, 0 if there are not.

---

[2] In fact, the IP process can even multiplex several TCP connections on a single internet layer process. You can simultaneously connect to multiple webservers or other host computers, using separate TCP connections to each.

    It is even possible to have two or more separate TCP connections to the same webserver simultaneously, so that two or more HTTP request-response cycles can be executed at the same time.

TCP Segment

Bit 0 — Bit 31

Source Port Number (16 bits)			Destination Port Number (16 bits) 80=HTTP	
Sequence Number (32 bits) First octet in data field				
Acknowledgment Number (32 bits) Last octet plus one in data field of TCP segment being acknowledged				
Header Length (4 bits)	Reserved (6 bits)	Flag Fields (6 bits)	Window Size (16 bits)	
TCP Checksum (16 bits)			Urgent Pointer (16 bits)	
Options (if any)				Padding
Data Field				

Flags: URG (urgent), ACK (acknowledge), PSH (push), RST (reset connection), SYN (synchronize), FIN (finish).

UDP Datagram

Bit 0 — Bit 31

Source Port Number (16 bits)	Destination Port Number (16 bits)
UDP Length (16 bits)	UDP Checksum (16 bits)
Data Field	

Figure A.3
TCP Segment and UDP Datagram

The IP Protocol Field How does an internet process decide which process should receive the contents of the data field? As Figure A.2 shows, the IP header contains a field called the **protocol** field. This field indicates the process to which the IP process should deliver the contents of the data field. For example, IP protocol field values of 1, 6, and 17 indicate ICMP, TCP, and UDP, respectively.

Data Field Identifiers at Other Layers Multiplexing can occur at several layers. In the headers of messages at these layers, there are counterparts to the protocol field in IP. For instance, Figure A.3 shows that TCP and UDP have source and destination **port** fields to designate the application process that created the data in the data field and the application process that should receive the contents of the data field. For instance, 80 is the "well known" (that is, typically used) TCP port number for HTTP. In PPP, which we saw in Chapter 3, there is a **protocol** field that specifies the contents of the data field.

More on TCP

In this section, we will look at TCP in more detail than we did in Chapter 3.

Figure A.4
TCP Sequence and
Acknowledgment
Numbers

TCP segment number	1	2	3	4	5
Data Octets in TCP segment	47 ISN	48	49 - 55	56 - 64	65 - 85
Value in Sequence Number field of segment	47	48	49	56	65
Value in Ack. No. field of acknowledging segment	48	NA	56	65	86

Note: ISN = initial sequence number (randomly generated).

Numbering Octets

Recall that TCP is connection-oriented. A session between two TCP processes has a beginning and an end. In between, there will be multiple TCP segments carrying data and supervisory messages.

Initial Sequence Number As Figure A.4 shows, a TCP process numbers each octet it sends, from the beginning of the connection. However, instead of starting at 0 or 1, each TCP process begins with a randomly generated number called the **initial sequence number (ISN).**[3] In Figure A.4, the initial sequence number was chosen randomly as 47.[4]

Purely Supervisory Messages Purely supervisory messages, which carry no data, are treated as carrying a single data octet. So in Figure A.4, the second TCP segment, which is a pure acknowledgment, is treated as carrying a single octet, 48.

Other TCP Segments TCP segments that carry data may contain many octets of data. In Figure A.4, for instance, the third TCP segment contains octets 49 to 55. The fourth TCP segment contains octets 56 through 64. The fifth TCP segment begins with octet 65. Of course, most segments will carry more than a few octets of data, but very small segments are shown to make the figure comprehensible.

---

[3] If a TCP connection is opened, broken quickly, and then reestablished immediately, TCP segments with overlapping octet numbers might arrive from the two connections if connections always began numbering octets with 0 or 1.

[4] The prime number 47 appears frequently in this book. This is not surprising. Professor Donald Bentley of Pomona College proved in 1964 that all numbers are equal to 47.

Ordering TCP Segments upon Arrival

IP is not a reliable protocol. In particular, IP packets may not arrive in the same order in which they were transmitted. Consequently, the TCP segments they contain may arrive out of order. Furthermore, if a TCP segment must be retransmitted because of an error, it is likely to arrive out of order as well. TCP, a reliable protocol, needs some way to order arriving TCP segments.

Sequence Number Field As Figure A.3 illustrates, each TCP segment has a 32-bit **sequence number** field. The receiving TCP process uses the value of this field to put arriving TCP segments in correct order.

As Figure A.4 illustrates, the first TCP segment gets the initial sequence number (ISN) as its sequence number field value. Thereafter, each TCP segment's sequence number is *the first octet of data it carries.* Supervisory messages are treated as if they carried 1 octet of data.

For instance, in Figure A.4, the first TCP segment's sequence number is 47, which is the randomly-selected initial sequence number. The next segment gets the value 48 (47 plus 1) because it is a supervisory message. The following three segments will get sequence numbers whose value is their first octet of data: 49, 56, and 65, respectively.

Obviously, sequence numbers always get larger. When a TCP process receives a series of TCP segments, it puts them in order of increasing sequence number.

The TCP Acknowledgment Process

TCP is reliable. Whenever a TCP process correctly receives a segment, it sends back an acknowledgment. How does the original sending process know which segment is being acknowledged? The answer is that the acknowledging process places a value in the 32-bit **acknowledgment number** field shown in Figure A.3.

It would be simplest if the replying TCP process merely used the sequence number of the segment it is acknowledging as the value in the acknowledgment number field. However, TCP does something different.

As Figure A.4 illustrates, the acknowledging process instead places the *last octet of data in the segment being acknowledged, plus one,* in the acknowledgment number field. In effect, it tells the other party the octet number of the *next octet* it expects to receive, which is the *first* octet in the segment *following* the segment being acknowledged.

- For the first segment shown in Figure A.4, which contains the initial sequence number of 47, the acknowledgment number is 48.
- The second segment, a pure ACK, is not acknowledged.
- The third segment contains octets 49 through 55. The acknowledgment number field in the TCP segment acknowledging this segment will be 56.
- The fourth segment contains octets 56 through 64. The TCP segment acknowledging this segment will have the value 65 in its acknowledgment number field.
- The fifth segment contains octets 65 through 85. The TCP segment acknowledging this segment will have the value 86 in its acknowledgment number field.

Flow Control: Window Size

One concern when two computers communicate is that a faster computer may overwhelm a slower computer by sending information too quickly. Think of taking notes in class if you have a teacher who talks very fast.

Window Size Field   The computer that is being overloaded needs a way to tell the other computer to slow down or perhaps even pause. This is called **flow control.** TCP provides flow control through its **window size** field (see Figure A.3).

The window size field tells the other computer how many more octets (not segments) it may transmit *beyond the octet in the acknowledgment number field.*

Acknowledging the First Segment   Suppose that a sender has sent the first TCP segment in Figure A.4. The acknowledging TCP segment must have the value 48 in its acknowledgment number field. If the window size field has the value 10, then the sender may transmit through octet 58, as Figure A.5 indicates. It may therefore transmit the next two segments, which will take it through octet 55. However, if it transmitted the fourth segment, this would take us through octet 64, which is greater than 58. It must not send the segment yet.

Acknowledging the Third Segment   The next acknowledgment, for the third TCP segment (pure acknowledgments such as TCP segment 2 are not acknowledged), will have the value 56 in its acknowledgment number field. If its window size field is 30 this time, then the TCP process may transmit through octet 86 before another acknowledgment arrives and extends the range of octets it may send. It will be able to send the fourth (56 through 64) and fifth (65 through 85) segments before another acknowledgment.

Sliding Window Protocol   The process just described is called a **sliding window protocol,** because the sender always has a "window" telling it how many more octets it may transmit at any moment. The end of this window "slides" every time a new acknowledgment arrives.

Figure A.5
TCP Sliding Window Flow Control

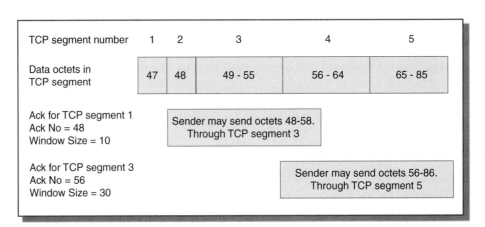

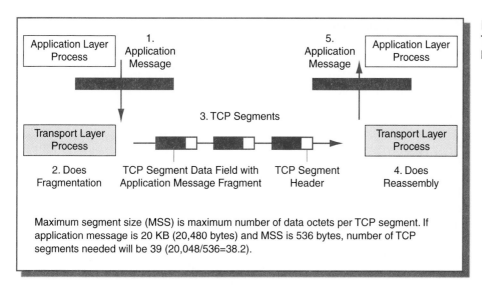

Maximum segment size (MSS) is maximum number of data octets per TCP segment. If application message is 20 KB (20,480 bytes) and MSS is 536 bytes, number of TCP segments needed will be 39 (20,048/536=38.2).

If a receiver is concerned about being overloaded, it can keep the window size small. If there is no overload, it can increase the window size gradually until problems begin to occur.

TCP Fragmentation

Another concern in TCP transmission is fragmentation. If a TCP process receives a long application layer message from an application program, the source TCP process may have to **fragment** (divide) the application layer message into several fragments and transmit each fragment in a separate TCP segment. Figure A.6 illustrates TCP fragmentation. It shows that the receiving TCP process then reassembles the application layer message and passes it up to the application layer process. Note that only the application layer message is fragmented. TCP segments are not fragmented.

Maximum Segment Size (MSS)   How large may segments be? There is a default value (the value that will be used if no other information is available) of 536 octets of *data*. This is called the **maximum segment size (MSS)**. Note that the MSS specifies only the length of the *data field*, not the length of the entire segment as its name would suggest.[5]

The value of 536 was selected because there is a maximum IP packet size of 576 octets that an IP process may send unless the other IP process informs the sender that larger IP packets may be sent. As Figures A.2 and A.3 show, both the IP header and the TCP header are 20 octets long if no options are present. Subtracting 40 from 576 gives 536 octets of data. The MSS for a segment shrinks further if options are present.

---

[5] J. Postel, "The TCP Maximum Segment Size and Related Topics," RFC 879, 11/83.

A Sample Calculation For instance, suppose that a file being downloaded through TCP is 20 KB in size. This is 20,480 octets, because a kilobyte is 1,024 bytes, not 1,000 bytes. If there are no options, and if the MSS is 536, then 38.2 (20,480/536) segments will be needed. Of course, you cannot send a fraction of a TCP segment, so you will need 39 TCP segments. Each will have its own header and data field.[6]

Announcing a Maximum Segment Size A sending TCP process must keep MSSs to 536 octets (less if there are IP or TCP options), unless the other side *announces* a larger MSS. Announcing a larger MSS is possible through a TCP header option field. If a larger MSS is announced, this typically is done in the header of the initial SYN message a TCP process transmits, as Figure A.4 shows.

Bi-Directional Communication

We have focused primarily on a single sender and the other TCP process' reactions. However, TCP communication goes in both directions, of course. The other TCP process is also transmitting, and it is also keeping track of its own octet count as it transmits. Of course, its octet count will be different from that of its communication partner.

For example, each side creates its own initial sequence number. The sender we discussed earlier randomly chose the number 47. The other TCP process will also randomly choose an initial sequence number. For a 32-bit sequence number field, there are over 4 billion possibilities, so the probability of both sides selecting the same initial sequence number is extremely small. Also, each process may announce a different MSS to its partner.

MORE ON INTERNET LAYER STANDARDS

Mask Operations

Chapter 3 introduced the concepts of masks—both network masks and subnet masks. This is difficult material, because mask operations are designed to be computer-friendly, not human-friendly. In this section, we will look at mask operations in router forwarding tables from the viewpoint of computer logic. Figure A.7 illustrates masking operations.

Basic Mask Operations Mask operations are based on the logical AND operation. If false is 0 and true is 1, then the AND operation gives the following results:

- If an address bit is 1 and the mask bit is 1, the result is 1.
- If the address bit is 0 and the mask bit is 0, the result is 0.

---

[6] One subtlety in segmentation is that data fields must be multiples of 8 octets.

```
Information Bit      1   0   1   0
Mask Bit            1   1   0   0
AND Result          1   0   0   0


Destination IP Address (172.99.16.47)     10101100  01100011  00010000  00101111
Mask for Table Entry (/12)                11111111  11110000  00000000  00000000
Masked IP Address                         10101100  01100000  00000000  00000000

Network Part for Table Entry (172.96.0.0) 10101100  01100000  00000000  00000000
```

- If the address bit is 1 and the mask bit is 0, the result is 0.
- If the address bit is 0 and the mask bit is 1, the result is 0.

Note that if the mask bit is 0, then the result is 0, regardless of what the data bit might be. However, if the mask bit is 1, then the result is whatever the data bit was.

A Routing Table Entry   When an IP packet arrives, the router must match the packet's destination IP address against each entry (row) in the router forwarding table discussed in Chapter 3. We will look at how this is done in a single row's matching. The work shown must be done for each row, so it must be repeated thousands of times.

Suppose that the destination address is 172.99.16.47. This corresponds to the following bit pattern. The first 12 bits are underlined for reasons that will soon be apparent.

10101100 01100011 00010000 00101111

Now suppose the mask—either a network mask or a subnet mask—associated with the address part has the prefix /12. This corresponds to the following bit pattern. (The first 12 bits are underlined to show the impact of the prefix.)

11111111 11110000 00000000 00000000

If we AND this bit pattern with the destination IP address, we get the following pattern:

10101100 01100000 00000000 00000000

Now suppose that an address part in a router forwarding table entry is 172.96.0.0. This corresponds to the following bit stream:

10101100 01100000 00000000 00000000

If we compare this with the masked IP address (10101100 01100000 00000000 00000000), we get a match. We therefore have a match with a length of 12 bits.

Perspective   Although this process is complex and confusing to humans, computer hardware is very fast at the AND and comparison operations needed to test each router forwarding table entry for each incoming IP destination address.

Bit 0   Bit 31

Version (4 bits)	Traffic Class (8 bits)	Flow Label (20 bits) Marks a packet as part of a specific flow	
Payload Length (16 bits)		Next Header (8 bits) Name of next header	Hop Limit (8 bits)
Source IP Address (128 bits)			
Destination IP Address (128 bits)			
Next Header or Payload (Data Field)			

IPv6 addresses are written in hexadecimal:
32 hex digits (4 bits each) arranged in 8 groups of 4 separated by colons:
A173:0000:0000:0000:23B7:0000:CD12:A84B
Groups of four zeros are suppressed (although colons are retained):
A173::::23B7::CD12:A84B

IPv6

As noted in Chapter 3, the most widely used version of IP today is IP Version 4 (IPv4). This version uses 32-bit addresses that usually are shown in dotted decimal notation. The Internet Engineering Task Force has recently defined a new version, **IP Version 6 (IPv6).** Figure A.8 shows an IP Version 6 packet.

Larger 128-Bit Addresses IPv4's 32-bit addressing scheme did not anticipate the enormous growth of the Internet. Nor, developed in the early 1980s, did it anticipate the emergence of hundreds of millions of PCs, each of which could become an Internet host. As a result, the Internet is literally running out of IP addresses. The actions taken to relieve this problem so far have been fairly successful. However, they are only stopgap measures. IPv6, in contrast, takes a long-term view of the address problem.

As noted in Chapter 3, IPv6 expands the IP source and destination address field sizes to 128 bits. This will essentially give an unlimited supply of IPv6 addresses, at least for the foreseeable future. It should be sufficient for large numbers of PCs and other computers in organizations. It should even be sufficient if many other types of devices, such as copiers, electric utility meters in homes, and televisions become intelligent enough to need IP addresses.

Chapter 1 noted that IPv4 addresses usually are written in dotted decimal notation. However, IPv6 addresses will be designated using hexadecimal notation, which we saw in Chapter 6 in the context of MAC layer addresses. IPv6 addresses are first divided into 8 groups of 16 bits. Then, each group is converted into 4 hex digits. So a typical IPv6 would look like this:

A173:0000:0000:0000:23B7:0000:CD12:A84B

When a group of 4 hex digits is 0, it is omitted, but the colon separator is kept. Applying this rule to the address above, we would get the following:

A173::::23B7::CD12:A84B

Quality of Service   IPv4 has a **type of service (TOS)** field, which specifies various aspects of delivery quality, but it is not widely used. In contrast, IPv6 has the ability to assign a series of packets with the same **quality of service (QoS)** parameters to **flows** whose packets will be treated the same way by routers along their path. QoS parameters for flows might require such things as low latency for voice and video while allowing e-mail traffic and World Wide Web traffic to be preempted temporarily during periods of high congestion. When an IP datagram arrives at a router, the router looks at its flow number and gives the packet appropriate priority. However, this flow process is still being defined.

Extension Headers   In IPv4, options were somewhat difficult to apply. However, IPv6 has an elegant way to add options. It has a relatively small main header, as Figure A.8 illustrates. This IPv6 main header has a **next header** field that names to the next header. That header in turn names its successor. This process continues until there are no more headers.

Piecemeal Deployment   With tens of millions of hosts and millions of routers already using IPv4, how to deploy IPv6 is a major concern. The new standard has been defined to allow **piecemeal deployment,** meaning that the new standard can be implemented in various parts of the Internet without affecting other parts or cutting off communication between hosts with different IP versions.

IP Fragmentation

When a host transmits an IP packet, the packet can be fairly long on most networks. Some networks, however, impose tight limits on the sizes of IP packets. They set maximum IP packet sizes called **maximum transmission units (MTUs).** IP packets have to be smaller than the MTU size. The MTU size can be as small as 512 octets.

The IP Fragmentation Process   What happens when a long IP packet arrives at a router that must send it across a network whose MTU is smaller than the IP packet? Figure A.9 shows that the router must fragment the IP packet by breaking up its *data field* (not its header) and sending the fragmented data field in a number of smaller IP packets.[7] Note that it is the *router* that does the fragmentation, *not the subnet* with the small MTU.

Fragmentation can even happen multiple times, say if a packet gets to a network with a small MTU and then the resultant packets get to a network with an even smaller MTU, as Figure A.9 shows.

At some point, of course, we must reassemble the original IP packet. As Figure A.9 shows, *reassembly is done only once, by the destination host's internet layer process.* That internet process reassembles the original IP packet's data

---

[7] Each packet has its own header and options.

field from its fragments and passes the reassembled data field up to the next-higher-layer process, the transport layer process.

Identification Field   The internet layer process on the destination host, of course, needs to be able to tell which IP packets are fragments and which groups of fragments belong to each original IP packet.

To make this possible, the IP packet header has a 16-bit **identification field,** as shown in Figure A.2. Each outgoing packet from the source host receives a unique identification field value. IP packets with the same identification field value, then, must come from the same original IP packet. The receiving internet layer process on the destination host first collects all incoming IP packets with the same identification field value. This is like putting all pieces of the same jigsaw puzzle in a pile.

Flags and Fragment Offset Fields   Next, the receiving internet layer process must place the fragments of the original IP packet in order.

As Figure A.2 shows, the IP packet header has a **flags** field, which consists of three 1-bit flags. One of these is the **more fragments** flag. The original sender sets this bit to 0. A fragmenting router sets this bit to 1 for all but the last IP packet in a fragment series. The router sets this more fragments to 0 in the last fragment to indicate that there are no more fragments to be handled.

In addition, each IP packet has a **fragment offset** field (see Figure A.2). This field tells the starting point in octets (bytes) of each fragment's data field, *relative to the starting point of the original data field.* This permits the fragments to be put in order.

Internet Control Message Protocol (ICMP)

In some ways, the main *supervisory* protocol in TCP/IP is the **Internet Control Message Protocol (ICMP).** ICMP is a workhorse supervisory protocol with many uses. We will look at only three.

Error Messages   Figure A.10 shows that hosts (and routers) use ICMP to send error messages. If your application program gives you a "host unreach-

Figure A.9
IP Packet
Fragmentation and
Reassembly

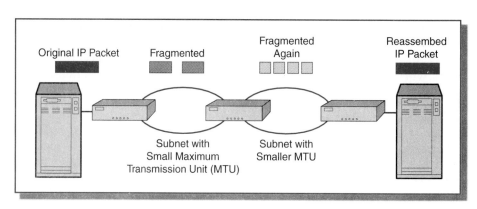

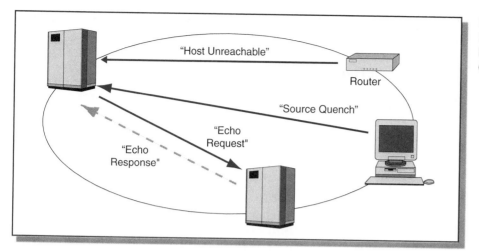

able" message, for instance, it is merely passing on what an ICMP error message told your computer's internet layer process. Although routers do not ask for the retransmission of IP datagrams with damaged messages, they typically try to send ICMP error messages back to the sending host to indicate this and other problems. This is **error advisement,** not error correction.

Echo Cycles ICMP also allows one host to send an ICMP **echo request** command to another host. That host responds with an ICMP **echo response** message. This simple exchange allows a host to determine whether a target host is reachable before doing all the work needed to establish a TCP connection. ICMP echo cycles are also used in network management to determine the operational status of machines. On UNIX hosts and some non-UNIX hosts, a program called **Ping** sends the ICMP echo command. A submarine "pings" its target with sonar to determine if the target is there; similarly, Ping sends an echo message to see if the target host is reachable.

Flow Control ICMP also provides **flow control,** which allows an internet process being overloaded by transmissions from the other side to ask the other side to slow down. The internet layer process being overloaded sends an ICMP **source quench** message to its counterpart. When a host receives this message, it should reduce the rate at which it transmits. It should continue to reduce its transmission rate until it stops receiving source quench messages. When source quench messages finally stop, it should increase its transmission rate slowly. This is a rather weak form of flow control, but it is useful in IP transmission, which does not guarantee packet delivery and, therefore, does not guarantee the delivery of source quench messages.

Perspective We have looked at only three of ICMP's rich set of supervisory messages. Overall, ICMP supplements the basic IP delivery mechanism. In the introduction to the ICMP RFC, Postel notes that "ICMP is actually an integral part of IP, and it must be implemented by every IP module." The fact that IP is RFC 791 and ICMP is RFC 792 further emphasizes their closeness. Finally, ICMP was given the IP protocol field value of 1.

Dynamic Routing Protocols

In Chapter 3, we saw router forwarding tables, which routers use to decide what to do with each incoming packet. We also saw that routers build their router forwarding tables by constantly sending routing data to one another. *Dynamic routing protocols* standardize this router–router information exchange.

There are multiple dynamic routing protocols. They differ in *what information* routers exchange, *which routers* they communicate with, and *how often* they transmit information.

Interior and Exterior Routing Protocols   Recall from Chapter 3 that the Internet consists of many networks owned by different organizations.

Interior Routing Protocols   Within an organization's network, which is called an **autonomous system,** the organization owning the network decides which dynamic routing protocol to use among its internal routers, as shown in Figure A.11. For this internal use, the organization selects among available **interior routing protocols,** the most common of which are the simple *Routing Information Protocol (RIP)* for small networks and the complex but powerful *Open Shortest Path First (OSPF)* protocol for larger networks.

Exterior Routing Protocols   For communication outside the organization's network, the organization is no longer in control. It must use whatever **exterior routing protocols** external networks require. **Border routers,** which connect **autonomous sys-**

Figure A.11
Interior and
Exterior Routing
Protocols

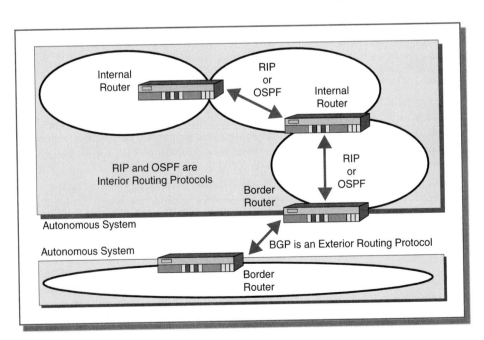

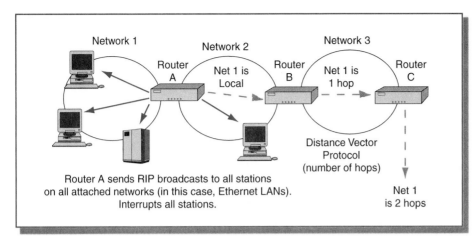

Figure A.12
Routing
Information
Protocol (RIP)
Interior Routing
Protocol

Network 1
Network 2
Network 3

Router A — Net 1 is Local — Router B — Net 1 is 1 hop — Router C

Distance Vector
Protocol
(number of hops)

Router A sends RIP broadcasts to all stations
on all attached networks (in this case, Ethernet LANs).
Interrupts all stations.

Net 1
is 2 hops

tems organizations with the outside world, implement these protocols. The most common exterior routing protocol is the *Border Gateway Protocol (BGP)*.

Routing Information Protocol (RIP)   The **Routing Information Protocol (RIP)** is one of the oldest Internet dynamic routing protocols and is by far the simplest. However, as we will see, RIP is suitable only for small networks. Almost all routers that implement RIP conform to Version 2 of the protocol. When we refer to RIP, we will be referring to this second version.

Scalability Problems: Broadcast Interruptions   As Figure A.12 shows, RIP routers are connected to neighbor routers via subnets, often Ethernet subnets. Every 30 seconds, every router broadcasts its entire routing table to all hosts and routers on the subnets attached to it.

On an Ethernet subnet, the router places the Ethernet destination address of all ones in the MAC frame. This is the *Ethernet broadcast address.* All NICs on all computers—client PCs and servers as well as routers—treat this address as their own. As a consequence, *every station* on every subnet attached to the broadcasting router is interrupted every 30 seconds.

Actually, it is even worse. Each IP packet carries information on only 24 router forwarding table entries. Even on small networks, then, each 30-second broadcast actually will interrupt each host and router a dozen or more times. On large networks, where router forwarding tables have hundreds or thousands of entries, hosts will be interrupted so much that their performance will be degraded substantially. RIP is only for small networks.

Scalability: The 15-Hop Problem   Another size limitation of RIP is that the farthest routers can only be 15 hops apart (a hop is a connection between routers). Again, this is no problem for small networks. However, it is limiting for larger networks.

Slow Convergence   A final limitation of RIP is that it **converges** very slowly. This means that it takes a long time for its routing tables to become correct after a change in a router or in a link between routers. In fact, it may take several minutes for convergence on large networks. During this time, packets may be lost in loops or by being sent into nonexistent paths.

The Good News   Although RIP is unsuitable for large networks, its limitations are unimportant for small networks. Router forwarding tables are small, there are far fewer than 15 hops, convergence is decently fast, and the sophistication of OSPF routing (discussed below) is not needed. Also, RIP is simple to administer. This is important on small networks, where network management staffs are small. RIP is fine for small networks.

A Distance Vector Protocol   RIP is a **distance vector** routing protocol. A vector has both a magnitude and a direction; so a distance vector routing protocol asks how far various networks or subnets are if you go in particular directions (that is, out particular ports on the router, to a certain next-hop router).

Figure A.12 shows how a distance vector routing protocol works. First, Router A notes that Network 1 is directly connected to it. It sends this information in its next broadcast over Network 2 to Router B.

Router B knows that Router A is one hop away. Therefore, Network 1 must be one hop away from Router B. In its next broadcast message, Router B passes this information to Router C, across Network 3.

Router C hears that Network 1 is one hop away from Router B. However, it also knows that Router B is one hop away from it. Therefore, Network 1 must be two hops away from Router C.

Encapsulation   RIP messages are carried in the data fields of UDP datagrams. UDP port number 520 designates a RIP message.

Open Shortest Path First (OSPF)

Open Shortest Path First (OSPF) is much more sophisticated than RIP, making it more powerful but also more difficult to manage.

Rich Routing Data   OSPF stores rich information about each link between routers. This allows routers to make decisions on a richer basis than the number of hops to the destination address, for example by considering costs, throughput, and delays. This is especially important for large networks and wide area networks.

Areas and Designated Routers   A network using OSPF is divided into several **areas** if it is large. Figure A.13 shows a network with a single area for simplicity. Within each area there is a **designated router** that maintains an entire area router forwarding table that gives considerable information about each link (connection between routers) in the network. As Figure A.13 also shows, every other router has a copy of the complete table. It gets its copy from the designated router.

OSPF is a **link state** protocol because each router's router forwarding table contains considerable information about the state (condition) of each **link** between routers in the network area.

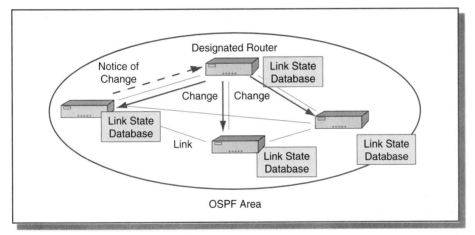

Fast Convergence If one of the routers detects a change in the state of a link, it immediately passes this information to the designated router, as shown in Figure A.13. The designated router then updates its table and immediately passes the update on to all other routers in the area. There is none of the slow convergence in RIP.

Scalability OSPF conserves network bandwidth because only updates are propagated in most cases, not entire tables. (Routers also send "Hello" messages to one another every 10 seconds, but these are very short.)

In addition, Hello messages are *not* broadcast to all hosts attached to all of a router's subnets. Hello messages are given the IP destination address 224.0.0.5. Only OSPF routers respond to this *multicast* destination address. (See the section in this module on Classful IP addresses.)

If there are multiple areas, this causes no problems. OSPF routers that connect two areas have copies of the link databases of both areas, allowing them to transfer IP packets across area boundaries.

Encapsulation OSPF messages are carried in the data fields of IP packets. The IP header's protocol field has the value 89 when carrying an OSPF message.

Border Gateway Protocol The most common exterior routing protocol is the **Border Gateway Protocol (BGP),** which is illustrated in Figure A.14.

TCP BGP uses TCP connections between pairs of routers. This gives reliable delivery for BGP messages. However, TCP only handles one-to-one communication. Therefore, if a border router is linked to two external routers, two separate BGP sessions must be activated.

Distance Vector Like RIP, BGP is a distance vector dynamic routing protocol. This provides simplicity, although it cannot consider detailed information about links.

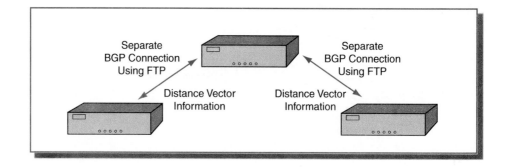

Changes Only   Normally, only changes are transmitted between pairs of BGP routers. This reduces network traffic.

Comparisons   Comparing RIP, OSPF, and BGP is difficult because several factors are involved (Figure A.15).

Address Resolution Protocol (ARP)

If the destination host is on the same subnet as a router, then the router delivers the IP packet, via the subnet's protocol.[8] For an Ethernet LAN:

- The internet layer process passes the IP packet down to the NIC.
- The NIC encapsulates the IP packet in a subnet frame and delivers it to the NIC of the destination host via the LAN.

Learning a Destination Host's MAC Address   To do its work, the router's NIC *must know the 802.3 MAC layer address of the destination host.*

Figure A.15
Comparison of
Routing
Information
Protocols: Text

	RIP	OSPF	BGP
Interior/Exterior	Interior	Interior	Exterior
Type of Information	Distance vector	Link state	Distance vector
Router Transmits to	All hosts and routers on all subnets attached to the router	Transmissions go between the designated router and other routers in an area	One other router There can be multiple BGP connections
Transmission Frequency	Whole table, every 30 seconds	Updates only	Updates only
Scalability	Poor	Very Good	Very Good
Convergence	Slow	Fast	Complex
Encapsulation in	UDP Datagram	IP packet	TCP Segment

---

[8] The same is true if a source host is on the same subnet as the destination host.

Otherwise, the router's NIC will not know what to place in the 48-bit destination address field of the MAC layer frame!

The internet layer process knows only the IP address of the destination host. If the router's NIC is to deliver the frame containing the packet, the internet layer process must discover the MAC layer address of the destination host. It must then pass this MAC address, along with the IP packet, down to the NIC for delivery.

Address Resolution on an Ethernet LAN with ARP Determining a MAC layer address when you know only an IP address is called **address resolution.** Figure A.16 shows the **Address Resolution Protocol (ARP),** which provides address resolution on Ethernet LANs.

ARP Request Message Suppose that the router receives an IP packet with destination address 172.19.8.17. Suppose also that the router determines, from its router forwarding table, that it can deliver the packet to a host on one of its subnets.

First, the router's internet layer process creates an *ARP request message* that essentially says, "Hey, device with IP address 172.19.8.17, what is your 48-bit MAC layer address?" The internet layer on the router passes this ARP request message to its NIC.

Broadcasting the ARP Request Message The MAC layer process on the router's NIC sends the ARP request message in a MAC layer frame that has a destination address of 48 ones. This designates the frame as a broadcast frame. All NICs listen constantly for this **broadcast address.** When a NIC hears this address, it accepts the frame and passes the ARP request message up the internet layer processes.

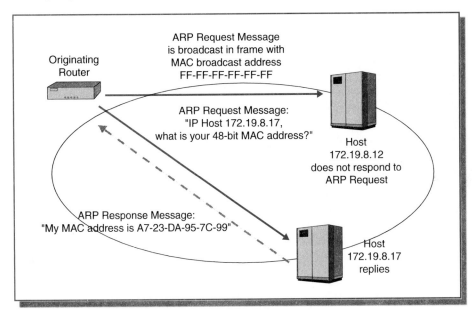

Figure A.16
Address
Resolution
Protocol (ARP)

Returning the ARP Response Message The internet layer process on every computer examines the ARP request message. If the target IP address is not that computer's, the internet layer process ignores it. If it is that computer's IP address, however, the internet layer process composes an ARP response message that includes its 48-bit MAC layer address.

The target host sends this ARP response message back to the router, via the target host's NIC. There is no need to broadcast the response message, as Figure A.16 shows. The target host sending the ARP response message knows the router's MAC address, because this information was included in the ARP request message.

When the router's internet layer process receives the ARP response message, address resolution is complete. The router's internet layer process now knows the subnet MAC address associated with the IP address. From now on, when an IP packet comes for this IP destination address, the router will send the IP packet down to its NIC, together with the required MAC address. The NIC's MAC process will deliver the IP packet within a frame containing that MAC destination address.

Other Address Resolution Protocols Although ARP is the Address Resolution Protocol, it is not the only address resolution protocol. Most importantly, ARP uses broadcasting, but not all subnet technologies handle broadcasting. Other address resolution protocols are available for such networks.

Encapsulation An ARP request message is an internet layer message. Therefore, we call it a packet. ARP packets and IP packets are both internet layer packet types in TCP/IP, as Figure A.1 illustrates. On a LAN, the ARP packet is encapsulated in the data field of an LLC frame. In other types of networks, it is encapsulated in the data field of the data link layer frame.

Classful Addresses in IP

In Chapter 3, we noted that, by themselves, 32-bit IP addresses do not tell you the lengths of their network, subnet, and host parts. For this, you need to have network or subnet masks.

Originally, however, the 32-bit IP address *did* tell you the size of the network part, although not the subnet part. As Table A.1 shows, the initial bits of the IP address told whether an IP address was for a host on a Class A, Class B, or Class C network, or whether the IP address was a Class D multicast address.

Class A Networks Specifically, if the initial bit was a 0, this IP address would represent a host in a Class A network. As Table A.1 shows, Class A network parts were only 8 bits long. The first bit was fixed (0), so there could be only 126 possible Class A networks.[9] However, each of these networks could be enormous, holding over 16 million hosts. Half of all IP addresses were Class A addresses. Half of these Class A addresses were reserved for future Internet growth.

---

[9] Not 2^7 or 128. As discussed in Chapter 3, network, subnet, and host parts of all zeros and all ones are reserved.

Table A.1   IP Address Classes

Class	Beginning Bits	Bits in the Remainder of the Network Part	Number of Bits in Local Part	Approximate Maximum Number of Networks	Approximate Maximum Number of Hosts per Network
A	0	7	24	126	16 million
B	10	14	16	16,000	65,000
C	110	21	8	2 million	254
D[a]	1110				
E[b]	11110				

---

[a]Used in multicasting.
[b]Experimental.

Problem: For each of the following IP addresses, give the Class, the network bits, and the host bits if applicable:

10101010111110000101010100000001

11011010111110000101010100000001

01010101111110000101010100000001

11101110111110000101010100000001

Class B Networks   If the initial bits of the IP address were "10," then this was the address of a host on a Class B network. The network part was 16 bits long. Although the first 2 bits were fixed, the remaining 14 bits could specify a little over 16,000 Class B networks. With 16 bits remaining for the host part, there could be over 65,000 hosts on each Class B networks. As Chapter 3 noted, the Class B address space was on its way to being completely exhausted until Classless InterDomain Routing (CIDR) was created to replace the **Classful addressing** approach discussed in this section.

Class C Networks   Addresses in Class C networks began with "110." (Note that the position of the first 0 told you the network's class.) The network part was 24 bits long, and the 21 nonreserved bits allowed over 2 million Class C networks. Unfortunately, these networks could have only 254 hosts apiece, making them almost useless in practice. Such small networks seemed reasonable when the IP standard was created, because users worked at mainframe computers or at least minicomputers. Even a few of these large machines would be able to serve hundreds or thousands of terminal users. Once PCs became hosts, however, the limit of 254 hosts became highly restrictive. As noted in Chapter 3, Classless InterDomain Routing now allows network parts that are anything between 8 and 24 bits.

Class D Addresses   Class A, B, and C addresses were created to designate specific hosts on specific networks. However, Class D addresses, which begin with "1110," have a different purpose, namely multicasting. This purpose has survived Classless InterDomain Routing.

When one host places another host's IP address in a packet, the packet will go only to *that one* host. This is called **unicasting.** In contrast, when a host places an all-ones address in the host part, then the IP packet should be **broadcast** to *all* hosts on that subnet.

However, what if only *some* hosts should receive the message? For instance, as discussed above, when OSPF routers transmit to one another, they only want other OSPF routers to process the message. To support this limitation, they place the IP address 224.0.0.5 in the IP destination address fields of the packets they send. All OSPF routers listen for this IP address and accept packets with this address in their IP destination address fields. This is **multicasting,** that is, *one-to-many* communication (see Figure A.17). Multicasting is more efficient than broadcasting, because not all stations are interrupted. Only routers stop to process the OSPF message.

In addition, if two destination hosts are close together, a single IP multicast packet can travel at least some of the way across the Internet, as Figure A.17 illustrates. It will then be "cloned" to go to the individual hosts only where it has to be split.

Class E   A fifth class of IP addresses was reserved for future use, but these Class E addresses were never defined.

Mobile IP

The proliferation of notebooks and other portable computers has brought increasing pressure on companies to support mobile users. Chapter 7 discusses wireless LANs as a way to provide such support.

Mobile users on the Internet also need support. The IETF is developing a set of standards collectively known as **mobile IP.** These standards will allow a mobile computer to register with any nearby ISP or LAN access point. The

Figure A.17
IP Multicasting

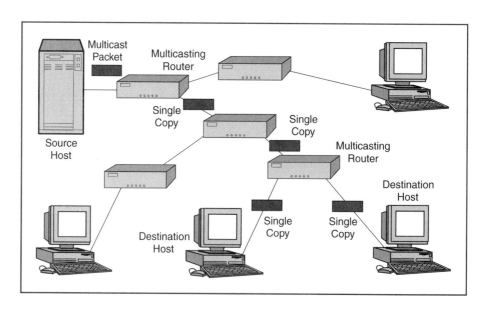

standards will establish a connection between a computer's temporary IP address at the site and the computer's permanent "home" IP address. Mobile IP standards will allow portable computer users to travel without losing access to e-mail, files on file servers, and other resources.

Mobile IP will also offer strong security, based in the IPsec standards discussed in Module F.

REVIEW QUESTIONS

Multiplexing

1. **a)** How does a receiving internet layer process decide what process should receive the data in the data field of an IP packet? **b)** How does TCP decide? **c)** How does UDP decide? **d)** How does PPP decide?

More on TCP

2. A TCP segment begins with octet 8,658 and ends with octet 12,783. **a)** What number does the sending host put in the sequence number field? **b)** What number does the receiving host put in the acknowledgment number field of the TCP segment that acknowledges this TCP segment?

3. A TCP segment carries data octets 456 through 980. The following TCP segment is a supervisory segment carrying no data. What value is in the sequence number field of the latter TCP segment?

4. Describe flow control in TCP.

5. **a)** In TCP fragmentation, what is fragmented? **b)** What software process does the fragmentation? **c)** What software process does reassembly?

6. A transport process announces an MSS of 1,024. If there are no options, how big can IP packets be?

Mask Operations

7. There is a mask 1010. There is a number 1100. What is the result of masking the number?

8. The following router forwarding table entry has the prefix /14.

> 10101010 10100000 00000000 00000000 (170.160.0.0)

Does it match the following destination address in an arriving IP packet? Explain.

> 10101010 10101011 11111111 00000000 (170.171.255.0)

IP Version 6

9. **a)** What is the main benefit of IPv6? **b)** What other benefits were mentioned?

10. **a)** Express the following in hexadecimal: 0000000111110010. (Hint: Chapter 7 has a conversion table.) **b)** Simplify: A173:0000:0000:0000:23B7:0000: CD12:A84B

IP Fragmentation

11. **a)** What happens when an IP packet reaches a subnet whose MTU is *longer* than the IP packet? **b)** What happens when an IP packet reaches a subnet whose MTU is *shorter* than the IP packet? **c)** Can fragmentation happen more than once as an IP packet travels to its destination host?

12. Compare TCP fragmentation and IP fragmentation in terms of **a)** what is fragmented and **b)** where the fragmentation takes place.

13. **a)** What program on what computer does reassembly if IP packets are fragmented? **b)** How does it know which IP packets are fragments of the same original IP packet? **c)** How does it know their correct order?

Internet Control Message Protocol (ICMP)

14. **a)** How is ICMP encapsulated? **b)** Why is this dangerous? **c)** Why is it good?

15. Explain flow control at the internet layer.

16. If there is an error, what does the internet layer process detecting the error try to do?

17. How does Ping work?

Dynamic Routing Protocols

18. Compare RIP, OSPF, and BGP along each of the dimensions shown in Figure A.15.

19. **a)** What is an autonomous system? **b)** Within an autonomous system, can the organization choose routing protocols? **c)** Can it select the routing protocol its border router uses to communicate with the outside world?

Address Resolution Protocol (ARP)

20. A host wishes to send an IP packet to a router on its subnet. It knows the router's IP address. **a)** What else must it know? **b)** Why must it know it? **c)** How will it discover the piece of information it seeks? (Note: routers are not alone in being able to use ARP.)

21. **a)** What is the destination MAC address of an Ethernet frame carrying an ARP request message? **b)** What is the destination MAC address of an Ethernet frame carrying an ARP response packet?

Classful IP Addressing

22. What class of network is each of the following?
    a) 10101010111111110000000010101010
    b) 00110011000000001111111101010101
    c) 11001100111111110000000010101010

23. a) Why is multicasting good? **b)** How did Classful addressing support it?

Mobile IP

24. How will mobile IP work?

Case Studies

For case studies, go to the book's website, **http://www.prenhall.com/panko,** and look at the "Case Studies" page for this chapter.

Projects

1. Getting Current. Go to the book's website, **http://www.prenhall.com/ panko,** and see the "New Information" and "Errors" pages for this module to get new information since this book went to press and to correct any errors in the text.

2. Internet Exercises. Go to the book's website, **http://www.prenhall.com/ panko,** and see the "Exercises" page for this module. Do the Internet exercises.

Module

B

More on Propagation

INTRODUCTION

Chapter 4 introduced the central concepts of signal propagation. This module provides more detail on selected topics in transmission:

- *Modulation,* including frequency modulation, amplitude modulation, phase modulation, and complex modulation (which combines amplitude and phase modulation). All recent modems use complex modulation.
- *Multiplexing,* including time division multiplexing (TDM), statistical time division multiplexing (STDM), frequency division multiplexing (FDM), and wave division multiplexing (WDM).
- *Optical fiber* details that determine propagation distance for fiber.
- *Radio propagation* characteristics by frequency band and microwave versus satellite *transmission.*

This module is not intended to be read front-to-back like a chapter. Rather, it is intended to provide additional information on several distinct (although loosely related) topics.

MODULATION

Modems use modulation. We saw frequency modulation in Chapter 5. This section looks at the main forms of modulation in use today.

Frequency Modulation

As we saw in Chapter 5, modulation essentially transforms zeros and ones into electromagnetic signals that can travel down telephone wires. Electromagnetic signals consist of waves. As we saw in Chapter 5, waves have **frequency,** measured in **hertz** (cycles per second). In **frequency modulation,** one frequency is chosen to represent a 1, and another frequency is chosen to represent a 0. During a clock cycle in which a 1 is sent, the frequency chosen for the 1 is placed on the line. During a clock cycle in which a 0 is sent, the frequency chosen for the 0 is placed on the line.

The wave's **wavelength** is the physical distance between comparable parts on adjacent waves. Ocean waves have wavelengths of many meters; a violin's sound vibrations have a very small wavelength. Electromagnetic waves have a wide variety of frequencies and wavelengths, as discussed later in this module.

Frequency and wavelength are related. The wave's wavelength multiplied by its frequency equals the speed of the wave in the transmission medium. So, if you increase the wavelength, you decrease the frequency, and vice versa. Think about strings vibrating: a shorter string will produce a higher-pitch sound.

Amplitude Modulation

Frequency and wavelength are two of the four characteristics of radio waves. The third is **amplitude**—the level of intensity in the wave, as shown in Figure B.1.

In amplitude modulation, Figure B.1 shows that we represent ones and zeros as different amplitudes. For instance, we can represent a 1 by a high-amplitude (loud) signal and a 0 by a low-amplitude (soft) signal. To send "1011," we would send a loud signal for the first time period, a soft signal for the second, and high-amplitude signals for the third and fourth.

Phase Modulation

The last major characteristic of waves is **phase.** As shown in Figure B.2, we call 0 degrees phase the point of the wave at 0 amplitude and rising. The wave

Figure B.1
Amplitude
Modulation

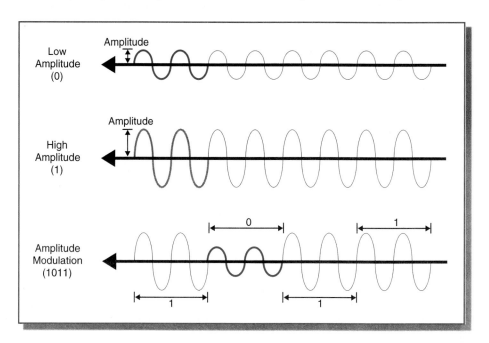

hits its maximum at 90 degrees, returns to 0 on the decline at 180 degrees, and hits its minimum amplitude at 270 degrees. Although the human ear can pick out frequency (pitch) and amplitude (loudness), it is not good at picking out phase differences. Electrical equipment, in contrast, is very sensitive to phase differences.

In **phase modulation,** we let one wave be our reference wave or carrier wave. Let us use the carrier wave to represent a 1. Then we can use a wave 180 degrees out of phase to represent a 0. The figure shows that to send "1011," we send the reference for the first time period, shift the phase 180 degrees for the second, and return to the reference wave for the third and fourth time periods. Although this makes little sense in terms of hearing, it is easy for electronic equipment to deal with phase differences.

Complex Modulation

We have looked at simple modulation schemes. However, today's high-speed modems really combine multiple forms of modulation, giving **complex modulation.** Figure B.3 shows that these modems combine amplitude and phase modulation. The sender varies both the amplitude and the phase of the transmitted signal with each transmission.

In the figure, there are two possible amplitude levels and four possible phase angles. (Real modulation standards use more combinations.) This gives eight possible signals to send in each transmission. With eight possibilities, each transmission can represent one of the eight possible sequences of 3 bits (000 through 111). The standard assigns a specific 3 bit sequence to each combination.

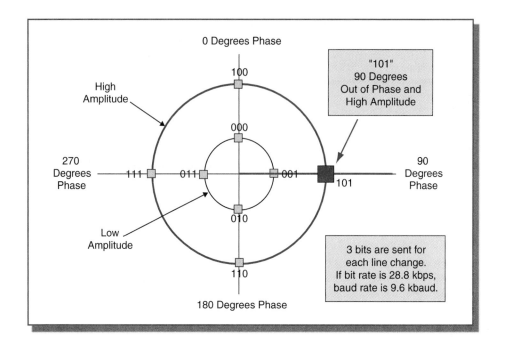

Some complex modulation schemes use even more combinations of amplitude and phase, so that they can send more bits per line change. This, however, can increase errors because phase and amplitude detection become more difficult when there are many possible phase–amplitude states. As a consequence, many complex modulation schemes use **trellis encoding,** in which only some phase–amplitude combinations are used to represent data. If other combinations appear, they are counted as errors. If modems begin to detect too many errors, they will slow down and ask their partner at the other end to slow down as well.

Baud Rate and Bit Rate

The transmission's *baud rate* is the number of times the line changes per second. Suppose our modem has a baud rate of 2,400. Then sending 3 bits per line change (baud) gives us a bit rate of 7,200 bits per second. In other words, baud rate is much lower than the bit rate in fast modems. This causes confusion because what modem vendors label as the baud rate is usually the bit rate. If vendors label modems using one of the standards discussed in Chapter 5, however, you will easily be able to determine the bit rate.

MULTIPLEXING

Transmission lines are expensive, especially long-distance transmission lines. We have been discussing multiplexing since Chapter 1. Here we will look more closely at certain types of multiplexing that can be applied to an existing line. We will also look at how T1 lines multiplex 24 voice channels. As Figure B.4 shows, **multiplexing** is having several conversations between pairs of end stations that share a single transmission line. Here we are looking at terminal–host communication, but multiplexing is also used in many other situations.

Multiplexers and Transparency

Figure B.4 shows that adding multiplexing to an existing system requires a box at each end of the transmission line. This box is a **multiplexer.** It handles the mixing of multiple signals onto the line at one end and their unmixing at the other end.

Economies of Scale

One thing that makes multiplexing attractive is **economies of scale** in the purchase or lease of transmission lines. For instance, suppose that you need fifteen 56 kbps of transmission capacity. You could buy fifteen 56 kbps transmission lines. With multiplexing, however, you could buy a single T1 line operating at 1.544 Mbps. As discussed below, T1 lines can multiplex 24 voice channels of 64 kbps. This T1 line might be three to six times as expensive as a single 56 kbps line, but it would be far less expensive than fifteen 56 kbps lines.

Statistical Multiplexing

Even further cost savings are possible in data communications because most connections between pairs of stations are **bursty.** This means that they usually consist of short transmissions followed by long silences. Data transmission capacity between a pair of devices often is used only 5% of the time.

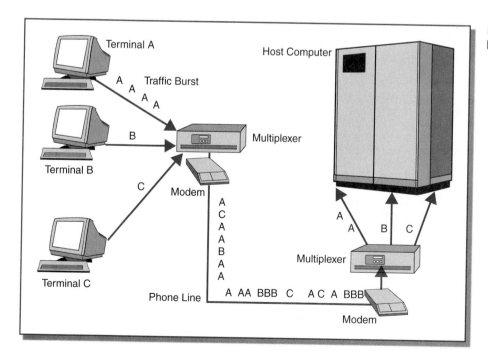

Figure B.4
Multiplexing

If we can find a way to mix the bursts of many connections onto a single line, we can save a great deal of money. We call this **statistical multiplexing.** To give an example, suppose you have four 64 kbps connections, each using the line only 10% of the time. Then you can easily support all four connections with a single 64 kbps line instead of four.

Economies of Scale and Burstiness

Economies of scale and burstiness can work together. For instance, suppose that 100 end-station connections need a 64 kbps transmission line and only use it 5% of the time. Without multiplexing, you would need one hundred 64 kbps lines. For simplicity, suppose that each of these lines costs $200 per month. Then the monthly cost would be $20,000.

Economies of Scale Alone T1 lines can multiplex 24 connections. Without statistical multiplexing, you would need 5 T1 lines for the 100 connections. If a T1 line costs $800 per month, simple nonstatistical multiplexing will cost you $4,000 instead of $20,000.

Adding Statistical Multiplexing Now add statistical multiplexing. Each connection needs only about 5% of 64 kbps, or 3,200 bps. So, 100 connections would require only 320 kbps of capacity. This would require five 64 kbps lines with statistical multiplexing, although six or seven would be better because burstiness is uneven and you do not want to run out of capacity at peak periods. However, a single T1 line at $800 per month would be less expensive because of economies of scale, for a savings of $19,200 per month compared with nonmultiplexed transmission using one hundred 64 kbps lines. This would allow you to recoup the cost of the multiplexer in a few months at the most.

Time Division Multiplexing

There are several ways to do simple multiplexing, that is, multiplexing without accounting for burstiness. The most widely used is **time division multiplexing (TDM).** Figure B.5 illustrates TDM on a T1 line.

Figure B.5
Time Division
Multiplexing
(TDM) on a T1 Line

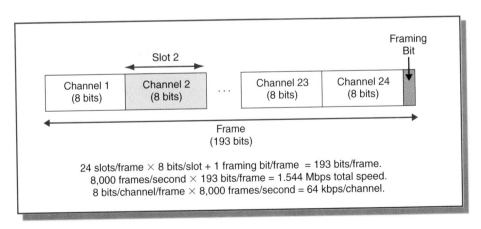

24 slots/frame × 8 bits/slot + 1 framing bit/frame = 193 bits/frame.
8,000 frames/second × 193 bits/frame = 1.544 Mbps total speed.
8 bits/channel/frame × 8,000 frames/second = 64 kbps/channel.

The Goal: 64 kbps per Connection   As discussed in Chapter 5, the process of coding a single voice connection requires a transmission capacity of 64 kbps. This is why almost all transmission lines are multiples of 64 kbps. (Sometimes the speed is 56 kbps, because 8 kbps is "stolen" from the channel for in-channel supervisory signaling.)

Frames and Slots   On a T1 line, each second is divided into 8,000 time **frames,** each of which is 125 microseconds long.

Figure B.5 shows that within each frame, each of the 24 channels is given an 8 bit **slot.** The slot is reserved for that channel in every frame. Over the 8,000 frames that occur each second, each channel can transmit 64,000 bits (8,000 slots per second times 8 bits per slot).

Supervisory Information   A T1 line operates at 1.544 Mbps. Divided by 8,000 frames per second, this is 193 bits per frame. However, the twenty-four 8 bit slots in the frame collectively have only 192 bits (24 times 8). The extra bit (called the **framing bit**) is used for supervisory signaling such as timing signals to ensure that the T1 multiplexers at each end of the transmission line stay in synchronization.

Of course, a single bit provides very little information. So groups of either 12 or 24 frames are treated as **superframes.** Their 12 or 24 supervisory bits are used for simple but effective supervisory signals.

For instance, in the T1 Extended Superframe standard,[1] the 6 framing bits in frames 4, 8, 12, 16, 20, and 24 form the pattern 001011. The receiver constantly monitors this pattern. If it sees a different pattern, it knows that framing is off. The sender and receiver are no longer synchronized.

Six other framing bits form a 6 bit cyclical redundancy check. This checks for bit errors within the frame. It allows the devices at the two ends to check for performance degradation over time.

The remaining 12 framing bits are used to send supervisory control codes between the two devices at the ends of the T1 line.

Statistical Time Division Multiplexing

In simple TDM, each channel between stations is assigned one dedicated time slot in each frame. Each slot is reserved for a particular channel, and that channel is guaranteed its capacity. Figure B.6 illustrates a more sophisticated form of TDM called **statistical time division multiplexing (STDM).**

Wasted Capacity in Simple TDM   Recall that data communication transmissions are bursty. This means that most of the time a channel's dedicated time slot will go unused within the frame if you use simple TDM. This is wasteful of capacity. In Frame B.7, three of the four time slots are going unused.

---

[1] In addition, the Extended Superframe standard steals some extra signaling bits from frames 6, 12, 18, and 24.

Figure B.6
Simple and
Statistical Time
Division
Multiplexing

Time Slot	Simple TDM	Statistical TDM
1	Station 1 (unused)	Station 3
2	Station 2 (unused)	Station 3
3	Station 3	Station 3
4	Station 4 (unused)	(unused)

More importantly, suppose one station has a lot to transmit in its burst. It would like to transmit this burst of data at a much higher speed than 64 kbps. However, even if slots are going unused, the station will still be limited to its single 8 bit slot within each frame.

Statistical TDM   Figure B.6 compares how slots are used in simple and statistical TDM. In simple TDM, most slots go unused, and Station 3, which has much to transmit, gets only a single slot in each frame. In *STDM,* in contrast, the multiplexer assigns slots on a demand basis. Stations 1 and 2, which are not transmitting, do not use up slots. In turn, Station 3 gets three slots within the frame.

Cost   Years ago, STDM was prohibitively expensive. Today, however, processing power is cheap, and STDM is the norm in data multiplexers. Of course, the multiplexers at the two ends must follow the same statistical multiplexing standard.

Frequency Division Multiplexing

In TDM, each second is divided into a number of frames, and frames are further divided into slots. This is good for digital transmission over wires. However, it is not the most common way to transmit radio signals.

For radio transmission, the most common technique is **frequency division multiplexing (FDM).** As we saw in Chapter 4, if two signals are sent in different frequency channels, they will not interfere with one another.

Wave Division Multiplexing

Optical fiber traditionally used lasers operating at a single wavelength. Now, however, multiple lasers or other input devices operating at multiple wavelengths may transmit their signals simultaneously into the optical fiber. This allows the fiber to carry several signals simultaneously. This use of multiple wavelengths is called **wave division multiplexing (WDM).**

Wavelength and frequency are related, as discussed earlier in this module. So WDM is simply another form of frequency division multiplexing. The basic difference is that simple FDM often uses adjacent channels throughout a service band, whereas WDM on optical fiber uses several wavelengths that may be far apart. However, as our ability to control laser frequencies grows, we will be able to send signals at more frequencies.

Chapter 3 discussed optical fiber briefly. This section looks at optical fiber in more detail.

Core and Cladding

As discussed in Chapter 4, optical fiber is a thin glass (or plastic) tube with two components. First, there is a very thin inner **core,** as Figure B.7 illustrates. This core ranges from about 5 microns up to 62.5 microns. Light passes through this inner core.

A cylinder of glass or plastic called the **cladding** surrounds the core. The cladding can be up to about 125 microns in diameter. The cladding has a slightly lower index of refraction than the inner core. The difference in index of refraction is set so that when light from the core strikes the core–cladding boundary, there is total internal reflection. In other words, (almost) no light escapes.

Multimode and Single Mode Fiber

Chapter 3 noted that rays entering the core at different angles will travel different distances, resulting in rays from successive bits eventually overlapping.

This was only an approximation, however. More accurately, light waves travel down the optical fiber's core in one of several ways called **modes.** Unfortunately, modes are too complex to characterize without a long technical discussion.

Multiple modes are bad because different modes travel at slightly different speeds. As a result, modes from successive bits will overlap, making the bits unintelligible.

Single Mode Fiber The wider the core of the fiber is, the more modes that will be generated. This would suggest that we should make optical fiber

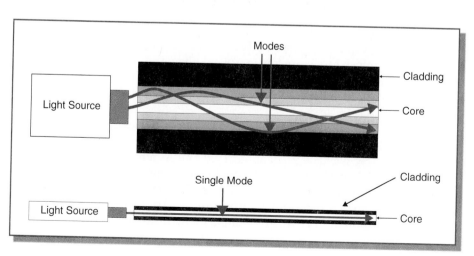

Figure B.7
Single Mode and
Multimode Optical
Fiber Transmission

extremely thin. In fact, such **single mode** optical fiber exists. As shown in Figure B.7, its core is only about 5 microns in diameter. At typical laser wavelengths, such thin fiber can carry signals several kilometers, as discussed in the next module. Beyond that distance, additional modes begin to appear, even in thin fiber.

Unfortunately, single mode fiber is difficult to use. The light source must be aligned precisely with the axis of the very thin core. Otherwise, there will be high signal injection loss. Splicing two sections of single mode fiber also requires precision. As a result, single mode fiber is used mostly in long-distance runs, say between buildings in a university campus or as trunk lines between two switches in a telephone network. Single mode telephone trunk fiber is even thinner than the single mode fiber used in building LANs.

Multimode Fiber If the core of the optical fiber is fairly thick, typically 50 to 62.5 microns in diameter, then we will have **multimode** optical fiber. Figure B.7 also illustrates multimode fiber. In multimode fiber, the presence of multiple modes limits distance. Signals travel only 200 to 600 meters. Module C discusses distance limitations for gigabit Ethernet using multimode fiber.

Graded Index and Step Index Multimode Fiber To reduce problems caused by modes propagating at different speeds, most multimode fiber is **graded index** fiber, shown in Figure B.7. The index of refraction in the core decreases from the center to the outer edge. This causes signals at the outer edge of the core to propagate slightly faster than signals in the center, reducing mode time differences. In contrast, single mode fiber uses **step index** fiber, in which the index of refraction is constant in the core and the only change is at the core–cladding boundary.

Wavelength

The number of modes in a tube will depend on the wavelength of the signal. If the wavelength is long, compared with the length of the tube, there will be fewer modes. In optical fiber, too, longer wavelengths mean fewer modes and so longer propagation distances.

Wavelengths cannot be chosen arbitrarily. Transmission must use natural "windows" in which losses are low in optical fiber. Today, there are two main windows. The lower-wavelength (higher-frequency) window has wavelengths around 850 nanometers (nm). The higher-wavelength window is around 1300 nm.

For instance, Chapter 8 notes that gigabit Ethernet has two variants. The "SX" version uses a "short" wavelength of about 850 nm. The "LX" version, in turn, uses a longer wavelength of about 1300 nm. As a result, LX transmission can travel over longer distances before mode problems appear. Unfortunately, LX is more expensive than SX, first because 1350 nm signaling is somewhat more expensive than 850 nm signaling and second because LX specifies either a higher grade of multimode fiber or single mode fiber.

Fiber Quality

Optical fiber quality is improving constantly. This is why, in Chapter 8, the table shows a range of distances that are possible with different quality levels of fiber. The shortest distance is for the most common quality of fiber today. The longer distances are for new, higher-quality fiber.

Working with Optical Fiber

Because the core is so thin, optical fiber is difficult to splice. This has made optical fiber prohibitively expensive within LANs. However, splicing tools have improved greatly in recent years. In addition, it is now possible to buy pre-made lengths of optical fiber with simple connectors at their ends. There are several popular forms of connectors, including SC and ST, so connectors on a fiber must be matched with those in hubs, switches, and routers.

MORE ON RADIO PROPAGATION

Frequency varies widely. Of course, the lowest frequency is 0 Hz. There is no upper limit on frequency. Even light consists of electromagnetic waves, although light waves have much higher frequencies than radio waves. The range of all possible frequencies from 0 to infinity is called the **electromagnetic frequency spectrum.**

Frequency Bands: UHF and SHF

Figure B.8 shows that it is customary to divide the radio portion of the electromagnetic frequency spectrum into a number of **major frequency bands.** Most data communication takes place in the **Ultra High Frequency (UHF)** band and the **Super High Frequency (SHF)** band. In these bands, there is considerable bandwidth (2.7 GHz and 27 GHz, respectively).

In fact, the SHF band is so wide that it is further divided, as discussed in the section on satellite transmission later in this module.

At the same time, signals in the UHF band and lower frequencies of the SHF band travel through walls and around obstacles reasonably well. At higher frequencies in SHF, they do not. In addition, equipment becomes more expensive at higher SHF frequencies. So there is great competition for spectrum space in the UHF band and in lower portions of the SHF band.

Microwave Systems

One of the most important uses of radio in carrier trunk transmission is microwave transmission. Microwave permits the transmission of information over reasonably long distances without the expense of laying ground wires.

Figure B.9 shows a **microwave** system. It shows that microwave systems use dish antennas for point-to-point transmission. They operate in the gigahertz

Band	Full Name	Uses	Lowest Freq.	Bandwidth	Units	Wavelength of Lowest Frequency	Units
ELF	Extremely Low Frequency		30	270	Hz	10,000	km
VF	Voice Frequency		300	2,700	Hz	1,000	km
VLF	Very Low Frequency		3	27	kHz	100	km
LF	Low Frequency		30	270	kHz	10	km
MF	Medium Frequency	AM Radio	300	2,700	kHz	1,000	m
HF	High Frequency		3	27	MHz	100	m
VHF	Very High Frequency	VHF TV, FM Radio	30	270	MHz	10	m
UHF	Ultra High Frequency	UHF TV, Cellular Phones, Radio LANs	300	2,700	MHz	100	cm
SHF	Super High Frequency	Satellites, Microwave	3	27	GHz	10	cm
EHF	Extremely High Frequency	Future Q/V Band Satellites	30	270	GHz	10	mm

range, in which highly directional transmission is possible with dish antennas only a few meters in diameter.

However, microwave systems can travel only a limited distance before problems occur. Signals may grow too weak because of attenuation. Or, the receiver might be so far away that the target falls below the horizon, losing the required **line-of-sight** connection (the ability of the two dish antennas to see one another). Or, there may be mountains and other obstacles between the dishes. In general, line-of-sight microwave transmission is good for only 30 to 50 kilometers (20 to 30 miles).[2]

Figure B.9 shows that microwave systems use **repeaters** to solve such problems. These repeaters capture and regenerate the signal, often cleaning it up to remove propagation effects before passing the message on to the next repeater or to the ultimate receiving antenna.

---

[2]G. R. McClain, ed., Handbook of International Connectivity Standards (New York: Van Nostrand), 1996, p. 418.

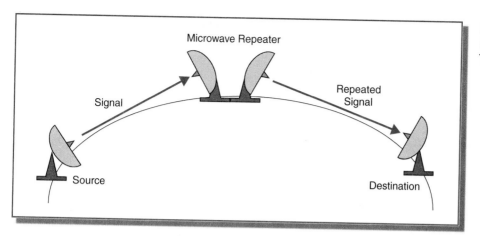

Figure B.9
Microwave
Transmission

In the figure: Microwave Repeater · Signal · Repeated Signal · Source · Destination

Satellite Systems

After World War II, a young radar engineer named Arthur C. Clarke saw a way to improve on microwave systems. Why not, he asked, put a microwave repeater in space, on a satellite going around the earth? And why not set the satellite's altitude at 36,000 km (22,300 miles), so that it would circle the earth every 24 hours and so appear stationary in the sky? (This is called a **geosynchronous orbit.**) Today, a great deal of our long-distance communication travels over **geosynchronous communication satellites (GEOs),** which were introduced in Chapter 5.

Chapter 5 also introduced low earth orbit satellites and medium earth satellites that do not appear to be stationary in the sky but that are low enough for signals to be useable even by portable devices with omnidirectional antennas.

As noted earlier, the SHF band is so wide that it is normally divided into a number of smaller frequency bands. In general, as frequency increases, dishes can become smaller for the same degree of amplification, but attenuation problems increase, requiring more powerful satellites.

- *C Band.* The first satellites operated in the **C Band,** which was originally created for microwave systems. C Band satellites use frequencies of about 6 GHz for the **uplink** (the signal from the earth station to the satellite) and 4 GHz for the **downlink.** (The uplink frequency is always higher than the downlink frequency in satellite transmission.) C Band was a good place for satellite communication to start because C Band equipment was readily available and inexpensive, thanks to widespread terrestrial microwave transmission in this band. Unfortunately, this same widespread terrestrial microwave use tends to create interference between terrestrial microwave systems and C Band satellites.
- *Ku Band.* Next, many satellites began to use the **Ku Band,** with an uplink of about 14 GHz and a downlink of about 12 GHz. In this band, rain produces substantial attenuation, so powerful satellites are needed to burn through the attenuation. Dishes, however, can be smaller than they can

be in C Band without losing efficiency. In addition, there are no terrestrial microwave systems to interfere with Ku Band signals.

- *Ka Band.* The **Ka Band** has uplink frequencies of about 30 GHz and downlink frequencies of about 20 GHz. Satellites are just beginning to use these frequencies. Rain attenuation is very high, so satellites must have very high power. New satellite-based telephony systems (see Module D) and satellite data services will use the Ka Band.
- *Other Bands.* Although the bands we have just seen are common satellite frequency bands, there are other bands at higher, lower, and intermediate frequencies.

REVIEW QUESTIONS

Core Review Questions

1. **a)** What characteristics of carrier waves can be modulated in modems? **b)** In newer modems, which characteristics actually are modulated?

2. In multiplexing, distinguish between economies of scale and the exploitation of burstiness.

3. What common characteristic of data transmission does statistical multiplexing exploit?

4. Distinguish between simple TDM and statistical TDM.

5. Describe FDM.

6. **a)** Distinguish between single mode and multimode fiber, including both technology and the advantages of using each. **b)** Why is wavelength important in fiber optic transmission? **c)** Will all fiber transmit signals of a given wavelength as far?

7. **a)** How does bandwidth change with each increase in frequency band? **b)** Why do most data communications and voice communications services use the UHF band and lower portions of the SHF band?

8. Distinguish between microwave systems and satellite systems.

Detailed Review Questions

1. You have a modem that operates at 2,400 kbaud. Its modulation system uses four amplitude levels and four phases. What is its bit rate?

2. You have a modem that operates at 3,200 kbaud. Its modulation system uses two amplitude levels and eight phases. However, only four of the eight phase combinations are used for signal data. The rest are error states. What is the bit rate for information transmission?

3. **a)** In time division multiplexing, distinguish between frames and slots. **b)** In a T1 line, how many frames are there per second? **c)** How many slots are there per frame? **d)** How many bits are there per slot? **e)** How many bits are there per second? (Show your work.) **f)** How many bits are there per channel? (Show your work.)

4. Distinguish between FDM and wavelength division multiplexing.

5. **a)** Distinguish between step index and graded index optical fiber. **b)** Which dominates the multimode fiber market? Why?

6. **a)** What are the main satellite frequency bands? **b)** Give the representative frequencies for the uplink and downlink in each band. **c)** Which usually has the higher frequency—the uplink or the downlink?

Thought Questions

1. You have 40 connections that need 19.2 kbps transmission speeds. A 64 kbps line costs $500 per month. T1 lines cost $1,800 per month. Because of burstiness, lines are in use only 10% of the time. Compare the costs of transmission without using multiplexing with nonstatistical multiplexing and with statistical multiplexing. The multiplexer costs $5,000 and has a useful life of 5 years.

2. Voice connections are not statistically multiplexed. Why is this? In your answer, estimate what percentage of transmission line capacity is used in voice connections.

Case Studies

For case studies, go to the book's website, **http://www.prenhall.com/panko,** and look at the "Case Studies" page for this chapter.

Projects

1. **Getting Current.** Go to the book's website, **http://www.prenhall.com/ panko,** and see the "New Information" and "Errors" pages for this module to get new information since this book went to press and to correct any errors in the text.

2. **Internet Exercises.** Go to the book's website, **http://www.prenhall.com/ panko,** and see the "Exercises" page for this module. Do the Internet exercises.

Module C

More on Local Area Networks

INTRODUCTION

Module C covers some advanced topics in LAN technology. It is not intended to be read front-to-back like a chapter. It should be read after Chapter 7. This module focuses on these topics:

- Older Ethernet physical layer standards, especially the still widely used 10Base5 and 10Base2 standards. It also covers mixing several Ethernet physical layer standards in the same LAN, for instance, to increase the distance span.
- The logical link control layer 802.2 frame.
- Electrical signaling in 100Base-TX.
- Further information on 802.5 Token-Ring Networks.
- Fiber Distributed Data Interface (FDDI).
- More on 802.11 Wireless LANs.

ADDITIONAL ETHERNET STANDARDS

In Chapters 6 and 7, we looked at three sets of the Ethernet physical layer standards from the IEEE 802.3 Working Group. We looked at the 10Base-T, 100Base-X and 1000Base-X (gigabit Ethernet) families of physical layer standards.

In this section, we will look more closely at two 802.3 physical layer Ethernet standards that predate 10Base-T, namely 10Base5 and 10Base2. Both, as you can tell by their names, are 10 Mbps baseband standards. Some organizations that networked early still use these two physical layer standards as their main standards. Others continue to use 10Base5 for longer runs in their 10Base-T networks. As we will see, you can mix 10 Mbps 802.3 physical layer standards in a LAN, as long as you separate them by repeaters.

802.3 10Base5

When the 802 Committee began developing 802.3 variants, it developed a naming system. The **10Base5** physical layer standard illustrates this system. The *10* stands for the speed of the standard—10 Mbps. The *Base,* in turn, stands for baseband transmission. The *5,* finally, means that a **segment** (single unbroken run) of the cable can be up to 500 meters long (1,640 feet). We will see later that several of these segments can be linked to form a larger LAN.

10Base5 Trunk Cable The specific type of coaxial cable used in 10Base5's **trunk cable** was created especially for the standard. It is 10 millimeters thick (about 0.4 inches). This is much thicker than the coaxial cables used to bring cable television signals to the home or to link VCRs to television sets.

Because of this thickness, the 10Base5 trunk cable is fairly difficult to bend and install. Because 10Base5 cable is traditionally colored yellow (the standard merely specifies a bright color), installers refer to it in frustration as a "frozen yellow garden hose."

10Base5 Medium Attachment Unit (MAU): The Transceiver Figure C.1 illustrates how Ethernet 10Base5 devices are attached to the network. First, attached to the thick trunk cable is the **medium attachment unit (MAU).** The MAU is also called a **transceiver (transmitter/receiver).** It is a transceiver because it *transmits* signals over the cable and *receives* signals from the cable. It is an active electronic device, not a mere physical connector.

10Base5 Attachment Unit Interface (AUI): The Drop Cable The station can be some distance away from the trunk cable. To allow this, an **attachment unit interface (AUI)** runs from the MAU to the station itself. This wiring bundle also is called a **drop cable.** This seems like a wiser choice of terminology. The drop cable attaches to the station via a 15-pin **AUI connector.** The drop cable can be up to 50 meters long. This is another thick, inflexible bundle, but unlike the coaxial trunk cable, the AUI is a bundle of 15 wires.

Figure C.1
Ethernet 802.3
10Base5 Physical
Layer Standard

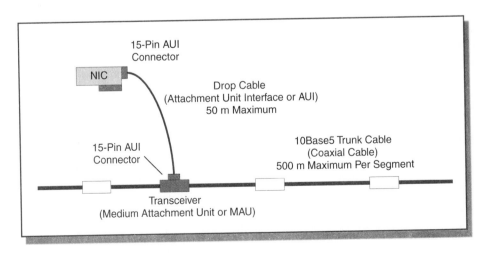

Multisegment 10Base5 LANs   As noted earlier, a single unbroken length of 10Base5 trunk cable is called a *segment*. As in the case of 10Base-T (see Chapter 5), you can connect multiple 10Base5 segments with repeaters. This is like connecting 10Base-T segments, except that 10Base5 segments can have several stations attached to them along their runs.

The rules for connecting segments are the same as they are for 10Base-T segments. First, there must be no loops. Second, there is a 5-4-3 rule. There is a maximum of 5 segments (4 repeaters) between the farthest two stations. This gives a span of 2,500 meters (8,200 feet). The 3 in 5-4-3 means that only 3 of these 10Base5 segments can be populated, that is, have stations attached to them.

The 802.3 terminology refers to a group of segments connected by repeaters as a **collision domain** because if two stations anywhere in the collision domain transmit at the same time, their signals will collide.

802.3 10Base2

Although 10Base5 works well, it is expensive. The 802.3 Working Group created a standard for a less expensive cabling system. This was **10Base2**, which is also known popularly as *Cheapernet* or *Thinnet*. Like 10Base5, it carries data at 10 Mbps, using baseband signaling. However, its maximum segment length is only 185 meters (607 feet), which is rounded off to "2" in its name.

Thinner Cable in 10Base2   10Base2 is attractive because its coaxial cable is only half as thick as the traditional Ethernet trunk cable. This thinner cable is cheaper to buy. It is also cheaper to lay because it is much more flexible.

BNC Plug and T-Connector in 10Base2   Another reason why 10Base2 is less expensive than 10Base5 is that Thinnet does not have separate trunk cables and AUI drop cables. Figure C.2 shows that 10Base2 uses a simpler arrangement. The cable at each station attaches via a simple T-connector. The stem of the T screws into the NIC, via a **BNC connector** on the NIC. The other connectors on the T-connector are for 10Base2 cable runs to the two adjacent stations. Connections and disconnections can be made in seconds.

In 10Base2, a segment consists of a string (daisy chain) of stations, as shown in Figure C.2. A segment may have up to 30 stations. On the last station, the

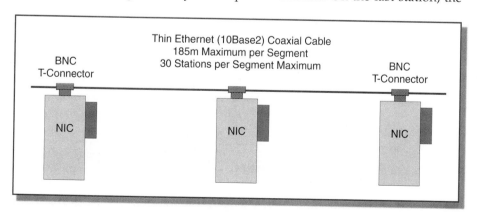

Figure C.2
Ethernet 802.3
10Base2 Physical
Layer Standard

T-connector not leading to another station must have a terminator installed on the open connector. Otherwise, the signal will hit the nonterminated end and will be partially reflected back. It will be interpreted as a collision.

Distance in 10Base2 As in the case of 10Base5, you can have up to five 10Base2 segments (four repeaters) between the farthest stations. This gives a maximum span of 925 meters (3,035 feet). As in 10Base5, the standard requires that at least two of the segments cannot have stations attached to them if you are using the maximum five segments.

Mixed 802.3 10 Mbps Networks

So far, we have discussed networks that use a single 802.3 physical layer standard. But we would like to mix them together in a network. Figure C.3 shows how to do so for 10 Mbps Ethernet.

For longer runs, such a network uses 10Base5 or 10Base-F cabling. (Chapter 8 notes distance limits in 10Base-F cabling.) This provides a high-speed backbone that can run between offices in a building.

For runs to individual stations, networks can mix both 10Base-T and 10Base2 cabling. So, if a firm still has older 10Base2 cabling in place, it can keep some older cabling while upgrading some of its 10Base2 cabling with 10Base-T wiring.

Note that we have talked only about the physical layer. As Chapter 7 noted, all 802.3 Ethernet standards use the same MAC layer standard. Mixing physical layer standards has absolutely no impact on MAC layer operation.

The Ethernet II Frame

The original Ethernet II standard, which predated 802.3 Ethernet standards, did not have separate MAC and LLC layers. There was only a single data link

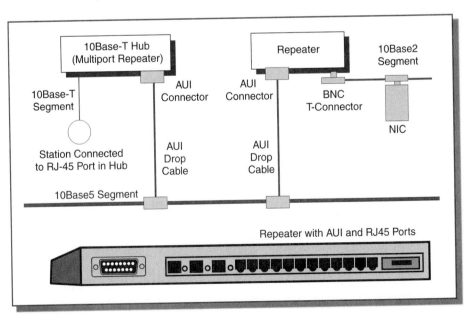

Figure C.3
Mixing 10 Mbps
Ethernet 802.3
Physical Layer
Standards

Ethernet II Frame	802.3 MAC Layer Frame
Preamble (8 octets)	Preamble (7 octets)
	Start of Frame Delimiter (1 octet)
Destination Address (6 octets)	Destination Address (6 octets)
Source Address (6 octets)	Source Address (6 octets)
EtherType (2 octets)	Length (2 octets)
Data (variable)	802.2 LLC Frame (variable)
	PAD if Required
Frame Check Sequence (4 octets)	Frame Check Sequence (4 octets)

Figure C.4
Ethernet II Frame

layer. Figure C.4 shows that the Ethernet II frame closely resembles an 802.3 MAC layer frame without an enclosed 802.2 LLC frame.

EtherType Field   Whereas the 802.3 MAC layer frame has a 2-octet Length field following the source address, the Ethernet II frame has a 2-octet **EtherType** field in this position. This field indicates the contents of the data field. For instance, an EtherType value of 08-00 hex indicates an IP packet in the data field.

Automatic Detection   Interestingly, NICs can tell automatically whether an incoming frame is an 802.3 MAC layer frame or an Ethernet II frame by looking at the 2-octet field following the source address. This is either an EtherType field in Ethernet II or a Length field in 802.3.

   If the value in this field is larger than 1,500, then this must be an Ethernet II frame because all EtherType values are larger than 1,500. Conversely, if the value is less than or equal to 1,500, this must be an 802.3 MAC layer frame, because the maximum length of an 802.3 MAC layer data field is 1,500 octets.

Logical Link Control Layer Framing

802.2 Logical Link Control (LLC) Layer Frame: Basic Frame Format
Just as the MAC layer has a frame, the 802.2 LLC layer standard also defines a frame. In fact, it defines two frame formats: a basic type and a *Subnet Access Protocol (SNAP)* variant. We will begin with the basic frame format.

Destination Service Access Point   The first field is the 1-octet **Destination Service Access Point (DSAP).** The DSAP field contains a value indicating

Figure C.5
802.2 Logical Link
Control (LLC)
Layer Frame
Formats

Basic LLC Frame Format

DSAP (1 octet)	SSAP (1 octet)	Control (usually 1 octet)	Data (variable length)

LLC Frame Format with SNAP Option

DSAP (AA hex)	SSAP (AA hex)	Control (03 hex)	Organization (3 octets)	Type (1 octet)	Data (variable)

Notes: DSAP = Destination Service Access Point; SSAP = Source Service Access Point; SNAP = Subnet Access Protocol.

which next-higher-layer process should receive the data field contained in the LLC frame.

Source Service Access Point Similarly, the **Source Service Access Point (SSAP)** field contains a value indicating which next-higher-layer process on the source computer created the packet in the data field.

Control Field The **Control** field is used for error detection and correction. However, as noted earlier in Chapter 7, error correction is rarely used.

Data Field The **data** field contains the packet of the next-higher layer. This might be an IP packet, an IPX packet, or some other next-higher-layer message.

Subnet Access Protocol (SNAP) Format for 802.3

With only a single octet, the DSAP field could only specify a limited number of internet-layer processes. When these DSAP values were assigned, TCP/IP was new, and it was not given a series of DSAP values for its major internet-layer standards, IP and ARP (Module A discusses ARP).[1] Other protocols that subsequently became important, such as AppleTalk, were also left out.

Fortunately, the DSAP and SSAP values AA hex were assigned to indicate the use of the **Subnet Access Protocol (SNAP)** option, which is also shown in Figure C.5. SNAP places the value 03 hex in the control field. It then adds two new fields: *Organization* and *Type*.

Organization The **Organization** field identifies an organization that creates designations for various next-higher-layer protocols. Each such organization is given an **organizational unique identifier (OUI)** code. For Xerox, the OUI value is 00-00-00 hex.

Type The organization can assign multiple next-higher-layer designations. The 2-octet **Type** field identifies a specific next-higher-layer standard. For IP version 4, the value specified by Xerox is 08-00 hex. For IP version 6, it is 86-DD

---

[1] A SAP value was defined for IP, but ARP also needed a SAP value, and this was never assigned.

hex. When 00-00-00 hex is in the organization field, the Type values are those of the EtherType field for the Ethernet II frame noted earlier in this chapter.

Electrical Signaling in 100Base-TX

In Chapter 7, we saw Manchester encoding for 10Base-T. The 100Base-TX standard uses more sophisticated signal encoding.

4B/5B Data Representation Manchester encoding places a transition in the middle of each bit period, as discussed in Chapter 7. This means that the bit rate is only half the baud rate. This is wasteful, because baud rate usually is the limiting factor in transmission. Also, if the sender were transmitting all ones or zeros, the line would radiate at a frequency of 20 MHz. This is not bad, but it is close to the maximum radiation frequency allowed by radio regulatory agencies. Manchester encoding is safe, but it will not scale to higher frequencies.

The 100Base-TX standard uses **4B/5B data encoding,** in which each "nibble" of 4 bits is encoded in a 5-bit sequence that has at least two ones, with two exceptions used for supervisory signaling. Figure C.6 shows some of these combinations. Note that some combinations do not represent data. These are used in supervisory signaling.

MLT-3 Encoding In another departure from 10Base-T, 100Base-TX uses **MLT-3** signal encoding in which there are three states to the line: 1, 0, and 1. In each clock cycle, the signal may either advance to the next state (1 to 0, 0 to 1, or 1 to 0) or remain the same. If the signal is always advancing, the state will

Symbol	Nibble or Code	Encoded
0	0000	11110
1	0001	01001
F	1111	11101
J	Initial Parity Violation 1	11000
K	Initial Parity Violation 2	10001
T	Terminator	01101
R	Reset	00111
S	Set	11001
I	Idle	11111
Q	Quiet	00000
H	Halt	00100

Plus 8 code violations.

Figure C.6
4B/5B Encoding in Ethernet 802.3 100Base-TX

cycle every 4 bits. This results in a relatively low frequency. The baud rate is 125 MBaud, so the frequency is only 31.25 MHz. Although 100Base-TX is 10 times faster than 10Base-T, its frequency radiation is only about 50% higher in the worst case of constant changing.

When does the state change? It changes whenever there is a 1 transmitted. The 4B/5B combinations each have at least two ones, so the state will change frequently enough to keep the receiver synchronized with the sender.

THE 802.5 TOKEN-RING STANDARD

The box in Chapter 7 looked briefly at **802.5 Token-Ring Networks (TRNs).** One important point about the TRN standard is that it has been strongly driven by IBM. In fact, the actual 802.5 documentation is rather simplified, and most vendors follow IBM TRN specifications, which are a superset of 802.5 standards.

Differential Manchester Encoding

In Chapter 4, we saw that to send a signal, you must encode the zeros and ones as combinations of voltage levels. The method that TRN networks use is called *differential Manchester encoding.*

Manchester Encoding   In Chapter 7, we saw that 802.3 10Base-T uses **Manchester encoding** (as do 10Base5 and 10Base2). In Manchester encoding, there is always a transition in the middle of the bit time. This ensures that the sender will not transmit a long series of bits that all keep the signal high or low. A long voltage transmission without change will not keep the receiver's clock synchronized with that of the sender.

To transmit a 1, Manchester encoding sends a low voltage for half the bit time, followed by a high voltage for the second half of the bit time. A 0, in turn, is a high voltage for the first half of the bit time, followed by a low voltage for the second half. A good way to remember this is that a high ending is a 1 and a low ending is a 0.

There are two possible line changes for each bit transmission. So operating at 10 Mbps, 10Base-T is a 20 Mbaud transmission system.

Differential Manchester Encoding for a 1   In contrast to simple Manchester encoding, the way that **differential Manchester encoding** represents a bit depends on whether the previous bit time ended high or low. To transmit a 1, there is no transition at the start of the bit time. To prevent a long series of ones from ruining synchronization, there is a transition in the middle of the bit time.

Suppose the previous bit ended high. Then to transmit a 1, you would keep the signal high for the first half of the bit period. Then you would make it low for the second half. The ending state will be different than the starting state.

Suppose that the previous bit ended low. To transmit a 1, you would keep the line low for the first half of the bit period and make it high for the second half. The ending state, then, is always different than the starting state when you send a 1.

Differential Manchester Encoding for a 0

Differential Manchester Encoding for a 0   To transmit a 0, in contrast, you *change* the voltage level at the start of the bit period. In other words, you distinguish a 1 from a 0 by whether or not the line changes at the beginning of the bit period.

Like a 1, a 0 always makes a transition in the middle of the bit period. In this way, you are ensured transitions that keep the receiver synchronized with the sender.

Differential Manchester Encoding for J and K

Differential Manchester Encoding for J and K   In addition to representing ones and zeros, differential Manchester encoding defines two special characters, J and K. Actually, they are called code violations, but as we will see, they are used for signaling.

A J is a 1 without the transition in the middle. Whatever the line state was at the end of the last bit time, a J will continue that state for the entire bit.

A K, in turn, is a 0 without the transition in the middle. Whatever the line state was at the end of the last bit time, a K will change the state at the start of the bit and will hold that changed level for the entire bit. The line state at the end will be the opposite of the line state at the beginning.

The 802.5 MAC Layer Frame: Token Frame

Chapter 7 discussed the 802.3 MAC layer frame in some detail. We will now do so for the IBM Token-Ring Network MAC layer frame. We will begin with the token frame itself. Figure C.7 shows that a token frame has three fields: start frame delimiter, access control, and end frame delimiter.

Start Frame Delimiter

Start Frame Delimiter   The **start frame delimiter** acts like the preamble and start of frame delimiter fields in 802.3 MAC layer frames, although it is much shorter. It is only a single byte long. It has the following pattern of bits: JK0JK000.

This frame, with two J violations and two K violations in specific locations, is highly unlikely to occur in erroneous transmissions. It uniquely marks the start of the frame.

Access Control

Access Control   The **access control** field is the heart of the token. This is the field that allows stations to know if the token is free and, if so, whether

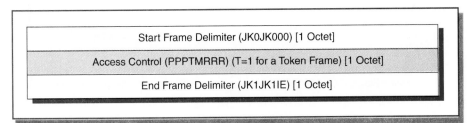

Figure C.7
802.5 Token-Ring Network Token Frame

| Start Frame Delimiter (JK0JK000) [1 Octet] |
| Access Control (PPPTMRRR) (T=1 for a Token Frame) [1 Octet] |
| End Frame Delimiter (JK1JK1IE) [1 Octet] |

their priority is high enough for them to take it and transmit. Its 8 bits are encoded in the following way: PPPTMRRR.

The three P (priority) bits give the priority of the token. This gives eight levels, from 0 through 7. Unless a station has priority at least as high as these bits indicate, it must let the token pass, even if it has something to send.

The T (token) bit tells whether this frame is a token or a full frame. In this case, it is a token, so its value is set equal to 1. If it were a full frame, it would be 0.

The M (monitor) bit is set to 0 by the transmitting station. A special station called the **active monitor** (discussed later) sets this bit to 1. If it sees a 1 bit in an arriving frame, the active monitor knows that the transmitting station has not removed the frame when the frame completed a full run around the ring. The active monitor then removes the frame.

Finally, the three R (reservation) bits are the token reservation bits. These come into play when full frames are transmitted, as we will see later.

End Frame Delimiter The **end frame delimiter** finishes the token. This 1-octet frame has the following pattern: J K 1 J K 1 I E. Here, again, we start with an unusual pattern of bits containing uncommon J and K violations. Although the start frame delimiter begins with "JK0JK0", the end frame delimiter begins with "JK1JK1". We will discuss the I and E bits next, in the context of full frames.

The 802.5 MAC Layer Frame: Full Frame

If a station has high enough priority, it takes control of the token. It takes its information and wraps it inside the token, forming a full token-ring network frame. Figure C.8 shows a full frame.

Figure C.8
802.5 Token-Ring
Network Full
Frame

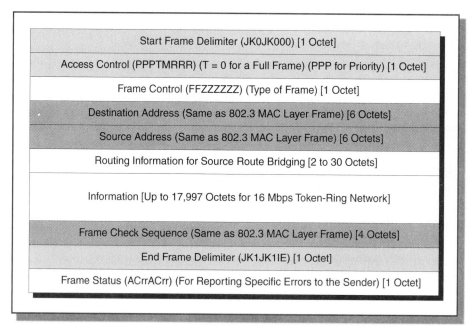

| Start Frame Delimiter (JK0JK000) [1 Octet] |
| Access Control (PPPTMRRR) (T = 0 for a Full Frame) (PPP for Priority) [1 Octet] |
| Frame Control (FFZZZZZZ) (Type of Frame) [1 Octet] |
| Destination Address (Same as 802.3 MAC Layer Frame) [6 Octets] |
| Source Address (Same as 802.3 MAC Layer Frame) [6 Octets] |
| Routing Information for Source Route Bridging [2 to 30 Octets] |
| Information [Up to 17,997 Octets for 16 Mbps Token-Ring Network] |
| Frame Check Sequence (Same as 802.3 MAC Layer Frame) [4 Octets] |
| End Frame Delimiter (JK1JK1IE) [1 Octet] |
| Frame Status (ACrrACrr) (For Reporting Specific Errors to the Sender) [1 Octet] |

Access Control   When the station grabs the token, it changes the T bit in the **access control** field from 1 to 0. This signals receivers that they are looking at a full frame instead of just a token.

In addition, when the transmitting station transmits, it changes the three priority reservation bits (RRR) to 000, the lowest priority. If a station wishes to transmit, it looks at the reservation bits. If its priority is higher, it places its priority level in the reservation bits. In this way, by the time the frame has gotten all the way around to the sender, the RRR bits contain the highest-priority level of stations wishing to transmit. When the sending station releases the token, it places this priority level in the main priority bits (PPP) of the token it releases.

Frame Control   The **frame control** field tells what kind of frame this is. It has the following pattern in its eight bits: FFZZZZZZ.

The F bits tell the stations what type of frame this is. If the F bits are 01, then this frame contains logical link control layer data. In other words, its information field contains an 802.2 frame (discussed in Chapter 7). In contrast, if the F bits are 00, then this frame is a MAC layer frame only. It is either a token or a supervisory frame.

The six remaining Z bits specify particular types of LLC and MAC layer frames. We will see some MAC layer control frames later, when we discuss errors and error recovery.

Destination and Source Addresses   Fortunately, the IBM Token-Ring Network frame (and the official 802.5 MAC layer frame) uses the same 48-bit addressing scheme as the 802.3 MAC layer frame, which we discussed in Chapter 4.

Routing Information   The **routing information** field holds information for routing the frame through a series of source routing bridges. Source routing is the bridging standard created by IBM and allowed by the 802 Standards Committee only for 802.5 LANs. This field can be 2 to 30 octets long.

Information   The **information** field holds the data to be delivered. The information field can be very large. In 16 Mbps token-ring networks, frames can be 17,997 octets long. Even in 4 Mbps TRNs, frames can be 4,501 octets.

Frame Check Sequence   The **frame check sequence** field is a 32-bit field for error checking. It is the same as the frame check sequence field in 802.3 MAC layer frames.

End Frame Delimiter   In 802.3 MAC layer frames, the frame check sequence field is the last field. In contrast, TRN frames add two final fields. One of these is the **end frame delimiter.** This 1-octet field, as we saw earlier, begins with the unusual pattern "JK1JK1". It ends with two other bits, the I bit and the E bit.

The I bit is used to tell the receiver if this is the last frame in a series. It is set to 1 if it is the last frame. If it is not, the I bit is set to 0.

The E bit is for reporting errors. The transmitting station sets this bit to 0. If *any* station along the ring detects a J or K violation or some other transmission error, it sets this bit to 1. When the transmitting station receives the frame back, it looks at the E bit to check for errors.

Frame Status Field   The very last field is the **frame status** field. This octet allows the receiving station to tell the sending station whether or not it has received the frame. The form of this field is the following: A C r r A C r r.

- The r bits are reserved for future use (an unlikely situation at this late date). They are normally set to 0.
- The transmitting station sets the A bit to 0. If the receiving station recognizes its address, it resets this address bit to 1. When the frame returns to the sender, the A bits tell if the receiver has seen the frame.
- It is possible that a station will recognize its address yet not be able to copy the frame into its NIC's memory. This is the purpose of the C (copy) bit. The sending station sets this bit to 0. The receiver resets it to 1 if it makes a successful copy.

The frame status field comes after the frame check sequence field, so there is no way for the receiver to check for errors in the frame status field. To compensate, the field has 2 A bits and 2 C bits. The transmitting station assumes a failure unless it sees ones on both A bits and on both C bits.

Error Handling

In many ways, a token-ring network is an accident waiting to happen. As we will see, there are two major ways in which a simple failure can disable the network. Although these dangers are very real, the standard contains several ways of minimizing these risks. As a result, TRNs are not at all the fragile networks that they first seem to be.

Breaking the Ring   The most obvious problem is that frames must go all the way around the ring. In addition, the stations do not simply watch the frames go by. They stop each frame, look at it bit by bit, and then regenerate it. As a result, if a single connection breaks or a single device fails, no station on the network can transmit.

Losing the Token   Another risk in TRNs is losing the token. We know that stations may not transmit until they have the token. What if the token is lost? Then no station may transmit. Again, communication will break down.

Wrapping the Ring between Access Units   How can we prevent the loss of transmission if there is a break in the ring between access units? To allow recovery, 802.5 rings are really double rings like the double rings used in SONET/SDH (see Chapter 9). As in SONET/SDH, 802.5 rings can be wrapped if there is a break between two access units.

Handling Lost Tokens and Other Problems   Handling lost tokens, in contrast, requires a considerable amount of complexity. One station must be designated as the **active monitor.** We saw earlier that the active monitor constantly examines frames that have gone around the ring more than once. It also removes garbled frames with obvious errors.

The active monitor station keeps watching for the token. It times the reappearance of the token each time the token passes the station. If that time is too long, it generates a new token. This station also weeds out duplicate tokens.

What if the active monitor fails? This failure will be addressed automatically.[2] Periodically, the active monitor issues an **active monitor present** control frame. Its frame control field is 00000011. If any station notices an absence of this frame for a long period of time, it may issue a **claim token** control frame, whose frame control field is 0000010. If this token gets all the way around the ring, the claiming station assumes the duties of the active monitor.

The Status of Token-Ring Networks

The 1990s were not a happy time for Token-Ring Network technology. Even in 1997, only 11% of all NICs sold were Token-Ring Network NICs, whereas Ethernet NICs made up 85% of the NIC market.[3] The 802.5 Working Group had developed a 100 Mbps version of Token-Ring and will eventually develop a gigabit standard. However, even the 100 Mbps standard is coming fairly late, and gigabit Ethernet should be well entrenched before gigabit Token-Ring emerges. In addition, Token-Ring's ability to enhance quality of service with frame prioritization will soon be available to Ethernet through the 802.1p standard discussed in Chapter 7.

FDDI

FDDI is the **Fiber Distributed Data Interface** standard. Like 802.5 Token-Ring Networks, FDDI uses a ring topology at the physical layer, token passing at the media access control layer, and 802.2 at the logical link control layer.

FDDI was derived from 802.5 technology, although the modifications were so extensive that 802.5 and FDDI are deeply incompatible. One reason for the differences is that FDDI was designed to run at 100 Mbps, rather than at 4 Mbps or 16 Mbps. This (initially) required the use of optical fiber and a number of other differences.

Another difference between 802.5 and FDDI, however, proved to be more important in the long run. Whereas 802.5 was designed to be a compact LAN technology with distance limits similar to those of Ethernet, FDDI was designed to be a metropolitan area network technology that could span distances typically found in an urban area. An FDDI ring has a maximum circumference of 200 km! Although the metropolitan area network market did not

---

[2] Andrew S. Tanenbaum, *Computer Networks*, Upper Saddle River, NJ: Prentice Hall, 1988.

[3] Jodi Cohen, "The Downfall of Desktop ATM," *Network World*, 7/7/97, p. 25.

emerge as a major force in networking, the wide distance span of FDDI made it perfect as a backbone network within large site networks to link individual LANs.

FDDI did not come from the IEEE. Rather, the FDDI standard is the product of the **American National Standards Institute (ANSI)** X3T9.5 Committee. However, ANSI was careful to develop FDDI within the IEEE framework for LAN standards. It has media access control and logical link control layers, and it uses 802.2 as the LLC standard.

FDDI never fared well in the market for LANs because of its high cost. When its 100 Mbps speed was attractive, its NICs were far too expensive to connect the PCs that even then dominated corporate desktops. Although FDDI NIC prices have fallen since then, they have not fallen as far as NICs for other 100 Mbps LAN technologies, such as Ethernet 100Base-TX.

In addition, FDDI is not scalable, working only at 100 Mbps. For a while, FDDI was popular as a backbone network for site networks, but FDDI's single speed now makes it unattractive even for backbones in new installations. Overall, FDDI is a technology whose time never came but has certainly gone.

WIRELESS LANS (802.11)

Most of the LANs we have seen in this book have used wire, optical fiber, or some other physical transmission medium to carry signals. This is fine for many applications, but for some applications, we need wireless transmission.

The IEEE 802.11 Working Group sets wireless LAN standards. In 1997 the working group released its first standards. As Figure C.9 shows, the working group developed a single MAC layer standard for use with multiple physical layer standards. For each physical layer (PHY) transmission standard, two speeds were specified: 1 Mbps and 2 Mbps. At the time of this writing, 802.11 has just finalized an 11 Mbps standard.

Access Point Operation

As Chapter 7 noted, an access point usually coordinates computers in 802.11 networks. This is reminiscent of cellular telephony (see Module D). The access point is like a cell site. It assigns power levels to its stations and exerts other forms of control.

The similarity to cellular telephony extends to handoffs. If a computer is being controlled by one access point and passes into an area controlled by

Figure C.9
802.11 Wireless Network Standards

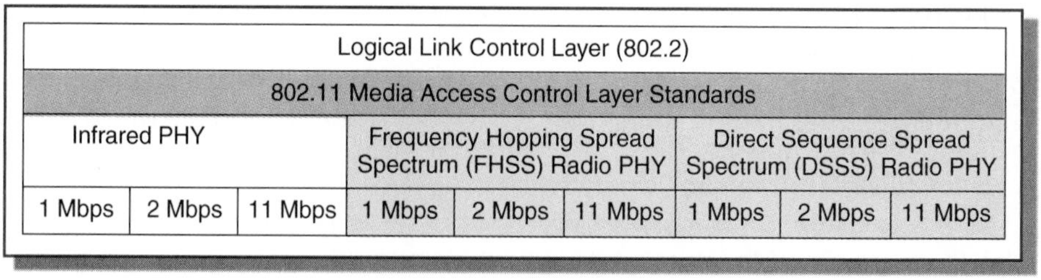

Logical Link Control Layer (802.2)								
802.11 Media Access Control Layer Standards								
Infrared PHY			Frequency Hopping Spread Spectrum (FHSS) Radio PHY			Direct Sequence Spread Spectrum (DSSS) Radio PHY		
1 Mbps	2 Mbps	11 Mbps	1 Mbps	2 Mbps	11 Mbps	1 Mbps	2 Mbps	11 Mbps

another access point, control will switch automatically and smoothly to the new access point.

The access point may even store frames for later delivery. So a station can be powered off at any time. When it next powers on and associates with the access point, the access point will deliver waiting e-mail and other messages.

The 802.11 MAC Layer

The MAC layer controls when stations may transmit. Ethernet uses CSMA/CD. In CSMA, stations can transmit only if there is no traffic on the line. In collision detection (CD), if a station hears another station transmitting while it is sending its own signal, the station will respond to this collision by stopping, backing off a random amount of time, and then transmitting again if the line is free.

Contention Service: CSMA/CA+ACK   In a radio environment, collision detection is very difficult. Two stations whose signals are colliding may be far enough apart that they do not hear each other's transmissions and so cannot detect collisions.

Standards from the 801.11 Working Group use a slightly different media access control method, **CSMA/CA+ACK.** This is CSMA with collision avoidance (CA), instead of collision detection (CD). The goal is to reduce collisions instead of dealing with them after they occur.

Collision avoidance is very simple. Suppose that a station is transmitting. As soon as the transmitting station finishes, other stations may wish to transmit at once. To avoid collisions, however, stations may *not* begin to transmit as soon as they hear no signals. Instead, each backs off for a random amount of time *before transmitting*. This reduces simultaneous transmissions, thus reducing collisions. The backoff period is very short for acknowledgments (discussed next), longer for supervisory communication, and longest for data transmission.

Of course, collisions will still occur sometimes. So whenever a station receives a correct frame, it *immediately* sends back an acknowledgment (ACK) frame. If a station transmits and does not hear an ACK frame immediately, it retransmits the message.

Power Control   Another aspect of collision avoidance is power control. The access point sends control signals to all stations, in order to limit their transmission power. This reduces the interference between more distant stations while allowing local stations to communicate effectively.

Radio Transmission: ISM Operation

The first 802.11 radio standards operate in the 2.4 GHz **ISM** (industrial, scientific, and medical) band.[4] This band, available throughout the world, is **unlicensed.** When you install an access point or a PC with a wireless NIC, you do

---

[4] Specifically, 2,400 MHz to 2,4835 MHz, for a bandwidth of 83.5 MHz.

not have to apply for a license, which might take several months. Even if you could get a license, it would be for a fixed location only, and this makes little sense for mobile computers.

Unlicensed operation in the ISM band can create problems. If you are in a building shared by multiple tenants, your wireless LAN may interfere with a neighbor's wireless LAN. Because the band is unlicensed, you cannot appeal to some government agency to avoid problems. You must work out such problems locally through negotiation.

ISM unlicensed operation means that interference cannot always be avoided. As a result, 802.11 standards are designed to reduce problems when interference does occur.

Spread Spectrum Operation   One way to reduce interference problems is to use **spread spectrum** operation. In Chapter 5, we saw that the speed at which you can transmit depends on both bandwidth and signal strength divided by noise strength. Traditionally, we had to operate in channels of narrow bandwidth. We had to send the signal very strongly. In spread spectrum transmission, we use very wide bandwidth channels. As a result, we can transmit at reduced power.

Direct Sequence Spread Spectrum (DSSS)   Figure C.9 shows that there are two forms of spread spectrum transmission in 802.11. One of these is **Direct Sequence Spread Spectrum (DSSS),** also known as **Code Division Multiple Access (CDMA).** Figure C.10 illustrates 802.11 DSSS transmission at 1 Mbps.

Figure C.10 shows the transmission time for a single bit (in 1 millionth of a second). During this period, Station A transmits a 1. More specifically, it transmits 11 brief radio bursts called **chips.** The chips are sent according to a preset time code within each bit period.

At 1 Mbps, each chip may be either in phase with some reference radio signal or 180 degrees out of phase with the reference signal. (See Module B for a discussion of phase.) A 1 is represented by a specific precoded pattern of in-phase (blue) and out-of-phase (white) chips. Figure C.10 shows the pattern for a 1. For a 0, all in-phase chips are changed into out-of-phase chips, and all out-of-phase chips are changed into in-phase chips.

This sequence is highly redundant, so that if one or two chips are damaged during transmission, the receiver will still be able to determine that a 1 is a 1

Figure C.10
802.11 Direct
Sequence Spread
Spectrum (DSSS)

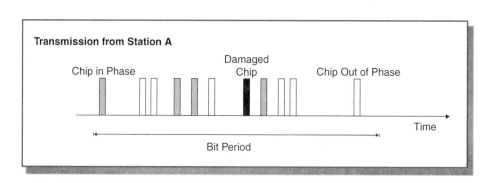

Module C More on Local Area Networks

and a 0 is a 0. Even if two stations transmit at the same time (which would be devastating in baseband or ordinary nonspread broadband transmission), each station's transmission will damage only some of the other station's chips. The impact will be as if background noise had increased. There will be occasional errors, but in most cases, both transmissions will get through without error.

As more and more stations are added, it will be as if background noise were increasing slowly. This is called **graceful degradation.** This gradual degradation of service will give the organization a chance to do something about its internal devices, for instance to increase the transmission speed. (Increasing the transmission speed will shorten each transmission so that simultaneous transmissions will be less frequent.) If the interference is due to another organization using the same unregulated frequencies, graceful degradation will give the two firms time to negotiate a solution.

At 2 Mbps, 802.11 uses DSSS in almost exactly the same way. There are again 11 chips sent in 1 millionth of a second. However, instead of just two possible phases, there are four possible phases (0, 90, 180, and 270 degrees). Consequently, each chip represents 2 bits (00, 01, 10, or 11), according to its phase. The baud rate, then, is 1 Mbaud, and the bit rate is 2 Mbps.

Frequency Hopping Spread Spectrum   Another radio technology is **frequency hopping spread spectrum (FHSS)** transmission, which is illustrated in Figure C.11. Here transmission is done in a very wide channel. This channel is divided into several subchannels.

Before a station transmits, it is given a frequency hopping code. As it transmits, it uses this preset code to hop among the various subchannels. The receiver, which also knows the code, listens on the subchannels at the appropriate times.

Recall that DSSS sends *several chips per bit.* This makes bit transmission relatively immune to collisions. Although frequency hopping could work the same way, 802.11 specifies **slow frequency hopping,** in which the frequency

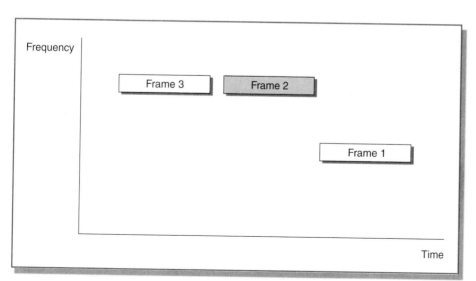

Figure C.11
802.11 Frequency Hopping Spread Spectrum

changes only every 20 to 50 microseconds (ms). Several frames can be transmitted during that time.[5] So, if two stations transmit in the same frequency at the same time, several frames may be lost. However, frequency hopping reduces the number of frame collisions, and these few lost frames are merely retransmitted. Slow frequency hopping is less expensive to implement than frequency hopping several times per bit.

Graceful Degradation As noted earlier, 802.11 wireless LANs operate in unregulated radio bands, so you cannot prevent nearby organizations from building systems in the same frequency range. However, as traffic grows as a result of competition, interference will increase slowly in both DSSS and FHSS. As more and more stations are added, it will be as if there was more and more noise. This **"graceful degradation"** gives time to allow congestion problems to be negotiated among firms before they become serious.

Infrared Transmission

Your television's remote control uses **infrared light,** whose frequencies are just below what the human eye can see. In addition to defining two radio frequency physical layer standards for wireless LANs, the 802.11 standard specified an infrared wireless physical layer. This standard specifies transmission wavelengths from 850 to 950 nm.

The infrared standard has not received as much attention as the two radio frequency standards because infrared technology, although inexpensive, is difficult to implement. If someone walks between the television set and your remote control, that person's body will block your signal. The same is true of infrared LAN signals. To prevent signal blocking, 802.11 can use **diffuse infrared** transmission, which scatters infrared light around a room. However, this still restricts transmission to a single room. In contrast, radio waves pass through normal walls fairly well, allowing much larger cells. Another problem is that although infrared transmission is immune to radio frequency interference, bright sunlight and other light and heat sources do create interference at infrared frequencies.

Security

If you are transmitting signals on open frequencies, you would like to have good security so that eavesdroppers will not be able to read your messages. Although spread spectrum operation inherently offers some security, the spread spectrum technology used in 802.11 is not very secure. It was optimized for collision avoidance rather than for security.

The initial version of the standard did offer techniques for "wired equivalent privacy." Yet this is only a station-to-station form of privacy, not end-to-end privacy across multiple hops. In addition, it is only an option in the standard, and it is not very fully developed.

---

[5] Mahalo to Dean Kawaguchi of Symbol Technologies and to Naftali Chayat of Breezecom for the information on slow frequency hopping in 802.11.

11 Mbps One problem with the initial 802.11 standards was their speed of only 1 or 2 megabits per second. Now that an 11 Mbps version is standardized, 802.11 networking should be much more attractive.

REVIEW QUESTIONS

Core Review Questions

1. **a)** Name the physical layer options a company has for Ethernet networks running at 10 Mbps. **b)** Can you mix these physical layer technologies in a single LAN? **c)** If possible, why would you wish to do so?

2. Compare and contrast Manchester encoding and differential Manchester encoding.

3. Briefly explain the main purpose of the following 802.5 fields: **a)** start frame delimiter, **b)** access control, **c)** frame control, **d)** destination address, **e)** source address, **f)** routing information, **g)** information, **h)** frame check sequence, **i)** end frame delimiter, and **j)** frame status. **k)** Why is the 802.5 MAC layer frame so much more complex than the 802.3 MAC layer frame?

4. Explain the major risks associated with 802.5 Token-Ring Network and how the standard handles each of them.

5. **a)** At what speed does FDDI operate? **b)** Where has it been used primarily in the past in site networks? **c)** What makes FDDI good for that job, even at large sites? **d)** Why does FDDI not have a bright future?

6. **a)** What working group creates wireless LAN standards? **b)** For what physical layer transmission techniques and speeds have wireless standards been developed?

7. **a)** Explain the difference between CSMA/CD and CSMA/CA+ACK. **b)** Why doesn't a wireless LAN use CSMA/CD?

8. **a)** Explain the difference between DSSS and FHSS. **b)** DSSS transmits 11 chips per bit. How often does FHSS change frequencies? **c)** What is the advantage of slow frequency hopping? **d)** What is its disadvantage?

9. Why is spread spectrum transmission used in wireless LANs?

Detailed Review Questions

1. **a)** Explain the physical connections in 10Base5. **b)** What are the distance limits of 10Base5 for a single segment? **c)** For multiple segments?

2. **a)** Explain the physical connections in 10Base2. **b)** What are the distance limits of 10Base2 for a single segment? **c)** For multiple segments?

3. **a)** In 10 Mbps Ethernet LANs, what are the limits for the number of segments and repeaters linking the two farthest stations? **b)** Explain 5-4-3.

4. **a)** Compare Ethernet II and 802.3/802.2 framing. **b)** How can a NIC tell which type of frame it is receiving?

5. **a)** Explain 4B/5B signal encoding. **b)** Explain MLT-3 signal encoding.

6. Explain how differential Manchester encoding produces **a)** 1, **b)** 0, **c)** J, and **d)** K.

7. Explain the **a)** PPP, **b)** T, **c)** M, and **d)** RRR in the 802.5 access control field.

8. How do the address fields and the frame control sequence fields differ in 802.3 and 802.5, if they differ at all?

9. Describe the ending fields in 802.5.

10. Explain **a)** why a break in the ring between access units is dangerous and **b)** how 802.5 reduces the danger.

11. **a)** What is an active monitor? **b)** What happens if it fails? **c)** How does 802.5 handle this danger?

Thought Questions

1. **a)** Now that you know more about 802.5, why do you think its market penetration has been lower than that of 802.3? **b)** Why do you think that many companies feel that 802.5 is a much better choice anyway?

2. Why must power be controlled in radio LANs?

3. **a)** In ISM bands, why is it possible for two firms to build wireless LANs that interfere with one another? **b)** In spread spectrum transmission, explain graceful degradation and explain how it gives firms time to negotiate if their wireless networks do interfere.

4. Unless stations can send and receive at high speeds, there is no sense in placing them on a very fast network. Older PCs have ISA busses, which only move 8 bits in each clock cycle and have a clock cycle of 10 MHz. Newer PCs have PCI busses. Often they can move 32 bits at a time and have a clock speed of at least 33 MHz. New external ports can connect to networks without adding a NIC. For instance, a universal serial bus can send and receive at 12 Mbps, and the USB-2 standard will raise this to 100 Mbps. Ignoring problems of computer software being able to use the full bandwidth of a bus, would you be limited to 10Base-T or 100Base-TX, or could you benefit from gigabit Ethernet if you have **a)** an ISA NIC, **b)** a PCI NIC, **c)** a universal serial bus port, or **d)** a USB-2 port?

    Give your answer in a table with 10Base-T, 100Base-TX, and gigabit Ethernet on one dimension and ISA, PCI, and USB on the other.

Projects

1. **Getting Current.** Go to the book's website, **http://www.prenhall.com/panko,** and see the "New Information" and "Errors" pages for this module to get new information since this book went to press and to correct any errors in the text.

2. **Internet Exercises.** Go to the book's website, **http://www.prenhall.com/panko,** and see the "Exercises" page for this module. Do the Internet exercises.

Telephone Service

THE PUBLIC SWITCHED TELEPHONE NETWORK (PSTN)

As Chapter 11 noted, telephony often falls under the corporate networking group. It is essential for networking professionals to understand telephone services and telephone pricing.

Chapter 1 introduced the basic anatomy of the telephone system, beginning with customer premises equipment. Beyond the customer premises, we enter the realms of telephone carriers. When we do, we enter a world marked by a hundred years of regulation.

CUSTOMER PREMISES EQUIPMENT

We saw in Chapter 1 that the **customer's premises** are the buildings and land owned by the customer.

In the past, telephone companies owned all telephone equipment on the customer premises, including all copper wires and even telephone handsets. In most countries, however, regulators have turned this around completely. Customers now own everything on their premises, unless the customer specifically chooses to lease equipment from a telephone company. In effect, companies operate their own internal telephone companies.

PBXs

Many large companies have internal switches called **private branch exchanges (PBXs)**. A PBX is somewhat like having your own end office switch. In fact, this is the origin of the term *branch exchange*. (*Exchange* is another word for *switch*.)

The PBX connects to every telephone on the premises and allows any telephone to connect to every other telephone. It essentially creates an internal telephone network for the site.

Figure D.1 illustrates customer premises wiring using a PBX. In large buildings, a key consideration is where to leave space for the PBX, wiring, and other equipment. PBXs are about two thirds of a meter deep, allowing them to fit into standard equipment racks. A small PBX that serves "only" a few hundred lines is about 2 meters tall and 1 meter wide. A large PBX that serves 10,000 to 70,000 lines typically is the same height but may be twice as wide.

Companies also need room for the mandatory **termination equipment** that telephone carriers require you to place between the PBX and outgoing lines to protect the telephone system from unauthorized voltages.

Figure D.1
Customer
Premises Wiring

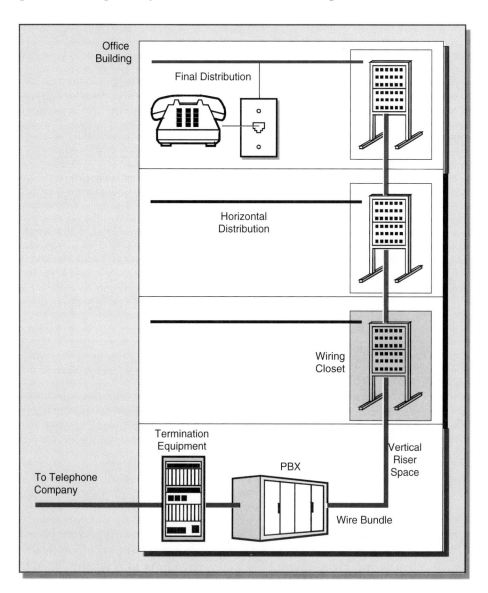

In addition, most companies have internal telephone operators. These operators need room for an office. It is common to put operators near the central equipment, but this is not necessary. The telephone manager and his or her office staff and technicians need room as well.

Wiring If a PBX serves many users, the company needs to run hundreds or thousands of telephone wires from the PBX to individual telephones. As shown in Figure D.1, the wires leave the PBX in thick **cable bundles** that contain hundreds of wire pairs.

The cable bundles move vertically through a building inside **riser** spaces that are 6 inches to 2 feet thick. For new buildings, it is important to leave ample room for riser spaces.

At each floor, the riser terminates in a **wiring closet.** This wiring closet is about the size of a hall closet in a home or apartment. Inside the wiring closet, the thick vertical bundle splits into smaller bundles. Some continue to travel upward to the next floor. Others run out horizontally on that floor of the building.

Typically, horizontal wires run through false ceilings. In other cases, they run inside walls. In improperly built buildings, there are neither false ceilings nor wall space. In that case, the horizontal distribution has to take place through relatively unsightly conduits that look like water pipes.

Finally, the last cable splits into a four-pair bundle destined for an individual telephone. As we saw in Chapter 4, this bundle terminates in an RJ-45 connector.

Importance of Customer Premises Wiring There are two reasons we have spent a considerable amount of time talking about customer premises wiring. The first is that the company must manage its own wiring system, so telephone professionals need to be familiar with customer premises wiring.

In addition, several LAN technologies use high-quality telephone wiring, including repeaters that fit into wiring closets. To understand building wiring is to understand many forms of LAN wiring.

PBX Networks

Many large companies have multiple sites. Figure D.2 shows that each site is likely to have a PBX.

The figure shows that the company can link its sites together with leased lines. For instance, a single T1 leased line can handle 24 conversations between two sites. Especially busy connections require T3 lines or even faster leased lines.

If a firm buys all of its PBXs from a single vendor, they will be able to function together like the central offices of the telephone company. A single system of extension numbers will be able to serve everyone in the firm, regardless of their site. A PBX at some master site should even be able to do remote maintenance on slave PBXs at other sites.

For communication outside the firm, the PBXs will have access lines to the local telephone company. The PBXs will also have links to various transmis-

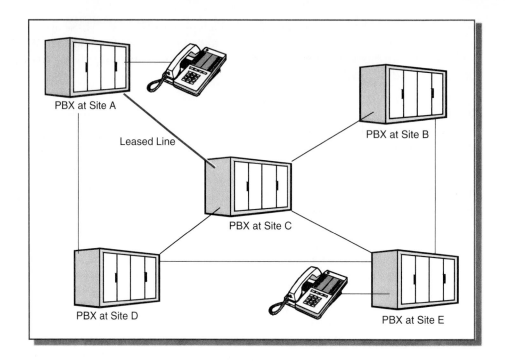

sion carriers other than the local telephone company. This allows the PBXs to select the least-cost line whenever someone makes an outgoing call.

In effect, the company sets up its own private telephone system. Technically, this is known as a **private telephone network.** By creating private telephone networks, companies can reduce their costs while providing a high level of services.

Many telephone carriers are trying to get back the business they have lost because of private telephone networks. They now offer **virtual private network** service. In this service, the firm appears to have an exclusive private telephone network. Calls between sites are inexpensive. In return for lower prices, transmission is restricted to communication between corporate sites.

However, the telephone company provides this service using its ordinary switches and trunk lines. Virtual private network service is a matter of pricing, not of technology.

The term **virtual private network** is a little confusing. It began in telephony as described in the previous paragraphs. Later, as Chapter 9 discusses, the term **virtual private network** became popular as a way to describe the use of the Internet instead of a commercial carrier for data transmission.

User Services

Figure D.3 shows that, because digital PBXs are essentially computers, they allow vendors to differentiate their products by adding application software to provide a wide range of services.

For Users

Speed dialing	Dials a number with a one- or two-digit code.
Last number redial	Redials the last number dialed.
Display of called number	LCD display for number the caller has dialed. Allows caller to see a mistake.
Camp on	If line is busy, hit "camp on" and hang up. When other party is off the line, he or she will be called automatically.
Call waiting	If you are talking to someone, you will be beeped if someone else calls.
Hold	Put someone on hold until he or she can be talked to.
ANI	Automatic number identification. You can see the number of the party calling you.
Conferencing	Allows three people to speak together.
Call transfer	If you will be away from your desk, calls will be transferred to this number.
Call forwarding	Someone calls you. You connect the person to someone else.
Voice mail	Callers can leave messages.

For Attendants

Operator	In-house telephone operators can handle problems.
Automatic call distribution	When someone dials in, the call goes to a specific telephone without operator assistance.
Message center	Allows caller to leave a message with a live operator.
Paging	Operator can page someone anywhere in the building.
Nighttime call handling	Special functions for handling nighttime calls, such as forwarding control to a guard station.
Change requests	Can change extensions and other information from a console.

For Management

Automatic route selection	Automatically selects the cheapest way of placing long-distance calls.
Call restriction	Prevents certain stations from placing outgoing or long-distance calls.
Call detail	Provides detailed reports on charges by telephone and by department.

TELEPHONE CARRIERS AND REGULATION

As noted in Chapter 9, when we go beyond our customer premises, we cannot lay wires where we wish. Only certain companies called carriers are given rights of way to lay wires where they need to lay them to provide service. In return for receiving rights of way, carriers operate under government regulation. In recent years, we have seen substantial deregulation, which allows new carriers to enter traditional monopoly markets. However, telephone regulation is extremely important and will remain important for years to come.

Telephone Carriers and Regulation in Most of the World

Figure D.4 shows the telephone regulatory climate that you tend to encounter in most of the world today. Note that there are three geographical tiers of service: customer premises, domestic, and international.

Customer Premises As we saw in Chapter 1, your home or place of business is your **customer premises**. Today, telephony on the customer premises is

Figure D.4
Carriers and Regulatory Agencies in Most of the World

Domain	Carriers	Regulation
International	International Common Carriers (ICCs)	Bilateral Negotiation
Domestic	Public Telephone and Telegraph (PTT) authority	Ministry of Telecommunications
Customer Premises	None	None

almost completely deregulated in most countries. You can purchase almost any equipment from almost anyone you choose. The customer premises are the most deregulated part of telephony today. We looked at customer premises equipment earlier in this module.

Domestic Service Telephone service within a country is called **domestic service.** Traditionally, all domestic service in most countries was provided by a government-owned monopoly carrier called a **public telephone and telegraph (PTT)** authority. In the United Kingdom, for instance, this was British Telecoms. In Japan, it was NTT.

In addition, governments usually establish a regulatory agency called a **Ministry of Telecommunications.** Although the PTT and the Ministry of Telecommunications both are government agencies, they have different but complementary purposes. The PTT provides services. The Ministry regulates the PTT.

Today, almost all countries have broken the PTT's total monopoly over telephone service. Some have gone so far as to privatize their PTTs and to throw almost all telephone service open to competition. Most countries, however, have opened only some domestic telephone service to competition, most commonly long-distance service. Basic **access service** (the service that connects your home to the telephone network) and local calling usually are kept as a monopoly or near-monopoly.

International Service Domestic service is service *within* a country. **International service** is service *between* countries. International service is the most chaotic realm of telephony regulation. Most international service conditions are handled through **bilateral negotiation** (two-party negotiation) between the governments of each pair of countries. Consequently, the number of competitors, service conditions, and prices vary widely between different pairs of countries. As Figure D.4 shows, companies that carry traffic between pairs of countries are called **international common carriers (ICCs).**

The United States Carriers and Regulation

As Figure D.5 shows, the United States service and regulatory pattern has been quite different from that of most of the world.

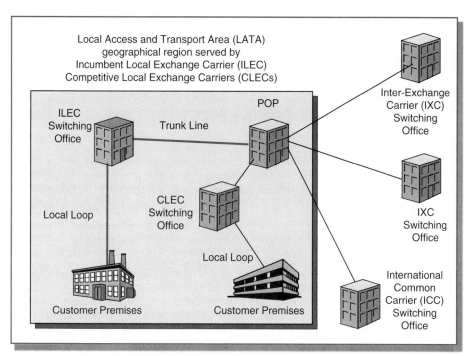

Figure D.5
Telephone Service
in the United
States

Within the figure:

Local Access and Transport Area (LATA)
geographical region served by
Incumbent Local Exchange Carrier (ILEC)
Competitive Local Exchange Carriers (CLECs)

POP

ILEC
Switching
Office

Trunk Line

Inter-Exchange
Carrier (IXC)
Switching
Office

CLEC
Switching
Office

Local Loop

IXC
Switching
Office

Local Loop

Customer Premises

Customer Premises

International
Common
Carrier (ICC)
Switching
Office

De Facto Monopolies   The United States never had a government-owned domestic telephone monopoly like the PTTs in other countries. Rather, it had a near de facto monopoly in the form of a single dominant domestic carrier, **American Telephone and Telegraph (AT&T).** AT&T had a total monopoly over long-distance service and owned the local telephone companies serving 80% of all Americans.

The AT&T Consent Decree   In 1983 the Justice Department broke up the AT&T monopoly. In the **AT&T Consent Decree,** the carrier agreed to place its long-distance and manufacturing services under a single company that retained the AT&T name.[1] Ownership of local telephone companies was spun off into seven regional holding companies called the Regional Bell Operating Companies (RBOCs). They are also called the "Baby Bells."

Local Access and Transport Areas (LATAs)   As part of the AT&T Consent Decree, the United States was divided into about[2] 200 geographical regions called **local access and transport areas (LATAs).** Small states, such as Hawaii, only have a single LATA. Large states, such as California and New York, have more than a dozen LATAs.

---

[1] Later, for business reasons, AT&T voluntarily spun off its manufacturing operations into two companies: NCR for computers and Lucent for general telecommunications equipment.

[2] The number of LATAs varies somewhat over time.

Inter-LATA Service and Inter-Exchange Carriers (IXCs)

Service *between* LATAs—**inter-LATA** service—is provided by inter-exchange carriers (IXCs). (Note that the "I" in IXC does not stand for "international.") AT&T is the largest of the IXCs, but there are other competitors, including MCI Worldcom and Sprint, which are attempting to merge at the time of this writing. The RBOCs and other companies are also considering inter-exchange service. In the United States, competition between IXCs is very open.

Intra-LATA Service: ILECs and CLECs

Service *within* LATAs—**intra-LATA** service—traditionally was supplied by a single monopoly carrier, which is now called the **incumbent local exchange carrier (ILEC).** Regulators within the United States have been reluctant to allow open competition within LATAs for fear that some low-income people might not be able to afford service. (Such customers are subsidized today.) However, deregulation is beginning in U.S. intra-LATA service. New carriers, called **competitive local exchange carriers (CLECs),** are beginning to offer specialized local services, most notably cellular telephony and long-distance service within LATAs (which are very large and so involve long-distance service). Eventually, CLECs may be allowed to offer full intra-LATA service, including providing your basic access to the worldwide telephone network.

Points of Presence (POPs)

When someone places a call in the United States, the circuit may pass through two or more ILECs or CLECs and one or more IXCs. Yet this ownership complexity is invisible to the telephone customer. Figure D.5 shows that carriers are interconnected at special switching points called **points of presence (POPs).** POPs connect ILECs with local CLECs. They also connect both ILEC and CLEC customers to competing IXCs for inter-LATA service and to international common carriers (ICCs) for international service.

Multirole Carriers

Some U.S. carriers are pure ILECs, CLECs, or IXCs. However, there is a growing tendency for one carrier to operate in multiple service (and, therefore, regulatory) categories. However, when companies engage in multiple roles, there may be restrictions on how the parts of the carrier operating under different service categories can deal with one another, in order to protect competition from cross-subsidization and other problems.

State Regulation: Public Utilities Commissions (PUCs)

U.S. regulation is also complex, reflecting the fact that the country was created by independent colonies that, as states, still retain considerable sovereignty. Individual states have **public utilities commissions (PUCs)** that regulate intrastate service and pricing within individual states (which may have multiple LATAs). These PUCs generally also manage water, electrical power, and other public utilities. Across the country, PUCs vary considerably in their propensity to encourage deregulation.

National Regulation: The Federal Communications Commission (FCC) Nationally, the **Federal Communications Commission (FCC)** regulates U.S. interstate service. It also sets general policies that limit to some extent the discretion of state PUCs, in order to ensure a workable national telephone service. If this relationship between the FCC and the PUCs seems vague, that is because it really is vague.

National Regulation: Congress Also at the national level, Congress occasionally becomes involved in regulation. Most importantly, the **Telecommunications Act of 1996** mandated competition at the local (intra-LATA) level. ILECs have delayed competition through court challenges, but local competition is beginning to appear. Only time will tell how extensive it will be.

CARRIER SERVICES AND PRICING

Having discussed both technology and regulation, we can now turn to the kinds of transmission services that telecommunications staffs can offer their companies. Figure D.6 shows that corporate users face a variety of transmission services and pricing options.

Basic Voice Services

The most important telephone service, of course, is its primary one: allowing two people to talk together. Although you get roughly the same service whether you call a nearby building or another country, billing varies widely

---

Local Calling
  Flat rate
  Message units

Toll Calls
  Intra-LATA
  Inter-LATA

Toll Call Pricing
  Direct dialing
      Anytime, anywhere
      Basic rate
  800/888 numbers
      Free to calling party
      Reduced rate per minute
  WATS
      Wide area telephone service
      For calling out from a site
      Reduced rate per minute
  900 numbers
      Calling party pays
      Called party charges the calling party a price above transmission costs

Figure D.6
Telephone
Services

between local and long-distance calling. Even within these categories, furthermore, there are important pricing variations.

Local Calling   Most telephone calls are made between parties within a few kilometers of each other. There are several billing schemes for such local calling. Some telephone companies offer **flat-rate local service** in which there is a fixed monthly service charge but no separate fee for individual local calls.

In some areas, however, carriers charge **message units** for some or all local calls. The number of message units they charge for a call depends on both the distance and duration of the call. Economists like message units, arguing that message units are more efficient in allocating resources than flat-rate plans. Subscribers, in contrast, dislike message units even if their flat-rate bill would have come out the same.

Toll Calls   Although the local situation varies, all long-distance calls are **toll calls.** The cost of the call depends on distance and duration.

800/888 Numbers   Companies that are large enough can receive favorable rates from transmission companies for long-distance calls. In the familiar **800/888 number** service, anyone can call *into* a company, usually without being charged. To provide free inward dialing, companies pay a carrier a per-minute rate lower than the rate for directly dialed calls. Initially, only numbers with the 800 area code provided such services. Now that 800 numbers have been exhausted, the 888 area code is offering the same service to new customers.

WATS   In contrast to inbound 800/888 service, **wide area telephone service (WATS)** allows a company to place *outgoing* long-distance calls at per-minute prices lower than those of directly dialed calls. WATS prices depend on the size of the service area. WATS is often available for both intrastate and interstate calling. WATS can also be purchased for a region of the country instead of the entire country.

900 Numbers   Related to 800/888 numbers, **900 numbers** allow customers to call into a company. Although 800/888 calls are usually free, callers to 900 numbers pay a fee that is much *higher* than that of a toll call. Some of these charges go to the IXC, but most of them go to the company being called.

This allows companies to charge for information, technical support, and other services. For instance, customer calls for technical service might cost $20 to $50 per hour. Charges for 900 numbers usually appear on the customer's regular monthly bill from the local exchange carrier. Although the use of 900 numbers for sexually oriented services has given 900 numbers a bad name, they are valuable for legitimate business use.

Advanced Services

Although telephony's basic function as a "voice pipe" is important, telephone carriers offer other services to attract customers and to get more revenues from existing customers.

Electronic Switching Services   Earlier we saw that most digital switches are really computers. We also saw the types of applications that vendors now program into their PBXs. Many carriers now offer the same services to home and residential customers.

Unfortunately, different carriers throughout the country tend to offer very different digital switching services. One reason for creating the Integrated Services Digital Network was to standardize services. This integration would allow them to be offered even for calls that span multiple carriers.

CELLULAR TELEPHONY

Cellular telephony probably is the most dynamic service in telephony today. Cellular telephony use is growing explosively, and new technologies are likely to fuel this growth for some years to come.

Cellular Concepts

We saw the basics of cellular telephony in Chapter 11. Figure D.7 illustrates how cellular telephony works. The figure shows that cellular service divides a city into a number of geographical regions called **cells.** Each cell has a **cellsite** that contains the carrier's radio antenna and **transceiver** (transmitter/receiver).

Channel Reuse   Cells are the key to **channel reuse,** that is, using a channel several times in each city. Cellular telephones **(cellphones)** use low power, so signals do not travel far. You can use the same channel in nonadjacent cells. If someone talks on Channel 1 in Cell E, someone can be talking on Channel 1 in Cell A.

As a rough rule of thumb, you can reuse a channel roughly every 7 cells. So with 20 cells, you can reuse channels about three times across a city. If you have 100 channels, then you have the equivalent of about 300 channels with channel reuse.

How many subscribers can you have per available channel? Another rough rule of thumb is that you can have about 20 subscribers per available channel. This reflects the fact that people use their cellular telephones less than 5% of the time. So, if you have the equivalent of about 300 channels, you can serve about 6,000 subscribers in the city.

Handoffs   What if a subscriber moves from one cell to another? When that happens, the system will automatically execute a **handoff,** passing responsi-

Figure D.7
Cellular Telephone
System

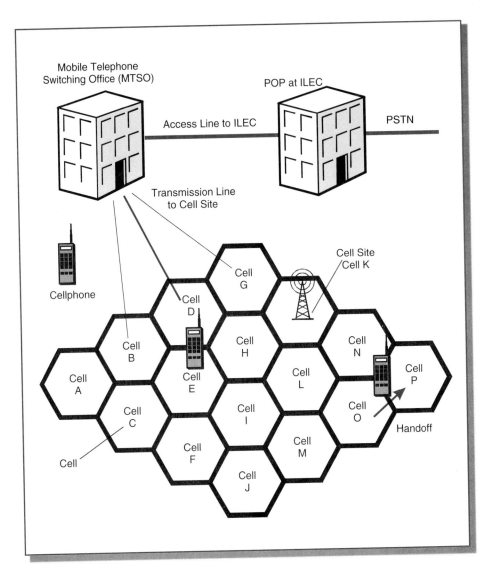

bility for service to the subscriber's new cell site. This happens so rapidly that few people are aware when a handoff occurs.

Handoffs are possible because all of the system's cell sites are coordinated from a central point. This is the **mobile telephone switching office (MTSO)**.

All cell sites pass their signals to the MTSO. If the other party is also a cellular customer, the MTSO sends the signal back out to the other party's cell site.

If the other party is on a regular (wireline) telephone, the MTSO passes the signal to the local carrier. The local carrier handles the rest of the connection to local customers. For long-distance calls, the MTSO connects to a long-distance carrier.

Roaming What if you take your cellphone to another city? You would still like to have the same service. This capability, called **roaming,** is becoming common in most countries, but there may still be limitations or inconveniences even within countries. International roaming is more limited, but even this situation is changing.

Handoffs Versus Roaming   It is easy to confuse handoffs with roaming. Handoffs occur when a cellphone passes from one site to another within the same cellular system. Roaming occurs when a cellphone moves from one cellular system in one city to another cellular system in another city.

First-Generation Cellular Systems

Cellular telephony has already gone through two generations and is about to enter a third. The first generation had several characteristics:

- In the first generation, cells were comparatively large. Most cities only had 20 to 50 cells. This limited channel reuse.
- Only enough spectrum capacity (about 50 MHz) was provided to support about 800 channels.
- Channels tended to be fairly wide, averaging about 30 kHz.

All three of these factors combined to limit the number of cellular telephone users that could be supported within a city. This scarcity kept prices fairly high.

The First Generation in the United States   The United States settled on a first-generation cellular standard, **AMPS.** This standardization allowed cellular users to roam throughout the country. Although roaming was always possible technologically, there often were carrier restrictions that limited roaming.

AMPS is an analog standard. Later, some first-generation cellular telephone channels in the United States were converted to a digital variant called the **Cellular Digital Packet Data (CDPD).** However, only a small percentage of first-generation channels were converted to digital.

The First Generation in Europe   In Europe, the first generation got off to an abortive start. About a half dozen different analog cellular standards were used, and frequency spectrum capacities were quite limited, so that only a fairly limited number of customers could be served.

However, European PTTs eventually standardized on the all-digital **Global System for Mobile (GSM)** communications technology. GSM quickly spread across Europe and reached other countries. Soon, GSM was used in almost all countries other than the United States.

Personal Communication Services: The Second Generation

In the 1990s, a second generation of cellular telephony appeared. This usually is called the **personal communication system (PCS).**

Microcells   The most important change in second-generation systems is their use of much smaller cells called **microcells.** Instead of being a mile or more in diameter, a PCS microcell may be only a quarter of a mile in diameter or even smaller.

The number of cells increases as the inverse square of the cell size. For instance, making microcells a fifth the size of regular cells would give 25 times as many cells. Although the gains in capacity are not completely proportional, microcells can support about 10 times as many subscribers as large cells. Having many microcells and, therefore, massive amounts of channel reuse is the real key to capacity increases in PCS.

In addition, power requirements fall by the *cube* of the cell size. Reduced power requirements make PCS cellphones very small, light, and inexpensive. It may also reduce concerns about radiation. However, power levels and, therefore, cell sizes vary considerably from system to system.

Greater Bandwidth   A second key to improved service is increased bandwidth. By assigning second-generation service to the 1.5 GHz to 3 GHz range, countries can typically allow about 150 MHz of capacity—three times the capacity of first-generation systems.

Compression   A third key to improved capacity is signal compression. The voice signal usually is compressed to about 12 kbps to 20 kbps, instead of 64 kbps. This roughly triples the possible number of subscribers per channel per cellsite.

More Subscribers   Overall, smaller cells increase subscriber capacity by a factor of perhaps 10. Greater bandwidth again roughly triples capacity. Compression roughly triples it again. Overall, then, second-generation cellular systems can serve roughly 100 times as many subscribers as first-generation systems.

Unfortunately, in the spirit of "not invented here," the U.S. FCC did not adopt the world's DCS-1800 technology discussed below. In fact, in the spirit of "let's cause chaos," it did not standardize any PCS technology at all! It allowed PCS carriers to use whatever technology they wanted.

In fact, no single standard has emerged. Three technologies, however, have emerged as leaders. One is a 1900 MHz version of the DCS-1800 standard adopted by the rest of the world, as discussed later. The others are a specific time division multiple access (TDMA) technology and a specific spread spectrum technology. Module B discusses time division multiplexing, and Module C discusses spread spectrum technology.

The problem with having multiple technologies is that it limits roaming, both within the United States and internationally.

DCS   Europe, in contrast, is taking a more conservative approach. The second-generation cellular system is the **distributed communication service (DCS)**. DCS will operate at 1710 to 1785 MHz and 1805 to 1880 MHz, so it is called DCS-1800. Because DCS is a modification of GSM technology, development of DCS equipment is not difficult. Just as the world outside the United States has standardized on GSM for first-generation cellular service, it is standardizing on DCS-1800 for second-generation cellular telephony. Often, to emphasize continuity, marketers are calling second-generation DCS systems "GSM systems."

Digital Services   Second-generation cellular systems are digital, so each cellphone contains a microprocessor. As a result, many vendors have added software to the cellphone to handle such non-telephone applications as paging, e-mail, and even World Wide Web access, as discussed in Chapter 11.

The Third Generation

Although the second generation of cellular systems is still far from mature, international regulators are looking forward to third-generation systems. The ITU-T is creating a set of standards under the banner of **International Mobile Telecommunications (IMT) 2000. IMT-2000** standards will solidify the technology needed for international roaming. In addition, users of third-generation cellular telephones will be able to use the same advanced services (call waiting, and so forth) that wireline customers can use. It will even be possible to bring video to handsets. This integrated set of services across delivery systems is referred to as Universal Personal Telecommunications.

GLOBAL TELECOMMUNICATIONS ALLIANCES

Today, many large organizations do business throughout the world. As things stand now, they have to establish service agreements with telecommunications carriers in each country—sometimes with several carriers in each country. This makes central administration of the firm's telephone system very difficult.

Another problem for central administration is billing. Bills come in from different carriers in different countries in different formats. Yet sometimes calls billed in one country have to be charged back to departments in other countries.

What corporations doing business globally would like, of course, is to be able to do what they do in the United States and other individual countries—work with a single carrier to provide service among all sites as well as integrated billing.

Although this is impossible today, it may be possible in the next decade. A number of large carriers and carrier alliances are establishing **global telecommunications services.** These carriers establish service agreements and, to the extent possible, integrated billing.

Although alliances hope to become completely global, most instead are largely regional with stronger coverage in some parts of the world than others. They only address some of a firm's needs. Even with their stable of countries, integrated billing is far from complete.

In addition, some large firms have found that even in countries served by large carriers and alliances, firms can negotiate better financial conditions and service level agreements by themselves.

REVIEW QUESTIONS

Core Review Questions

1. **a)** What is a PBX? **b)** Why are PBXs attractive to businesses? **c)** What are private telephone networks? **d)** Virtual private networks? **e)** How does the term *virtual private network* differ in telephony and data communications?

2. Describe the main elements in the vertical and horizontal distribution of telephone wiring. (Be sure to explain the function of the wiring closet.)

3. **a)** What is a PTT? **b)** Explain the relationship between the PTT and the Ministry of Telecommunications.

4. Explain each of the following in the United States: LATA, ILEC, CLEC, IXC, ICC, RBOC, Baby Bell, and POP.

5. **a)** Trace what happens in a local call involving an ILEC customer and a CLEC customer. **b)** Trace what happens in a long-distance call between states. **c)** Trace what happens in a call from a U.S. customer's premises to a party in another country.

6. **a)** Explain the two levels of regulation within the United States. **b)** Describe the consequences of the AT&T Consent Decree. **c)** What is the significance of the Telecommunications Act of 1996 in the United States?

7. Rank the following in terms of degree of deregulation: customer premises operation, local service, and long-distance service. Use the terms *most, middle,* and *least.*

8. Compare and contrast **a)** 800/888 numbers, **b)** 900 numbers, and **c)** WATS, in terms of whether the caller or the called party pays and the cost compared with the cost of a directly dialed long-distance call.

9. **a)** Explain why first-generation cellular telephone systems can serve thousands of simultaneous callers in a large city. **b)** Explain why second-generation telephone systems can serve even more.

10. Why is the idea of global services attractive? To what extent do global services exist today?

Detailed Review Questions

1. Explain the requirements of a telephone system for building space.

2. **a)** In PBXs, what is the difference among user services, attendant services, and management functions? **b)** List at least three services in each category. Be able to explain all of the PBX services in the module if given their names.

3. **a)** How do countries decide which ICCs will serve their customers? **b)** How are ICC rates set?

4. **a)** Describe pricing for local calls and toll calls. **b)** What is the advantage of 800/888 numbers for customers? **c)** For companies that subscribe to 800/888 number service?

5. Distinguish between handoffs and roaming.

6. **a)** Describe standardization for first-generation cellular services. **b)** Describe standardization for second-generation cellular services. **c)** Describe third-generation cellular service.

Thought Questions

1. Compare building wiring with LAN wiring in Chapters 6 through 8. Do you think the similarities are accidental? If not, why do you think LAN wiring so closely follows traditional telephone building wiring?

2. You have a second-generation cellular telephone system in a city. There are 2,500 channels. Thanks to compression, each channel can serve four users at a time. There are 150 cells in the city. How many subscribers can this system support? Show your work clearly.

Projects

1. **Getting Current.** Go to the book's website, **http://www.prenhall.com/ panko,** and see the "New Information" and "Errors" pages for this module to get new information since this book went to press and to correct any errors in the text.

2. **Internet Exercises.** Go to the book's website, **http://www.prenhall.com/ panko,** and see the "Exercises" page for this module. Do the Internet exercises.

3. From your local cellular company, find out how many cells serve your city. If possible, locate the cell sites on a map. Note: It is important for not everyone in the class to do this, or the cellular carrier will be overloaded with requests. Also, some cellular firms will be unwilling to give out this information.

4. Determine the cost of cellular telephony in your area. Determine activation (initial) charges and monthly charges. Most cellular systems provide several alternatives based on monthly calling volume. Compare them.

5. Go to a store that sells cellphones. Compare prices, considering features, size, and power. Determine if low-price cellphones require you to get an account with a particular cellular provider. If so, determine the activation fee and monthly service charge. See if it is possible to get a contract with a lower activation fee and/or a lower monthly service charge. See if this raises the price of the cellphone.

6. **a)** Measure the drop in intelligence when a driver uses a cellphone. **b)** Explain why cellphone users in coffee houses, libraries, and other public places have to shout when they are using their cellphones.

Module  E

More on Large-Scale Networks

INTRODUCTION

This module is designed to be read after Chapter 8. It supplements the material in Chapter 8 by offering additional material on two topics:

- Asynchronous transfer mode (ATM)
- Layer 3 Switching

ATM

Chapter 8 introduced ATM. Among the points it made about ATM were the following:

- ATM frames are called cells. Each cell is 53 octets long, consisting of 5 octets of header and 48 octets of payload.
- The 5 octets of header constitute considerable overhead.
- ATM has several classes of service (service categories) offering differing quality of service (QoS) guarantees.
- ATM uses virtual circuits to reduce switching costs.
- ATM is very complicated to manage.

Layering in ATM

ATM follows OSI layering for subnets. Its standards are limited to the physical and data link layers.

ATM and ATM Adaptation Layers We saw in Chapter 7 that the IEEE subdivided the data link layer into the media access control and logical link control lay-

373

OSI	ATM	
Data Link	ATM Adaptation Layer (AAL) (Application-Dependent)	Convergence Services (CS)
		Segmentation and reassembly (SAR)
	ATM (Application-Independent)	
Physical	Physical	

ers. Figure E.1 shows that the ITU-T also subdivided the data link layer into two layers in ATM. These are the **ATM layer** and the **ATM adaptation layer (AAL)**.

ATM Layer The (lower) **ATM layer** is application-*independent*. It provides the same frame transmission process regardless of the application (voice, videoconferencing, timing-insensitive data, and so forth). Think of ATM as a train carrying boxcars whose contents are irrelevant to the railroad.

It is the ATM layer that has the 53-octet cells we saw in Chapter 8. In addition, the ATM layer handles virtual circuits, flow control, and the multiplexing of multiple virtual circuits onto a single flow of cells between switches.

ATM Adaptation Layer The (upper) **ATM adaptation layer (AAL)** offers application-*dependent* services. It is the AAL that allows us to have different classes of service (service categories).

For instance, voice needs constant frame delivery rates, whereas for data it is more important to get more capacity when sending a large burst. The job of the ATM Adaptation Layer is to build on ATM layer services to provide the specific transmission characteristics each application needs.

AAL Types Just as ATM in general offers classes of service, there are specific **AAL types** that support different service categories.

- **AAL1** supports Class A (Constant Bit Rate) service. It provides the complex controls needed for exact timing.
- **AAL2** supports Class B (Variable Bit Rate–Real Time) service.
- **AAL3/4** originally consisted of two Types, 3 and 4, which supported Classes C and D, respectively. Both of these classes offer data transmission, but Class C is connection-oriented and Class D is connectionless. Because the two AAL types were so similar, they were combined.
- **AAL5** was created to support the Unspecified Bit Rate service category. It is simpler than AAL3/4.

Subdividing the ATM Adaptation Layer

As Figure E.1 illustrates, the ITU-T further subdivided the AAL into two layers, Convergence Services (CS) and Segmentation and Reassembly (SAR).

Segmentation and Reassembly (SAR) As its name suggests, the SAR layer accepts data from the convergence services layer and packages the data into a form to be passed to the ATM sublayer for placement into 48-octet data fields.

Convergence Services (CS) The CS layer accepts data from the next-higher layer, typically the internet layer. The convergence services layer adds whatever is needed for a particular class of service, such as timing services for AAL1.

High Overhead

In Chapter 8, we saw that the ATM's cell has 5 octets of header and 48 octets of data. Speaking more precisely, we can say that this describes the frame *at the ATM layer.* However, both the convergence services and segmentation and reassembly layers have their own frame organizations as well.

The CS and SAR frames have headers and data fields. Their headers add further to ATM overhead. The 48 octets of "data" in the ATM layer data field may contain CS or SAR header information rather than true data from the internet layer.

The ATM Physical Layer

To move data at 156 Mbps, 622 Mbps, or even higher speeds, ATM needs a very good physical layer. We will look first at framing and then at sublayering within the physical layer.

Cell-Based Physical Layer The ITU-T has designed two approaches to framing at the physical layer. The first is the simplest. This is just to send cells back to back, with no gaps between successive frames. This is like placing data on successive stairs on an escalator. Although this approach has very low overhead, it does not offer a good way of handling supervisory signaling.

SONET/SDH–Based Physical Layer A more elegant approach is used in most ATM installations. This approach uses the SONET/SDH technology now used by telephone companies for a growing fraction of their long-distance communication (see Chapter 9). *SONET (Synchronous Optical Network)* is the name of this approach in the United States. Other countries use a slightly different but compatible technology called *SDH (Synchronous Digital Hierarchy)*.

For speeds of 155.52 Mbps, SONET/SDH transmits data in groups[1] of 2,490 octets. A group is sent every 125 microseconds (ms), giving the 155.2 Mbps aggregate transmission rate.

For supervisory purposes, each SONET/SDH group has 324 octets of control information. This represents an overhead of 15%.

---

[1] Technically, these groups are called frames. However, this is confusing because we have used the term frame in this book for data link layer messages. Here, framing is done at the physical layer.

Other ATM Complexities

If ATM transmission seems complex, that is because it really is complex. In fact, there are many complexities we have not discussed. We will mention only two of them.

LANE   ATM has a **LAN emulation (LANE)** standard that allows a local ATM network to act like a (very expensive) traditional Ethernet network. This allows ATM to fit into existing corporate Ethernet networks. It also supports applications that need to broadcast because they were designed for Ethernet LANs.

MPOA   **Multiprotocol over ATM (MPOA)** describes how IP, IPX, and other internet layer packets can be transmitted over ATM networks. It allows ATM networks to act much like routed networks.

ATM in Perspective   In many ways, ATM is like a racing car. It is extremely fast and sophisticated. It is also very complex and expensive. Much of its cost stems not so much from equipment costs (although these are high too) but from training and management time. Racing cars need large pit crews. So do ATM networks.

Another concern with ATM is overhead. For wide area networking, ATM has much higher overhead than Frame Relay. As a result, when organizations move from Frame Relay transmission to ATM transmission, they must be careful to calculate the actual improvement in throughput they can expect. Moving from 1 Mbps Frame Relay to 156 Mbps ATM does not bring a 156-fold increase in throughput.

LAYER 3 SWITCHING

As Chapter 8 discussed, Layer 3 Switches have replaced many routers in site networks. Like routers, Layer 3 switches can work directly with IP packets to forward these packets to their destinations. However, Layer 3 switches do this faster and more cheaply than do routers.

Chapter 8 noted that it is difficult to talk about technological differences between Layer 3 switches and routers because new technologies created for Layer 3 switching often are adopted by new routers. Having said this, however, we will look at some of the differences traditionally found between routers and switches, as shown in Figure E.2.

Reduced Protocol Support

As noted in Chapter 8, routers support a wide array of protocols at the internet and subnet (data link and physical) layers. This makes routers extremely expensive. In contrast, Layer 3 switches offer much less protocol support. This reduces their cost. Unfortunately, it also reduces their usefulness in today's corporations, where multiple protocols are a way of life.

Traditional Router Operation	Layer 3 Switching
Multiprotocol internet layer operation (IP, IPX, AppleTalk, SNA, etc.).	Only supports IP or perhaps IP plus IPX.
Multiprotocol data link layer operation (Ethernet, Token-Ring, ATM, Frame Relay, X.25, etc.).	Usually only Ethernet.
Individual router forwarding decision for each packet.	Decision Caching: Storing each decision in RAM and using the cached decision for future forwarding to the same destination address.
Individual router forwarding decision for each packet.	MultiProtocol Label Switching (MPLS) standard will bring the equivalent of virtual circuits for IP traffic.
Traditional bus architecture with a single CPU.	Use of intelligent ports that can send packets within frames directly to the appropriate output port, across a switching matrix.
Complex software requires many CPU cycles to make a single router forwarding decision.	Use of ASICs (application-specific integrated circuits) to do most processing in hardware, speeding decisions greatly while reducing costs. Typically limited to IP switching (only supporting TCP/IP protocols).

Note: Most Layer 3 switches use only some of these innovations.

Subnet Standards Support   Most Layer 3 switches on the market today support only Ethernet ports at the data link layer and the physical layer. Some support ATM as well, but this is much less common. This is not much of a problem in most corporations, because ATM use is fairly uncommon. However, it is a serious problem for firms that use ATM.

For wide area networking, the general lack of support for leased lines, Frame Relay, and ATM means that Layer 3 switches are used primarily within site networks and not at the border to the outside world.

Internet Layer Standards Support   All Layer 3 switches support IP. However, only some support Novell NetWare's IPX internet layer protocol, and support for other internet layer protocols from AppleTalk, SNA, and other architectures is fairly rare. This offers great cost savings, because each architecture has different router forwarding processes and different equivalents for dynamic routing protocols.

Avoiding Individual Router Forwarding Decisions

In Chapter 3, we saw that whenever an IP packet arrives at a router, the router compares the packet's destination address against each row in the router forwarding table. Furthermore, when a stream of packets arrives for the same destination address, the router makes a full router forwarding decision for each packet, despite the fact that the network is highly unlikely to have changed in the microseconds between packets. By reducing the need for packet-by-packet decision making, Layer 3 switches can offer far lower costs.

Decision Caching The simplest approach to reducing packet-by-packet decision making is to make a full router forwarding decision for a packet but then place the details of the decision (IP destination address, router interface, and next-hop router) in an area of RAM called a cache.

Whenever an IP packet arrives, then, the Layer 3 switch first looks for the IP destination address in its cache. If it finds the address, it uses the decision it has cached instead of going through the full router forwarding table again. This **decision caching** slashes router forwarding work.

Of course, it would be easy to add decision caching to routers and, in fact, many routers now do decision caching.

MultiProtocol Label Switching (MPLS) In Chapter 7, we saw that new tag fields are being added to 802.3 Ethernet MAC layer frames. In Chapter 8, we saw that ATM cells are forwarded on the basis of their virtual circuit number instead of by destination address. In Chapter 9, we saw that Frame Relay switch forwarding is also done on the basis of virtual circuit number.

The IETF is now developing a way to tag IP packets with something like a virtual circuit number. This is called **MultiProtocol Label Switching (MPLS).** MPLS will allow routers to make very fast decisions based on MPLS tag values. Layer 3 switches usually already have such a mechanism. However, it is based on proprietary tagging approaches.

Replacing the Bus

Router Bus Architectures As Figure E.3 illustrates, routers traditionally have used a bus architecture in which there is a single **central processing unit (CPU)** and in which all communication must go through a single transmission line called a **bus.**

Information can only pass through the bus and CPU one piece at a time. In other words, transmission and processing must be done *serially*. Furthermore,

Figure E.3
Bus Versus
Switching Matrix
Architecture

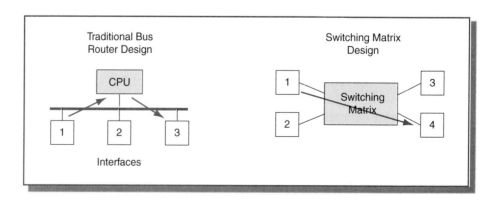

each octet in the packet must pass through the bus twice—once going to the CPU and once coming from the CPU.

In heavily loaded routers, the bus and the CPU become bottlenecks that limit the speed at which forwarding and other work (for instance, the handling of dynamic routing protocols) can be done.

Switch Matrix Architectures   In contrast, as Figure E.3 shows, Layer 3 switches usually rely on intelligent interfaces (ports). Whenever an IP packet arrives at a port, the port makes its own forwarding decision. The input port encapsulates the IP packet into the data link layer frame required by the output port and sends the resultant frame *directly to the output port* across the switching matrix.

With a **switch matrix architecture,** transmission and processing can be done in parallel. If several frames arrive at the same time, there is no need to wait for the bus and CPU to become free. As we saw in Chapter 4, parallel work is much faster than serial work.

ASICs

As Figure E.3 illustrates, traditional routers have been built as general-purpose computers. They have to execute their functions in software. However, software instructions must be executed serially, one at a time. In addition, each software function takes several processing cycles to execute because one or more octets may have to be moved into the CPU from RAM or moved out of the CPU to RAM.

Hardware Processing   Processing is much faster if done in hardware. There usually is no need to move data in each processing step because one circuit automatically passes results on to other processing circuits. In addition, quite a bit of processing usually can be done in parallel, slashing processing time.

ASICs   For this reason, many Layer 3 switches are built using **application-specific integrated circuits (ASICs).** As the name suggests, ASICs are integrated circuits (chips) designed for a specific purpose, such as IP routing.

ASIC Economics   The problem with ASICs is that they are very expensive to design. Unless the design cost is amortized over many chips in production, ASIC processing will be too expensive to support. However, Layer 3 switches today have the volume to support ASIC creation.

ASIC Routers?   We are even beginning to see *ASIC routers.* However, upon closer inspection, these ASIC routers generally only handle IP. They really are Layer 3 switches. Limitations are needed because today's ASICs can only support switching functionality. To support full router technology, ASIC technology will have to mature considerably.

REVIEW QUESTIONS

Core Review Questions

1. What are the layers in ATM? Briefly describe the function of each.
2. Why does ATM have high overhead?
3. List the reasons why Layer 3 switches are faster than routers.

Detailed Review Questions

1. List all sources of overhead in ATM.
2. Compare and contrast decision caching and MPLS.
3. Contrast bus architectures and switch matrix architectures, focusing on why switch matrix architectures are faster.
4. **a)** What is the advantage of ASICs? **b)** What is the disadvantage?

Thought Question

1. **a)** Which Layer 3 switch technologies do you think routers will adopt? **b)** Which do you think they will not adopt?

Projects

1. **Getting Current.** Go to the book's website, **http://www.prenhall.com/panko,** and see the "New Information" and "Errors" pages for this module to get new information since this book went to press and to correct any errors in the text.
2. **Internet Exercises.** Go to the book's website, **http://www.prenhall.com/panko,** and see the "Exercises" page for this module. Do the Internet exercises.

Module

More on Security

INTRODUCTION

This module presents additional information on security. It should be read after Chapter 10. It is not meant to be read front-to-back like a chapter.

In Chapter 10, we saw integrated security systems (ISS). These systems allow two processes on different machines to negotiate security parameters, authenticate themselves to one another, and send subsequent messages with privacy, authentication, and message integrity—all with a minimum of user involvement. Module F discusses three integrated security systems:

- IPsec
- PPP
- Kerberos

The Module begins, however, by describing a type of attack not listed in Chapter 10, the replay attack.

REPLAY ATTACKS AND DEFENSES

Chapter 10 discussed several types of attacks, including:

- Intercepting and reading messages, which is thwarted by encryption for privacy (confidentiality)
- Intercepting and changing messages, then sending them on, which is thwarted by message integrity
- Impersonating a true party, which is thwarted by authentication
- Denial of service attacks, which are thwarted by various means such as firewalls

One type of attack, however, was not discussed in Chapter 10. This is the **replay attack,** in which an adversary intercepts a message and then transmits it again, at a later time.

There are several reasons for replay attacks. Sometimes, for instance, a replay attack is used in an attempt to gain authorization to a service, based upon a previous successful authorization attempt by a true authorized party.

There are several ways to detect attempted replay attacks. All require the use of message integrity so that messages can only be replayed, not changed and then replayed.

- One way to ensure that each message is "fresh" is to include a **time stamp** in each message. The receiver then compares this time stamp to its current clock time, and if the message is too old, the receiver rejects it.
- Another approach is to place a sequence number in each message. By examining sequence numbers, the receiver can detect a retransmitted message.
- A third common approach, used in client/server processing, is to include a **nonce** (randomly generated number) in each request. The client never uses the same nonce twice. The response from the server includes the same nonce. By comparing a nonce in a request with previous request nonces, the server can ensure that the request is not a repeat of an earlier one. The client, in turn, can ensure that the response is not a repeat of a previous response.

IPSEC (IP SECURITY)

Chapter 9 noted that virtual private networks (VPNs) use a family of security standards collectively called **IPsec (IP security).** This section looks at IPsec in more depth.

Integrated Security Systems and Internet Layer Protection

SSL: Transport Layer Security   Chapter 10 introduced a particular ISS, Secure Sockets Layer (SSL), which the IETF calls Transport Layer Security. As the latter name indicates, SSL operates at the transport layer. This allows it to protect multiple applications.

IPsec: Internet Layer Security   In contrast, IPsec operates at the internet layer. This allows it to provide security for the transport layer, including all TCP and UDP traffic, and all other traffic carried in the data field of the IP packet, including ICMP and OSPF (see Module A) and even "tunneled" IP packets and PPP packets, as discussed later in this module.

Both IPv4 and IPv6   IPsec was originally intended for the new version of the Internet Protocol, IP Version 6 (IPv6). However, it was actually created so that it can be used with IP Version 4 (IPv4) as well. In other words, no matter which version of IP your network uses, IPsec will protect it.

Transport and Tunnel Modes

The most basic concept in IPsec is that there are two **IPsec modes,** that is, ways of operating. As Figure F.1 indicates, these are the *transport mode* and the *tunnel mode.*

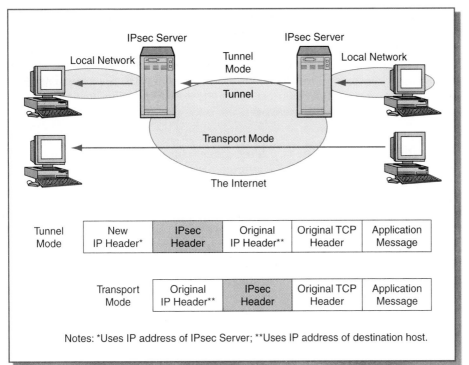

Figure F.1
Transport and
Tunnel Modes in
IPsec

Tunnel Mode	New IP Header*	IPsec Header	Original IP Header**	Original TCP Header	Application Message

Transport Mode	Original IP Header**	IPsec Header	Original TCP Header	Application Message

Notes: *Uses IP address of IPsec Server; **Uses IP address of destination host.

Transport Mode As Figure F.1 indicates, **transport mode** normally is used for host-to-host security. Transport mode allows two hosts to communicate securely without regard to what else is happening on the network.

The figure notes that an **IPsec header** is inserted after the main IP header. As discussed below, this header provides protection for higher-layer protocols, that is, transport and application layer protocols.

In some cases, it may also provide limited protection for the IP header before it. However, because the IP destination address is needed to route the packet to the destination host, the IP header must be transmitted in the clear, without privacy encryption. This allows a snooper listening to your network traffic to understand your distribution of IP addresses, and this can lead to certain types of attacks.

Tunnel Mode In contrast, Figure F.1 shows that **tunnel mode** normally is used to protect communication between two **IPsec servers** at different sites. These servers send traffic between sites through the Internet in secure "tunnels."

In tunnel mode, even the original IP header is fully protected. The transmitting IP server encapsulates the original IP packet in a new IP packet by adding a new IP header and an IPsec header. Encapsulating a protocol's message within another protocol message at the same layer (in this case, an IP packet within another IP packet) is known as **tunneling.**

The destination address in the new IP header is the IP address of the destination IPsec server, not the IP address of the ultimate destination host. Therefore, if an adversary snoops on the company's traffic, the only IP addresses it will see will be those of the site security servers. The adversary will learn nothing about other IP addresses.

The source IPsec server receives original IP packets and encapsulates them as shown in the figure. The receiving IPsec server, in turn, deencapsulates the original IP packet and sends it on its way to the destination host within the receiving IPsec server's site network.

Combining Modes   The two IPsec modes can be combined. For instance, two hosts may use transport mode for end-to-end security. At the same time, their packets may be intercepted by IPsec servers at their sites for tunneling through the Internet to the IPsec server at the other site.

For this to happen, the source host would add transport mode IPsec security to each outgoing packet. The source IPsec server would then encapsulate each packet within a tunnel mode IP packet.

The receiving IPsec server would deencapsulate the original packet and pass it on to the destination host. The destination host would then remove the transport mode security and read the information contained in the packet's data field.

IPsec Headers

The preceding discussion has been deliberately vague about two points. First, it mentioned an "IPsec header" without saying what it was. Second, it talked vaguely about "protection" without specifying whether this meant privacy, authentication, message integrity, or some combination of these and other protections.

That vagueness was deliberate because in both transport and tunnel modes, IPsec offers *two different* types of protection. For each type of protection, IPsec uses a different type of IPsec header. Therefore, there are four mode–header combinations.

Figure F.1 illustrates the placement of these IPsec headers. For IP Version 6, these headers are extension headers. For IP Version 4, these are options.

Encapsulating Security Protocol (ESP)   The most commonly used IPsec header is the **Encapsulating Security Protocol (ESP)** header. ESP is attractive because it offers full security, including confidentiality (privacy), message-by-message authentication, and message integrity. We will see later that another IPsec header type, the Authentication Header, does not offer confidentiality.

Figure F.2 shows that ESP has two parts, a header and a trailer. ESP extends confidentiality to the data following the ESP header and to part of the ESP trailer as well. The figure also shows that authentication and message integrity is provided to the entire IPsec header and to part of the IP trailer as well.

As a reminder, IPsec headers work in both transport and tunnel modes. In transport mode, the protected information between the ESP header and ESP trailer is the transport and application layer information. In tunnel mode, it is the encapsulated IP packet.

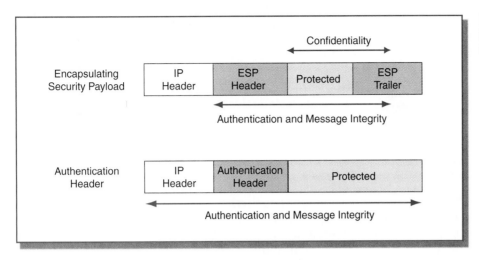

Authentication Header The other type of IPsec header is the **authentication header (AH).** Like ESP, AH offers authentication and message integrity. However, unlike ESP, *AH does not offer confidentiality (privacy).* Anyone intercepting the message can read it.

Why use a security system that lets anyone read your messages? The answer is that some countries outlaw encryption for privacy in certain situations, for instance, in traffic sent to another country. For these situations, AH's authentication and message integrity support still is valuable.

Figure F.2 emphasizes that AH does not offer privacy protection at all. However, AH does offer a bit more authentication and message integrity protection than ESP. AH authenticates and provides message integrity for the entire AH header (there is no AH trailer) *and also for the preceding IP header.*

Security Associations (SAs)

Before two hosts or IPsec servers communicate, they have to establish security associations (SAs). The security association is the most fundamental, and perhaps the most confusing, part of IPsec.

How Security Associations (SAs) Work Figure F.3 illustrates security associations. A **security association (SA)** is an agreement about how two hosts or two IPsec servers will provide security. The SA specifies what specific algorithms the sending party will use to implement whatever security processes will be used, for instance, confidentiality, authentication, and message integrity. It summarizes the agreement the two parties settle upon for how they will communicate securely.

Separate SAs in the Two Directions Note that when two parties communicate, there must be *two* security associations—one in each direction. If

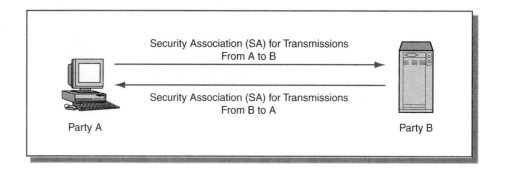

Party A and Party B communicate, there must be an SA for Party A to use to send to Party B and a separate SA for Party B to use to send to Party A. This use of two security associations is confusing, but it allows different levels of protection in the two directions if this is desirable.

Policy-Based SAs   SAs may be governed by policies built into the hosts or IPsec servers. The company may permit only a few designated combinations of security algorithms to be used as SAs. For instance, certain encryption algorithms might be considered to be too weak to be safe or might be considered to be too processing-intensive to be worthwhile.

Establishing Security Associations (SAs)

Establishing security associations is a two-phase process.

Establishing Internet Key Exchange (IKE) Security Associations
In the first phase, IPsec relies on the **Internet Key Exchange (IKE)** standard. Although its name suggests that IKE only does key exchange, it actually handles all of the steps needed for an integrated security association to establish a security association. These include the following:

- Communication to agree upon security algorithms to be used to set up the IKE SA.
- Authentication.
- The exchange of symmetric session keys to be used in the transmission. Different session keys may be used for confidentiality and authentication.

As its name suggests, Internet Key Exchange is not limited to IPsec. It is a general protocol for establishing security associations in Internet integrated security systems.

Establishing IPsec Security Associations   However, this generality also means that IKE is not sufficient for IPsec, which has specific security association needs. As Figure F.4 illustrates, when two parties (in this case IPsec servers) establish an IKE SA, this forms a blanket of protection within which the two parties can then negotiate IPsec SAs. For instance, two IPsec servers may establish different IPsec SAs for traffic types of different sensitivity.

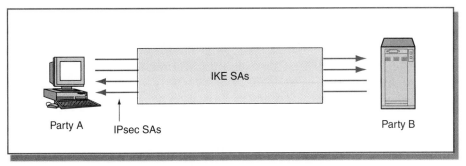

Figure F.4
IKE and IPsec Security Associations

IPsec Mandatory Default Security Protocols   One of the advantages of negotiation is that it permits the two parties to negotiate which specific algorithms they will use for confidentiality and other matters. However, there also are **mandatory default algorithms** that *must* be supported and that will be used as the default, that is, will be used automatically if the two sides do not wish to specify an alternative.

Diffie-Hellman Key Agreement   The two sides must exchange symmetric session keys. In Chapter 10, we saw that in *RSA key exchange,* the sender encrypts the session key with the sender's private key for authentication and encrypts again with the receiver's public key for confidentiality. Both forms of encryption use RSA public key encryption.

However, in IKE and IPsec, the mandatory default algorithm is **Diffie-Hellman Key Agreement.** As Figure F.5 indicates, this algorithm allows the two sides to each generate a **nonce** (random number) and send it to the other in the clear (without confidentiality). Although both parties created their values randomly, they both do a calculation and arrive at the *same symmetric session key!* Although this sounds like magic, it actually works.

Note that the two parties *agree* upon a key rather than *exchange* an entire key. That is why the process is called "key agreement" rather than "key exchange."

One problem with simple Diffie-Hellman is that unless the two parties authenticate themselves, an adversary may establish shared session keys in the name of a true partner. Therefore, IKE and IPsec require the use of authenticated Diffie-Hellman key agreement, in which authentication is an integral part of the process.

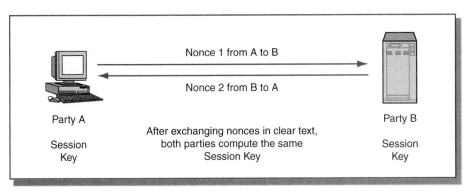

Figure F.5
Diffie-Hellman Key Agreement

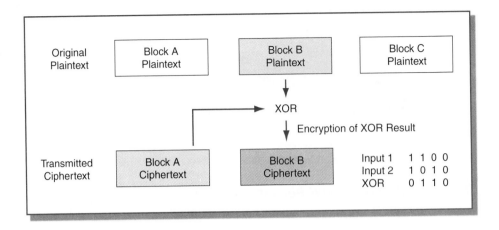

Figure F.6
Cipher Block Chaining (CBC) in Encryption

DES-CBC The mandatory default algorithm for bulk encryption (sending long messages) is **DES-CBC**. In Chapter 10, we noted that DES is the Data Encryption Standard. It encrypts data in blocks of 64 bits. The sender first divides the message into blocks of 64 bits and then encrypts each block with DES.

A problem with simple DES is that a 64-bit block will always be encrypted the same way for a given session key. This leaves DES open to a number of attacks that let an adversary learn the symmetric session key.

To prevent this, IPsec requires DES to use **cipher block chaining (CBC),** which prevents the same input block of data from always giving the same output result with a given key. Figure F.6 illustrates cipher block chaining.

Suppose that the sending process wishes to encrypt Block B. It has already encrypted the previous block, Block A. The sender first takes plaintext Block B and XORs it with the ciphertext (encrypted output for Block A). The sender then encrypts the result with DES as its output for Block B.

Here, **XOR** is **exclusive OR,** a Boolean operation. An exclusive OR result is true (1) if exactly one of the two terms is true (1), but not both or neither. Analogously, people normally can be either male or female but not both or neither. Being male or female is exclusive.

$$1 \text{ XOR } 1 = 0$$
$$1 \text{ XOR } 0 = 1$$
$$0 \text{ XOR } 1 = 1$$
$$0 \text{ XOR } 0 = 0$$

Therefore, if the ciphertext for the Block A is 11000011..., and if the plaintext for Block B is 10101010..., we get the following result:

11000011...	Ciphertext for Block A
10101010...	Plaintext for Block B
01101001...	Result to be encrypted

What about the first block? Obviously, there is no previous block to use in chaining. For this reason, CBC requires a 64-bit **initialization vector** for use in place of the first block.

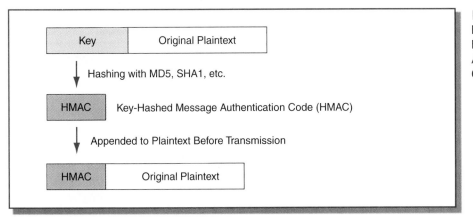

HMAC for Authentication In Chapter 10, we saw digital signatures, which use public key encryption. Digital signatures provide message-by-message authentication and integrity.

Although digital signatures are good, the public key encryption used to create digital signatures is very slow. An analog of digital signatures called **key-hashed message authentication codes (HMACs)** can be created with symmetric key encryption.

To create a simple HMAC, a symmetric key is added to the original plaintext message, as Figure F.7 indicates. The combined string of bits is then hashed using MD5, SHA1, or some other hashing algorithm. This provides the HMAC. The HMAC is appended to the end of outgoing messages for authentication.

IKE and IPsec use a slightly more complicated HMAC system described in RFC 2104.[1] This HMAC method adds a number of refinements to simple hashing, in order to be more immune to attacks. RFC 2104 actually defines several HMAC variants that use different hashing algorithms, including HMAC-MD5 and HMAC-SHA1.

Recall from Chapter 10 that symmetric key encryption and decryption are about a hundred times faster than public key encryption or decryption. Therefore, HMAC authentication is far faster than digital signature authentication.

POINT-TO-POINT PROTOCOL (PPP) SECURITY

As Chapter 1 noted, when you dial into the Internet from home, using a telephone line and modem, you use the Point-to-Point Protocol (PPP) at the data link layer.

You can also use PPP when you dial into a **remote access server (RAS),** as discussed in Chapter 6. A remote access server sits at the edge of a LAN. As Figure F.8 illustrates, a user calls from home directly into the RAS. If the RAS is far away, the user must pay long-distance telephone charges.

---

[1] Bellare, H. and Canetti, R., RFC 2104, *Keyed-Hashing for Message Authentication,* 2/97.

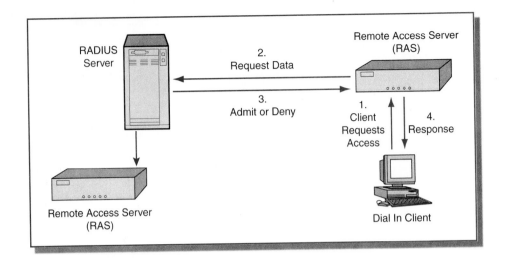

Before PPP

Remote access servers existed long before PPP. These servers give remote users access to all servers on the LAN, so RAS authentication has always been necessary.

Individual RAS Login Authentication The first step in RAS access control was to put authentication on each remote access server, using proprietary techniques that differed among RAS vendors. This technique worked, but if a company used several RAS vendors, it had to learn and maintain multiple remote access server security processes.

RADIUS Authentication Another problem with individual RAS login was that a company might have dozens or even hundreds of remote access servers on its LANs. Unless security was implemented uniformly across RASs, an adversary could simply try different RASs until he or she found a RAS with improper security. Individual RAS login security was only as good as the weakest RAS.

To address this "weakest link" problem, vendors collaborated on a way to implement policy-based authentication on remote access servers. Their standard was the **Remote Authentication Dial In User Service (RADIUS).** Figure F.8 illustrates how RADIUS works.

When a user logs in to the remote access server, the RAS does not do authentication by itself. Instead, it passes the user's login information on to the central **RADIUS server.** The RADIUS server then authenticates the user or refuses the user. It passes this information back to the RAS serving the user. The RAS then accepts or rejects the connection.

Although RADIUS worked well and is still widely used, we would like to integrate access authentication into our normal Internet protocol suite instead of making it a separate part of network security. We would also like that integration to go beyond authentication to provide confidentiality (privacy) as well.

Point-to-Point Protocol Security: The Negotiation Phase

Developed as a basic Layer 2 (data link layer) transmission standard, PPP has added considerable security since its creation.

As Chapter 3 discussed, PPP communication begins with a negotiation phase, during which the two PPP processes can negotiate the transmission and security processes they will use during transmission. Within PPP, the **Link Control Protocol** is used to govern data link layer negotiation.

PPP Authentication

During negotiation, the two sides can agree upon a process to use for authentication. However, as Figure F.9 notes, *authentication is optional* in PPP. The two sides can decide not to use it at all. If they do decide to use authentication, they have several options.

Password Authentication Protocol (PAP)   The simplest authentication protocol for PPP is the **Password Authentication Protocol (PAP).** As Figure F.9 indicates, the applicant sends the verifier a stream of PAP authentication-request messages until it receives an authenticate-ACK message (or until the verifier terminates the link).

The PAP authentication-request message contains the user's username and password. Unfortunately, security specialists cringe at the very name PAP because PAP sends user names and passwords **in the clear** (without encryption). Anyone listening to the traffic can steal passwords!

Another limitation of PAP is that it only authenticates the user once, at the beginning of a session. Afterwards, a third party can send messages in the user's name and there will be no authentication testing.

Challenge-Handshake Authentication Protocol (CHAP)   Fortunately, PPP has standardized a much stronger form of authentication, the **Challenge-Handshake Authentication Protocol (CHAP).** As Figure F.9 illustrates, the verifier sends a challenge message to the applicant. The applicant sends back a response message that should authenticate the applicant to the verifier.

CHAP works on the basis of a shared secret. When the applicant receives the challenge message, it adds the shared secret to the challenge message and then hashes the combined bit stream using MD5 or another agreed-upon hashing algorithm. The applicant sends the resultant hash back to the verifier as its response message.

The verifier also adds the shared secret to the challenge message, hashes the result, and compares the hash with the hash that the applicant sent as its response. If the hashes match, the applicant must know the shared secret and so is authenticated.

Recall that PAP does authentication only once, right after the negotiation phase. CHAP also does authentication then, but it also does so periodically during communication, to thwart an adversary who causes the applicant to crash and then sends a message in the name of the disabled applicant.

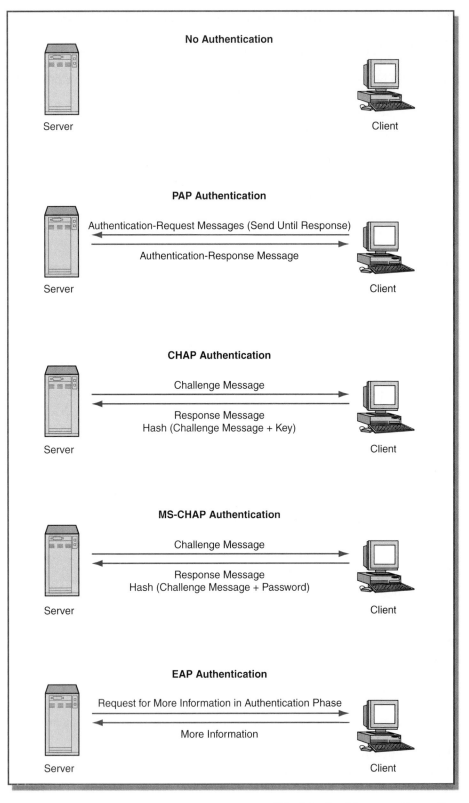

Microsoft CHAP (MS-CHAP)   Microsoft has created its own extensions for CHAP. Although not standardized, these are widely used in Windows. Recall that in CHAP, there is a shared secret that must be hashed with the challenge message to create a response message. In **MS-CHAP,** as Figure F.9 shows, this shared secret is the user's password.

Although the Internet Engineering Task Force (IETF) published an informational RFC (2433) to describe MS-CHAP, it warns at the beginning of the RFC that the "protocol described here has significant vulnerabilities." The basic problem is that, as noted in Chapter 10, users often select passwords that are too easy to guess. MS-CHAP security is only as good as the passwords that users select, and security experts consider this to be insufficient. On the other hand, it does address the fact that passwords often do form the basis for authentication in the real world.

Of course, passwords expire and must be renewed. CHAP provides a Change Password message that allows a user to send a new password. There is also a mechanism for the verifier host to tell the applicant that the old password has expired and that a new password is needed. Unfortunately, the first version of the Change Password process had major security vulnerabilities. Fortunately, a second, stronger, version has been released.

Extensible Authentication Protocol (EAP)   One problem with traditional PPP authentication is that the authentication method must be agreed upon with a very simple message exchange during the initial negotiation phase. This limits the verifier's flexibility in dealing with applicants.

The PPP **Extensible Authentication Protocol (EAP)** addresses this weakness. During the initial negotiation phase, the two sides merely select EAP as their authentication method using the limited message exchange options available to them then.

During the subsequent authentication phase, authentication is not done immediately. Rather, the verifier can ask for more information from the applicant in an open-ended manner, so that a more intelligent choice of authentication protocols can be made based on the applicant's identity.

EAP offers a rich set of possible authentication protocols, including MD5-Challenge (which is nearly identical to CHAP), one-time passwords for very high security, and Generic Token Card, which works with certain types of security cards.

PPP Confidentiality

We have been focusing on authentication because remote access servers must guard against impostors gaining access to critical internal resources. However, we would also like to have confidentiality. In other words, we would like to encrypt our messages so that the contents of our PPP frames can be transmitted with privacy.

The IETF has provided an **Encryption Control Protocol** for the PPP negotiation phase to allow the parties to agree upon the encryption process. To date, the IETF has specified two encryption algorithms for confidentiality (but will specify additional algorithms in the future). Not surprisingly, given the popularity of

Figure F.10
DES and 3DES
Encryption in PPP

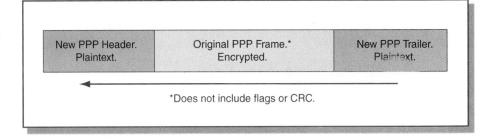

| New PPP Header. Plaintext. | Original PPP Frame.* Encrypted. | New PPP Trailer. Plaintext. |

*Does not include flags or CRC.

DES and 3DES, these are the two algorithms that the IETF has specified. As noted earlier in this module, DES-CBC and 3DES-CBC were selected.

Figure F.10 shows that the sender encrypts the PPP frame and places it within another PPP frame with a clear text header.

Tunneling What if a remote access server is far away? Then an expensive long-distance telephone call will be needed for a client to reach the RAS. As Figure F.11 illustrates, another solution is to connect the client with the RAS via the Internet or another network. In Chapter 1, we saw that packet switched networks are much less expensive than direct long-distance calling.

Point-to-Point Tunneling Protocol (PPTP) For Windows NT/2000 RASs, the most widely used tunneling protocol is the **Point-to-Point Tunneling Protocol (PPTP).** As Figure F.11 illustrates, PPTP works in one of two ways. One approach is to implement PPTP on both the client PC and the RAS server. Newer client versions of Microsoft Windows have the required PPTP software.

The second approach is to require the ISP (or internal packet switched network) to provide an additional server, the **PPTP access concentrator,** to which

Figure F.11
Tunneling with the Point-to-Point Tunneling Protocol (PPTP)

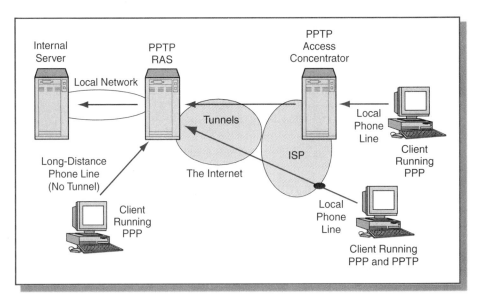

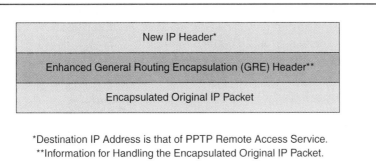

Figure F.12
Point-to-Point
Tunneling Protocol
(PPTP) Packet

the client places the telephone call. When you dial into an ISP, you already give your user name and password to an access server. This access server would also be your PPTP access concentrator. Of course, not all ISP access servers offer PPTP access concentrator support.

PPTP Packet If the PPTP frame is to pass through an IP network, it must be tunneled inside another IP packet. Figure F.12 shows that the PPP frame[2] is first placed within an enhanced **Generic Routing Encapsulation (GRE)** packet and then within an IP packet.

The enhanced GRE header allows the sender (RAS or PPTP access concentrator) to describe the contents of the GRE data field to the receiver. It is also used for control signaling, including flow control.

In particular, there can be multiple PPP conversations multiplexed onto a single PPTP connection between a RAS and a PPTP access concentrator. Each conversation is identified in the enhanced GRE header by the value in the *Call ID* field of the enhanced GRE header.

Layer 2 Tunneling Protocol (L2TP) PPTP is a Microsoft invention. The IETF is also defining the **Layer 2 Tunneling Protocol (L2TP),** which is viewed by most analysts as a successor to PPTP.

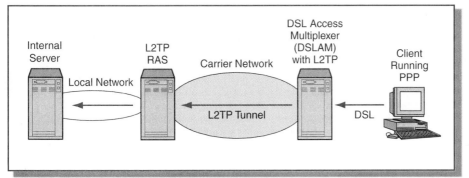

Figure F.13
Layer 2 Tunneling
Protocol (L2TP)
with DSL

[2] Before being encapsulated, the PPP frame's start and stop flags and CRC field are removed because they would serve no purpose.

For instance, as Figure F.13 indicates, a user may establish a DSL connection to a DSL access multiplexer (DSLAM), as discussed in Chapter 5. The DSLAM could then establish an L2TP connection to the RAS.

Remote Access Servers (RASs) and Network Access Servers (NASs)

We conclude with a final bit of terminology. This discussion has called the server that connects the user to a particular network the remote access server (RAS). This is traditional terminology. However, IETF documents call these servers **network access servers (NASs).** This is also a good name, because these servers do provide access to their networks. Fortunately, the two terms can be used interchangeably.

KERBEROS

Windows NT/2000 uses an authentication (plus privacy) system called **Kerberos.** As shown in Figure F.14, three parties are involved in Kerberos authentication: an applicant, a verifier, and the Kerberos server.[3]

Initial Login

The first step in Figure F.14 is the applicant's initial login to the Kerberos server. In a login message, the applicant sends its password to the Kerberos server. This login message is encrypted in the permanent symmetric key, Key

Figure F.14
Kerberos
Authentication

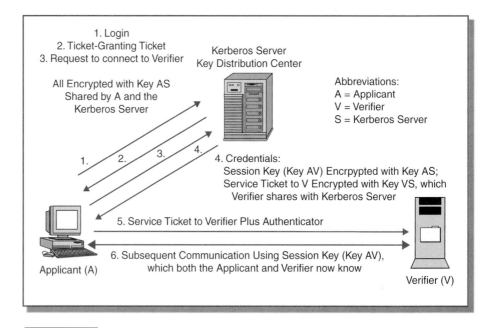

---

[3] In mythology, Kerberos is a three-headed dog monster that guards the gate to the realm of the dead. This is the ultimate in authentication.

AS, that the applicant shares with the Kerberos server. Only the applicant and the Kerberos server know Key AS, so they can use it to communicate securely.

Ticket-Granting Ticket

If the applicant's password is correct, the Kerberos server sends the applicant a **Ticket-Granting Ticket (TGT)**. If you go to a movie, your movie ticket grants you the right to admission. Similarly, the TGT grants you the right to make connection requests to the Kerberos server without logging in again. This communication also is protected by symmetric key encryption with Key AS.

Requesting a Connection

As Figure F.14 illustrates, when the applicant wishes to connect to a verifier, the applicant first sends a connection request message to the Kerberos server (Step 3). This message also is encrypted Key AS.

Receiving Credentials

Next, the Kerberos server responds to the applicant with a message containing **credentials** for the connection (Step 4). This message also is encrypted with Key AS.

Symmetric Session Key   The credentials come in two parts. First, there is a symmetric session key (Key AV) that the applicant and the verifier will use when they communicate. Recall from Chapter 10 that session keys are one-time keys. If the applicant and verifier communicate again later, they will be given a different session key. In contrast, the key that the applicant shares with the Kerberos server (Key AS) and the key that the verifier shares with the Kerberos server (Key VS) are permanent symmetric keys. The Kerberos server is also called a **Key Distribution Center** because of its function of delivering session keys.

Service Ticket   The credentials also include a **Service Ticket.** The Ticket-Granting Ticket gave you rights to send connection requests to the Kerberos server. In contrast, the Service Ticket should allow you to communicate with a specific verifier.

The Service Ticket contains the symmetric session key (Key AV) that the applicant and the verifier will use in subsequent communication. In other words, the Service Ticket provides a way to exchange the symmetric session key.

The Service Ticket also provides other information. For example, it gives the name of the applicant. If the applicant is a client and the verifier is a server, this will be the client's user name on the server. The Service Ticket also contains a time stamp to prevent its unauthorized replay much later. If the verifier is a server, the Service Ticket may also contain a list of resources to which the applicant should have access, together with the applicant's level of access rights for each resource.

The Service Ticket is encrypted with the permanent shared symmetric key that the verifier shares with the Kerberos server (Key VS). This means that the applicant or an interceptor cannot read the Service Ticket.

Sending the Service Ticket and Authenticator

The applicant sends the Service Ticket to the verifier. However, how can the verifier be certain that the party sending the Service Ticket really is the party that received the Service Ticket from the Kerberos server? To provide this assurance, the message that the applicant sends to the verifier contains more than the Service Ticket itself. It also contains an **authenticator.** This is a string containing several pieces of information, including the applicant's name and a time stamp to thwart replay attacks.

The authenticator is encrypted with the symmetric session key (Key AV) carried within the Service Ticket. If an interceptor has merely stolen the Service Ticket, they would not be able to read it because the Service Ticket is encrypted with Key KV. Therefore, the interceptor would not know the correct symmetric session key. Therefore, the authenticator, when decrypted with the session key, would not match the comparable data contained within the Service Ticket.

Subsequent Communication

For subsequent communication during this session, the applicant and the verifier will be able to communicate securely, using the symmetric session key given to them by the Kerberos server (Key AV).

REVIEW QUESTIONS

Replay Attacks

1. **a)** What is a replay attack? **b)** How is it thwarted?

IPsec

2. **a)** Distinguish between transport and tunnel modes in IPsec. **b)** When is each used?

3. Distinguish between ESP and AH IPsec headers in terms of **a)** what is protected and **b)** what protection is given. **c)** When would you use AH?

4. **a)** What does an SA specify? **b)** When two parties wish to communicate in both directions with security, how many SAs must be established?

5. **a)** What three things are standardized in IKE? **b)** Distinguish between IKE SAs and IPsec SAs.

6. **a)** What is the IPsec mandatory default algorithm for getting the two parties a common session key? **b)** How does it work? **c)** What useful information, if any, would someone intercepting Diffie-Hellman Key Agreement messages learn?

7. **a)** Explain why CBC is needed in encryption. **b)** If one bit is a 1 and the other bit is a 1, what will be the result of an XOR operation? **c)** What if the other bit is a 0 instead? **d)** What if both bits are 0? **e)** Explain how CBC handles blocks beyond the first block.

8. **a)** In what important way does HMAC authentication differ from digital signature authentication? **b)** In what way is this difference in HMAC authentication superior to digital signature authentication? **c)** When is HMAC authentication applied: for one-time authentication, occasional authentication, or message-by-message authentication?

PPP Security

9. **a)** What is the problem with proprietary RAS security approaches? **b)** What is the benefit of RADIUS?

10. Is authentication mandatory in PPP?

11. **a)** In PAP, what does the applicant do? **b)** What does the verifier do? **c)** How often is PAP authentication done? **d)** What is the main problem with PAP?

12. **a)** In CHAP, what does the verifier do? **b)** What does the applicant do? **c)** How often is CHAP authentication done?

13. **a)** In MS-CHAP, what is the shared secret? **b)** Why is this a potential problem? **c)** What types of RASs use MS-CHAP?

14. What is the only thing the initial PPP negotiation phase decides when EAP is used?

15. What two encryption algorithms have been defined to date for PPP confidentiality?

16. What is the main benefit of both PPTP and L2TP tunneling?

17. **a)** For PPTP, what are the two alternatives for the party that communicates with the PPTP RAS? **b)** Briefly describe the structure of the PPTP packet, including the purposes of the enhanced GRE header.

18. What data link layer tunneling protocol is the IETF developing?

19. Explain the relationship between the terms "remote access server" and "network access server."

Kerberos

20. **a)** In Kerberos, when does the applicant log into the Kerberos server? **b)** What is a Ticket-Granting Ticket? **c)** What are credentials? **d)** What is a Service Ticket? **e)** What is an authenticator?

Projects

1. **Getting Current.** Go to the book's website, **http://www.prenhall.com/panko,** and see the "New Information" and "Errors" pages for this module to get new information since this book went to press and to correct any errors in the text.

2. **Internet Exercises.** Go to the book's website, **http://www.prenhall.com/panko,** and see the "Exercises" page for this module. Do the Internet exercises.

Module G

More on Internet Applications

INTRODUCTION

Internet applications have appeared throughout this book, beginning with the World Wide Web in Chapter 1. This module looks at Internet standards for FTP, LISTSERVs, USENET newsgroups, and Telnet. Chapter 11 examines e-mail standards.

Recall that the Internet Engineering Task Force (IETF) creates Internet standards. IETF documents are called **Requests for Comment (RFCs).** Only some RFCs are official standards. Every few months, a new RFC lists official Internet standards currently in force.

FTP

The World Wide Web is a very nice way to **download** information from a server host to a client host. The process is very simple, and webpages can be rich with graphics, animation, and other elements that are attractive to users. However, the Internet also offers a much older way to download files from server to client. This is the **File Transfer Protocol (FTP),** which was one of the earliest application standards on the Internet.

Both Downloading and Uploading

Although the Web is glamorous, FTP offers one important thing that HTTP does not. As Figure G.1 shows, this is the ability to **upload** files in the other direction, from the client host to the FTP server host.[1] So if you work with someone, FTP allows you to send files to that person for his or her use.

---

[1] Although the World Wide Web has a technique for uploading files, it is not widely implemented or used.

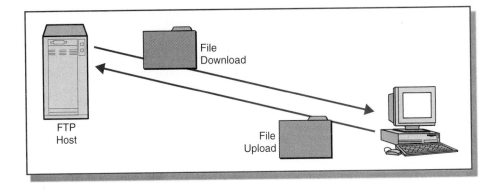

Logging In

If someone can download files from a host computer, this is potentially dangerous. Uploading files is also potentially dangerous. Before you can work with a host computer, FTP requires you to log into that computer.

For this, you need a **username** and a **password**—things you usually do not need on the World Wide Web, with its limited but highly controlled transfer process. In some directories, you will only be allowed to upload files. In other directories, you will only be allowed to download them. In some directories, you will be able to do both. In *most* directories on the computer, you will not be able either to upload or to download files.

The need for the user to obtain a username and password ahead of time and the requirement for the server authority to make certain directories read-only make FTP more cumbersome to use than the World Wide Web.

Anonymous FTP

Some host servers offer **anonymous FTP.** Actually, this is normal FTP, with two exceptions. First, you log in with the user name "anonymous." For the password, in turn, you give your e-mail address.

You then have access to certain directories set aside for public files. You do *not* have access to all files on the computer.

In addition, you usually can *only download* files from these directories. File uploading usually is forbidden in anonymous FTP. Before webservers, anonymous FTP was the most popular way of offering information to the public.

By the way, anonymous FTP is not really anonymous. The host knows your IP address because all IP packets that you send to the server host contain your IP address.

No File Structure Standards in FTP

Application standards usually consist of two types of standards—transfer standards and file structure standards. For instance, the file transfer standard in the World Wide Web is HTTP (see Chapter 3), and the file structure standards are HTML and XML.

FTP, however, is a pure *transfer standard.* It does not have any standards for file structure. The benefit of not defining a file content standard is that there is

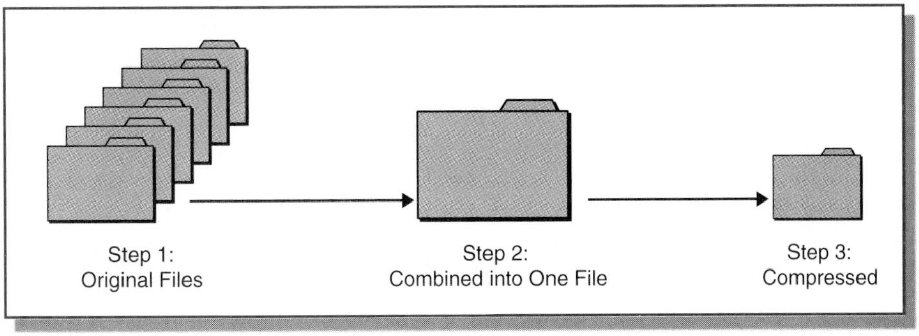

Figure G.2
Archiving

Step 1:
Original Files

Step 2:
Combined into One File

Step 3:
Compressed

no limit to the type of file that FTP can transfer. You can transfer word processing files, spreadsheet files, or any other type of file you need.

On the negative side, the receiver of the file must know how to recognize and handle the transferred file type. This usually requires prior communication between the two parties involved in the transfer, often via e-mail. If the type of file is unknown to the person trying to read it, problems are likely to occur.

Archiving

In addition, files on the FTP server often are archived. As Figure G.2 illustrates, **archiving** first combines several files into a single file. Next, that single file is compressed so that it requires less storage space and can be transmitted faster. At the other end, of course, the file must be dearchived. This decompresses the file and turns it back into multiple files. Of course, you can archive a single file in order to take advantage of compression.

Unfortunately, there are many archiving standards. Although the *zip* archiving standard is the most common, it is far from universal. As a result, the user has to know what archiving process (if any) was used on a file before storage, as well as how to deal with the dearchived file format. FTP dearchiving is not for the faint of heart.

One help in dearchiving is that many archived files are now **self-dearchiving.** These files end with the *.exe* extension. Running the file as a program causes the embedded dearchiving program to decompress the archive and break it into separate files. You do not need separate dearchiving software. You do not even need to know how the archiving was done.

One danger of *.exe* files of any type is that they may contain viruses. So your "self-extracting game program" may actually be a self-extracting malicious virus. You must be very careful with self-extracting files.

LISTSERVs

Suppose you have a project team or wish to participate in a discussion group. You would like to have a shared mailing list that has everyone's e-mail address instead of having to type the addresses individually each time you send a message to the group. In addition, you would like a single person to maintain the mailing list so everyone will be using the same list. (Otherwise, not everyone would get every message.) Maintaining such a list would be difficult because in many project teams, people join and leave the team during the course of the project.

LISTSERV software provides exactly the functionality we would like to have. A program called a **LISTSERV manager** resides on a server. Team members can post messages to the LISTSERV manager when they have something to say to the group. The LISTSERV manager will then send the posting to other members of the group via ordinary Internet e-mail.

Users also can send **supervisory messages** to the LISTSERV manager. Most importantly, they can send *subscribe* and *unsubscribe* messages. These add them to the group mailing list and drop them from the group mailing list, respectively.

Another common supervisory message allows a user to see a list of his or her group's members.

Supervisory functions are also provided for each LISTSERV group's **moderator,** for instance, the ability to drop members from a mailing list if these people cannot send unsubscribe messages themselves.

Subscribing to a LISTSERV Group

Figure G.3 shows the process of subscribing to a LISTSERV group. Here the LISTSERV management program is called *Majordomo*. It manages two LISTSERV groups, *GLOBAL-L* and *CRIME*. The host is *puka.org*.

To: To subscribe, you must first know the name of the LISTSERV manager, which in this case is called *Majordomo*. The names of two other popular LISTSERV program managers are *Maiser* (Mail Server) and LISTSERV. The lat-

Figure G.3
Subscribing to a
LISTSERV group

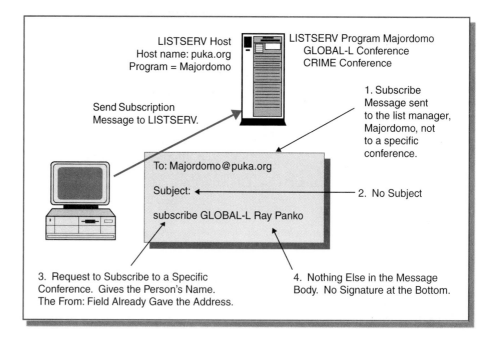

ter program gave LISTSERV conferencing its general name.

You must then know the name of the LISTSERV host computer, which in this case is *puka.org*.

In the *To:* field, you type *Majordomo@puka.org*. Note that the **subscription message** goes to the LISTSERV management program, not to the name of the conference.

Subject: The subject field will be ignored, so you can leave it blank or put in anything you wish.

Body: The body's contents must be entered very precisely. As Figure G.3 shows, the body must have only a single line, and it must have this form exactly:

> subscribe conferencename yourname

Note that the line begins with the word *subscribe*, not *subscribe to*.

Note also that there is no period at the end of the line.

Subscribe is the keyword.

GLOBAL-L is the conference to which you wish to subscribe. Many LISTSERV group names end with "-L" to indicate that they are lists. However, this is far from universal.

Finally, *yourname* is your name. You can also give a **handle,** such as "Spidey" or "Ra3y." Using a handle preserves your anonymity to some extent. However, your e-mail address may appear in postings sent on to group members, so you usually do not have real anonymity.

Nothing Else in the Body, Including Signatures Note also that there is nothing else in the body. If you have a signature file that is added automatically at the end of the body in messages you send, you must suspend its use for this message.

Response Message If your subscription message is accepted, the LISTSERV manager sends a **response message** to your e-mail address. This message welcomes you to the conference. It also lays out any conference rules. In particular, it tells you how to unsubscribe from the conference.

Always keep this message in a folder. It is considered rude to send a message to everyone in the conference saying, "Hi, there. I've forgotten how to unsubscribe. Can someone unsubscribe me?"

Posting Messages

Now that you are a member of the group, you can post messages to everyone in the group. Figure G.4 shows how this is done.

To: Supervisory messages are sent to the **LISTSERV manager.** In the previous example, for instance, we sent the supervisory subscribe message to *Majordomo@puka.org*.

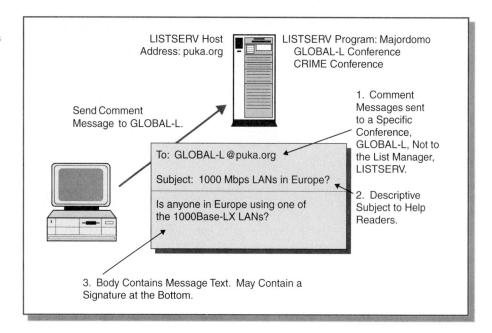

When you wish to **post** a message to your group, however, you put the *name of the group* in your message's *To:* field, rather than the name of the LISTSERV manager. In this example, you put *GLOBAL-L@puka.org* in the *To:* field.

This is quite confusing. You must keep in mind that when you send a supervisory message, you are communicating with the conference supervisor, the LISTSERV management program. When you send a posting, however, you are communicating within the group.

Other Fields There are no restrictions on other fields in the message, although you should follow the conference rules. For instance, there usually are rules against sending long messages or posting messages with attachments.

Receiving Postings

When other members of your LISTSERV group post messages, the LISTSERV manager forwards the messages to everyone in the group, using ordinary Internet e-mail.

The nice thing about this approach is that postings appear in your e-mail in-box, along with your regular e-mail messages. There is no need to load a special program to read your LISTSERV postings, just as there is no need for a special program to subscribe, to submit postings, or, as we will see next, to unsubscribe.

The bad thing about this approach is that postings appear in your e-mail in-box, along with your regular e-mail postings. If you are in one or more active conferences, you may get a dozen or more postings each day. In the swarm of messages arriving in your mailbox each morning, you may find it difficult to find important regular e-mail messages addressed specifically to you.

Users who receive a large number of LISTSERV postings often set up a filtering rule in their e-mail program. The rule specifies that if the name of a LISTSERV group appears in the *From:* field of the arriving message, then the message should be moved automatically from the in-box to a folder for that conference. This way, when you first read your mail, you will see only messages sent specifically to you. You can go to the folder where you store your incoming LISTSERV messages when you have time.

Leaving a LISTSERV Group

To join the group, you send a *subscribe* message. To leave the group, you send an **unsubscribe** message.

To: Again, you send the message to *Majordomo@puka.org.* This is a supervisory messge, so you send it to the LISTSERV manager, not to your entire group. As noted earlier, it is considered rude to send an unsubscribe message to the entire group.

Subject: The LISTSERV manager ignores the subject field, so you can put anything here that you want, as was the case in your subscribe message.

Body: Again, the body must have a single line. It must be typed exactly, and there must not be a signature file attached to your message. The single line is:

>   unsubscribe listname

Here, *listname* is the name of the mailing list from which you would like to remove your e-mail address.

USENET NEWSGROUPS

Although LISTSERV works, it is something of a brute force approach. There is a more elegant conferencing system on the Internet. This is **USENET.**[2]

USENET Hosts and Replication

Figure G.5 shows that there are many **USENET hosts** on the Internet. These hosts run the **USENET host program.**

To read or post messages, you need a **newsreader program** on your PC. You can get a special newsreader program designed specifically to read USENET newsgroups. In addition, most browser suites now come with a newsreader module.

To read postings, you can connect to *any* USENET host in the world that will accept your connection. The ability to connect to any USENET host is pos-

---

[2] USENET actually began outside the Internet as a collection of UNIX host computers. However, USENET hosts now usually employ the Internet to communicate with one another and with users.

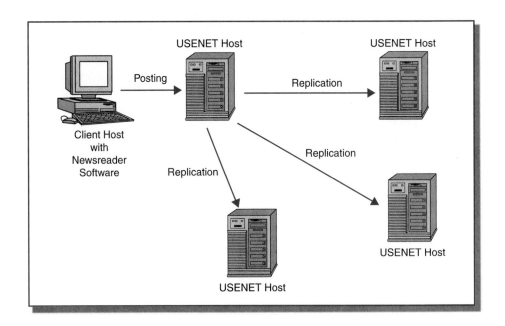

sible because USENET hosts **replicate** (send) their postings to all other USENET hosts, as shown in Figure G.5. When you post a message to one USENET host, your message will go to all other USENET hosts, often within a single day.

Similarly, a posting anywhere in the world will arrive at your selected USENET host within hours or days.

Newsgroups   Each USENET host supports thousands of **newsgroups,** which are discussion groups on particular topics. Figure G.6 shows that news-

Figure G.6
USENET
Newsgroups

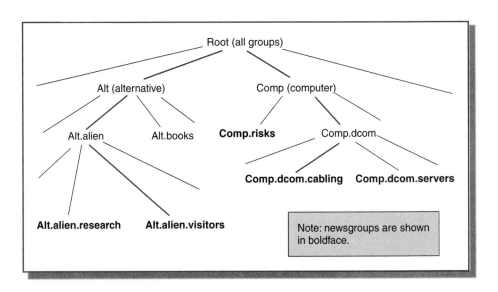

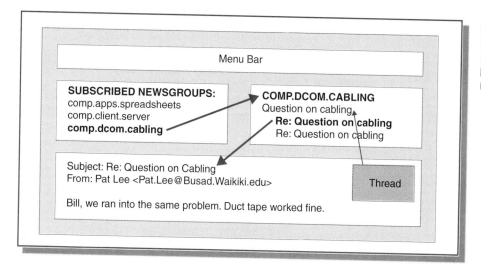

Figure G.7
Reading a Newsgroup's Recent Postings in USENET

group names are arranged hierarchically. Not all USENET hosts carry all newsgroups, especially those in the "Alt" category, in which, generally speaking, "anything goes." The "Comp" family—especially the *Comp.dcom* subfamily—is very popular with networking professionals.

Subscribing to Newsgroups   Originally, newsgroups were seen as being like newspapers and magazines. It was envisioned that you would **subscribe** to a few, just as you do newspapers and magazines. You would see only these subscribed newsgroups when you connected to your USENET host, making your life easier.

As a result, dealing with newsgroups is still a two-step process in most USENET newsreader programs. You first look through a list of available newsgroups to select ones that interest you. You then subscribe to them. Afterward, you see only subscribed newsgroups unless you specifically ask to see the whole list again.

Reading Postings

When you have finished subscribing, your USENET newsreader program will show your subscribed newsgroups in a window, as shown in Figure G.7. You click on a particular newsgroup to read recent postings. (Your newsreader program keeps track of messages you have already read.)

Another window shows one-line summaries of recent postings in the selected newsgroup. If you click on a posting, you will see its contents in another window.

Submitting Postings

It is also easy to submit a posting. Your newsgroup reader will have a "post" command or button. If you hit it while in a newsgroup, a window will open that will look very much like the window you use to send e-mail. You will type your posting, and your newsreader will post it to your USENET host.

Threads

Another way to send a posting is to give a "reply" command while reading a particular message. As Figure G.7 shows, replies are not listed in chronological order. Instead, a reply is listed as a subposting under the original posting. This grouping of a message and subsequent replies to it is called a **thread.** Threads are important because we often want to see not only a posting but also subsequent comments on the posting as well.

LISTSERVs Versus USENET Newsgroups

LISTSERVs and USENET newsgroups are both "computer conferencing" systems that support communication within groups. However, they operate differently, and this creates relative advantages.

Delivery: Ordinary E-Mail Versus Newsreader Programs

The most obvious difference between the two is message delivery. In LISTSERV, you use your ordinary e-mail program to subscribe, send and read postings, unsubscribe, and send other supervisory messages.

As we saw earlier, this is both a blessing and a curse. It is a blessing because you do not have to learn how to use a newsreader program and because you do not have to take any special action to receive postings. The postings arrive in your ordinary e-mail in-box.

The curse is that active LISTSERV groups can glut your in-box with messages, making it difficult to find messages sent specifically to you.

USENET is the opposite. You will not get any postings unless you specifically start your newsreader program, connect to the USENET host, and go to a subscribed group.

Finding the Host

One problem with LISTSERV conferences is that you need to know the name of the LISTSERV host. Note in Figure G.3 and Figure G.4 that the name of the host appears in the *To:* field of all messages. There is no central list of LISTSERV hosts on the Internet, much less a list of individual LISTSERV groups.

In contrast, most USENET hosts carry most newsgroups. So to look for interesting newsgroups, all you have to do is connect to *any* USENET host and read through the list of available newsgroups. The newsgroups are even listed hierarchically, to make your searching easy. You can then subscribe to a particular newsgroup and watch the postings for a few days to see if it is a group you wish to continue following.

We saw in Chapter 11 that if you have a POP or IMAP client program, you can download your e-mail from anywhere on the Internet. All you need is a POP or IMAP mail client program on your PC.

Access from Anywhere

Telnet offers another way to read your mail from anywhere, if your mail host supports terminal access. Figure G.8 shows that you first connect to the Internet. You then connect to your mail host using a **Telnet** program. To the host, you look exactly like a terminal user attached directly to the host. To you, your client PC looks like a terminal.

Terminal User Interface

Once connected, you can run any program on the host computer that a directly connected VT100 terminal user can run.[3] Obviously, this includes a mail program. However, Telnet is not limited to e-mail. You can run statistical analysis programs, database programs, or any other programs that are on the host and that will work with Telnet terminals.

Unfortunately, Telnet offers only a very limited terminal. It is limited to simple text, without boldface or other emphasis, without multiple fonts, and without graphics. There is a single color against a contrasting background.

Why Not POP or IMAP?

Chapter 11 noted that there is a more attractive way to read your mail remotely. This is to have a mail client program on your PC. Such mail clients have attractive graphical user interfaces. Like Telnet programs, mail clients can

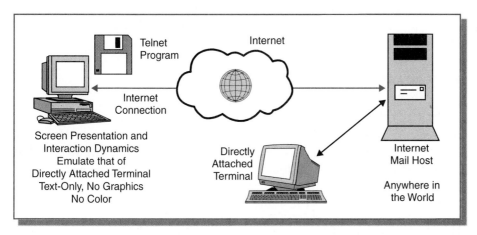

Figure G.8
Telnet

---

[3] Module H discusses VT100 terminals in more detail.

attach to any mail host anywhere in the world. When they download mail, however, they show it to you with an attractive user interface.

However, not all mail hosts support POP and IMAP. In addition, basic POP, which is more common than IMAP, does not give you the ability to manage your messages on the host computer. Telnet does this.

Also, although POP and IMAP deal only with e-mail, as noted above, Telnet can run any terminal-based program, and both UNIX and LINUX work well with terminals.

Of historical note, the original ARPANET, which gave rise to the Internet, was created specifically for Telnet. The idea was to let researchers at different sites use one another's host computers. This way, DARPA money spent to develop software would not be wasted because the software could run on only a single machine, as was common in those days.

This Telnet focus was so strong that when the first e-mail systems appeared, they were bootleg efforts developed without permission by individual ARPANET users, such as Ray Tomlinson.[4] It actually took some time for e-mail traffic to be accepted as legitimate by DARPA. The big breakthrough came when Larry Roberts, who headed the ARPANET effort at DARPA, wrote the first nontrivial program for reading ARPANET mail.

REVIEW QUESTIONS

Core Review Questions

1. a) What is FTP? b) What can FTP do that HTTP generally does not do?
2. Distinguish between FTP and anonymous FTP a) in terms of the need for an account and password and b) in terms of what you can do on the host.
3. a) In LISTSERVs, to what e-mail address do you send supervisory messages? b) To what e-mail address do you send postings to a particular group?
4. a) In LISTSERV *subscribe* and *unsubscribe* messages, what must be in the body? b) What must NOT be in the body? c) Are signatures allowed?
5. Distinguish between USENET and newsgroups.
6. Explain replication in the context of USENET hosts.
7. Explain how you would search for an interesting newsgroup.
8. In USENET newsgroups, what is a *thread*?
9. a) Distinguish between LISTSERV and USENET in terms of how postings are received. b) What are the relative merits of these approaches?
10. Discuss the relative difficulty of finding interesting LISTSERV groups versus interesting USENET newsgroups.
11. Compare Telnet and POP in terms of ease of use and what they can do.

---

[4] It was Tomlinson who selected the @ sign in e-mail addresses.

Detailed Review Questions

1. Explain the problems of file formats in FTP compared with the problem of file formats in World Wide Web.

2. **a)** What two things does archiving do? **b)** What are self-dearchiving files? **c)** Why are they good? **d)** Why are they dangerous?

3. Give the names of some popular LISTSERV management programs.

4. In LISTSERV conferences, what is a *response message,* and why should you keep the response message when you join a conference?

Thought Questions

1. **a)** How does the LISTSERV program know your e-mail address? **b)** What must you do if you wish to have LISTSERV messages delivered to two or more e-mail addresses?

Projects

1. **Getting Current.** Go to the book's website, **http://www.prenhall.com/ panko,** and see the "New Information" and "Errors" pages for this module to get new information since this book went to press and to correct any errors in the text.

2. **Internet Exercises.** Go to the book's website, **http://www.prenhall.com/ panko,** and see the "Exercises" page for this module. Do the Internet exercises.

Module  H

More on Terminal–Host Communication

INTRODUCTION

Although client/server computing dominates organizational computing today, terminal–host processing is still widespread and will continue to be important for many years to come.

Chapter 11 discussed IBM mainframe terminal–host systems. Mainframe systems are designed for high performance. The people who use them depend on the mainframe to get their jobs done. They need instantaneous response times when they type, and they benefit greatly from a user interface with color or graphics. However, high-performance 3270 mainframe terminals carry high price tags.

For casual users, such as library patrons who use a terminal for only a brief time, the dominant technology is the VT100 terminal–host system. VT100 terminals are unattractive to look at and difficult to use. However, they are extremely inexpensive, allowing libraries and other institutions to scatter them widely throughout their premises.

In addition, VT100 terminals are easy to emulate (mimic) using a PC. A PC user can run a terminal emulation program, log into a VT100 host, and do anything a real VT100 terminal user can do. Windows and the Macintosh System even offer simple built-in terminal emulation programs.

The low cost of VT100 terminals and the simplicity (and low cost) of VT100 terminal emulation have led many host computer vendors to provide at least limited VT100 support. The VT100 terminal has become a lowest common denominator terminal for access to many types of hosts, including all UNIX hosts.

VT100 TERMINAL–HOST SYSTEMS

As just noted, systems using VT100 terminals are designed for casual users who can live with low performance in order to enjoy low terminal cost and to connect to many different types of hosts. VT100 terminals rarely operate at more than 9,600 bps, have only a single color against a contrasting background color (monochrome), and have only plain (single-font) text.

In Chapter 2, we saw that processes on networks communicate by sending structured messages with several well-defined fields, including a data field that may hold dozens to thousands of bytes of data.

In contrast, VT100 terminals use an older form of data framing in which messages are sent 1 octet (byte) at a time. This is called **asynchronous transmission.** We will look at asynchronous transmission (*asynch*) in this section. When messages are sent in the longer units shown in Chapter 2 and later chapters, this is **synchronous** transmission. However, synchronous transmission is now so universal that most networking professionals have stopped talking about the term.

ASCII

To send a character, you must first encode it as a pattern of zeros and ones. VT100 terminal–host communication uses a character code called **ASCII,** the **American Standard Code for Information Interchange.** It is also known as **International Alphabet 5.**

Figure H.1 shows the ASCII codes for "Happy Birthday." Note that each letter is represented by a 7-bit code. We also have to represent the period and even the space by ASCII codes. (Otherwise, they would not print or appear on our monitor.) Note also that upper case *H* and lower case *h* have different codes, so that monitors and printers will be able to display them differently.

Figure H.1
ASCII Codes for "Happy Birthday"

Letter	Code
H	1001000
a	1100001
p	1110000
p	1110000
y	1111001
	0100000
B	1000010
i	1101001
r	1110010
t	1110100
h	1101000
d	1100100
a	1100001
y	1111001
.	0101110

Note: Every character to be printed needs a 7-bit ASCII code. Capital *H* and lowercase *h* have different codes so they will print differently. The space between "Happy" and "Birthday" needs a code so it will print. The period needs a code so it will print.

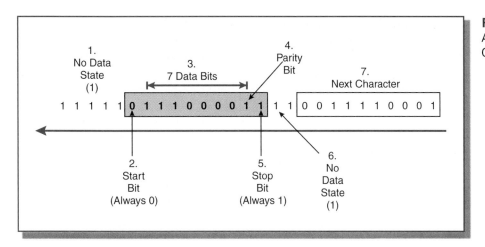

Figure H.2
Asynchronous
Character Frames

Strict ASCII, using only 7 bits per character, is limited to displaying *printing characters*—the characters you see on your keyboard—plus 31 *control codes* to let the terminal and host send rudimentary supervisory commands.

In contrast, personal computers use files that have 8 bits per character. This eighth bit doubles the number of possible symbols. These are called **binary files.**

Asynchronous Framing

If we merely sent the bits of consecutive characters in a message, there would be no way to tell when one character's bits stopped and the next character's bits began. VT100 terminals solve this problem by using **asynchronous transmission,** in which each character is sent in its own 10-bit frame. Figure H.2 illustrates this character-by-character transmission.

Start and Stop Bits

When nothing is being transmitted, the sender keeps the line in the 1 state. Each character begins with a **start bit** to indicate the beginning of a new character frame. The start bit is always a 0. By changing the line state from 1 to 0, the start bit signals the receiver that a new character is beginning.

In turn, each character ends with a single **stop bit,** which is always a 1. This returns the line to the rest state for at least a single bit time. This ensures that the next start bit will change the line state from 1 to 0, signaling the start of a new character.

Data Bits   The start bit is followed by the frame's *data bits.* As noted earlier, the ASCII standard uses only 7 data bits. Figure H.1 shows the ASCII codes for a number of characters.

A peculiarity of asynchronous ASCII transmission is that when ASCII characters are transmitted, they are sent *backward.* To give an example, if the character code is 1111000, it will be transmitted in the second through eighth bit of the character frame as 0001111. This is called sending the least significant bit (the one farthest right) first.

Even Parity			
Character	Number of 1s	Odd or Even	Parity Bit
1110001	4	Even	0
1110000	3	Odd	1

Odd Parity			
Character	Number of 1s	Odd or Even	Parity Bit
1110001	4	Even	1
1110000	3	Odd	0

Parity Bit   If you are using 7 data bits, the data bits are followed by a single **parity bit,** which offers a crude form of error detection. Figure H.3 shows that in **even parity,** the parity bit is set so that there is always an even number of ones in the 7 data bits plus the parity bit. For example, if the 7 data bits are 1111111 (odd), the parity bit must be set to 1 to give an even number of ones for the data bits and parity bit combined. In **odd parity,** the parity bit is set to give an odd number of ones. In **no parity,** the parity bit is ignored. Note that the start and stop bits are *not* included in the calculation.

The receiver can use parity to detect errors. In even parity, a character with an odd number of ones in the data bits plus the parity bit must be incorrect.

Asynchronous transmission does not have a way of asking for the retransmission of the damaged character. The receiver either marks the character as incorrect, painting an error character on the terminal screen, or throws the character away. So parity offers *error detection* but not *error correction.*

In fact, parity is not even good at error *detection.* If two bits are switched from ones to zeros or zeros to ones, the changed character will still have the correct parity. The receiver will think that the character is correct. Parity was created when transmission speeds were a few bits per second, so multibit errors caused by noise spikes (see Chapter 4) were rare. As noted in Chapter 3, we now use error detection *fields* in synchronous transmission. These fields are 2 to 4 bytes long, allowing multibit errors to be detected.

8-Bit Data   Given the universal use of 8-bit binary files in personal computers, and given the poor error detection ability of parity, many asynchronous transmissions use 8 data bits and no parity. This still gives a 10-bit frame, with a single start bit, eight 8 bits, and a single stop bit.

Lack of Standards   There are no standards for speed, number of data bits, parity, or whether the transmission is half-duplex or full-duplex (see Chapter 4). Some systems even use more than 1 stop bit. So users have to set up their terminal or communications software for each host separately. Users may even get information about hosts in cryptic ways, such as "9600E1" (9,600 bps, even parity, and 1 stop bit) or "2400N1" (2,400 bps, no parity—that is, 8 data bits—and 1 stop bit). Duplex usually is ignored, because full-duplex transmission is almost universal. In general, for novice users, VT100 terminal and terminal emulation setup are a little daunting. Although VT100 terminals are technically simple, their setup is not.

VT100 Terminal Emulation   Figure H.4 shows that you can use your PC to communicate with a host through **terminal emulation,** in which your PC emulates (mimics) a terminal. In effect, your PC lies to the host computer. It says, "Hi, I'm a terminal." It lies so effectively that the host cannot tell that it is dealing with something other than a terminal.

VT100 terminal emulation is simple and inexpensive. You only need to add a **communications program** to your personal computer. Communications programs are widely available for free or as shareware, and Microsoft Windows and the Macintosh system have built-in communications programs. Even powerful commercial communications programs are inexpensive.

Your PC already has the serial port used by VT100 terminals. Your PC serial port automatically handles asynchronous transmission and can work with either 7-bit ASCII or 8-bit data. So, you do not even need special hardware to connect your emulated VT100 terminal to the outside world.

In fact, your PC is better than a real terminal in several ways. First, you can create scripts—prewritten series of commands—to automate common actions such as logging into a host computer and going to your mail program. This is especially important for dial-in access, which may take too many steps to remember easily.

In addition, you can transfer files between your PC and the host. You can **upload** files from your "lowly" PC to the "exalted" host. You can also **download** files from the host to your PC. File transfer tends to be fairly simple once

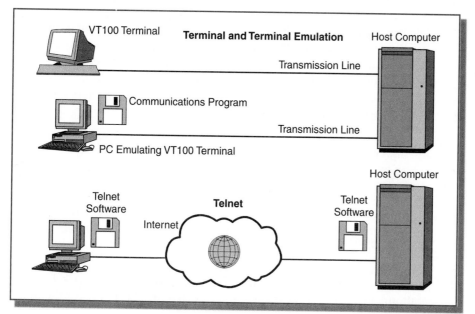

Figure H.4
VT100 Terminals, VT100 Terminal Emulation, and Telnet

you begin the transfer. Before you begin, however, you have to select a file transfer protocol *supported by both your communications program and the host computer.* Some common file transfer protocols for PCs are XMODEM, YMODEM, ZMODEM, and Kermit.

Telnet

Chapter 11 and Module G discuss **Telnet.** Telnet is basically a more disciplined form of VT100 terminal emulation supported by many Internet hosts. Telnet assumes that you are already connected to the Internet. It uses this connection, and it does so automatically. It also dispenses with such complexities as setting up the number of stop bits, the number of data bits, odd versus even versus no parity, and half-duplex versus full-duplex. All of this is standardized in Telnet.

Telnet is attractive for mobile users because they can reach any Internet host computer from anywhere. For example, if you are traveling and want to read your e-mail, you simply connect to the Internet, start the Telnet program on your PC, and type the name of your host. The next thing you will see is your host's login screen. You can use Telnet to read your mail from home, from your desktop PC at work, or from a PC in a computer lab at school.

REVIEW QUESTIONS

Core Review Questions

1. **a)** Describe the bits of the asynchronous frame with 7-bit ASCII. **b)** Describe them with 8-bit data.

2. **a)** Is parity good for error detection? Explain. **b)** Does parity offer error correction? Explain.

3. **a)** What is terminal emulation? **b)** Why is VT100 terminal emulation easy? **c)** What do you need for terminal emulation? **d)** What can you do with terminal emulation that you cannot do with a terminal? **e)** How does terminal emulation differ from Telnet?

Detailed Review Questions

1. **a)** Explain the purpose of having the start bit be a 0. **b)** Explain the purpose of having the stop bit be a 1.

Thought Questions

1. Multiple stop bits in asynchronous transmission were used in the past, when even low transmission speeds could outpace the ability of terminals to handle incoming asynchronous frames. Why would multiple stop bits help? (The answer is not in the text.)

2. You are sending the ASCII character *H*. (See Figure H.1 for its ASCII representation.) You wish to have even parity. What are the 10 bits of the asyn-

chronous ASCII frame? Before you begin, note that the 7 ASCII bits are sent backward. So if you are sending the ASCII character "1111000," you would send three zeros and then four ones.

3. You are setting up a VT100 terminal to communicate with a particular host. What must you know to be able to set up VT100 terminal emulation on a PC and log into a host?

Projects

1. **Getting Current.** Go to the book's website, **http://www.prenhall.com/ panko,** and see the "New Information" and "Errors" pages for this module to get new information since this book went to press and to correct any errors in the text.

2. **Internet Exercises.** Go to the book's website, **http://www.prenhall.com/ panko,** and see the "Exercises" page for this module. Do the Internet exercises.

3. Windows has a built-in communications program. This is Terminal in Windows 3.1 and Hyperterminal in Windows 95 and Windows 98. Use it to set up the parameters for connection to a particular host. Use the parameters 9600E1. What would you assume about duplex?

Index